DEBATES ON SOCIAL INEQUALITY

CLASS, GENDER, AND ETHNICITY IN CANADA

160201

M. REZA NAKHAIE
UNIVERSITY OF WINDSOR

HARCOURT
BRACE
CANADA

Harcourt Brace & Company, Canada

Toronto Montreal Fort Worth New York Orlando
Philadelphia San Diego London Sydney Tokyo

Canadian Cataloguing in Publication Data

Main entry under title:

Debates on social inequality : class, gender, and ethnicity

Includes bibliographical references.
ISBN 0-7747-3663-1

1. Equality — Canada.   2. Canada — Social conditions — 1971–   .
3. Racism — Canada.   4. Canada — Race relations.   5. Canada — Ethnic relations.   6. Sexism — Canada.   7. Discrimination — Canada.   I. Nakhaie, Mahmoud Reza, 1952–   .

HN110.Z9S6 1999   305'.0971   C98-932776-0

Senior Acquisitions Editor: Heather McWhinney
Developmental Editor: Camille Isaacs
Production Editors: Stacey Roderick and Semareh Al-Hillal
Senior Production Co-ordinator: Sue-Ann Becker

Copy Editors: Adrianna and Ron Edwards/Focus Strategic Communications
Cover and Interior Design: The Brookview Group
Typesetting and Assembly: Carolyn Hutchings
Printing and Binding: Transcontinental Printing Inc.

Cover Art: Copyright © John Reuter, *Your Point of View*. Courtesy of The Image Bank. Used with permission.

Harcourt Brace & Company Canada, Ltd.
55 Horner Avenue, Toronto, ON, Canada M8Z 4X6
Customer Service
Toll-Free Tel.: 1-800-387-7278
Toll-Free Fax: 1-800-665-7307

This book was printed in Canada.

1 2 3 4 5   03 02 01 00 99

Preface

This volume is intended to serve as a textbook for undergraduate students interested in social inequality in Canada. It has two objectives. The first is to introduce the key issues in social inequality so undergraduate students can grasp the ways sociologists themselves do research and critique on this topic. In this regard, each article presents an in-depth look at a specific issue pertaining to class, gender, and ethnicity. The second objective is to teach critical thinking by studying sociologists as they debate one another. Each article is followed by a criticism of the theoretical, methodological, and empirical issues discussed. Thus, students will learn how significant class, gender, and ethnicity are in all aspects of the social world, the importance of theory building to all areas of sociological inquiry, and how critical thinking is part and parcel of the sociological enterprise.

I undertook this task because I felt that available texts rarely conveyed to students the real sense of excitement in the controversy and heated debate common in the everyday activities of sociologists. These texts, at least in my mind, failed to develop critical thinking that is so much a part of the sociological endeavour. Students tend to think of their professors as infallible and their sociology texts as bibles, and, as such, they may be wary of criticizing these "idols," believing that the evaluation of academics should be left to the academics themselves. Moreover, students may get the impression that sociologists are immune to the tension and conflict that they themselves write about. Students need to acquire the necessary tools in order to be able to critically evaluate social inequality. Failing to do so may produce, in Herbert Marcuse's words, "repressive tolerance." Not only does such an attitude produce a sort of benevolent neutrality, which is dangerous in and of itself, but it is also dangerous because students do not have access to authentic information and methods of weighing and considering various sociological theories and assumptions. They need to have access to a clear and concise rebuttal of the existing knowledge in order to be able to see both sides of an issue, evaluate the arguments on their merits, and choose on the basis of their own autonomous thought. In the absence of such knowledge, what they perceive as "impartiality" and "objectivity" may mean that they fail to distinguish between information and indoctrination. It is hoped that the point–counterpoint method, as presented in this textbook, will help students to acquire a realistic image of the processes of sociological theorizing and to develop autonomous, authentic, and critical knowledge.

However, as we all know, anyone who intends to write or edit a book on social inequality is immediately confronted with the problem of choosing what materials to include and what to exclude. It is impossible for any book to encompass more than a small selection of the vast array of research on this topic. Therefore, it is important to understand the inadequacies of this book by stating what it does and does not include. This text includes sixteen articles that were written about class, gender, and race/ethnicity, followed by sixteen direct comments and criticisms of these articles. Although an attempt was made to include all of the important recent debates on social inequality, this has not been possible. First, not all of the important issues have received critical examinations. Some that had were either not available, space did not allow me to include them, or they were too theoretically and methodologically complex. As a method of dealing with this shortcoming, I have included a bibliographical list of other debates for those who are interested in pursuing these or similar issues. Second, although some of the articles and debates are slightly dated, the issues raised are still with us, and their controversies are still unresolved. Some examples include causes of inequality, multiculturalism, French–English relations, employment equity, capitalism, patriarchy, gender inequality, and violence against women. Third, these articles are often written by scholars for scholars, and the language and methodology can make them inaccessible for undergraduate students. In such cases, I have tried to eliminate the complex statistics and methodologies that are not easily understood, while keeping the integrity of the author's main message intact. Furthermore, in order to make this text more accessible, I have added an introduction at the beginning of each part in order to summarize key issues and place these issues within a wider research framework. These introductions are attempts at clarifying the basic terms and concepts and making them relevant to the everyday lives of students.

There are some additional points about the presentation of this book that need further comment. It is divided into three parts. Generally, Part One introduces some of the key arguments in Marxist class analysis, Part Two contains a feminist critique of Marxist theory, and Part Three includes a critique of (white middle-class) feminism. More specifically, Part One begins with the classic functionalist debates on the causes of social inequality, introduces Marx's and Weber's views on class, and then suggests the possibility that the class concept is irrelevant in modern times. Finally, Canadian research on class exploitation, elite accessibility, and economic dependency are introduced and criticized. Part Two deals with the relationship between capitalism and patriarchy, gender income inequality, pay equity, sexual violence, and the economic consequences of divorce. Part Three deals with ethnicity/race. Here, issues such as systemic racism, language legislation and French–English relations, First Nation issues, multiculturalism, and causes of racial inequality are critically examined.

There are two ways of reading this book. The reader who starts with the first article and goes through to the end will be introduced systematically to the debates on class, gender, and ethnicity. Alternatively, the reader can dip in and out, reading any pair of articles in any order, since they are self-contained pedagogical units. Students and professors are free to choose any number of articles as class readings. The introductions to each part present more debates on each issue.

Finally, three types of learning aids are included to help the student understand the key issues: (1) most articles are followed by samples of clippings from popular Canadian newspapers and magazines on recent events, governmental and/or private corporate policies, and public opinions pertaining to social inequality; (2) at the end of each set of paired articles, a series of questions and assignments are included in order to encourage students to rethink major issues and debates presented by the articles; and (3) a glossary is provided at the back of the book to help students untangle some of the key concepts mentioned in the text.

ACKNOWLEDGEMENTS

In preparing this book, I have benefited from the unrelenting encouragement and hard work of Heather McWhinney, Senior Acquisitions Editor; Camille Isaacs, Developmental Editor; Stacey Roderick, Production Editor; and Sue-Ann Becker, Senior Production Co-ordinator from Harcourt Brace. Arshia Zaidi at the University of Windsor was always available to assist me in preparing this book. I thank them all deeply. My colleagues at the University of Windsor — Steven Baron, Willem DeLint, Alan Hall, Lynn Phillips, and Alan Sears — helped me tremendously with their good humour and great suggestions. I thank my colleagues Bob Pike and Roberta Hamilton at Queen's University, Bob Brym at the University of Toronto, and Susan McDaniel at the University of Alberta for their seasoned advice. My thanks also to several people who reviewed the book during its development and provided their suggestions: Gordon Darroch, York University; Polo Diaz,

University of Regina; Berkeley Fleming, Mount Allison University; Richard Ogmundson, University of Victoria; and Gregg Olsen, University of Manitoba. I am fortunate to have buddies such as Vince Sacco and Larry Comeau who have always been there for me. Thank you Larry and Vince.

Last, but not least, I can't image writing this book without the love and support of my dearest *hamsar* Abby and our three children, Sheeva, Farrah, and Ali. They have provided continuous emotional support and limitless love. I thank them from the bottom of my heart.

M.R.N.
Windsor, Ontario

A Note from the Publisher

Thank you for selecting *Debates on Social Inequality: Class, Gender, and Ethnicity in Canada*, by M. Reza Nakhaie. The author and publisher have devoted considerable time to the careful development of this book. We appreciate your recognition of this effort and accomplishment.

We want to hear what you think about *Debates on Social Inequality: Class, Gender, and Ethnicity in Canada*. Please take a few minutes to fill in the stamped reader reply card at the back of the book. Your comments and suggestions will be valuable to us as we prepare new editions and other books.

Contents

List of Exhibits

Part One

CLASS INEQUALITIES

INTRODUCTION

What accounts for social inequality? Why are there large differences in rank, status, education, occupation, income, wealth, and property? Are these differences achieved or ascribed, acquired or inherited? Karl Marx and Max Weber are two of the most important sociologists who have attempted to provide illuminating answers to these questions. For Marx, the unequal distribution of economic resources is a consequence of the more fundamental phenomenon of class relations. He starts from the premise that in order to live, we need to eat, and in order to eat, we need to produce. Therefore, those who control the production processes are also able to control other aspects of life such as the distribution of rewards. For example, capitalists own the means of production such as factories, technology, and land. They decide who to hire, for how long, and in what capacity, as well as what to produce, how to produce it, and in what quantity. In contrast, workers, not having any ownership of the means of production, are forced to sell their labour to the capitalists for wages that allow them to maintain a minimum level of subsistence. The difference in the wages paid to the workers and the income received by the capitalist from selling the products produced is what constitutes surplus labour. Therefore, the more the workers produce, the richer the capitalists become, while the workers remain at a subsistence level. That is to say, for Marx, the difference in income or rewards among people is a function of class relations.

Max Weber objected to Marx's emphasis on production as the only axis of class relations. He introduced his own concepts of class, status, power, and party. Weber defined *class* as a number of people who share similar opportunities for acquiring material goods in the market. He agreed that property relations are an important determinant of class but so, too, he felt, are marketable skills. *Status*, in contrast, refers to the relative prestige of an individual and the positive or negative perception by others. Variation in status can be determined by people's evaluation of education, occupation, ethnicity, and/or gender, among other things. Thus, we value some occupations more than others even though those who occupy them may be paid less than others. For example, persons operating locomotives or supervisors in machining occupations often have a higher income than teachers, yet they have a lower social status (Blishen et al. 1987). In some societies, there is a tendency to value certain groups such as males and Caucasians (they are viewed as having higher status) more than others. *Power* refers to a person's ability to influence others even against their will. Thus, the more power one has, the more one is able to put his or her wishes into practice at the expense of others. Finally, *party* refers to a group organized for the purpose of acquiring power. For Weber, therefore, social inequality is multidimensional and each of the concepts defined above can have an impact on one's access to economic rewards. For debates on political ideology and social classes, see Bell (1989a), Sinclair (1989), Bell's reply (1989b), Knight (1979), Smith (1979), Schreiber (1980), Ogmundson (1980), Langford (1994), Glaberman (1996), Mouffe (1989), Meiksins and Meiksins-Wood (1985), Guimond et al. (1989), Baer and Lambert (1990), Guimond and Palmer's reply (1994), Warskett (1988), and Bakker (1991). On poverty, see Johnson (1974) and Hamilton and Pinard (1977). On occupational mobility, see Harvey and Chartner (1975) and Weaver and Parton (1979).

In a classic article, Kingsley Davis and Wilbert Moore (1945) use functionalist theory to shift the analysis of inequality from a structural to an individual explanation. They argue that social inequality is an unintended consequence of the need to ensure that the most important occupations and social positions are filled by the most talented and qualified individuals. We need to motivate individuals to undergo training for the most important and necessary jobs (for example, doctors). Alternatively, we need to encourage individuals to perform less pleasant jobs (such as garbage collecting). How do we motivate people to make sure all these jobs are filled with qualified individuals and thus ensure that society survives and functions properly? Davis and Moore (1945) suggest that the lure of high rewards (material, recreational, and/or symbolic) induces individuals to make the sacrifice to acquire many years of education and training to improve their skills or to perform jobs that are highly undesirable.

Melvin Tumin systematically questions Davis and Moore's theory of stratification. He argued that: (1) There is no way of knowing what is functionally important for society except through illegitimate tautology — important occupations are those that now enjoy the highest reward. Moreover, the theory fails to account for the low rewards allocated to occupations that are crucial for survival of society such as farming or motherhood; (2) In a highly stratified society, there will be substantial difficulty in discovering the most talented individuals because those at the top of the hierarchy limit the access for those at the bottom. Thus, inequality is dysfunctional and counter-productive to the survival of society; (3) The argument that higher rewards should be given to those who sacrifice money and time in order to train themselves is a rationalization on the part of the powerful. For example, in Canada, children of the privileged class sacrifice little since the education system is largely subsidized by the taxpayers. Even if we accept that there is such a sacrifice, it is not often the individuals who undergo the sacrifice but their parents. Thus, the privileged parents are better able to help their children attain higher education than the less privileged parents (Pike 1981; Nakhaie and Curtis 1998); (4) There are motivation schemes other than differential rewards that could induce individuals to undertake advanced training. People could have a sincere interest in an occupation, enjoy specific work, want to help people, and so on; (5) Societies and cultures differ in their display of differential economic advantage. For example, numerous societies view conspicuous display of differential economic advantage as extremely bad taste; (6)According to the functional theory of stratification, those who conform to the normative order of society deserve the highest rewards; and finally, (7) Tumin concludes that social inequality is *not* functional, desirable, or inevitable. This debate continues (Davis 1953; Moore 1953, 1963; Tumin 1953). For debates on education and inequality, see Anisef et al. (1992), Guppy (1992), Vaillancourt and Henriques (1986), Krashinsky (1987), Brantlinger (1985), Weir (1986), Hodgkinson (1982a, 1982b), and Anderson (1982). On meritocracy, see Saunders (1995) and Lampard (1996).

Marx and Weber developed their views on class about a hundred years ago. There have been significant changes since. Many argue that our society is now more industrial and modern, or even postindustrial and postmodern. Then the question is: Can Marx's or Weber's views on class apply today? Terry Nichols Clark and Seymour Martin Lipset argue that social class, both in the Marxian and Weberian models, is an irrelevant sociological concept nowadays. They show that the tendency for people to vote along class lines has declined, and economic growth, technological advancement, and smaller family sizes have all undermined the hierarchical class stratification. Mike Hout, Clem Brooks, and Jeff Manza provide counter-evidence and argue that class voting has not declined, that there are significant income gaps among classes, and that classes are not dying. For more debates on the importance (or lack) of class analysis see Pahl (1989, 1991, 1993), Scott (1994), Crompton (1991), Marshal (1991), Goldthorpe and Marshal (1992), Pakulski (1993), Pakulski and

Waters (1996a, 1996b), Wright (1996), Manza and Brooks (1996), and Szelenyi and Olvera (1996).

More specifically, Marxist theory of inequality has also been criticized for ignoring recent structural changes in the process of production such as the decline in the blue-collar, manufacturing sector and the rise in the white-collar, service sector. Moreover, it has been argued that the real wages of the working class as well as the proportion of the middle class have both increased, thus suggesting that Marx's theory of class polarization and class conflict is inapplicable in the postindustrial societies. Carl Cuneo reacts to these criticisms and argues that the most central aspect of Marx's theory of inequality — class exploitation — has often been ignored by research. Thus, any attempt to refute Marx's theory is premature. He investigates the pattern of class exploitation in Canada from 1917 to 1971 by calculating eleven different indices of rates of surplus value. Taking into account wages, cost of production, depreciation, number of workers employed, and so on, he shows that the rate of surplus value or class exploitation has increased in Canada over time. Moreover, this rate is strongly correlated to class conflict manifested in strikes and lockouts, and he finds that the higher the class exploitation, the higher the class conflict. That is to say, as Marx argued, the more workers are exploited, the more they experience impoverishment, and the more they fight back. In other words, since there is a causal link between the wealth of capitalists and the poverty of workers, higher exploitation means more wealth for the capitalists and less for workers, resulting in workers' protest.

Cuneo's analyses are questioned by Axel van den Berg and Michael Smith for methodological problems and for misinterpreting Marx. They quote Marx to the effect that, contrary to Cuneo's conceptualization, the number of workers does not affect the rate of surplus value or the degree of exploitation. They insist that if we look at just the number of production workers in calculating the rate of surplus value, we might conclude that workers in a large plant in which an employer extracts no surplus at all are as much exploited as workers in a small plant in which over 90 percent of the value of production goes to the workers. Van den Berg and Smith further dispute Cuneo's finding on the relationship between the rate of surplus value and strike/lockout; this is meaningless, they say, since as the number of workers in Canadian industries has increased (a factor Cuneo takes into account for calculating the rate of surplus value), so have the number of workers involved per year in strikes and lockouts, days lost per year for strikes and lockouts, and number of strikes and lockouts per year. Furthermore, for van den Berg and Smith, the increase in the indicators of industrial conflicts are more likely to be due to an increase in unionization, extension of the right to strike, increase in real income, and in number of women in the labour force, which allows workers to stay on strike for a longer period. For example, the increasing labour force participation of women increases the probability of strike per se. More importantly, it increases the available disposable income to the household, allowing the partner to stay on strike for a longer period. Thus, van den Berg and Smith argue that the increasing rate of strike and lockout is not due to the increase in the rate of exploitation, as suggested by Cuneo. This debate continues: see Emmerson and Rowe 1982; Cuneo 1982, 1984; van den Berg and Smith 1984.

One can perhaps believe that there is nothing unfair about capitalists being able to use their ownership of the means of production, employ propertyless workers, and in the process become rich by extracting what Marxists call surplus value from these workers. After all, the capitalists risk losing the money they invest in a business. But is it also fair that individuals from different backgrounds do not have equal access to the positions of power and wealth? On the one hand, the liberal–pluralist tradition argues that with advanced industrialization, the class structure becomes less rigid, and there is a greater likelihood of mobility among and between the generations. Industrialization entails technological advancement, a greater division of labour, and more rational organization of employment. Traditional authoritarian ascriptive norms are replaced by new norms based on universalism and equality of opportunity. On the other hand, critics rooted in Marxist tradition argue that with advanced industrialization, there is no evidence of a trend of increasing equality of opportunity. Upper classes are able to pass on to their offspring wealth, better education, and the use of their club network to assure them of important occupations or higher social class positions. The critics insist that there is a persistent pattern of the elites recruiting and reproducing themselves in capitalist societies such as in Canada.

Is entry into the upper classes open or closed? What are the avenues of mobility into these classes? Has there been any change over time in terms of mobility opportunities into upper classes? Answers to these questions are important because they will enable us to determine the extent to which Canadian society is open or closed.

Wallace Clement bases his study on John Porter's classic analysis and shows that there exists a persistent pattern of the upper class dominating the corporate elite. The Canadian corporate elite is significantly more likely to come from an upper-class background. They are more likely to have had fathers (or other family members) among corporate CEOs, to have had private schooling and a post-secondary education, and to be members of private clubs, as well as to have used engineering, science, finance, and law in order to pursue an elite career. Clement also shows that from 1951 to 1972, entry into the elite did not open for the lower classes, and, in fact, there were signs of less mobility. Rick Ogmundson (1990) questions the Porter–Clement tradition on methodological grounds and in terms of their interpretations of results. He insists that Clement failed to replicate Porter's study and, therefore, one cannot infer trends over time with any confidence. Moreover, measures of class origin based on education ignore a significant proportion of the working class who attended university. In addition, Porter and Clement only included data for individuals with complete biographical information, excluding the rest from their analysis. One consequence of this is that lower-class origins are less likely to be included since fewer have complete biographical data. Finally, Ogmundson suggests that the Canadian elite structure is no different than that of other societies, including socialist ones. For more debate on these issues, see Heap (1972), Porter (1965, 1972), Black (1974), Rich (1976a, 1976b, 1991), Berkowitz (1984), Brym and Fox (1989), Clement (1975, 1990), and Ogmundson (1990, 1993).

We finish this section with an article and a response that address the nature of Canadian economic dependency. One of the important debates on the nature of Canadian economic development centres around the relative strength of Canadian capitalist fractions (financial, industrial, and commercial) vis-a-vis each other and those of multinational foreign corporations in Canada. Empirical evidence on the relative strength of these fractions and on the pattern of change across time will enable us to determine the extent of: (1) foreign domination; (2) capital accumulation by the financial and industrial Canadian capitalist fractions and their impact on economic development; and finally (3) the relative influence of foreign and Canadian capitalists in the Canadian state and on its policies. Let's consider the potential influence of each of the Canadian capitalist fractions separately. To the extent that the Canadian commercial capitalist fraction dominates the economy, the Canadian economy will centre around staple resources (fur, wheat, forest products, oil and gas, and other industrial raw materials) intended for export largely to England and/or the United States. One consequence of such an economy is vulnerability to the international market fluctuation. When the international demand for these commodities weakens, unemployment and poverty increases. However, during periods of high demand, Canada experiences prosperity. Similarly, foreign ownership of Canadian economic sectors will result in limiting the power of the Canadian state to influence affairs of the society. These foreign corporations, for example, can influence state policies by demanding changes in employment insurance, minimum wages, and/or health and safety laws. If the Canadian government fails to accommodate them, these companies can withdraw their capital and move to where wages are lower and state laws are more relaxed — an investment strike. However, to the extent that the Canadian financial capitalist fraction exercises control over domestic financial institutions as well as over the large-scale industrial capitalist fraction, it will be able to appropriate the surplus value produced in Canada and to control Canadian economic development and capital accumulation. Otherwise, it will have to rely on foreign capitalist fractions for capital funds, research and development, and economic policies. In the former case, the Canadian state will rely on the Canadian capitalist (financial and industrial) fraction for sound economic advice and policies, while in the latter case, the Canadian state has to rely on foreign corporation for advice. It is only when financial and industrial capitalist fractions in Canada are effectively integrated that Canada can experience a relatively autonomous economic and political development. In sum, the development of independent Canadian capitalist production depends on the extent to which indigenous finance capital is tied with industrial capital, and that both are able to dominate the production process, appropriate surplus value, control the home market, and enhance capital accumulation independent of foreign control.

William Carroll evaluates the extent of interlocking directors between various capitalist fractions as well as with foreign-owned corporations. He shows that indigenous Canadian capitalists owned and controlled a substantial portion of financial and industrial capital throughout the postwar period, and that among this group, there were more interlocking multiple directorships than there were between Canadian capitalists and foreign-owned corporations. In fact, over time, the trend shows decreasing ties between Canadian-controlled financial institutions and U.S.-controlled industrial companies. His evidence points to a more independent Canadian economic and political process than previously believed. Paul Stevenson comments that the declining American control of Canadian corporations is not surprising given that since the 1950s, American investors have shifted their attention to Europe and away from Canada and the Third World. However, this does not indicate a radical decline in American control of the Canadian economy. As well, Stevenson questions Carroll's research implication that indigenous Canadian capitalists have supplanted American capitalists from the dominant position in the Canadian state. On the contrary, Stevenson argues that the Canadian state is a mediator of conflicting interests and pressures from fractions of capital, classes, regions, ethnic groups, men and women, political ideologies, and other groups. Students interested in this debate should consult Brym (1985), Carroll (1984, 1986), Clement (1975, 1977), Richardson (1982), Laxer (1985), and Fox and Ornstein (1986). Also see the free trade debate in Smith (1989), Marchak (1989), Lebowitz (1988), McNally (1990), and Lebowitz's response (1990). On the role of state, see Usher (1980a, 1980b), West and Winer (1980), Chorney et al. (1977), and Veltmeyer (1977).

MOTIVATION AND INEQUALITY

Some Principles of Stratification
Kingsley Davis and Wilbert E. Moore

THE FUNCTIONAL NECESSITY OF STRATIFICATION

[T]he main functional necessity explaining the universal presence of stratification is precisely the requirement faced by any society of placing and motivating individuals in the social structure. As a functioning mechanism, a society must somehow distribute its members in social positions and induce them to perform the duties of these positions. It must thus concern itself with motivation at two different levels: to instill in the proper individuals the desire to fill certain positions, and, once in these positions, the desire to perform the duties attached to them. Even though the social order may be relatively static in form, there is a continuous process of metabolism as new individuals are born into it, shift with age, and die off. Their absorption into the positional system must somehow be arranged and motivated. This is true whether the system is competitive or non-competitive. A competitive system gives greater importance to the motivation to achieve positions, whereas a non-competitive system gives perhaps greater importance to the motivation to perform the duties of the positions; but in any system, both types of motivation are required.

If the duties associated with the various positions were all equally pleasant to the human organism, all equally important to societal survival, and all equally in need of the same ability or talent, it would make no difference who got into which positions, and the problem of social placement would be greatly reduced. But actually it does make a great deal of difference who gets into which positions not only because some positions are inherently more agreeable than others, but also because some require special talents or training, and some are functionally more important than others. Also, it is essential that the duties of the positions be performed with the diligence that their importance requires. Inevitably, then, a society must have, first, some kind of rewards that it can use as inducements, and, second, some way of distributing these rewards differentially according to positions. The rewards and their distribution become a part of the social order and thus give rise to stratification.

One may ask what kind of rewards a society has at its disposal in distributing its personnel and securing essential services. It has, first of all, the things that contribute to sustenance and comfort. It has, second, the things that contribute to humor and diversion. And it has, finally, the things that contribute to self-respect and ego expansion. The last, because of the peculiarly social character of the self, is largely a function of the opinion of others, but it nonetheless ranks in importance with the first two. In any social system, all three kinds of rewards must be dispensed differentially according to positions.

In a sense, the rewards are "built into" the position. They consist in the "rights" associated with the position plus what may be called its accompaniments or perquisites. Often the rights, and sometimes the accompaniments, are functionally related to the duties of the position. (Rights as viewed by the incumbent are usually duties as viewed by other members of the community.) However, there may be a host of subsidiary rights and perquisites that are not essential to the function of the position and have only an indirect and symbolic connection with its duties, but which still may be of considerable importance in inducing people to seek the positions and fulfil the essential duties.

If the rights and perquisites of different positions in a society must be unequal, then the society must be stratified because that is precisely what stratification means. Social inequality is thus an unconsciously evolved device by which societies insure that the most important positions are conscientiously filled by the most qualified persons. Hence, every society, no matter how simple or complex, must differentiate persons in terms of both prestige and esteem, and must therefore possess a certain amount of institutionalized inequality.

It does not follow that the amount or type of inequality need be the same in all societies. This is largely a function of factors that will be discussed presently.

THE TWO DETERMINANTS OF POSITIONAL RANK

Granting the general function that inequality subserves, one can specify the two factors that determine the relative rank of different positions. In general, those positions convey the best reward, and hence have the highest rank, which (a) have the greatest importance for the society and (b) require the greatest training or talent. The first factor concerns function and is a matter of relative significance; the second concerns means and is a matter of scarcity.

Differential Functional Importance

Actually, a society does not need to reward positions in proportion to their functional importance. It merely needs to give sufficient reward to them to insure that they will be filled competently. In other words, it must see that less essential positions do not compete successfully with more essential ones. If a position is easily filled, it need not be heavily rewarded, even though important. On the other hand, if it is important but hard to fill, the reward must be high enough to get it filled anyway. Functional importance is therefore a necessary but not a sufficient cause of high rank being assigned to a position.[1]

Differential Scarcity of Personnel

Practically all positions, no matter how acquired, require some form of skill or capacity for performance. This is implicit in the very notion of position, which implies that the incumbent must, by virtue of his incumbency, accomplish certain things.

There are, ultimately, only two ways in which a person's qualifications come about: through inherent capacity or through training. Obviously, in concrete activities, both are always necessary, but from a practical standpoint, the scarcity may lie primarily in one or the other as well as in both. Some positions require innate talents of such high degree that the persons who fill them are bound to be rare. In many cases, however, talent is fairly abundant in the population, but the training process is so long, costly, and elaborate that relatively few can qualify. Modern medicine, for example, is within the mental capacity of most individuals, but a medical education is so burdensome and expensive that virtually none would undertake it if the position of the M.D. did not carry a reward commensurate with the sacrifice.

If the talents required for a position are abundant and the training easy, the method of acquiring the position may have little to do with its duties. There may be, in fact, a virtually accidental relationship. But if the skills required are scarce by reason of the rarity of talent or the costliness of training, the position, if functionally important, must have an attractive power than will draw the necessary skills in competition with other positions. This means, in effect, that the position must be high in the social scale — must command great prestige, high salary, ample leisure, and the like.

How Variations Are to Be Understood

Insofar as there is a difference between one system of stratification and another, it is attributable to whatever factors affects the two determinants of differential reward — namely, functional importance and scarcity of personnel. Positions important in one society may not be important in another because the conditions faced by the societies, or their degree of internal development, may be different. The same conditions, in turn, may affect the question of scarcity; for in some societies, the stage of development, or the external situation, may wholly obviate the necessity of certain kinds of skill or talent. Any particular system of stratification, then, can be understood as a product of the special conditions affecting the two aforementioned grounds of differential reward.

MAJOR SOCIETAL FUNCTIONS AND STRATIFICATION

Religion

The reason why religion is necessary is apparently to be found in the fact that human society achieves its unity primarily through the possession by its members of certain ultimate values and ends in common. Although these values and ends are subjective, they influence behavior, and their integration enables the society to operate as a system. Derived neither from inherited nor from external nature, they have evolved as a part of culture by communication and moral pressure. They must, however, appear to the members of the society to have some reality, and it is the role of religious belief and ritual to supply and reinforce this appearance of reality. Through belief and ritual, the common ends and values are connected with an imaginary world symbolized by concrete sacred objects, which world in turn is related in a meaningful way to the facts and trials of the individual's life. Through the worship of the sacred objects and the beings they symbolize and the acceptance of supernatural prescriptions that are at the same time codes of behavior, a powerful control over human conduct is exercised, guiding it along lines sustaining the institutional structure and conforming to the ultimate ends and values.

If this conception of the role of religion is true, one can understand why in every known society, the religious activities tend to be under the charge of particular persons who tend thereby to enjoy greater rewards than the ordinary societal member. Certain of the rewards and special privileges may attach to only the highest religious functionaries, but others usually apply, if such exists, to the entire sacerdotal class.

Moreover, there is a peculiar relation between the duties of the religious official and the special privileges he enjoys. If the supernatural world governs the destinies of men more ultimately than does the real world, its earthly representative, the person through whom one may communicate with the supernatural, must be a powerful individual. He is a keeper of sacred tradition, a skilled performer of the ritual, and an interpreter of lore and myth. He is in such close contact with the gods that he is viewed as possessing some of their characteristics. He is, in short, a bit sacred, and hence free from some of the more vulgar necessities and controls.

It is no accident, therefore, that religious functionaries have been associated with the very highest positions of power, as in theocratic regimes. Indeed, looking at it from this point of view, one may wonder why it is that they do not get *entire* control over their societies. The factors that prevent this are worthy of note.

In the first place, the amount of technical competence necessary for the performance of religious duties is small. Scientific or artistic capacity is not required. Anyone can set himself up as enjoying an intimate relation with deities, and nobody can successfully dispute him. Therefore, the factor of scarcity of personnel does not operate in the technical sense.

One may assert, on the other hand, that religious ritual is often elaborate and religious lore abstruse, and that priestly ministrations require tact, if not intelligence. This is true, but the technical requirements of the profession are, for the most part, adventitious, not related to the end in the same way that science is related to air travel. The priest can never be free from competition since the criteria of whether or not one has genuine contact with the supernatural are never strictly clear. It is this competition that debases the priestly position below what might be expected at first glance. That is why priestly prestige is highest in those societies where membership in the profession is rigidly controlled by the priestly guild itself. That is why, in part, at least, elaborate devices are utilized to stress the identification of the person with his office — spectacular costume, abnormal conduct, special diet, segregated residence, celibacy, conspicuous leisure, and the like. In fact, the priest is always in danger of becoming somewhat discredited — as happens in a secularized society — because in a world of stubborn fact, ritual and sacred knowledge alone will not grow crops or build houses. Furthermore, unless he is protected by a professional guild, the priest's identification with the supernatural tends to preclude his acquisition of abundant worldly goods.

Government

Like religion, government plays a unique and indispensable part in society. But in contrast to religion, which provides integration in terms of sentiments, beliefs, and rituals, it organizes the society in terms of law and authority. Furthermore, it orients the society to the actual rather than the unseen world.

The main functions of government are, internally, the ultimate enforcement of norms, the final arbitration of conflicting interests, and the overall planning and direction of society; and externally, the handling of war and diplomacy. To carry out these functions, it acts as the agent of the entire people, enjoys a monopoly of force, and controls all individuals within its territory.

Political action, by definition, implies authority. An official can command because he has authority, and the citizen must obey because he is subject to that authority. For this reason, stratification is inherent in the nature of political relationships.

So clear is the power embodied in political position that political inequality is sometimes thought to comprise all inequality. But it can be shown that there are other bases of stratification, that the following controls operate in practice to keep political power from becoming complete: (a) the fact that the actual holders of political office, and especially those determining top policy, must necessarily be few in number compared to the total population; (b) the fact that the rulers represent the interest of the group rather than of themselves and are therefore restricted in their behavior by rules and mores designed to enforce this limitation of interest; (c) the fact that the holder of political office has his authority by virtue of his office and nothing else, and therefore, any special knowledge, talent, or capacity he may claim is purely incidental so that he often has to depend upon others for technical assistance.

In view of these limiting factors, it is not strange that the rulers often have less power and prestige than a literal enumeration of their formal rights would lead one to expect.

Wealth, Property, and Labor

Every position that secures for its incumbent a livelihood is, by definition, economically rewarded. For this reason, there is an economic aspect to those positions (e.g., political and religious) the main function of which is not economic. It therefore becomes convenient for the society to use unequal economic returns as a principal means of controlling the entrance of persons into positions and stimulating the performance of their duties. The amount of the economic return therefore becomes one of the main indices of social status.

It should be stressed, however, that a position does not bring power and prestige *because* it draws a high income. Rather, it draws a high income because it is functionally important, and the available personnel is for one reason or another scarce. It is therefore superficial and erroneous to regard high income as the cause of a man's power and prestige, just as it is erroneous to think that a man's fever is the cause of his disease.

The economic source of power and prestige is not income primarily, but the ownership of capital goods (including patents, good will, and professional reputation). Such ownership should be distinguished from the possession of consumers' goods, which is an index rather than a cause of social standing. In other words, the ownership of producers' goods is, properly speaking, a source of income like other positions, the income itself remaining an index. Even in situations where social values are widely commercialized and earnings are the readiest method of judging social position, income does not confer prestige on a position so much as it induces people to compete for the position. It is true that a man who has a high income as a result of one position may find this money helpful in climbing into another position as well, but this again reflects the effect of his initial, economically advantageous status, which exercises its influence through the medium of money.

In a system of private property in productive enterprise, an income above what an individual spends can give rise to possession of capital wealth. Presumably, such possession is a reward for the proper management of one's finances originally and of the productive enterprise later. But as social differentiation becomes highly advanced and yet the institution of inheritance persists, the phenomenon of pure ownership and reward for pure ownership emerges. In such a case, it is difficult to prove that the position is functionally important or that the scarcity involved is anything other than extrinsic and accidental. It is for this reason, doubtless, that the institution of private property in productive goods becomes more subject to criticism as social development proceeds toward industrialization. It is only this pure, that is, strictly legal and functionless ownership, however, that is open to attack; for some form of active ownership, whether private or public, is indispensable.

One kind of ownership of production goods consists in rights over the labor of others. The most extremely concentrated and exclusive of such rights are found in slavery, but the essential principle remains in serfdom, peonage, encomienda, and indenture. Naturally, this kind of ownership has the greatest significance for stratification because it necessarily entails an unequal relationship.

But property in capital goods inevitably introduces a compulsive element even into the nominally free contractual relationship. Indeed, in some respects, the authority of the contractual employers is greater than that of the feudal landlord inasmuch as the latter is more limited by traditional reciprocities. Even the classical economics recognized that competitors would fare unequally, but it did not pursue this fact to its necessary conclusion that, however it might be acquired, unequal control of goods and services must give unequal advantage to the parties to a contract.

Technical Knowledge

The function of finding means to single goals, without any concern with the choice between goals, is the exclusively technical sphere. The explanation of why positions requiring great technical skill receive fairly high rewards is easy to see, for it is the simplest case of the rewards being so distributed as to draw talent and motivate training. Why they seldom if ever receive the highest rewards is also clear: the importance of technical knowledge from a societal point of view is never so great as the integration of goals, which takes place on the religious, political, and economic levels. Since the technological level is concerned solely with means, a purely technical position must ultimately be subordinate to other positions that are religious, political, or economic in character.

Nevertheless, the distinction between expert and layman in any social order is fundamental and cannot be entirely reduced to other terms. Methods of recruitment, as well as of reward, sometimes lead to the erroneous interpretation that technical positions are economically determined. Actually, however, the acquisition of knowledge and skill cannot be accomplished by purchase, although the opportunity to learn may be. The control of the avenues of training may inhere as a sort of property right in certain families or classes, giving them power and prestige in consequence. Such a situation adds an artificial scarcity to the natural scarcity of skills and talents. On the other hand, it is possible for an opposite situation to arise. The rewards of technical position may be so great that a condition of excess supply is created, leading to at least temporary devaluation of the rewards. Thus "unemployment in the learned professions" may result in a debasement of the prestige of those positions. Such adjustments and readjustments are constantly occurring in changing societies; and it is always well to bear in mind that the efficiency of a stratified structure may be affected by the modes of recruitment for positions. The social order itself, however, sets limits to the inflation or deflation of the prestige of experts: an over-supply tends to debase the rewards and discourage recruitment or produce revolution, whereas an under-supply tends to increase the rewards or weaken the society in competition with other societies.

Particular systems of stratification show a wide range with respect to the exact position of technically competent persons. This range is perhaps most evident in the degree of specialization. Extreme division of labor tends to create many specialists without high prestige since the training is short and the required native capacity relatively small. On the other hand, it also tends to accentuate the high position of the true experts — scientists, engineers, and administrators — by increasing their authority relative to other functionally important positions. But the idea of a technocratic social order or a government or priesthood of engineers or social scientists neglects the limitations of knowledge and skills as a basic for performing social functions. To the extent that the social structure is truly specialized, the prestige of the technical person must also be circumscribed.

NOTES

[1] Unfortunately, functional importance is difficult to establish. To use the position's prestige to establish it, as is often unconsciously done, constitutes circular reasoning from our point of view. There are, however, two independent clues: (a) the degree to which a position is functionally unique, there being no other positions that can perform the same function satisfactorily; (b) the degree to which other positions are dependent on the one in question. Both clues are best exemplified in organized systems of positions built around one major function. Thus, in most complex societies, the religious, political, economic, and educational functions are handled by distinct structures not easily interchangeable. In addition, each structure possesses many different positions, some clearly dependent on, if not subordinate to, others. In sum, when an institutional nucleus becomes differentiated around one main function and at the same time organizes a large portion of the population into its relationships, the *key* positions in it are of the highest functional importance. The absence of such specialization does not prove functional unimportance, for the whole society may be relatively unspecialized; but it is safe to assume that the more important functions receive the first and clearest structural differentiation.

Some Principles of Stratification: A Critical Analysis
Melvin M. Tumin

The fact of social inequality in human society is marked by its ubiquity and its antiquity. Every known society, past and present, distributes its scarce and demanded goods and services unequally. And there are attached to the positions which command unequal amounts of such goods and services certain highly morally toned evaluations of their importance for the society.

The ubiquity and the antiquity of such inequality has given rise to the assumption that there must be something both inevitable and positively functional about such social arrangements.

Clearly, the truth or falsity of such an assumption is a strategic question for any general theory of social organization. It is therefore most curious that the basic premises and implications of the assumption have only been most casually explored by American sociologists.

The central argument advanced by Kingsley Davis and Wilbert Moore can be stated in a number of sequential propositions [and critiqued accordingly], as follows:

(1) Certain positions in any society are more functionally important than others and require special skills for their performance.

The key term here is "functionally important." The functionalist theory of social organization is by no means clear and explicit about this term. The minimum common referent is to something known as the "survival value" of a social structure. This concept immediately involves a number of perplexing questions. Among these are: (a) the issue of minimum vs. maximum survival and the possible empirical referents which can be given to those terms; (b) whether such a proposition is a useless tautology since any *status quo* at any given moment is nothing more and nothing less than everything present in the *status quo*. In these terms, all acts and structures must be judged positively functional in that they constitute essential portions of the *status quo;* (c) what kind of calculus of functionality exists which will enable us, at this point in our development, to add and subtract long- and short-range consequences, with their mixed qualities, and arrive at some summative judgment regarding the rating an act or structure should receive on a scale of greater or lesser functionality? At best, we tend to make primarily intuitive judgments. Often enough, these judgments involve the use of value-laden criteria or, at least, criteria which are chosen in preference to others not for any sociologically systematic reasons, but by reason of certain implicit value preferences.

Thus, to judge that the engineers in a factory are functionally more important to the factory than the unskilled workmen involves a notion regarding the dispensability of the unskilled workmen, or their replaceability, relative to that of the engineers. But this is not a process of choice with infinite time dimensions. For at some point along the line, one must face the problem of adequate motivation for *all* workers at all levels of skill in the factory. In the long run, *some* labor force of unskilled workmen is as important and as indispensable to the factory as *some* labor force of engineers. Often enough, the labor force situation is such that this fact is brought home sharply to the entrepreneur in the short run rather than in the long run.

A generalized theory of social stratification must recognize that the prevailing system of inducements and rewards is only one of many variants in the whole range of possible systems of motivation which, at least theoretically, are capable of working in human society. It is quite conceivable, of course, that a system of norms could be institutionalized in which the idea of threatened withdrawal of services, except under the most extreme circumstances, would be considered as absolute moral anathema. In such a case, the whole notion of relative functionality, as advanced by Davis and Moore, would have to be radically revised.

(2) Only a limited number of individuals in any society have the talents which can be trained into the skills appropriate to these positions (i.e., the more functionally important positions).

If all that is meant is that in every society, there is a *range* of talent and that some members of any society are by nature more talented than others, no sensible contradiction can be offered, but a question must be raised here regarding the amount of sound knowledge present in any society concerning the presence of talent in the population.

For, in every society, there is some demonstrable ignorance regarding the amount of talent present in the population. *And the more rigidly stratified a society is, the less chance does that society have of discovering any new facts about the talents of its members.* Smoothly working and stable systems of stratification, wherever found, tend to build in obstacles to the further exploration of the range of available talent. This is especially true in those societies where the opportunity to discover talent in any one generation varies with the differential resources of the parent generation. Where, for instance, access to education depends upon the wealth of one's parents and where wealth is differentially distributed, large segments of the population are likely to be deprived of the chance even to *discover* what are their talents.

Whether or not differential rewards and opportunities are functional in any one generation, it is clear that if those differentials are allowed to be socially inherited by the next generation, then the stratification system is specifically dysfunctional for the discovery of talents in the next generation. In this fashion, systems of social stratification tend to limit the chances available to maximize the efficiency of discovery, recruitment and training of "functionally important talent."

Additionally, the unequal distribution of rewards in one generation tends to result in the unequal distribution of motivation in the succeeding generation. Since motivation to succeed is clearly an important element in the entire process of education, the unequal distribution of motivation tends to set limits on the possible extensions of the education system, and hence, upon the efficient recruitment and training of the widest body of skills available in the population.[1]

Lastly, in this context, it may be asserted that there is some noticeable tendency for elites to restrict further access to their privileged positions once they have sufficient power to enforce such restrictions. This is especially true in a culture where it is possible for an elite to contrive a high demand and a proportionately higher reward for its work by restricting the numbers of the elite available to do the work. The recruitment and training of doctors in modern United States is at least partly a case in point.

Here, then, are three ways, among others, which could be cited in which stratification systems, once operative, tend to reduce the survival value of a society by limiting the search, recruitment and training of functionally important personnel far more sharply than the facts of available talent would appear to justify. It is only when there is genuinely equal access to recruitment and training for all potentially talented persons that differential rewards can conceivably be justified as functional. And stratification systems are apparently *inherently antagonistic* to the development of such full equality of opportunity.

(3) The conversion of talents into skills involves a training period during which sacrifices of one kind or another are made by those undergoing the training.

Davis and Moore introduce here a concept, "sacrifice," which comes closer than any of the rest of their vocabulary of analysis to being a direct reflection of the rationalizations, offered by the more fortunate members of a society, of the rightness of their occupancy of privileged positions. It is the least critically thought-out concept in the repertoire and can also be shown to be least supported by the actual facts.

In our present society, for example, what are the sacrifices which talented persons undergo in the training period? The possibly serious losses involve the surrender of earning power and the cost of the training. The latter is generally borne by the parents of the talented youth undergoing training and not by the trainees themselves. But this cost tends to be paid out of income which the parents were able to earn generally by virtue of *their* privileged positions in the hierarchy of stratification. That is to say, the parents' ability to pay for the training of their children is part of the differential *reward* they, the parents, received for their privileged positions in the society. And to charge this sum up against sacrifices made by the youth is falsely to perpetrate a bill or a debt already paid by the society to the parents.

So far as the sacrifice of earning power by the trainees themselves is concerned, the loss may be measured relative to what they might have earned had they gone into the labor market instead of into advanced training for the "important" skills. There are several ways to judge this. One way is to take all the average earnings of age peers who did go into the labor market for a period equal to the average length of the training period. The total income, so calculated, roughly equals an amount which the elite can, on the average, earn back in the first decade of professional work, over and above the earnings of his age peers who are not trained. Ten years is probably the maximum amount needed to equalize the differential.[2] There remains, on the average, twenty years of work during each of which the skilled person then goes on to earn far more than his unskilled age peers. And, what is often forgotten, there is then still another ten- or fifteen-year period during which the unskilled person continues to work and earn when his unskilled age peer is either totally or partially out of the labor market by virtue of the attrition of his strength and capabilities.

One might say that the first ten years of differential pay is perhaps justified in order to regain for the trained person what he lost during his training period. But it is difficult to imagine what would justify continuing such differential rewards beyond that period.

There seems to be no good theoretical grounds for insisting on this assumption. For, while under any system, certain costs will be involved in training persons for skilled positions, these costs could easily be assumed by the society-at-large. Under these circumstances, there would be no need to compensate anyone in terms of differential rewards once the skilled positions were staffed. In short, there would be no need or justification for stratifying social positions on *these* grounds.

(4) In order to induce the talented persons to undergo these sacrifices and acquire the training, their future positions must carry an inducement value in the form of differential, i.e., privileged and disproportionate access to the scarce and desired rewards which the society has to offer.

Let us assume, for the purposes of the discussion, that the training period is sacrificial and the talent is rare in every conceivable human society. There is still the basic problem as to whether the allocation of differential rewards in scarce and desired goods and services is the only or the most efficient way of recruiting the appropriate talent to these positions.

For there are a number of alternative motivational schemes whose efficiency and adequacy ought at least to be considered in this context. What can be said, for instance, on behalf of the motivation which De Man called "joy in work," Veblen termed "instinct for workmanship" and which we latterly have come to identify as "intrinsic work satisfaction?" Or, to what extent could the motivation of "social duty" be institutionalized in such a fashion that self-interest and social interest come closely to coincide? Or, how much prospective confidence can be placed in the possibilities of institutionalizing "social service" as a widespread motivation for seeking one's appropriate position and fulfilling it conscientiously?

Are not these types of motivations, we may ask, likely to prove most appropriate for precisely the "most functionally important positions?" Especially in a mass industrial society, where the vast majority of positions become standardized and routinized, it is the skilled jobs which are likely to retain most of the quality of "intrinsic job satisfaction" and be most readily identifiable as socially serviceable. Is it indeed impossible, then, to build these motivations into the socialization pattern to which we expose our talented youth?

(5) These scarce and desired goods consist of rights and perquisites attached to, or built into, the positions and can be classified into those things which contribute to (a) sustenance and comfort; (b) humor and diversion; (c) self-respect and ego expansion.

(6) This differential access to the basic rewards of the society has as a consequence the differentiation of the prestige and esteem which various strata acquire. This may be said, along with the rights and perquisites, to constitute institutionalized social inequality, i.e., stratification.

With the classification of the rewards offered by Davis and Moore there need be little argument. Some questions must be raised, however, as to whether any reward system, built into a general stratification system, must allocate equal amounts of all three types of reward in order to function effectively, or whether one type of reward may be emphasized to the virtual neglect of others. This raises the further question regarding which type of emphasis is likely to prove most effective as a differential inducer. Nothing in the known facts about human motivation impels us to favor one type of reward over the other or to insist that all three types of reward must be built into the positions in comparable amounts if the position is to have an inducement value.

It is well known, of course, that societies differ considerably in the kinds of rewards they emphasize in their efforts to maintain a reasonable balance between responsibility and reward. There are, for instance, numerous societies in which the conspicuous display of differential economic advantage is considered in extremely bad taste. In short, our present knowledge commends to us the possibility of considerable plasticity in the way in which different types of rewards can be structured into a functioning society. This is to say, it cannot yet be demonstrated that it is *unavoidable* that differential prestige and esteem shall accrue to positions which command differential rewards in power and property.

What does seem to be unavoidable is that differential prestige shall be given to those in any society who conform to the normative order as against those who deviate from that order in a way judged immoral and detrimental. On the assumption that the continuity of a society depends on the continuity and stability of its normative order, some such distinction between conformists and deviants seems inescapable.

It also seems to be unavoidable that in any society, no matter how literate its tradition, the older, wiser and more experienced individuals who are charged with the enculturation and socialization of the young must have more power than the young on the assumption that the task of effective socialization demands such differential power.

But this differentiation in prestige between the conformist and the deviant is by no means the same distinction as that between strata of individuals, each of which operates *within* the normative order and is composed of adults. The *latter* distinction, in the form of differentiated rewards and prestige between social strata is what Davis and Moore and most sociologists consider the structure of a stratification system. The *former* distinctions have nothing necessarily to do with the workings of such a system nor with the efficiency of motivation and recruitment of functionally important personnel.

Nor does the differentiation of power between young and old necessarily create differentially valued strata. For no society rates its young as less morally worthy than its older persons no matter how much differential power the older ones may temporarily enjoy.

(7) Therefore, social inequality among different strata in the amounts of scarce and desired goods, and the amounts of prestige and esteem which they receive, is both positively functional and inevitable in any society.

If the objections which have heretofore been raised are taken as reasonable, then it may be stated that the only items which any society *must* distribute unequally are the power and property necessary for the performance of different tasks. If such differential power and property are viewed by all as commensurate with the differential responsibilities, and if they are culturally defined as *resources* and not as rewards, then no differentials in prestige and esteem need follow.

Historically, the evidence seems to be that every time power and property are distributed unequally, no matter what the cultural definition, prestige and esteem differentiations have tended to result as well. Historically, however, no systematic effort has ever been made, under propitious circumstances, to develop the tradition that each man is as socially worthy as all other men so long as he performs his appropriate tasks conscientiously. While such a tradition seems utterly utopian, no known facts in psychological or social science have yet demonstrated its impossibility or its dysfunctionality for the continuity of a society. The achievement of a full institutionalization of such a tradition seems far too remote to contemplate. Some successive approximations at such a tradition, however, are not out of the range of prospective social innovation.

What, then, of the "positive functionality" of social stratification? Are there other, negative, functions of institutionalized social inequality which can be identified, if only tentatively? Some such dysfunctions of stratification have already been suggested in the body of this paper. Along with others, they may now be stated, in the form of provisional assertions, as follows:

1. Social stratification systems function to limit the possibility of discovery of the full range of talent available in a society. This results from the fact of unequal access to appropriate motivation, channels of recruitment and centers of training.

2. In foreshortening the range of available talent, social stratification systems function to set limits upon the possibility of expanding the productive resources of the society, at least relative to what might be the case under conditions of greater equality of opportunity.

3. Social stratification systems function to provide the elite with the political power necessary to procure acceptance and dominance

of an ideology which rationalizes the *status quo,* whatever it may be, as "logical," "natural" and "morally right." In this manner, social stratification systems function as essentially conservative influences in the societies in which they are found.

4. Social stratification systems function to distribute favorable self-images unequally throughout a population. To the extent that such favorable self-images are requisite to the development of the creative potential inherent in men, to that extent stratification systems function to limit the development of this creative potential.

5. To the extent that inequalities in social rewards cannot be made fully acceptable to the less privileged in a society, social stratification systems function to encourage hostility, suspicion and distrust among the various segments of a society and thus to limit the possibilities of extensive social integration.

6. To the extent that the sense of significant membership in a society depends on one's place on the prestige ladder of the society, social stratification systems function to distribute unequally the sense of significant membership in the population.

7. To the extent that loyalty to a society depends on a sense of significant membership in the society, social stratification systems function to distribute loyalty unequally in the population.

8. To the extent that participation and apathy depend upon the sense of significant membership in the society, social stratification systems function to distribute the motivation to participate unequally in a population.

Each of the eight foregoing propositions contains implicit hypotheses regarding the consequences of unequal distribution of rewards in a society in accordance with some notion of the functional importance of various positions. These are empirical hypotheses, subject to test. They are offered here only as exemplary of the kinds of consequences of social stratification which are not often taken into account in dealing with the problem. They should also serve to reinforce the doubt that social inequality is a device which is uniformly functional for the role of guaranteeing that the most important tasks in a society will be performed conscientiously by the most competent persons.

The obviously mixed character of the functions of social inequality should come as no surprise to anyone. If sociology is sophisticated in any sense, it is certainly with regard to its awareness of the mixed nature of any social arrangement when the observer takes into account long- as well as short-range consequences and latent as well as manifest dimensions.

NOTES

[1] In the United States, for instance, we are only now becoming aware of the amount of productivity we, as a society, lost by allocating inferior opportunities and rewards, and hence, inferior motivation, to our Negro population. The actual amount of loss is difficult to specify precisely. Some rough estimate can be made, however, on the assumption that there is present in the Negro population about the same range of talent that is found in the White population.

[2] These are only very rough estimates, of course, and it is certain that there is considerable income variation within the so-called elite group, so that the proposition holds only relatively more or less.

DISCUSSION QUESTIONS

1. List some of the factors that motivated you to attend university. As well, what are your main reasons for studying, writing assignments, and attending classes? Why do you think some of your classmates do not attend classes or study as much as you do? How does your motivation differ from theirs? To what extent do these reasons correspond with Davis and Moore's conceptualization of inequality?

2. What factors do you think helped your parents achieve their present occupational position? What are the factors that prevented them from moving further up the occupational ladder? Do you think a lack of motivation on your parents' part was responsible for them not moving higher up the occupational ladder? How is their situation different from that of your classmates' parents?

3. List the ten most "functionally important" and ten least "functionally important" occupations. Also, list the approximate levels of education and skill required by each occupation. Finally, list the approximate level of income for these occupations (Statistics Canada is a good source for acquiring the mean education and income of various occupations). Do you think that there is a close correlation between education, skill, and income of these occupations? How does this experiment support or reject Davis and Moore's theory?

4. In what ways do you think inheritance of family wealth or one's sex or ethnicity can effect one's position in the system of inequality?

5. Why is Davis and Moore's theory tautological?

RELEVANCE OF CLASS

Are Social Classes Dying?
Terry Nichols Clark and
Seymour Martin Lipset

New forms of social stratification are emerging. Much of our thinking about stratification — from Marx, Weber, and others — must be recast to capture these new developments. Social class was the key theme of past stratification work. Yet class is an increasingly outmoded concept, although it is sometimes appropriate to earlier historical periods. Class stratification implies that people can be differentiated hierarchically on one or more criteria into distinct layers, classes. Class analysis has grown increasingly inadequate in recent decades as traditional hierarchies have declined and new social differences have emerged. The cumulative impact of these changes is fundamentally altering the nature of social stratification — placing past theories in need of substantial modification.

CLASSICAL FORMULATIONS: MARX AND WEBER

Marx and Weber developed an approach to class stratification which heavily influenced most later work.[1] We briefly summarise their contributions, then assess how they need revision.

Karl Marx

[Karl Marx] started from the premise that the primary function of social organisation is the satisfaction of basic human needs — food, clothing, and shelter. Hence, the productive system (the economy) is the nucleus around which society is organised. From the assumption of the primacy of production flows the Marxist definition of class: any aggregate of persons who play the same part in the production mechanism. Marx, in *Capital,* outlined three main classes differentiated according to their relations to the means of production: (1) capitalist, or owners of the means of production; (2) workers, or all those who are employed by others; (3) land-owners, who are regarded as survivors of feudalism. Although Marx differentiated classes in objective terms, his primary interest was to understand and facilitate the emergence of class consciousness among the depressed strata. He wished to see them create a sense of shared class interests as a basis for conflict with the dominant class. The fact that a group held a number of objective characteristics in common but lacked class consciousness meant for Marx that it could not play the role of an historically significant class. He analysed many conditions that facilitate working-class consciousness: consolidation of small into larger workplaces, nationalisation of communication, etc.

Max Weber

While Marx emphasised economic factors as determinants of social class, Weber suggested that economic interests were only a special case of the larger category of "values," which included many things that are neither economic nor interests. For Weber, the Marxist model was a source of fruitful hypotheses, yet it remained too simple to handle the complexity of stratification. He therefore sought to develop an analytical alternative, one which distinguished the various sources of hierarchical differentiation and potential cleavage. Weber's key contributions to social stratification were in showing how class, status, and bureaucracy can operate independently, such as to influence political decisions.

Class

Weber reserved the concept of class for economically determined stratification. He defined a class as composed of people who have life chances in common, as determined by their power to dispose of goods and skills for the sake of income. Property is a class asset but not the only criterion of class. For Weber, the crucial aspect of a class situation is, ultimately, the market. His examination of past class struggles suggested that conflicts between creditors and debtors are perhaps the most visible economic cleavage. The conflict between employers and workers is highly visible under capitalism but is just a special case of the more common struggle between buyers and sellers. Weber, like Marx, was concerned to identify conditions encouraging class consciousness. Yet for him, there was no single set of classes or form of class consciousness. Rather, which groups develop a consciousness of common interest opposing other groups is a specific empirical question; different groups join or conflict at different times and places. Variations depend heavily on the general culture of a society, including its religion and fundamental beliefs. These can foster or inhibit the emergence of class-conscious groups in ways that cannot be understood solely from a society's economic base.

Status

Writing about class, Weber broadened the concept but did not essentially break from Marx. His dramatic difference came in relativising class by introducing his second major dimension of stratification, status, which Weber defined as the positive or negative estimation of honour, or prestige, received by individuals or positions. Thus, it involves the felt perceptions of people. Since status involves the perception of how much one is valued by others, people value it more than economic gain. Status may flow from wealth, religion, race, physical attractiveness, or social skills.

Power, Status, and Bureaucracy

Power, which in the Marxist analysis derives from class position, is a much more complex phenomenon in the Weberian model. Weber defined power as the chance of a person or group to realise their will even against the opposition of others. Power may be a function of resources possessed in the economic, status, and political systems; both status and class are power resources. Since people want higher status, they tend to try to orient their behaviour to that approved by those with the higher status which they value. Power resources can also be found in institutions that command the allegiance of people — religions, parties, trade unions, and the like. Anyone with followers or, like the military, with control of force, may have access to power. In large measure, the relative weight of different power resources is determined by the rules of the political game, which vary in different societies. Such rules of the game are found in the structure of legal authority and its degree of legitimacy, which, in turn, influence how power is secured.

RECONCEPTUALISING CLASS: POST MARX AND WEBER

If one looks closely at class theories in recent decades, it is striking how much class has changed. This is not immediately obvious since most theorists claim direct descendance from Marx and Weber. But many have, in fact, fundamentally altered the concept of class toward what we term the fragmentation of stratification. Consider some examples of class theory and social stratification. Dahrendorf (1959: 157–206) stressed that many lines of social cleavage have not erupted into class conflict. For a Marxian revolution, the working class should suffer immiseration and grow more homogenous; capitalists should join in combat against them. But Dahrendorf points instead to the "decomposition of labour": workers have become more differentiated by skill level — into skilled, semi-skilled, and unskilled. Unions often separate more than join these groups. Perhaps even more important is the expansion of the "middle class" of white-collar non-manual workers. Such a middle class was largely ignored by Marx; it was expected to join the capitalists or workers. Instead, it has grown substantially and differentiated internally, especially between lower-level salaried employees and managers. Dahrendorf might have abandoned the concept of class, but instead retained the term while redefining it to include all sorts of groups in political or social conflict: " 'class' signifies conflict groups that are generated by the differential distribution of authority in imperatively coordinated associations" (Dahrendorf 1959: 204).

Many writers have, like Dahrendorf, retained terms from Marx while substantially changing their meaning. Erik Wright (1985: 64–104) has sought to capture some of the same changes as Dahrendorf. He does so by developing a 12-category "typology of class location in capitalist society" that includes: 1. bourgeoisie, 2. small employers, 4. expert managers, 5. expert supervisors, 8. semi-credentialed supervisors, and continues up to 12. proletarians. It explicitly incorporates not just ownership, but skill level and managerial responsibility. It is striking that Wright, a self-defined Marxist, incorporates so much post-Weberian multi-dimensionality.

Giddens (1980: 108–12) similarly emphasises the emergence of multiple cleavages within the workplace, the distinct importance of management, and the rise of an autonomous middle class as undermining the classical Marxist approach.

These analyses stress changes in workplace relations. Yet social relations outside the workplace are increasingly important for social stratification. If "proletarians" are visibly distinct in dress, food, and life-style, they are more likely to think of themselves and act as a politically distinct class. In the nineteenth and early twentieth century, this was often the case, as novels and sociologists report. The decreasing distinctiveness of social classes is stressed by Parkin (1979: 69), who holds that this brings the "progressive erosion of the communal components of proletarian status." Specifically, "the absence of clearly visible and unambiguous marks of inferior status has made the enforcement of an all-pervasive deference system almost impossible to sustain outside the immediate work situation. It would take an unusually sharp eye to detect the social class of Saturday morning shoppers in the High Street, whereas to any earlier generation, it would have been the most elementary task."

Should the social class concept be abandoned? In a 1959 exchange, Nisbet suggested that class "is nearly valueless for the clarification of the data of wealth, power, and social status in the contemporary United States" (1959: 11). Commenting on Nisbet in the same journal, Bernard Barber and O.D. Duncan (1959) both argued that his position had not been substantiated, and that a sharper analysis and evidence were necessary. This was over 30 years ago. Yet today, class remains salient in sociologists' theories and commentaries. We do not suggest it be altogether abandoned, but complemented by other factors.

THE DECLINE OF SOCIAL CLASS AND THE MULTIPLICATION OF STATUS DIMENSIONS

Theories lag behind social changes. Major social changes have occurred since Marx and Weber wrote and have accelerated since 1970. Their cumulative effects remain inadequately conceptualised. We extend the critique of Marx that Weber began and others continued. But we push further.

What do these changes imply for theories of stratification? A critical point is that traditional hierarchies are declining; economic and family hierarchies determine much less than just a generation or two ago.

We consider next separate situses [or separate vertical dimension, e.g., economic institutions, government organizations, and families] of social stratification. In each situs, we consider some of the specific dynamics by which social classes have declined or are declining. The cumulative effect, across situses, is emergence of a new system of social stratification.

POLITICS: LESS CLASS, MORE FRAGMENTATION

Political behaviour is an ideal area to assess changes in stratification. It was central to Marx and Weber; it is highly visible today; it has been studied in detail; it permits tests of competing hypotheses. A striking illustration of this change is in the results from the 1940s to 1980s on the Alford Index of Class Voting. This index is based on the percentage of persons by social class who vote for Left or Right parties. For instance, if 75 per cent of the working class votes for the Left, and only 25 per cent of the middle class does so, the Alford index score is 50 (the difference between these two figures).

Figure 2.1 shows that the Alford Index has declined in every country for which data are available.

Figure 2.1
Class Voting Has Declined in All Western Democracies from 1947 to 1986

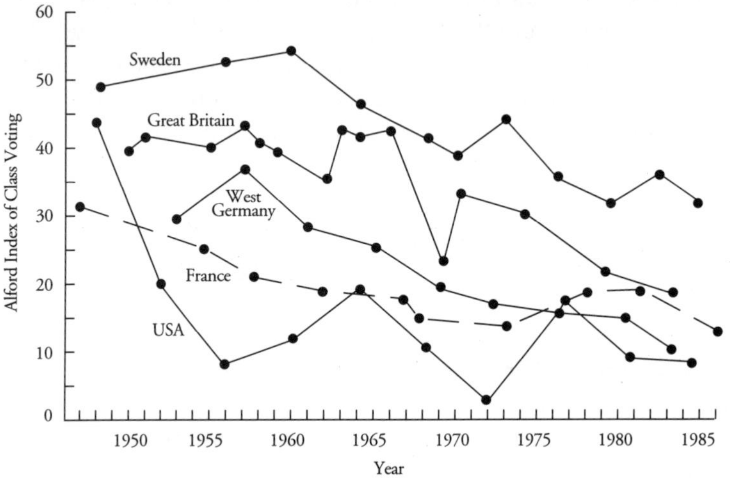

Source: Lipset (1981), updated in Clark and Inglehart (1991).

ECONOMIC ORGANISATION CHANGES: SOURCES OF A NEW MARKET INDIVIDUALISM

One simple, powerful change has affected the economy: growth. And economic growth undermines hierarchical class stratification.

The more advanced the technology and knowledge base, the harder it is to plan in advance and control administratively, both within a large firm and still more by central government planners.

Technological changes illustrate how new economic patterns are no longer an issue of public versus private sector control, but bring inevitable frustrations for hierarchical control by anyone. As research and development grow increasingly important for new products and technologies, they are harder to direct or define in advance for distant administrators of that firm and even harder for outside regulators or political officials seeking to plan centrally (as in a Soviet five-year plan, to use an extreme case). Certain plastics firms have as much as one-third of staff developing the chemistry for new products. Computers, biological engineering, and robotics illustrate the dozens of areas that are only vaguely amenable to forecast and hence central control.

A major implication for social stratification of these economic changes is the *decline in traditional authority, hierarchy, and class relations*. Current technologies require fewer unskilled workers performing routine tasks or a large middle management to coordinate them than did traditional manufacturing of steel, automobiles, etc. High tech means increasing automation of routine tasks. It also demands more professional autonomous decisions. More egalitarian, collegial decision-making is thus increasingly seen as a hallmark of modern society by analysts from Habermas and Parsons to Daniel Bell and Zbigniew Brzezinski and to consultants in business schools who teach the importance of a new "corporate culture" — as illustrated by *In Search of Excellence* (Peters and Waterman 1982), the number one non-fiction bestseller in the United States for some time and widely read by business leaders in the United States and Europe.

The occupations that are expanding are white-collar, technical, professional, and service-oriented. The class structure increasingly resembles a diamond bulging at the middle rather than a pyramid. Higher levels of education are needed in such occupations; the numbers of students pursuing more advanced studies has rapidly increased in the past few decades.

The larger the extent of the market, the less likely are particularistic decisions (preference for family members, city residents, or nationals) likely to prevail. Local stratification hierarchies are correspondingly undermined as markets grow — regionally, nationally, and internationally.

The force of this proposition has grown in the 1970s and 1980s with the globalisation of markets for manpower, capital, and sales. Big and small firms have experienced major consolidations — enhanced by the growth of multinationals, the 1970s' oil boom and subsequent bust, leveraged buy-outs, the rise of the Eurodollar market, and worldwide trade expansion. The growth of the US economy has been fuelled by massive in-migration, especially from Mexico, Latin America, and Asia. More immigrants came into the United States in the 1980s than in any decade since before World War I. These factors combine to undermine the familistic-quasi-monopolistic tradition of business hierarchy and class stratification patterns.

A SLIMMER FAMILY

Major trends here parallel those in the economy.

The family and intimate personal relations have increasingly become characterised by more egalitarian relations, more flexible roles, and more tolerance for a wider range of behaviour. Hierarchical stratification has weakened.

The traditional family has been slimmed. The authoritarian paternalistic family is decreasingly the model for stratification in the rest of society. Fewer young people marry, they wed later, have fewer children, far more women work outside the home, divorce rates have risen, parents and grandparents live less often with children (e.g., Cherlin 1981; Forse 1986). Paralleling these socio-demographic changes are changes in attitudes and roles concerning the family. Children and wives have grown substantially more egalitarian in a very short period of time. Indeed, attitudes toward the family have changed more than almost any other social or political factor in the past 20–30 years, especially questions like, should women work outside the home?

SOCIAL MOBILITY

Besides these internal family dynamics, the slimmer family determines less the education and jobs of individual family members. Increased wealth and government support programmes gave expanded choices to individuals and cumulatively transferred more functions than ever away from the family. The magnitude of these changes rose in the 1970s and 1980s.

The family has grown less important as a basis of stratification in relation to education and jobs.

Families are decreasingly responsible for raising children and placing them in jobs. Fewer children work in family firms (farms, shops, etc.). Social mobility studies show decreasing effects of parents' education and income in explaining children's occupational success; simultaneously, the effects of education have increased.[2] The proportions of wives and mothers working in jobs outside the home have grown dramatically, first and especially in the United States, but in many European countries too.

CONCLUSION

New patterns of social stratification are emerging. The key trend could be described as one of "fragmentation of stratification":

- The weakening of class stratification, especially as shown in distinct class-differentiated life-styles.
- The decline of economic determinism and the increased importance of social and cultural factors.
- Politics is less organised by class and more by other loyalties.
- The slimming of the family.
- Social mobility is less family-determined, more ability and education-determined.

NOTES

[1] A further discussion of Marx, Weber, and functionalist contributions to stratification can be found in Lipset (1985: Ch. 2).

[2] US mobility studies from the late nineteenth century onward report few changes until the 1960s (Lipset and Bendix 1991; Grusky 1986), but major changes since: Hout's (1988) replication of Featherman and Hauser (1978) showed that the effect of origin status on destination status declined by 28 per cent from 1962 to 1973 and by 1/3 from 1972 to 1985. Hauser and Grusky (1984, 1987) analyse 16 and 22 countries, finding more mobility in countries with socialist and social democratic political leadership. This reflects the dramatic changes in the occupational and ownership structure across many societies in recent years.

The Persistence of Classes in Post-Industrial Societies
Mike Hout, Clem Brooks, and Jeff Manza

THE PERSISTENCE OF CLASSES

Sociologists did not invent the concept of class. But we have made more out of it than others have mainly by emphasising the point that it is how one makes a living that determines life chances and material interests. We differ from economists' nearly exclusive focus on the quantity of income or wealth and commonsense conceptions that blend life-style and morality with economic and sociological considerations (Jencks and Petersen 1991).[1] The part-time school teacher, the semi-skilled factory worker and the struggling shopkeeper may all report the same income on their tax returns, but we recognise that as salaried, hourly and self-employed workers, they have different sources of income and, consequently, different life chances.

At various points in their paper, Clark and Lipset (1991: 397, 401–2, 405) seem to equate class and hierarchy, but they are separate dimensions. Hierarchy, in sociological usage, could refer to any rankable distinctions. Class refers to a person's relationship to the means of production and/or labour markets, and it is an important determinant of an individual's income, wealth and social standing. Hierarchy or related concepts might be used as an explanation of stratification processes, as in Erikson and Goldthorpe (1992) or Hout and Hauser (1992), but to use the concepts as explanadum and explanans, they must be defined independently, and the relationship must be spelled out.

Class is an indispensable concept for sociology because: (1) class is a key determinate of material interests; (2) structurally defined classes give rise to — or influence the formation of — collective actors seeking to bring about social change; and (3) class membership affects the life chances and behaviour of individuals. The first concern refers to the intrinsic importance of class. The other two are relevant for "class analysis" — the investigation of how class affects other aspects of social life. Clark and Lipset state their case — which refers to all three of these concerns — without acknowledging that each raises different sets of issues. As a result of these confusions, Clark and Lipset's argument collapses analytically distinct processes.

Clark and Lipset also confuse trends in society with trends in writing about society. To be sure, our conceptions of class have grown more complex over the years. Marx's initial codification of the importance of whether one works for a living or expropriates a profit from the sale of goods produced by others has been supplemented over the years by additional distinctions, most of which are ignored by Clark and Lipset. In addition to workers and capitalists, contemporary Marxist accounts of class structure recognise professionals and crafts persons, who extract rents on their expertise, and managers and supervisors, who extract rents on their organisational assets (Wright 1985). These are not mere status distinctions, as Clark and Lipset would have it. They are class distinctions because they specify economic roles with respect to labour markets and material interests. Contemporary Weberian theories of class also admit to complexity without negating the existence of classes. Weberians focus on the closure strategies that professionals and skilled workers use to influence labour markets to their collective advantage (Parkin 1979; Goldthorpe 1980: 39–46; Erickson and Goldthorpe

1992: 42–3; Manza 1992) and the internal labour markets that select managers and supervisors (Parking 1979; Kalleberg and Berg 1987). While sociologists' models of class are a lot more complicated than they used to be, complexity alone does not imply that class is dead or dying.

Clark and Lipset's conclusions about the decline of class in post-industrial societies hinge on the claim that "traditional hierarchies are declining; economic and family hierarchies determine much less than just a generation or two ago" (Clark and Lipset 1991: 401 [p. 33 in this book]). However, hierarchy is never defined, and the assumed link between *hierarchy* and *class* in their formulation is at best vague. In moving back and forth between a materialist analysis of class to the vaguer concept of "hierarchy," Clark and Lipset are tacitly shifting the terrain of debate away from class *per se*. This conceptual slippage makes it easier for them to conclude that classes are dying. Their emphasis on hierarchy is also potentially misleading in that forms of hierarchy could decline without any change in class structure or the general importance of class for systems of stratification or political behaviour.[2] They persistently conflate class-based inequalities with non-class forms of stratification. Perhaps as a consequence, Clark and Lipset conveniently ignore some of the most salient aspects of class inequalities in contemporary capitalist societies. First, they completely ignore the remarkable persistence in the high levels of wealth controlled by the bourgeoisie in these societies.[3] Further, they ignore the capacity of wealth-holders to influence political processes, either directly through financial contributions, intra-class organisational and political networks and government agencies, or indirectly through control over investment decisions (Clawson, Neustadt, and Scott 1992; Domhoff 1990; Useem 1984; and Bottomore and Brym 1989 on direct control; and Block 1987, 1992; Lindblom 1977 on indirect control).[4]

Private fortunes are still predicted on ownership of the means of production. During the 1980s when inequality of wealth and earnings was growing in the United States and elsewhere, the private fortunes at the forefront of resurgent inequality were in almost all cases built through ownership. High-tech champions like Gates, merchandisers like Walton and developers like Trump got rich because they owned the means of production. Arbitragers collected high fees, and executives were "overcompensated," but they gained more from ownership of shares of stock than from their wages and salaries (Crystal 1991).

One important test for class analysis is the demonstration that some classes have material advantages over others. If classes are dying, then we would expect incumbents of different classes to earn similar amounts, i.e., all of the income or earnings inequality should be within classes. Table 2.1 shows previously unpublished evidence regarding the rela-

tionship between class and earnings in the United States in late 1991.
The two leading class schemes in the current literature — Wright

Table 2.1
Earnings by Class: United States, 1991 (n=1,557)

Class	Annual Earnings[a]		Annual Earnings (Adjusted)[b]	
	Men	*Women*	*Men*	*Women*
Wright Schema				
Employers				
10 or more employees	$71,300	$27,800	$52,200	$22,300
1–9 employees	$34,400	$23,000	$29,900	$19,100
No employees (petty bourgeoisie)	$20,800	$9,200	$21,200	$11,200
Employees				
Expert managers	$46,500	$30,600	$32,100	$22,000
Expert supervisors	$44,900	$26,600	$37,500	$23,700
Expert nonmanagers	$32,500	$24,900	$27,200	$20,800
Semi-credentialled managers	$32,300	$22,100	$31,500	$20,800
Semi-credentialled supervisors	$20,800	$19,700	$23,100	$21,600
Semi-credentialled nonmanagers	$25,800	$17,700	$26,700	$17,000
Uncredentialled managers	$22,200	$14,400	$26,000	$16,800
Uncredentialled supervisors	$23,100	$16,300	$23,600	$17,500
Workers	$16,800	$11,400	$20,900	$14,600
Erikson–Goldthorpe Schema				
Upper professional (Ia)	$39,200	$28,400	$32,300	$21,700
Upper manager (Ib)	$56,200	$27,200	$40,300	$22,400
Lower professional (IIa)	$24,400	$18,700	$23,400	$17,400
Lower manager (IIb)	$33,400	$18,100	$30,300	$18,000
Clerk or sales worker (IIIb)	$22,800	$13,300	$23,300	$15,900
Service worker (IIIb)	$14,500	$7,800	$20,300	$12,000
Employer (IVa)	$41,800	$21,600	$35,300	$19,000
Petty bourgeosie (IVb)	$20,000	$9,000	$22,000	$11,100
Technician or supervisor (V)	$24,700	$17,000	$26,300	$18,700
Skilled worker (VI)	$22,600	$15,100	$26,000	$15,100
Semi-skilled worker (VIIss)	$19,100	$13,500	$21,500	$14,500
Unskilled worker (VIIus)	$11,500	$10,000	$16,800	$12,500
Farmer w/employees (IVc)	$27,400	— [c]	$24,400	— [c]
Farmer, no employees (IVd)	$26,600	$4,500	$18,100	$3,300
Farm labourer (VIIf)	$16,700	— [c]	$17,600	— [c]

[a] We calculated the geometric mean instead of the usual arithmetic mean because of the well-known positive skew of the earnings distribution.
[b] We adjusted the geometric mean for the effects of education, age (including a term for age-squared), hours worked and class (dummy variables) by regressing the log of earnings on these variables for men and women separately. The adjusted means are the antilog of the value expected for a 40-year-old person with a high school diploma who worked 40 hours per week for a full year.
[c] Fewer than five cases.

(1985) and Erikson and Goldthorpe (1992) — are used. We are confident that other carefully crafted class schemes would also show significant variation in earnings levels.

The class differences in earnings are statistically and substantively significant. Wright's capitalist class are at the top of the earnings distribution and his bottom class — workers — are at the bottom. The ratio of earnings from top to bottom is 4.2:1 for men and 2.5:1 for women. Wright's class scheme explains 20 per cent of the variance in earnings. Adjusting for sex, education, age and hours worked mediates some of the class differences, but the adjusted means show significant variation. The Erikson–Goldthorpe scheme also shows a pattern of significant variation. The ratio of the top class's earnings to the earnings of their lowest class is 4.9:1 among men and 3.6:1 among women. The ratio of between class variance to total variance in the Erikson–Goldthorpe schema is .17. From both class schemes, it is clear that changes in the class structure have not eroded the important effects of class on earnings.

The growth of the proportion of the population that is middle class and the proliferation of middle classes has also not negated the persistence of income inequality (Smeeding 1991) and the growing proportions of the populations of industrial societies that are living in extreme poverty. The broad outlines of this "new poverty" (Markland 1990) are becoming increasingly clear (Wacquant 1993).[5] The existence of long-term joblessness or occupational marginality among sectors of the populations of these societies and the growth of low-income areas characterised by multiple sources of deprivation for residents (Massey 1990; Massey and Eggers 1990) does not fit very well with Clark and Lipset's claims about the decline of "traditional hierarchies."

In general, the persistence of wealth and power at the top and growing poverty and degradation at the bottom of contemporary class structures suggests that Clark and Lipset's conclusions about the impending death of classes is premature. In the United States, the country which we know best, it is becoming increasingly common in urban communities for privileged professionals and managers to live in secluded enclaves and suburbs (often behind locked gates) or in secured high-rise condominiums, while marginalised sectors of the population are crowded into increasingly dangerous inner-city areas (a trend discussed at length by the new Secretary of Labor in the United States, Robert Reich, in a recent book — Reich 1991; Davis 1991). As long as such conditions prevail, we are sceptical that sociologists would be wise to abandon the concept of class, whatever other evidence might be adduced to show that the importance of class is declining.

ARE SOCIAL CLASSES DYING? NO

Politics

To demonstrate the declining significance of class in the political arena, Clark and Lipset attempt to show class voting has declined. Their evidence is based on the claim that "the Alford Index [of class voting] has declined in every country for which data are available" (Clark and Lipset 1991: 403 [p. 33 in this book]). Four observations about their data undermine these assertions, however.

First, their reliance on the Alford Index as the proper measure of class voting is highly dubious. That index is based on a two-class model of society. It is computed by simply subtracting the percentage of non-manual occupations voting for left parties from the percentage of persons in manual occupations voting for left parties (Alford 1963: 79–80). By lumping together all persons employed in non-manual occupations in one "class" and all persons working in manual occupations into the other "class," the Alford Index creates artificially high levels of cross-class voting among both groups. For example, secretaries, low-level clerks and service-sector employees, who may have very similar class interests to manual workers, are counted as deviant if they vote for left parties. It has been apparent for some time that the two-class model used in the Alford Index is overly simplistic and does not capture the full complexity of class voting (Korpi 1972; Robertson 1984). The two "classes" invoked by Alford have no relation to Marxist class categories and are far too crude for Weberian or functionalist approaches (Blau and Duncan 1967b: 432–33), so it is useless for testing hypotheses.

It will come as no surprise, then, to learn that the crude two-class model significantly underestimates the extent of class voting. By constructing a much more careful conception of the class structure than that employed by Clark and Lipset, Przeworski and Sprague (1986) derived very different estimates of both the cross-sectional differences and trends in class voting. They found that class voting between 1900 and 1975 was relatively stable in three countries (Germany, Norway and Finland), declined in one country (Denmark), and *increased* in the other three countries (Sweden, Belgium and France) (Przeworski and Sprague 1986: Ch. 5). Przeworski and Sprague's evidence is not above criticism, but it leads us to reject Clark and Lipset's generalisation about a monotonic decline in class voting in advanced capitalist societies.

[Second], the cross-national differences among the five countries they consider raise serious doubts about their proposition that "hierarchy generates and maintains rigid class relations" (Clark and Lipset 1991: 402). Problems with the Alford Index notwithstanding, reasonable estimates of class voting are likely to show Sweden as the nation with the strongest association between class and voting (among the five countries considered by Clark and Lipset) and the United States as the weakest. And yet, with respect to income inequality, Sweden is the most egalitarian country among the five by most indicators and the United States the least among the five (Esping-Anderson 1990). Parkin (1971), Korpi (1983) and Esping-Anderson (1990), among others, have advanced the converse proposition that Sweden's class politics have produced the social policies responsible for Sweden's low levels of inequality. Not only are the data inconsistent, but the causal order between egalitarianism and class voting is reversed.

[Third], Clark and Lipset seem to assume an unmediated connection between class and voting, ignoring completely the decisive role of unions, social movement organisations and political parties in shaping the conditions under which voters make choices. When parties and other political organisations are organised around class, high levels of class voting can be expected. Przeworski and Sprague's (1986) analysis of the dynamics of social democratic parties based originally on working-class votes suggests that the strategic decision of these parties to weaken their class-based appeals to seek middle-class votes — a trend celebrated in Lipset (1990) — has had a profound effect on the social bases of their political support. If workers' parties abandon or compromise their specific interests, does it mean those interests no longer exist? We say "no." Class interests may remain latent in the political arena, but this does not mean they do not exist.

In short, Clark and Lipset's evidence on class politics is incomplete and unconvincing. They have failed to make the case that class is declining in importance for politics. Class never was the all-powerful explanatory variable that some intellectual traditions assumed in earlier periods; class was always only one source of political identity and action alongside race, religion, nationality, gender and others. To say that class matters less now than it used to requires that one exaggerate its importance in the past and understate its importance at present. Class is important for politics to the extent that political organisations actively organise around class themes. Hence, in some periods, the political consequences of class may appear latent even if the underlying logic of class is unchanged. We believe that on balance, however, the evidence shows that class remains important and that Clark and Lipset fail to demonstrate that class voting and traditional political values have declined.

Post-Industrial Economic Trends

Clark and Lipset argue that more advanced technologies make it "harder ... to plan in advance and control administratively" and that these economic changes are leading to a "*decline in traditional authority, hierarchy and class relations*" (Clark and Lipset 1991: 406 [pp. 34–35 in this book]; emphasis in the original). Their discussion of technology takes the most optimistic conceivable scenarios as reality, ignoring the more complex institutional patterns actually emerging in post-industrial societies. The use of new management styles in response to the appearance of high technology is heavily dependent on the context in which it is embedded (Zuboff 1988; Shaiken 1984). In many firms, managers resist any transfer of authority to lower-level employees even if the new "smart machines" make possible a democratisation of decision-making within firms (Zuboff 1988). Far from eliminating class struggle, the introduction of new technology and management styles often creates new forms of class conflict. The jury is still out on the fate of hierarchy in post-industrial firms.

Finally, Clark and Lipset argue that economic growth is undermining "local stratification hierarchies as markets grow — regionally, nationally, internationally" (Clark and Lipset 1991: 406 [p. 35 in this book]). Mills (1946) effectively countered such observations nearly half a century ago by arguing that the gulf between decision centres in metropolitan skyscrapers and the dispersed loci of production and consumption was yet another layer of stratification, not a pattern that "combine[s] to undermine the familistic-quasi-monopolistic tradition of business hierarchy and class stratification patterns" (Clark and Lipset 1991: 407 [p. 35 in this book]), as Clark and Lipset would have it.

Family

Clark and Lipset argue that the "slimmed" family in post-industrial society has "increasingly become characterised by more egalitarian relations ... [as] hierarchical stratification has weakened" (Clark and Lipset 1991: 407 [p. 36 in this book]). While the patterns they refer to in support of these arguments (greater freedom of marriage and divorce, greater opportunities for women to work in the paid labour force and the decline of extended family arrangements) are clearly important, they provide no evidence that the "slimmed" family is a more egalitarian one. The modern family is a good deal more complex than Clark and Lipset imply (Connell 1987: 120–25). Research on contemporary family life suggests that while egalitarian *beliefs* are more widespread than in earlier periods, a clear gender division of labour remains in place in most families (Hochschild 1989). In the United States, for example, the evidence overwhelmingly suggests that the rise in female-headed "slimmed" families with the liberalisation of divorce law has led to *rising* rates of poverty in female-headed families (Thistle 1992: Ch. 4; Weitzman 1985). For the urban poor, the "slimmed family" celebrated by Clark and Lipset is a major source of poverty and inequality (Wilson 1987). This is attributable in part to the positive association between husbands' and wives' occupations that *increases* differences among families even as differences within families decrease (Bianchi 1981; Hout 1982).

Under "family," Clark and Lipset also address recent changes in social mobility, arguing that "the slimmer family determines less the education and jobs of individual family members" and that "social mobility studies show decreasing effects of parents' education and income in explaining children's occupational success" (citing Featherman and Hauser 1978; Hout 1988). However, Clark and Lipset fail to take due note of the sources of those changes. It is true that class origin affects students' progress through the educational systems of most industrial societies less than it used to, but the cause of diminished educational stratification is *not* less class-based selection but less selection of any kind at the early transitions where class matters most (Mare 1980, 1981). Replications of Mare's results for the United States in 15 industrial societies show that only Sweden, Hungary and the former Czechoslovakia had real declines in class-based selection (Shavit and Blossfeld 1991; Raftery and Hout 1993). In Hungary and Czechoslovakia, political party tests replaced class selection; only Sweden saw a real growth in the openness of the educational stratification process.

Likewise, falling class barriers to social mobility cannot be attributed to "affluence" or other indirect forces. The expansion of higher education in the United States — a class-conscious policy designed to benefit youth of lower-middle and working-class origins — has brought down class barriers to achievement (Hout 1988). It works because throughout this century, a college diploma served to cancel the effect of social origins on occupational success. By making college accessible to working-class youth, the expansion of higher education in the United States removed class barriers for those who took advantage. Elsewhere, different mechanisms affected mobility. In Sweden, the social democratic welfare state assured more equal access not only to universities, but also to jobs in desirable occupations (Esping-Anderson 1990: 144–61). In Hungary, political tests for professions and managerial positions guaranteed a dramatic weakening of class barriers during the first generation of communist rule; it slacked after the first generation (Wong and Hauser 1992). Where class-conscious action does not organise opportunity, as in Ireland (Hout 1989: Ch. 11), class barriers are unshaken — even by industrialisation on a scale that might be said to lead to an increase in "affluence."

CONCLUSION: CLASSES ARE NOT DYING

Class structures have undergone important changes in recent decades with the rise of post-industrial societies. The birth of new sources of inequality does not imply the death of the old ones. In arguing that Clark and Lipset have failed to show that social classes are dying, we do not wish to imply that there have been no changes in the class structures of advanced capitalist societies or in the association between class and other social phenomena. The manual working class *has* declined in size in recent decades in most countries, while the proportion of the labour force working in the service sector has increased. Such changes are important: they tell us that nineteenth-century models of class are no longer adequate. Yet moving to more complex, multidimensional models of class does not imply that classes are dying. The persistence of class-based inequalities in capitalist societies suggests that in the foreseeable future, the concept of class will — and should — play an important role in sociological research.

NOTES

[1] We note, however, that Clark and Lipset (1991: 400 [p. 32 in this book]) put great stock in life-style when they cite Parkin's contention that "the absence of clearly visible and unambiguous marks of inferior *status* has made the enforcement of an all-pervasive deference system almost impossible to sustain outside the immediate work situation. It would take an unusually sharp eye to detect the social class of Saturday morning shoppers in the High Street, whereas to any earlier generation, it would have been the most elementary task" (Parkin 1979: 69; our emphasis). To our minds, this is evidence of waning status distinctions, not waning class distinctions. Thus, it *counters* Clark and Lipset's general point that status distinctions are on the rise as class is on the wane. See Manza (1992) for a discussion of the class themes latent in Parkin's "closure theory."

[2] For example, one could imagine a class society in which traditional hierarchies based on gender or race had completely disappeared if one's life chances were completely uninfluenced by one's gender or race. Wright (1990) compares the logic of classless versus genderless societies.

[3] The pattern of the amount of wealth controlled by the richest 1 per cent of the populations of different capitalist societies seems to be remarkably consistent and seems to hold across different societies. Wolff's (1991) careful reconstruction of trends in the distribution of

household wealth in Sweden, Britain and the United States shows a common decline from the early 1920s to the early 1970s and no change or actual *increases* in bourgeois wealth over the last two decades (see also Levy 1987 and Phillips 1991 on the United States; Shorrocks 1987 on Britain; and Spånt 1987 on Sweden). Including an augmented measure of household wealth which includes retirement benefits, Wolff concludes that the top 1 per cent in all three societies control more than 20 per cent of all household wealth. The essays contained in Bottomore and Brym (1989) provide useful overviews of the persistence of the economic power controlled by the capitalist class in seven countries. Maurice Zeitlin's (1989) provocative essays have influenced our thinking on these issues.

4 We would further note that elite educational institutions play an important role in transmitting privilege from one generation to another. For a discussion of these issues, see Baltzell (1958) and Domhoff (1970) on the general mechanisms of transmission of privilege, and Useem and Karabel (1986) on the way such privileges operate in pathways to corporate hierarchies in the United States; see Marceau (1977) on France; and the essays in Bottomore and Brym (1989) on capital class privileges in seven leading countries. Finally, Marceau (1989) discusses the making of an international capitalist elite.

5 For discussions of the new poverty in the United States, England, Italy and the Netherlands respectively, see Jencks and Peterson (1991); Townsend et al. (1987); Mingione (1991); Engbersen (1989). See also Wacquant (1993) for an excellent analysis of some of the similarities and differences of the new poverty in France and the United States.

DISCUSSION QUESTIONS

1. Compare and contrast Marx's and Weber's view of class. How do they differ and/or how are they similar? How do they explain the relationship between class position and class consciousness?

2. Is the concept of class still important today? First, compare the education and occupation of individuals that you know who are from different class backgrounds. Do these individuals have the same level of education and occupational position? Second, compare the income, wealth, and power of some of the CEOs, managers, or owners of large and small companies with blue- and white-collar workers that you know in your community. To what extent are the differences between these groups significant? Finally,

informally ask the individuals who seem to be from upper and lower classes about their political attitudes, ideas, and behaviours, such as which Canadian political party do they support/vote, what do they think about the taxation system, what are their views on helping the poor and/or on employment insurance, and so on. You can also ask them about the types of books they read and the number of times they attend museums or art galleries. Is there a difference among people of different classes? For more information on income, education, and income of Canadians, see Statistics Canada, particularly the census data. You can also look at the business and local sections of some Canadian newspapers.

3. Study Exhibits 1.1 and 1.2 on poverty and income of Canadians. What is the main thrust of the tables? What type of trend do they suggest? Are there changes in the status of the lower, middle, and/or upper classes? How? Are classes dying? Why or why not?

Exhibit 1.1

Distribution of Total Canadian Income by Household, Quintile Shares, 1951-1988

Year	Bottom	Second	Middle	Fourth	Top
1951	4.4%	11.2%	18.3%	23.3%	42.8%
1961	4.2	11.9	18.3	24.5	41.1
1971	3.6	10.6	17.6	24.9	43.3
1981	4.6	10.9	17.6	25.2	41.8
1988	4.6	10.4	16.9	24.9	43.2

Source: Statistics Canada, *Income Distributions by Size*, Cat. No. 13-207, various years. In Christopher A. Sarlo, *Poverty in Canada.* Vancouver: Fraser Institute, 1992, p. 208. Used with permission.

Exhibit 1.2

Poverty Rates and Total Numbers in Poverty, 1973, 1981, 1986, 1991 — Statistics Canada and CCSD Definitions

	1973		1981		1986		1991	
	Number (Thousands)	*Rate (%)*	*Number (Thousands)*	*Rate (%)*	*Number (Thousands)*	*Rate (%)*	*Number (Thousands)*	*Rate (%)*
Families								
Statistics Canada	701	13.4	721	11.3	801	11.8	949	13.0
CCSD	908	17.4	1307	20.5	1444	21.2	1543	21.1
Unattached Individuals								
Statistics Canada	767	40.2	940	37.5	1004	34.5	1259	36.6
CCSD	756	39.7	991	39.5	1103	37.9	1280	37.1
Total Households								
Statistics Canada	1468	20.6	1661	18.7	1805	18.6	2209	20.6
65 years and over	506	41.0	533	33.7	433	24.2	522	25.0
Under 65 years	962	16.3	1129	15.4	1372	17.3	1687	19.5
CCSD	1664	23.3	2297	25.9	2547	26.2	2822	26.3
65 years and over	582	48.3	1495	20.5	1782	22.5	2043	23.6
Under 65 years	1082	18.2	803	34.9	765	30.0	779	27.6
Total Persons								
Statistics Canada	3269	16.2	3339	14.0	3597	14.4	4230	15.9

Editor's Note:
Definitions
Statistics Canada uses a cutoff point to determine the poverty rate. Basically, if a family spent significantly more than one-half of its income (i.e., 20 percentage points more) on food, shelter, and clothing, they are in poverty. This cutoff point is determined by other

(continued)

Exhibit 1.2 *(continued)*

factors such as community size. The larger the community, the higher the low-income cutoffs for any family. The Canadian Council on Social Development (CCSD) takes a purely relative approach to the definition of poverty. It uses the average Canadian family income and deems one-half of average family income to be the poverty line for a family of three members. Furthermore, it adjusts its poverty line for each additional member by 16.7 percent, which is a rough estimate of annual living costs of the additional family member (Ross et al. 1994: 12–16).

Source: David P. Ross, E. Richard Shillington, and Clarence Lochhead, *The Canadian Fact Book on Poverty 1994.* Ottawa: Canadian Council on Social Development, 1994. Tabulations based on Statistics Canada's Survey of Consumer Finances micro-data tapes. Reprinted by permission.

plus or numerator of the rate of surplus value was calculated by sub-tracting total wages of production and related workers from "value-added" in manufacturing production. "Value-added" is equal to the selling price of manufacturing products minus the cost of material, fuel, and electricity consumed in production. Since the latter two items were not calculated by the Dominion Bureau of Statistics before 1917, this date was the earliest from which rates of surplus value could be calculated. The rates of surplus value are summarized in Table 3.1. The first rate of sur-plus value, RSV_1, is equal to value-added minus total wages of production and related workers, all of which is divided by these wages. This is the crudest rate since no allowances are made for changes in the costs of constant and variable capital and in the number of production workers. These considerations are introduced into the other ten series. RSV_2 is equivalent to RSV_1, except that fluctuations in the "cost of living" are taken into account. This was measured by the Consumer Price Index (standardized to 1949) which was applied to total wages.[4] RSV_3 is equiv-alent to RSV_2, except that fluctuations in the costs of constant capital are taken into account. The most suitable index of such costs for this his-torical time period is the General Wholesale Price Index which was standardized to 1949.[5] The standardized index was applied to the constant capital in the numerator of RSV_3. In RSV_4 to RSV_6, total wages are

Table 3.1
Summary of the Eleven Rates of Surplus Value

Rate of Surplus Value	Controls
RSV_1	None
RSV_2	Inflation in variable capital
RSV_3	Inflation in variable and constant capital
RSV_4	No. of production workers
RSV_5	Inflation in variable capital; no. of production workers
RSV_6	Inflation in variable and constant capital; no. of production workers
RSV_7	Inflation in variable and constant capital; no. of production workers; 3.7 per cent depreciation in non-financial tangible assets
RSV_8	Inflation in variable and constant capital; no. of production workers; 5.8 per cent depreciation in fixed assets
RSV_9	Inflation in variable and constant capital; no. of production workers; 10 per cent depreciation in non-financial tangible assets
RSV_{10}	Inflation in variable and constant capital; no. of production workers; 31.9 per cent depreciation in non-financial tangible assets
RSV_{11}	Inflation in variable and constant capital; no. of production workers; 25.7 per cent depreciation in total assets

controlled by the number of production and related workers in manufacturing standardized to 1949.[6] RSV_4 is equivalent to RSV_1 controlling for the number of production workers. RSV_5 is equal to RSV_2 controlling for the number of production workers. And, RSV_6 is equivalent to RSV_3 with the number of production workers controlled. The remaining five rates of surplus value introduced various estimates of depreciation into RSV_6 since in this rate of surplus value, all of the previous modifications are taken into account. That is, RSV_7 to RSV_{11} take into account various estimates of depreciation (to be specified shortly), and variations in the costs of constant and variable capital and in the number of production and related workers.

RATES OF SURPLUS VALUE IN CANADA

The eleven series of rates of surplus value from 1917 to 1971 are shown in Table 3.2 so that their relationships with one another and over time will be immediately apparent.

The crudest rate of surplus value, RSV_1, appears to fluctuate over time, although it does have a moderate tendency to rise, showing a +.15 correlation with time (see bottom of Table 3.2).[7] The effect of controlling for the cost of variable capital in RSV_2 is to lower this rate below that of RSV_1 before 1949 and to raise it after this date. The reason for this is that before 1949, real wages were greater than gross wages. This decreases surplus value but increases the level of variable capital, resulting in a decline in the rate of surplus value. After 1949, real wages were less than gross wages. This increases the surplus value but decreases variable capital, resulting in an increase in the rate of surplus value. From 1917 to 1949, the Consumer Price Index increased by 54 per cent, but from 1949 to 1971, it increased by 167 per cent. But the increase in gross wages of production workers *decreased* from 394 per cent from 1917–49 to 298 per cent from 1947–71. In general terms, these changes mean that inflation in the cost of the reproduction of labour power increases the rate of class exploitation over time. This is indicated by the correlation of +.86 between RSV_2 and time (see bottom of Table 3.2). The control by the capitalist class over prices and its drive for higher consumer prices increases the rate of surplus value, resulting in a transfer of wealth from the working class to the capitalist class. However, this benefit to the capitalist class is mitigated somewhat by increases in the costs of capital which, along with the costs of variable capital, are taken into account in RSV_3. Before 1949, the real price of constant capital was greater than its gross price. This increases surplus value and therefore the rate of surplus value. Thus, during this time, RSV_3 is greater than RSV_2. After 1949, the real price of constant capital declined to less than its gross price (that is, costs in constant capital have soared). This decreases surplus value and therefore the rate of surplus value. Thus, during this latter period, RSV_3 is less than RSV_2. The effect of these changes is to produce a general negative correlation of $-.11$ between RSV_3 and time.

The weakness in the above three measures of the rate of surplus value is that they are based on widely different numbers of wage labourers which increases from 523,491 in 1917 to 1,167,810 in 1971. This variation is therefore taken into account in RSV_4 to RSV_6. The effect of this control is to generally lower the rates before 1942 and raise them slightly after 1942. Thus, before 1942, RSV_4 is lower than RSV_1 (with which it should be compared), RSV_5 is lower than RSV_2, and RSV_6 is lower than RSV_3. After 1942, the reverse occurs except for a few years. These changes occur because before 1942, total wages "appear low" partly because fewer workers are employed. This artificially drives up during this period the estimate of rates of surplus value unless the variation in the number of workers is taken into account. Similarly for most years after 1942, wages "appear high" partly because more workers are employed so that rates of surplus value are artificially low. Controlling for the number of wage labourers between 1917 and 1971 suggests that class exploitation increases with time. The correlation between time and these rates of surplus value are: RSV_4 (.95), RSV_5 (.93), and RSV_6 (.97).

Finally, five estimates of depreciation were applied to RSV_6, as outlined above. These were entered into RSV_7 to RSV_{11}. The correlations of these rates of surplus value with time are nearly identical with one another, being either +.97 or +.96. The general effect of taking depreciation into account is to lower the rate of surplus value (see Table 3.2). RSV_7 and RSV_8, in which 3.7 per cent and 5.8 per cent depreciation estimates are taken into account respectively, are only slightly lower than RSV_6. RSV_7 and RSV_8 are virtually identical with one another, suggesting that small changes in depreciation have no effect on rates of surplus value. However, when larger amounts of depreciation are taken into account in RSV_9 to RSV_{11}, the rates drop by a greater amount. RSV_9, in which a 10 per cent depreciation is taken into account, is slightly lower than RSV_6 to RSV_8 but higher than RSV_{10} and RSV_{11}. In the latter two rates, in which 31.9 per cent and 25.7 per cent depreciation are taken into account respectively, the rates in the early years are negative! (This also happens on a less extensive scale in RSV_5.) Since Marx would have predicted that such rates, if valid, imply the absence of capitalism, and since it would be difficult to argue that this state of affairs existed in Canada during these early years, it would seem that these depreciation estimates are too high and that these rates are not very valid. Of the prior three rates, RSV_9 is the least preferable since it has a rather arbitrary

Table 3.2
Eleven Alternative Estimates of Rates of Surplus Value in Manufacturing, 1917–71 (in Percentages)

Year	RSV_1	RSV_2	RSV_3	RSV_4	RSV_5	RSV_6	RSV_7	RSV_8	RSV_9	RSV_{10}	RSV_{11}
1917	194	91	160	62	6	43	33	33	15	-49	-48
1918	180	106	152	54	13	38	27	27	9	-55	-55
1919	182	128	165	47	19	38	28	28	10	-54	-53
1920	174	157	157	44	35	35	24	24	7	-55	-55
1921	182	132	228	10	-9	28	19	19	2	-55	-54
1922	184	114	241	16	-13	39	29	29	11	-48	-48
1923	170	104	224	24	-6	49	38	38	19	-47	-46
1924	166	98	209	17	-13	36	26	26	8	-52	-52
1925	168	101	204	27	-5	44	33	33	15	-50	-50
1926	170	105	216	38	4	61	49	49	28	-43	-42
1927	179	108	229	52	13	79	66	66	44	-32	-31
1928	186	114	242	65	23	97	83	83	60	-23	-22
1929	192	121	257	78	34	117	102	102	76	-13	-13
1930	189	117	286	61	21	115	101	101	76	-11	-10
1931	202	104	335	39	-6	100	87	87	65	-11	-10
1932	197	83	323	19	-26	70	59	59	40	-26	-25
1933	210	82	312	25	-27	66	55	55	36	-30	-29
1934	206	82	293	38	-19	77	65	65	44	-29	-28
1935	189	73	264	40	-16	76	63	63	41	-34	-33
1936	194	80	268	52	-7	90	76	76	52	-30	-30
1937	187	81	233	65	4	91	76	76	52	-34	-33
1938	187	83	255	57	0	95	81	80	56	-29	-28
1939	194	86	272	65	4	109	94	94	69	-20	-19
1940	186	88	245	89	24	128	111	111	82	-16	-16
1941	166	85	216	125	56	167	147	147	114	-2	-1
1942	146	79	189	152	84	196	175	175	139	13	14
1943	139	77	175	163	96	203	181	181	144	15	16

(continued)

Table 3.2 *(continued)*

Year	RSV_1	RSV_2	RSV_3	RSV_4	RSV_5	RSV_6	RSV_7	RSV_8	RSV_9	RSV_{10}	RSV_{11}
1944	149	86	182	170	102	206	184	184	147	18	20
1945	150	87	181	144	83	175	155	155	121	2	3
1946	161	102	188	141	87	166	147	147	114	-1	0
1947	166	126	174	164	124	172	152	152	117	-2	0
1948	163	155	162	165	157	164	144	152	110	-8	-7
1949	172	172	172	172	172	172	152	151	117	-1	0
1950	186	194	176	187	195	177	157	157	122	2	3
1951	182	221	165	200	241	182	161	161	125	1	2
1952	174	220	180	196	245	203	181	181	144	15	16
1953	172	214	182	202	248	213	191	191	154	24	25
1954	180	225	197	198	239	210	188	188	151	23	24
1955	192	240	208	211	262	228	205	205	166	30	31
1956	191	244	202	222	281	235	211	211	171	30	31
1957	188	250	206	216	286	236	212	212	172	30	31
1958	186	258	211	193	266	219	196	196	157	23	24
1959	189	265	214	201	280	227	204	204	164	27	29
1960	191	272	220	198	281	227	204	204	165	28	29
1961	195	282	224	192	278	221	198	198	160	25	26
1962	198	290	222	206	300	230	207	207	167	28	29
1963	200	298	223	217	321	241	217	217	175	30	31
1964	200	306	228	234	352	265	240	239	194	39	41
1965	198	313	227	250	385	284	257	257	210	47	49
1966	193	322	222	262	421	298	270	270	221	52	53
1967	190	332	224	257	431	299	270	270	221	51	52
1968	192	349	230	257	448	303	274	274	224	52	53
1969	191	363	224	264	480	306	276	276	227	54	56
1970	177	353	213	241	456	285	257	257	209	43	45
1971	178	364	218	242	471	290	262	262	214	45	47
Correlation with time	.15	.86	-.11	.95	.93	.97	.97	.97	.97	.96	.96

estimate of depreciation (10 per cent) contained in it. RSV_7 and RSV_8 seem the most valid and meaningful rates.

This leads me to conclude that *the rate of surplus value or class exploitation in Canada has increased dramatically over time.* Further, it appears that the correlations between time and class exploitation are stronger in a positive direction after the Second World War than before (see Table 3.3). This suggests that *not only is class exploitation in Canada increasing over time, but also that the rate of increase in exploitation is increasing over time.* Since monopoly capitalism has increased in Canada especially since the end of the Second World War, these findings confirm Marx's prediction that as the capitalist mode of production develops, the rate of class exploitation increases. This means that the capitalist class in manufacturing in Canada has increasingly extracted wealth out of the working class by its control over the means of production and the subordinate position in which this places the working class.

One of the weaknesses in correlational data is that they gloss over interesting variations over time in the rates of surplus value. When the rates [in RSV_6 to RSV_{11}] are inspected more closely, it appears that the sharpest increases in class exploitation in Canada have occurred during periods when the capitalist mode of production has developed the most rapidly: the boom of the 1920s, the Second World War, and the expansion of the 1960s. One of the sharpest declines in the rates of surplus value occurred during the depression when, of course, the capitalist system itself was in a state of deep crisis. These patterns suggest that when capitalism is healthy or expanding, class exploitation increases very sharply. My own findings are similar to those found by other researchers in other countries using somewhat similar methods (Varga n.d.: 174–75; Varley 1938: 395; Corey 1934: 83; Mandel 1975b: 174–75).

Table 3.3
Correlations between Rates of Surplus Value and Time

	1917–44	1945–71
RSV_1	−.22	.68
RSV_2	−.71	.98
RSV_3	.30	.87
RSV_4	.68	.90
RSV_5	.46	.97
RSV_6	.86	.95
RSV_7	.86	.95
RSV_8	.86	.95
RSV_9	.86	.95
RSV_{10}	.85	.94
RSV_{11}	.85	.94

Such rates of class exploitation are not very useful unless they help us understand better other aspects of the class structure as well as broader socioeconomic and political forces operating within society. A traditional Marxian hypothesis has been that as class exploitation increases, more overt forms of class conflict become more likely. This hypothesis was tested through measuring overt class conflict by three measures of strikes and lockouts in manufacturing between 1917 and 1971: days lost per year in strikes and lockouts, workers involved per year in strikes and lockouts, and number of strikes and lockouts per year (obtained from Department of Labour, various years *(a)*, *(b)*). These measures were regressed onto the eleven series of rates of surplus value. The results of the analysis appear in Table 3.4. The majority, or 55 out of 66, of the regressions are positive. The most valid rates of surplus value, RSV_7 and RSV_8, generally have the greatest effects on strikes and lockouts, depending upon which way the latter measured. Class exploitation explains up to 56 per cent of the variance in overt class conflict. This suggests that Marx's conception of class relations and its empirical application to Canada cannot be considered irrelevant or relegated only to objective dimensions of class, but that is also useful for understanding some of the behavioural dimensions of class conflict. The increasing extraction of wealth by the capitalist class from the working class places the latter in a defensive position from which it is forced to take more overt kinds of actions in the form of strikes in order to prevent an even greater redistribution of wealth from itself to the capitalist class.

CONCLUSIONS

There are three main conclusions to be drawn from the analysis in this paper. First, Marxian propositions are useful for understanding the dynamics of class relations in Canadian society. There is little support here for those who would dismiss many of Marx's propositions on an *ad hominem* basis. Second, class exploitation in Canada, as measured by the rate of surplus value in manufacturing, has increased dramatically over time, especially since the Second World War. As previously noted, this has been a period during which monopoly capitalism in Canada has had its greatest advance. Third, class exploitation brings about an increase in the level of open class conflict in the form of strikes and lockouts. The analysis presented here provides us with a more meaningful understanding of this kind of class conflict than the meaningless correlating of indexes of economic growth with strikes and lockouts which ignores the question of the influences of class relations on class conflict (Rees 1954; Smith 1972; Snyder 1975). Future research should be directed to an analysis of the determinants of class exploitation.

Table 3.4
Standardized Regression of Strikes and Lockouts in Manufacturing on Rates of Surplus Value (with Percentage of Variance in Strikes and Lockouts Explained by Rates of Surplus Value in Parentheses)

	RSV_1	RSV_2	RSV_3	RSV_4	RSV_5	RSV_6	RSV_7	RSV_8	RSV_9	RSV_{10}	RSV_{11}	T
SL_1	-.04	.61	-.22	.61	.66	.61	.61	.61	.61	.58	.58	.60
	(0)	(37)	(5)	(37)	(44)	(37)	(37)	(37)	(37)	(34)	(34)	
SL_2	-.06	.42	-.24	.37	.44	.36	.36	.36	.35	.32	.32	.34
	(0)	(18)	(6)	(14)	(19)	(13)	(13)	(13)	(12)	(10)	(10)	
SL_3	-.22	.54	-.33	.70	.67	.71	.70	.70	.70	.66	.66	.65
	(5)	(29)	(11)	(49)	(45)	(50)	(49)	(49)	(49)	(44)	(44)	
SL_4	-.22	.32	-.34	.45	.42	.43	.43	.43	.42	.38	.38	.37
	(5)	(10)	(12)	(20)	(18)	(18)	(18)	(18)	(18)	(14)	(14)	
SL_5	-.04	.66	-.24	.71	.75	.72	.72	.72	.72	.68	.68	.69
	(0)	(44)	(6)	(50)	(56)	(52)	(52)	(52)	(52)	(46)	(46)	
SL_6	.06	.25	-.10	.17	.25	.17	.17	.17	.17	.13	.13	.16
	(0)	(6)	(1)	(3)	(6)	(3)	(3)	(3)	(3)	(2)	(2)	

SL_1 = days lost per year in strikes and lockouts
SL_2 = days lost per year in strikes and lockouts per thousand production workers
SL_3 = workers involved per year in strikes and lockouts
SL_4 = workers involved per year in strikes and lockouts per thousand production workers
SL_5 = number of strikes and lockouts per year
SL_6 = number of strikes and lockouts per year per thousand production workers
T = time from 1917 to 1971; this column shows correlations between time and strikes and lockouts

NOTES

[1] At one point (Marx 1967: I, 303–11), Marx called the *rate* of surplus value the *mass* of surplus value wherever the rate of surplus value is generalized to the societal level. However, later (Marx 1967: III, 143) he used the *mass* of surplus value to refer only to the *numerator* of the *rate* of surplus value. To avoid confusion, I use Marx's *rate* of surplus value at both the individual and societal level while reserving the *mass* of surplus value to mean the *numerator* of the rate of surplus value.

[2] Marx's "profits" are not to be confused with contemporary notions of profits which are less inclusive in that they exclude such items as the salaries of administrative workers and interest payments.

[3] Marx distinguished productive wage labourers who produce surplus value from non-productive wage labourers who do not produce surplus value but only allow it to be realized in commercial and financial trans-actions (Gough 1972; O'Conner 1975). This paper concerns only productive wage labourers.

[4] Derived from Urquhart and Buckley (1965: 304) and Dominion Bureau of Statistics (1961–72).

[5] Derived from Urquhart and Buckley (1965: 293) and Dominion Bureau of Statistics (1961–72).

[6] Derived from Urquhart and Buckley (1965: 463) and Statistics Canada (1974, 1975).

[7] RSV_1 is analogous to Gardner's (1975) rates, except that the number of years covered is different, and he expresses his rates in proportions while I express mine in percentages.

On "Class Exploitation" in Canada
Axel van den Berg and Michael R. Smith

Marx often expressed the rate of surplus value in terms of a division of the working day of the average worker into "necessary labour time" (the part of the day necessary to produce the amount of value equal to the worker's daily wage) and "surplus" or "free" labour time (the part of the day in which the worker produces the surplus for the capitalist (Marx 1906: 212–18)). Obviously, the ratio of free to necessary labour time is identical to the ratio of total surplus to total variable capital (Marx 1906: 241). What this means is that the *rate* of surplus value depends *only* on the relation between the wage *rate* or the average wage and the productivity of labour (assuming, again, that prices reflect value).

It is very important that we stress this point since, as we will see, it appears to be something over which Cuneo is wholly confused. The total number of workers engaged in production is irrelevant to the *rate* of surplus value. It is the relation between wages and productivity which counts. An increase in the number of workers does increase the *total amount* of surplus value, but as long as labour productivity and wages remain the same, those additional workers are no more and no less exploited than those who are already employed. Since they add the same proportion to the wage bill as they add to the total amount of surplus value, the rate of surplus value remains unchanged. It is hard to envisage a useful rate of surplus value which would do otherwise.

That the degree of exploitation depends only on the relation between wages and productivity has one other important implication. It means that if increasingly technologically advanced machinery raises the productivity of labour in real terms, and if real wages remain constant at the subsistence level, then the degree of exploitation will increase proportionately with the increase in productivity. If real wages increase slowly with some sociocultural definition of "subsistence," then the rate of exploitation will increase by the difference between the rate of increase of productivity and the rate of increase in real wages. Thus, with rising productivity as a result of technological progress, the degree of exploitation may increase indefinitely, barring fatal "realization" crises.

CUNEO'S RATES OF EXPLOITATION

RSV_1 is constructed as follows: the numerator — the surplus — is calculated by subtracting total wages of production workers in manufacturing from total value added (the selling price minus the cost of material, fuel, and electricity consumed in production); the denominator is total wages. For Cuneo, this measure is flawed for two reasons. The first is that there is no control for the relative cost of constant capital built into it. If machinery, for instance, becomes increasingly expensive to replace, the recorded surplus in manufacturing overstates the actual surplus skimmed off by entrepreneurs. Cuneo is surely correct here. His other objection is that there is no control for numbers of production workers in this measure. As we shall see shortly, on this he is quite mistaken. What is important to note about this measure is that it indicates hardly any trend at all for the period considered (r = .15). Clearly, there is no dramatic increase in the rate of exploitation reflected in this measure.

RSV_2 does increase steeply after 1944. Prior to that, it displays a marked negative trend. It appears to be constructed by subtracting the wage aggregate deflated by the *CPI* (1949 = 100) from value added and dividing the result by aggregate wages, again deflated by the *CPI*. The effect of this is to increase wages above their nominal level prior to 1949, thereby reducing the rate of surplus value (since the value added from which wages are subtracted is not controlled for price increases); after 1949, the aggregates of wages are diminished and the rate of surplus value correspondingly increased. RSV_2 tends to decline from 1917 to 1944 but to increase dramatically from then onwards. This dramatic increase, then, is simply the result of the fact that wages are deflated by a substantial post-war rate of inflation, whereas the measure ignores the diminishing value of the surplus that goes to capital. Cuneo acknowledges this difficulty; consequently, it is not at all clear why he wasted the time of the reader by including it in his paper. Certainly, the positive trend it displays is meaningless.

Cuneo's RSV_3 appears to be a more acceptable measure. It is identical to RSV_2 except that "fluctuations in the costs of constant capital are taken into account" (Cuneo 1978: 290 [p. 53 in this book]). This was apparently done by dividing the amount of value added in the numerator by the General Wholesale Price Index. What is missing, however, is an allowance for depreciation in order for the numerator to appropriately approximate Marx's concept of surplus value. On the other hand, it is possible that RSV_3 has a slight conservative bias. On the whole, then, RSV_3 seems to be a fair surrogate for the Marxian rate of surplus value. However, since the "costs of constant capital" have apparently soared after 1949 (Cuneo 1978: 296 [p. 55 in this book]), RSV_3 actually displays a slight decrease over time (r = −.11). Hence, Cuneo's conclusions cannot be based on this rate.

The rates of surplus value upon which Cuneo does base his conclusions are RSV_4 through RSV_{11}. We will focus on RSV_4 in some detail because the same serious problem that renders RSV_4 preposterous also renders each of his other rates of surplus value preposterous.

RSV_4 is identical to RSV_1 except that "total wages are controlled by the number of production and related workers in manufacturing standardized to 1949" (Cuneo 1978: 290 [p. 54 in this book]). What Cuneo has done is construct an index of the number of production workers in Canadian Manufacturing on the basis of the number employed in 1949 (1949 = 1) and then to divide the wage sums in the numerator and the denominator by this index. The computing formula for RSV_4 thus looks as follows: $((VA - (W/I)/(W/I)) \times 100$ where VA stands for value added, W for the aggregate wage sum, and I for the index of the number of workers.

This rate of surplus value rises quite dramatically during the 1917 to 1971 period. Cuneo reports correlations with time of well over .9 for all his remaining rates of surplus value. What then accounts for the greatly differing results for RSV_4 as compared to RSV_3? Of RSV_1 through 3, Cuneo writes: "The weakness in the above three measures of the rate of surplus is that they are based on widely different numbers of wage labourers which increase from 523,491 in 1917 to 1,167,810 in 1971. This variation is therefore taken into account in RSV_4 to RSV_6" (Cuneo 1978: 296 [p. 55 in this book]). Taking the number of workers into account causes such changes in the rates because, "before 1942, total wages 'appear low' partly because fewer workers are employed. This artificially drives up during this period the estimate of rates of surplus value unless the variation in the number of workers is taken into account. Similarly, for most years after 1942, wages 'appear high' partly because more workers are employed so that rates of surplus value are artificially low" (Cuneo 1978: 296 [p. 55 in this book]).

Is this a sensible argument? That is, is an estimate of the rate of surplus value which contains such controls in some sense a better estimate of the Marxian process of exploitation than one that lacks such controls? We think the answer to this question is that it certainly is not.

Cuneo is claiming then, that such fluctuations in the number of workers, output, and wages will not be adequately reflected in a rate of surplus calculated by dividing the surplus (s) by total wages (v) without controlling for the number of workers. We can show, however, that this is nonsense with the help of Table 3.5 below.

As can be seen, Table 3.5 shows precisely the hypothetical cases considered by Cuneo. The change from period 1 to period 2 is his first

Table 3.5
Hypothetical Rates of Surplus Value for Different Combinations of Numbers of Workers, Wages, and Output

Period	Number of Workers	Average Production Per worker	Total Production	Total Wages (v)	Average Wage	s (Total Production − Total Wages)	s/v (%)
1	10	1	10	5	.5	5	100
2	20	1	20	7.5	.375	12.5	167
3	25	1	25	10	.4	15	150

hypothetical case. The number of workers rises from 10 to 20, or by 100 per cent, which is faster than the increase in total wages which is from 5 to 7.5, or a rise of 50 per cent. Productivity remains constant at 1 per worker (if it had been allowed to rise, the results would hold *a fortiori*, of course). What happens to the crude rate of surplus value, simply calculated as the ratio of total surplus to total wages, without any adjustments for the rising number of workers? It increases from 100 to 167 per cent, thus faithfully reflecting the increase in the degree of exploitation. Hence, there is no need at all to make special allowances for the number of workers. Now, the change from period 2 to period 3 is Cuneo's second hypothetical case. The number of workers increases from 20 to 25, or by 25 per cent, which is less than the increase in total wages from 7.5 to 10, or by 33 1/3 per cent. Again, productivity remains constant (letting it decrease only reinforces the results). And again, the decrease in the degree of exploitation is perfectly shown by the "simple" rate of surplus declining from 167 to 150 per cent! Thus, we may conclude that Cuneo's adjustments for the number of workers in his RSV_4 are completely superfluous because such fluctuations in the number of workers as occurred are already reflected quite satisfactorily in his RSV_1 and RSV_3.

It will now become clear why we have insisted earlier that the *rate* of surplus value only depends on the relation between productivity and wages, and that it has nothing to do with the number of workers, while the *mass* of surplus value, as Marx calls it, *does* depend on the number of workers, other things (that is, the rate) being equal. Cuneo appears to have confused the two. In fact, his argument consists of a complete *non sequitur*. What he really does in his hypothetical examples of numbers of workers increasing faster or more slowly than the total wage sum at constant productivity, is to change the relation between wages and output. If the number of workers increases faster than the total wage sum, this simply means that average wages, or the wage rate, must drop, as can be seen to occur between period 1 and 2 in Table 3.5, where the wage rate drops from .5 to .375. If the wage rate drops while productivity remains constant or rises, then obviously the capitalist must be appropriating a larger share of the proceeds, and thus the rate of surplus value rises. If the number of workers increases more slowly than the wage bill (period 2 to 3), the reverse takes place. Such hypothetical examples which implicitly vary the relation between wages and productivity *do not at all* suggest "that changes in the number of workers *independently* affect rates of surplus value" (Cuneo 1978: 288, emphasis ours), and, as a matter of fact, *they do not*.

It is all the more surprising that Cuneo should refer to precisely that section of the first volume of *Capital* in which Marx makes it perfectly clear that whereas the *mass* of surplus value can, at a constant *rate* of surplus value, be increased or decreased by hiring more or fewer workers, the *rate* of surplus value remains unaffected by changes in the number of workers. It can only be increased by reducing necessary relative to surplus labour-time; that is, by reducing the wage rate relative to productivity (Marx 1906: Ch. XI entitled: "Rate and Mass of Surplus-Value").[1] Thus, Cuneo's "correction" of Marx is quite unnecessary since Marx (unlike Cuneo) knew full well that the *rate* of surplus-value would not and should not be affected by the number of workers. As a matter of fact, a few pages after the one referred to by Cuneo, Marx clearly states once again, to avoid any possible confusion, "… that the surplus-value produced by a given capital is equal to the surplus-value produced by each workman simultaneously employed. *The number of workmen in itself does not affect either the rate of surplus-value or the degree of exploitation of labour-power*" (Marx 1906: 353, emphasis ours). Therefore, Marx was perfectly correct in ignoring the number of workers (with a few mistaken exceptions, see Note 1) when he was analysing the *rate* of surplus value, and this has nothing to do with Marx's time horizon being presumably shorter than Cuneo's. This is not meant as a defence of Marx; we simply wish to show that Cuneo does not understand Marxian economics.

Rates of surplus value RSV_5 through RSV_{11} are derivative of RSV_4. RSV_5 and 6 are not of interest here since they are the equivalents of RSV_2 and RSV_3 but with the adjustment for the number of workers incorporated in RSV_4 added. RSV_7 through 11 result from the application of various rates of depreciation of non-financial tangible assets, fixed assets, or total assets, to RSV_5 (presumably, that is, to the amount of value-added in the numerator of RSV_6; see Cuneo 1978: 291–92). For the sake of computing and data-searching convenience, Cuneo assumes that the stocks of these various assets remain a constant proportion of gross sales over time on the grounds that he has found little fluctuation during the period 1944 to 1964 (Cuneo 1978: 291–92), and thus his depreciation amounts to subtracting a series of fixed percentages from value-added (since the latter is also highly dependent on gross sales) which, in turn, amounts to simply varying the absolute levels of the rate of surplus value. Indeed, the zero-order correlations between RSV_6 through 11 are all either .99 or 1.00. Since Cuneo himself had already warned us that "not much validity can be placed on the absolute size of the rates of surplus value offered" (Cuneo 1978: 287), the whole exercise seems rather pointless.

CUNEO'S "RATES OF EXPLOITATION" AND "OVERT FORMS OF CLASS CONFLICT"

At this point, the reader might be disposed to make the following objection: how, if Cuneo's rates of surplus value are entirely worthless, is it possible that they can be used to predict amounts of industrial conflict in Canada? Cuneo, as a matter of fact, uses the correlations that he reports in Table 3.4 as evidence of the utility of his measures. And he uses the same correlations as a justification for describing the studies of industrial conflict by Smith (1972) and Snyder (1975) as "meaningless." Now, let us assume for the moment that Cuneo's *RSV*s 4 to 11 are actually sensible measures of what Marx had in mind, at least, of some reasonably interesting social process.

Cuneo [states] that "class exploitation explains up to 56 per cent of the variance in overt class conflict." It should be clear, however, that amounts of variance explained of that sort of magnitude are only found where Cuneo has not deflated the industrial disputes measure by growth in labour force. Since the number of workers in Canada has grown, one would expect the amount of industrial conflict to increase independently of whatever happened to the rate of exploitation. Because Cuneo's preferred *RSV*s are strongly associated with time, one would expect substantial correlations between his undeflated industrial disputes measures and those *RSV*s that display positive trends. What is more to the point in appraising the utility of Cuneo's *RSV*s is that the correlations involving industrial disputes deflated by labour force are by no means spectacular. For RSV_7, Cuneo's preferred measure, the largest bivariate correlation between rate of exploitation and an industrial disputes measure deflated by number of production workers in manufacturing is only .43 (or about 18 per cent variance explained). For RSV_3, which we view as the only reasonable approximation to what Marx had in mind, the relationship is weakly negative.

But even this .43 correlation between RSV_7 and numbers of workers involved in industrial disputes deflated by number of production workers is meaningless. There are other methodological deficiencies. It is, for instance, normal to include a trend term in time series regressions. Deflating by labour force is not enough. Not only does the size of the labour force increase with time; in Western capitalist countries, several aspects of workers' conditions and the legal framework of industrial relations have changed in ways that are likely to have increased the willingness of workers to strike. The proportion of the labour force unionized, for instance, has increased substantially. The right to strike has been extended to public service workers. Real incomes have increased such that it is conceivable that some workers are in a stronger position to finance themselves through a long strike. Female labour force participation has increased, thereby making available second incomes in a number of families to provide support during a strike. There are no doubt other factors. What the inclusion of a trend term in a time series regression does is provide a way of controlling for these kinds of effects that are not measured directly. That is especially important in a time regression covering a very long period of time. Now, it happens that for Cuneo's preferred RSVs, one could not sensibly introduce a trend term as one independent variable in a multiple regression in which RSV_7, for instance, was another independent variable. The reason is that Cuneo's preferred RSVs are almost perfectly correlated with time (e.g., .97 in the case of RSV_7). Multicollinearity, in other words, would render the estimates of the regression coefficients for each variable wholly unreliable. But that does not make the potential effect of unionization, increased female labour force participation, or changes in labour laws any less relevant. It simply means that one cannot separate out the effects of those variables from the effects of Cuneo's preferred RSVs (we are assuming for the moment, you will recall, that Cuneo's preferred RSVs are sensible measures) with the data at hand. Cuneo's preferred RSVs, being so closely correlated with time, can be most intelligently interpreted as an index for time whose association with measures of industrial disputes incorporates the effect of the various factors that a trend term normally incorporates.

CONCLUSION

Cuneo makes two principal claims in this paper. The first is that the rate of exploitation in Canada has increased dramatically over time. The second is that Canadian workers respond to increases in the rate of exploitation by being more prone to go on strike. Cuneo's evidence does not support either claim. The first claim is based upon a method of calculating the rate of surplus value which not only has nothing to do with what Marx actually says about the rate of surplus value but, worse yet, has the absurd implication that a worker in a large plant in which an employer extracts no surplus at all is as much exploited as a worker in a small plant in which 9/10ths of the value of production goes to the employer. Cuneo only manages to show that the rate of class exploitation in Canada has increased by using a method of calculation which makes complete nonsense of Marx's original ideas. Similarly, he is only able to show that industrial disputes are related to his somewhat eccentric conception of surplus value using methods much less than minimally adequate.

It remains true that the distributional questions that Cuneo addresses are very important indeed. But the methodological sloppiness of his paper suggests an unreasonable determination to have his data fit his preconceptions. It is the kind of willingness to compromise the facts in the interests of doctrine on the part of some Marxists that gives Marxists in general a bad name. With friends like Cuneo, Marxism does not need any enemies.

NOTES

[1] It must be admitted, however, that Marx occasionally creates confusion among his disciples by obscuring the relation between wages and productivity with arguments that are inconsistent with the overall theory. Thus, for instance, he argues that when the number of workers decreases, the mass of surplus may be kept constant by a compensating increase in the rate of surplus value, but that such increases have a limit due to the naturally fixed length of the day. After all, there comes a point where workers will simply starve to death, he argues, or where the amount of surplus labour time can simply not be further increased by lengthening the working day (Marx 1906: 333–34). However, this only holds if productivity remains constant. If productivity rises by as much as the number of workers declines, the amount *and* the rate of surplus value can remain unchanged and the working day need not be lengthened. Elsewhere, Marx similarly argues that the use of more productive machinery may decrease necessary to surplus labour time and thus raise the degree of exploitation, but at the same time, it reduces the number of workers employed by a given amount of capital. And since you cannot "squeeze as much surplus value out of 2 as out of 24 labourers," there is a limit to this (Marx 1906: 444–45). Again, this is not so. Given sufficient increases in productivity (without which the number of workers would not be reduced anyway), the rate of exploitation can be increased indefinitely, and it is quite possible to squeeze as much or more out of 2 than out of 24 workers.

DISCUSSION QUESTIONS

1. How do we know if someone is exploited? What would happen to the income/profit of the capitalists if workers withdrew their labour? Can capitalists produce commodities and/or acquire profit if workers stop working?

2. Consider two factories that are the same in every aspect except that one is owned collectively by workers and the other by a capitalist. In which of these factories would you expect workers to have a higher income? Why?

3. In which of the following conditions do you think workers are more likely to complain about their pay: when the company profit is high or when it is low? Why?

4. In what way does technology, double shift work, and/or high unemployment influence capitalist profit?

5. How are the increasing numbers of females in the labour force, higher real wages, and unionization affecting the rate at which strikes occur?

6. Read Exhibit 1.3, "Class out of the Shadows." What is the central message of the article. What type of theoretical paradigm does it follow? How would you go about criticizing it?

Exhibit 1.3

Class out of the Shadows

On any Sunday in Mexico City, you can take a stroll in Chapultepec Park and find it crowded with life: clowns, stalls selling gaudy trinkets, bandstands and dancers by the lakes, multi-coloured balloons, thousands of people taking it easy and enjoying each other's company. All of them are *mestizo*, from the "mixed" ancestry that accounts for a large proportion of the Mexican people. Switch on the television or leaf through the newspapers, however, and the faces of the rich and famous you see there are noticeably different: *criollo*, the descendants of Europeans.

"Sometimes I wonder why we bothered with the Revolution at all," said a Mexican friend despairingly. "We're still ruled by the *conquistadores*."

In Mexico, throughout most of Latin America and indeed across the countries of the Majority World, it is impossible to ignore the visible evidence of a class system at work, separating small and immensely powerful élites from the great majority of the people.

In the Minority World — the rich industrial countries of the North — on the other hand, we have lived for a couple of generations at least with the general idea that class is a thing of the past. Among the chattering classes, it hardly gets a reference unless someone happens to mention it in passing or by mistake. Our images of it are antique, sepia-tinted: male, downtrodden masses toiling away with hot metal in gigantic factories and a cloud of smog; bloated capitalists counting their cash in stately piles. The class system has simply evaporated, according to this theory. Life for the majority has changed beyond recognition, improved beyond measure. We are all middle class now.

(continued)

Exhibit 1.3 *(continued)*

But hang on a minute. It is worth remembering that class divisions are created at the top, where there is a vested interest in keeping as quiet as possible about them, at least in public. And consider the implications of the following story — it comes from the United States but could equally have come from almost anywhere in the world:

"On 25 February 1991, the compensation committee of the board of directors of General Dynamics met to consider revising the compensation package of its chief executive officer, William Anders, and 24 other top executives. Under the plan they approved, the executives would receive a bonus equal to their yearly salary if General Dynamics stock rose ten points, from $25.56 per share to $35.56 per share, and stayed there for ten days. If the stock went up another ten points to $45.56 per share and stayed *there* for ten days, they would receive a bonus equal to twice their yearly salary, and so on until the plan expired in 1994 ...

"So what do you suppose that Mr Anders and those other executives did? They announced a massive layoff of more than 12,000 of the company's 86,000 employees, cut spending in other areas and froze the salaries of anyone below their ranks. By the end of the year, they had amassed $600 million in cash, which they promised to spread among the shareholders, and earned themselves $18 million in bonuses as the stock price held to the $45.56 mark for the tenth day. Anders personally received more than $9 million in salary and bonuses" (Downs 1995).

Mr Anders and his kind have congealed into what has come to be called in North America an "overclass": immensely wealthy corporate executives and the "interests" of capital they represent. Twenty years ago, the chief executive officers of large companies in the US were paid about 35 times more than the average worker they employed; today, the ratio is 187 times as much (Cockburn 1996). By 1989, the top ten per cent of Americans controlled 80 per cent of the country's financial assets; the wealthiest 0.5 per cent of families (some 400 000 people) could have paid off the entire US national debt and still have been worth ten per cent more than they were in 1983 (Democratic Policy Committee 1996).

Underclass

This — the rich getting richer — is familiar fare. But the statistics tell a story that is about more than money. In effect, each of the 24 board members of General Dynamics pocketed the wages, the self-respect

(continued)

Exhibit 1.3 *(continued)*

and the aspirations of 500 employees. Their ability to do this, and to get away with it, presupposes the existence of a whole structure which empowers one small group of people to do this to another much larger group of people — and eventually to cast out upwards of 30 million people into an "underclass" beyond the outer parameters of the American Dream.

Class is about this kind of power over people. It is about ownership, control and exclusion, and about the way in which human aspiration is wasted and belittled.

The evidence for the persistence of class divisions in the North is, in fact, quite compelling. International research conducted over a long period has now demonstrated beyond dispute that the patterns of mobility up and down the social scale (and no-one denies the existence of a scale of some sort) in these countries have remained basically the same throughout most of this *century*. The patterns are remarkably similar, too, from one country to the next, including the US, Japan and Germany, which — unlike "class-ridden" Britain — are often thought of as "open" societies. In Germany, for example, you are 5.39 times more likely to stay in the top-earning "salariat" — and avoid moving down into the working class — if you are born into it, compared with the reverse for someone born into the working class. In Britain, the figure is 5.48 times; in the US, it is 3.72 times (Marshall and Swift 1995).

One consequence of this is that the much-hyped "equality of opportunity" in rich countries, the idea that all of us are free to "succeed" regardless of our class origin, is illusory. The inequity of birth, inheritance and class still prevail.

All the same, what has happened to the working class in the North? Traditionally employed in manufacturing industries which have now largely disappeared from our shores, the working class has been displaced into the service sector. But somebody must be *making* things, somewhere.

Indeed they are: 80 per cent of the world's manufacturing workforce is now to be found in the South, particularly in a belt around the tropics that was once best known for its rainforests (The World Bank 1995). Millions of people — most of them women — in Latin America, Asia and the Indian sub-continent, work in factories that make the electricial goods we buy, the clothes we wear, the shoes we walk in, the toys we play with. The conditions in which they work, and the rewards they receive for doing so, are little different from those in the industrial countries of the North one hundred years ago.

(continued)

Exhibit 1.3 *(continued)*

When you endure or witness these conditions at first hand — as I have witnessed them in Mexico — there is only one word that can accurately describe the experience: exploitation. Such conditions could only have been devised *for* people who have no choice in the matter, and *by* people who have lost any sense of common humanity, though they exercise great power over others nonetheless.

Chameleon

The existence of this kind of exploitation completes the picture of a fully fledged class system at work. To see this picture clearly, all we have to do is to think of the earth as one place and take an international view.

Why should we take any other? We know well enough that capitalism went global some time ago, but perhaps we have still to catch up with the full implications, the dramatic impact this has had on all our lives. There is not so much a "growing divide" or "deeper gulf" between rich and poor *countries*, as a higher wall between *classes* in all countries everywhere. Dramatic changes in appearance do not alter the nature of a chameleon: capitalism and class go together like profit and loss.

Class hasn't ceased to matter simply because communism failed. Quite the reverse. In formerly communist countries, a class system persisted beneath a veneer of equality so that commissars have transformed themselves into entrepreneurs and scarcely noticed the difference. In Hungary, a destitute underclass has its ancestry in exclusion under the communist regime prior to 1989 (Szalai 1996). The legal minimum wage in Hungary now provides for no more than 64 per cent of basic subsistence needs — in Russia for just 20 per cent. In Bulgaria, the value of the real minimum wage was halved in 1991; by mid-1992, three-quarters of Bulgarian households had incomes below the social minimum (International Confederation of Free Trade Unions 1996).

In the brand-new industrializing "tigers" of Asia, too, an old-fashioned class system is duly emerging. In China, 50,000 people a day visit McDonald's in Beijing and spend the equivalent of two weeks' wages for an average Chinese worker on a single burger. In South Korea, an immensely wealthy management élite hacks its way around the fairways of privilege at exclusive golf clubs that can cost upwards of $200,000 to join. In Malaysia, a class of NQTs — "Not Quite Theres" — has been characterized as "halfway up the ladder of success ... intro-

(continued)

Exhibit 1.3 *(continued)*

verted, spending-oriented, neurotic, unadventurous, traditional and lacking in confidence" (Robinson and Goodman 1996).

The idea that "we are all middle class now" (a middle with no top or bottom) is plainly ridiculous. All the arguments advanced to promote it eventually turn to nothing. For example, because half the shares on the London Stock Exchange are now owned by pension funds and insurance companies (HMSO 1995), it is suggested that there is a form of "popular capitalism" in Britain. But who owns the insurance companies? And which pensions have the right to tell their pension funds what to do with the money? The middle class may search for a location somewhere between servant of the system and lord of the universe, but like any pig in the middle, it tends to get dizzy.

The "hidden hand" of market forces has reached into the farthest corners of the earth and touched every one of us, marking us with our class, our part in the performance. To be honest, I could sit for ever in the depths of the Amazon rainforest watching a rubber-tapper in a long green robe singing plaintive songs and performing rituals with hallucinogenic *hayauasca*, without my getting any clearer idea of what on earth he was up to. Set us talking about rubber, however, and before long — even without mentioning glamour — we'd share a pretty good notion of our general drift.

Big-Shot Barons

Chances are that at the same time as this conversation, somewhere in the skies above our heads, big-shot rubber barons and their multinational chums would be winging their way between Sheraton Hotels, talking with just as much facility across cultural boundaries about the very same thing.

Our two conversations would, however, be entirely different: the one about how to strengthen the hand of the rubber-tappers against the grip of the barons; the other about how to grab their rubber for as little as possible and turn the rainforest into real estate.

There's no middle ground here and no way for one side to ignore the other. These are the active ingredients that decide, day by day, whether the rainforest will survive; whether the environment, genders, races and indigenous peoples will prosper or live in subjection. All too often, it is still the barons, and subjection, that win. There are sides and sooner or later, we all have to decide which one we are on.

(continued)

Exhibit 1.3 *(continued)*

Confronted with the class system, we have a limited number of options open to us. We can continue to deny that it exists. We can ignore it. We can think of it as a natural feature of the human landscape. We can try to scale it. We can denounce it. Or we can look to each other in solidarity and decide to do something about it. We may be up against a dictatorship more subtle, impersonal and absolute than anything previously conceived, but once we have decided to act, it is wonderfully liberating to discover what might then be created.

As consumers, we can discover the people who produce what we consume; we can refuse to embrace the process of exploitation; we can seek out and promote those products that challenge it best and restrain the craving for blind consumption.

As producers and workers, we can look to each other in a spirit of co-operation and solidarity in place of competition, fear and hatred — competition is for games, co-operation is for real on a lonely planet. We can push forward the long, slow process of building links across international boundaries between labour unions and activist organizations. We can transform the function of work from the systematic destruction of human talent into the celebration of human dignity and ingenuity.

As citizens, we can construct forms of government that express these needs rather than enforce the rule of free-market capitalism — *it* doesn't need democracy, but we do. We are many; they are few.

The seed of dissent holds the bloom of a new season.

Source: David Ransom, "Class out of the Shadows," *New Internationalist*, July 1996, pp. 7–10. Reprinted by permission.

ACCESS TO ELITE POSITIONS

Inequality of Access: Characteristics of the Canadian Corporate Elite
Wallace Clement

Embedded in the capitalist economic order of Canada and perpetuated through the sanctity of private property, the corporate elite during the post–second world war period has concentrated its base of power (Clement 1974: 18–25) and consolidated avenues of access into its inner circles. Important transformations have occurred in the economic structure, and rapid industrialization has been evident, but the corporate elite remains as closed as it was in 1951, even tighter in some key respects. Contrary to liberal ideology, which holds that greater mobility will characterize "postindustrialism," Canada remains capitalist, industrial, and closed at the upper levels of corporate power. Many sociologists who celebrate existing structures assert that corporate capitalism, with time and industrialization, will reduce inequalities based on ascription. Talcott Parsons, for example, argues that religion, ethnicity, regionalism, and social class based on ascriptive characteristics "have lost much of their force" (Parsons 1970: 14–15). Evidence now exists which shows that this has not been the case for Canada between 1951 and 1972.

ELITES AND SOCIAL CLASS

Corporate elite positions reflect Marx's analysis of the accumulation and concentration of capital into fewer and larger units and the "Pareto principle" of "separating the trivial many from the vital few." The corporate elite are synonymous in many respects with the "big bourgeoisie." Within the 113 dominant corporations in Canada in 1972, two dimensions of inequality are important. One involves positions within corporations, their stratification and power differentials, and the other, recruitment to these positions. The first is concerned with condition and the second with opportunity. In other words, the first is concerned about the structure of inequality, the second about the processes of maintaining inequality. To show that a corporate elite exists demonstrates the existence of inequality of condition; to show that there is differential access to elite positions demonstrates that there is an unequal opportunity structure.

This dichotomy is similar to that outlined by Frank Parkin (1972) when he distinguished between the "egalitarian critique" and the "meritocratic critique." The first focuses on "objection to the wide disparities of reward accruing to different positions," while the second is concerned about "the process of recruitment to these positions ... Seen from this angle, social justice entails not so much the equalization of rewards as the equalization of opportunities to compete for the most privileged positions" (Parkin 1972: 13). Parkin suggests the importance of synthesizing the two critiques since they are analytically distinct aspects of inequality but actually closely related. One concept used to integrate the two is kinship, whereby families are able to pass on their accumulated advantages intergenerationally, thus perpetuating class continuity through the ascriptive institutions of kinship and inheritance.[1] Of course, it is not kinship per se that perpetuates existing class structures. This is accomplished by the persistence of an economic order organized on the basis of corporate capitalism which determines which types of occupations will be created, how many there will be, how the economy will expand, its direction and scope, and the level of technology which will exist. Class structures, therefore, are a product of the way a society's economy is organized, and class continuity, a product of the way privilege is transferred. In Canada, as with all capitalist societies, there is a high correlation between class structures and class continuity. Those with advantages are able to pass them on, while those without are not able to provide their offspring with the same privileges.

Hierarchies within economic organizations and the existence of dominant corporations create positions of power to which social classes are differentially recruited, thus perpetuating dominant classes and reinforcing power disparities. By examining inequalities of power associated with key corporate positions and the perpetuation of class advantages, a corporate elite with roots firmly embedded in the upper class will be illustrated.

SOCIAL CHARACTERISTICS OF THE CORPORATE ELITE

The findings of the present study show that access into elite positions has become more difficult for persons outside the upper class. Since 1951, there has been a crystallization of the upper levels of power beyond the already rigid power structure identified by Porter in 1951. Directors and senior executives were identified from the 113 dominant corporations in Canada, and it was shown that a total of 946 individuals resident in Canada hold 1,456 of the corporate directorships. Adequate biographical data was found for 775 persons (81.9 per cent) who between them account for 1,276 positions (87.8 per cent). This compared favourably with Porter's coverage of 77.8 per cent of the members and 82 per cent of the positions for 1951.

Career Avenues into the Elite

Several important changes have occurred in the career patterns for members of the corporate elite. The proportion of members of the elite technically trained in science and engineering has declined. It would be expected that greater proportions of technical men would have made their way into the elite if specialized technical skills were now more central to decision-making as the "post-industrial" thesis would suggest, but this has not been the case [see Table 4.1].

Financial executives have remained stable, with one significant change occurring in terms of educational backgrounds for this group.

Table 4.1
Main Career Patterns of the Corporate Elite, 1951[a] and 1972

	Canadian-Born (%)		Canadian- and Foreign-Born (%)	
	1951	1972	1951	1972
Engineering and science	19.3	12.1	22.3	13.9
Financier and finance exec.	18.0	17.9	16.7	17.9
Law	17.7	21.7	14.2	19.0
Finance department	6.0	6.6	6.7	7.6
Main career in other elites	2.1	6.4	1.8	5.8
Career in family firms	16.8	18.8	14.9	17.2
Own account	7.5	2.1	7.6	2.2
Commerce	—	4.6	—	4.4
Unclassified	12.4	10.1	15.6	12.0
Total	100.0	100.0	100.0	100.0
N	(611)	(673)	(760)	(775)

[a]   See Porter (1965: 275, Table 27).

While in 1951 only 45 per cent had attended university, now 60 per cent of the financiers, 70 per cent of the insurance company executives, and 57 per cent of the other financial executives have done so. While only a quarter of the banking executives have attended university, these seven represent a substantial increase from the one in twenty-three who had in 1951. Porter indicates that in 1951, 39 per cent of the financiers had elite connections, with such connections being most prevalent among the youngest group. This is borne out in the present set of financiers, 46 per cent of whom have family connections in the elite. Bankers also have a high percentage (35 per cent) of elite connections. A high proportion of individuals in this group attended private school. Enjoying this advantage were 23 (46 per cent) financiers, nine (31 per cent) bankers, seven (23 per cent) insurance executives, and eleven (37 per cent) other financial executives. Private schools have provided large numbers of the individuals in this category with common experiences at an early age, as well as allowing extensive contacts to be developed with other upper class peers. These initial contacts have been fostered in later life within the confines of one or more of the exclusive national men's clubs (Rideau, Mont Royal, St James, York, Toronto, and National). Sixty-six per cent of the financiers, 90 per cent of the bank executives, 47 per cent of the life insurance company executives, and 70 per cent of the other financial executives belong to one or more of these six clubs.

Lawyers tend to be of upper class origin, and many have inherited law firms and directorships from their fathers. There has been a substantial increase in the proportion of lawyers entering the corporate elite. This change is due almost exclusively to those who have law degrees but choose to enter the elite via the corporation legal department rather than the law firm. While only 9 per cent of the lawyers came through the legal departments of corporations in 1951, 24 per cent were internal recruits in 1972. This suggests an increasing number who have chosen law as a general education suited to the corporate world and not primarily as a means of entering private practice. Law partnerships, however, remain an important linking institution. Porter (1965) reports for 1951 that thirteen sets of partners had more than one member in the elite. This number has increased to 23 in 1972. Together, they include 60 partners and 106 dominant directorships. Many lawyers share a common social experience in their educational careers; for example, four went to the University of Toronto Schools for their private schooling together, each going to the University of Toronto for their LLBs and then on to Osgoode Hall "finishing school." This included one pair of twins, John A. and James M. Tory, who followed their lawyer father's footsteps, together taking over five of his dominant corporate directorships. All the lawyers are training in Canada, with half attending Osgoode Hall. About one-fifth go to the University of Toronto and one-fifth to McGill University. Private school education is not uncommon for lawyers in the elite; 46 per cent of those in law practice and 29 per cent of the internal lawyers have this advantage.

Similar proportions in both periods made it into the elite through the finance departments. Of the 44 Canadian-born, 33 are chartered accountants, nine have economics or administrative training and two appear to be inside-trained, both of whom entered the corporate world after attending private schools. Only four of the fifteen foreign-born are chartered accountants. The others worked their way up as treasurers or comptrollers. For the most part, those entering the elite through the finance department have entered as inside directors and remained there; they also have fewer interlocks with other dominant companies than do those with other career patterns.

Porter did not include commerce as a career pattern in 1951, noting that "comparatively few persons in the elite have been trained in commerce or business administration" (Porter 1957: 381). Commerce careers have become more prevalent. Persons in commerce hold 5.1 per cent of the directorships in dominant corporations, 5.5 per cent of bank directorships, and 5.7 per cent of those in insurance. An additional 30 members of the elite have also received commerce degrees, but their main careers have been classified elsewhere.

The 133 individuals who have been characterized as gaining access to the elite through family firms have spent the majority of their business careers in corporations where their fathers, or in five cases maternal grandfathers, held key corporate positions. This does not include all those who began at or near the top of the class structure, nor does it include those who gained their access through their father-in-law's firms. There are 133 individuals in this category now compared to the 113 in 1951. The current figure includes 126 of the Canadian-born (18.8 per cent) and only seven foreign-born (6.8 per cent). Within the current elite who are Canadian-born with their main careers in family firms, there are 24 father/son combinations, and 32 are brothers. In examining the entire group of 133 individuals who inherited their positions, it becomes evident that private schools play a large part in their careers. Eighty-five attended private schools (64 per cent of the group), and 108 attended university (81 per cent). The power of this group extends further than does that of any other group in terms of interlocking directorships; they account for 18.7 per cent of the directorships in all dominant companies, 23 per cent in banks with 35 per cent of the group holding dominant bank directorships, and 21.4 per cent of the insurance directorships.

In contrast to those who enter the elite through family firms are those who manage to establish firms on their own account and gain the stature of becoming members of the elite in one generation. For 1951, Porter (1965) reports that 58 of the elite made it in this manner. A strong indicator that the structure of power in Canada has become more rigid over the past twenty years is the fact that only 26 members of the present elite have made it on their own account. They hold only 2 per cent of the dominant directorships and 1.5 per cent of the bank directorships.

Class Origins

Class origins are important from a number of perspectives. They show the extent of mobility existing at any given time and (if more than one time-frame is available, as in the present case) relative changes in class access to elite positions. When one is concerned with mobility, one assumes that talent is distributed throughout all classes in society, and if everyone had an equal chance at access to the elite, the total society would be better served. From the perspective of liberal democratic theory, the concern is focused on the value that everyone should have equal opportunity to participate in the management and direction of a society's future. From the social structural perspective, class access is an important indicator of the degree of openness present in the flow between different classes or, put differently, the extent of class crystallization there is in a society. The more difficult it is for people outside the upper class to enter the elite, the greater the exclusiveness of power in a particular society. With greater crystallization of power there is less opportunity for those outside the inner circles of power to actualize their concerns and desires, thus stifling equality of opportunity which forms the basis of liberal democratic ideology.

Table 4.2 presents a summary of class origins for the elite in 1951 and 1972. This table provides conclusive evidence that access to the corporate elite has become more exclusively the preserve of the upper class over the past twenty years. Using the same criteria as Porter, the present study replicates as close as possible both the spirit and methodology used earlier.

Comparing overall changes between 1951 and 1972, it is found for the Canadian-born members of the current elite that 28.5 per cent had fathers or, in a few cases, uncles in the corporate elite at some time. This represents an increase of 6.5 per cent from 1951 of the proportion of the elite enjoying the advantage of coming from a family directly in the inner circles of the corporate world in a previous generation. There is obviously a high degree of continuity when 192 members replicate their fathers' positions. Adding sixteen members who had fathers either in the political or bureaucratic elite gives an

Table 4.2
Class Origins of the Canadian-Born Members of the Corporate Elite, 1951 and 1972

	Population (%)[a] (Approximate)	Corporate Elite (%) 1951	Corporate Elite (%) 1972	Percentage Change 1951 to 1972
Upper class[b]	1–2	50	59.4	+9.4
Middle class	15	32	34.8	+2.8
Working class	85	18	5.8	−12.2
		100	100	
N		(611)	(673)	

[a] The population "at risk" breakdown is based on a calculation of occupations in 1941, the census year closest to when most members of the current elite entered the labour force. At that time, 12 per cent of the labour force was engaged in middle class occupations including professional, managerial, and proprietary. Only 8 per cent of the male population of the age group of the current elite had even some university. Taking into account the known high overlap between sons of the middle class and those entering university, the proportion from middle class origins is estimated at about 15 per cent of the population. Working class origins are less than middle class, thus including manual, service, and primary occupations. Upper class includes members of one of the corporate, political, or bureaucratic elites, fathers with large but not dominant corporations, and their families. See also private schools in note b below, and note b in Table 4.4.

[b] Includes attendance at one of the Headmaster's Association private schools or classical colleges. See Table 4.4 for detailed breakdowns of class categories.

increase to 30.9 per cent compared to 24 per cent in 1951. A further 39 not already included married into elite families. This means that 247 members of the current elite embarked on their careers with the initial advantage of having elite connections. This represents about a 6 per cent increase since 1951. Another 68 not thus far included had fathers who were in substantial businesses which, as far as could be determined, were not dominant but of sufficient size to provide an initial upper class avenue into the elite. This means that 46.8 per cent of the present elite began at or near the top of the class structure. The current figure for those who started with this initial advantage shows a full 9 per cent increase over the 1951 findings. Of the remainder, 85 had attended private schools. This brings to 400, or 59.4 per cent of the elite, the number who had upper class origins, a significantly higher percentage than the 50 per cent with the same origins in 1951 [see Table 4.2].

A further 57 had fathers who were engaged in middle class occupations such as engineers, doctors, lawyers, ministers, or managers. This brings the total to 457, accounting for almost 68 per cent of the elite. There are also 177 persons not included to this point who had attended university. The addition of this group brings the proportion accounted for to 94.2 per cent, while the same indicators accounted for only 82 per cent in 1951. The remaining percentage accounts for those who have made it into the elite from lower than middle class origins. While in 1951 18 per cent of the elite were in this bottom classification, only 5.8 per cent of the present elite are in the same position. The majority of the population, of course, had less than middle class origins as defined here, with over 80 per cent of the male population engaged in other than managerial, technical, or professional occupations (Kalbach and McVey 1971: 257). Each indicator shows that the current elite is of higher class origins than twenty years ago. The class structure of Canadian society has tightened in terms of gaining access into the corporate elite.

Table 4.2 illustrates that particularly the upper class, but also the middle class, are overrepresented compared to the general population. Moreover, this overrepresentation has increased over the last two decades. While there is no reason to believe that there have been any significant changes in the size of the upper class, the proportion of those of upper class origins in the elite has increased by 9.4 per cent over the period. The number of persons in the current elite who are of middle class origin has increased by 2.8 per cent, a change which could correspond to a change in the class composition of the population. Those with working class origins represent a significant decline of 12.2 per cent. The major difference between the two periods can be found in the 6.5 per cent increase in the proportion with fathers in the corporate elite and particularly those whose careers are in family firms, as discussed earlier.

It is recognized that there is differentiation within the elite based on length of time in the elite, by corporate positions, by control exercised as in the case of comprador and indigenous elites, by corporate activities or functions, and between single and multiple directorship holders. These will now be examined.

Elite Size and Concentration

Table 4.3 includes two further divisions, the "Top 100" and Multiple Directorship Holders. Porter introduced the division of the "Top 100," which is replicated here,[2] but another basis of differentiation which distinguishes between single and multiple directorship holders within dominant corporations has also been introduced. Although including only about 10 per cent of the entire elite, as it did in 1951, the "Top 100" have a scope well beyond their numbers. They hold 342 of the dominant directorships, i.e., 24 per cent of those held by Canadian

Table 4.3
Class Origins of Canadian-Born Members of the
Corporate Elite by Subgroups, 1972

	All	Top 100	Single Directorships	Multiple Directorships
Upper class[a]	59.4	65.0	52.8	72.8
Middle class	34.8	28.8	41.1	22.0
Working class	5.8	6.2	6.1	5.2
	100	100	100	100
N	(673)	(80)	(443)	(230)

[a] See Table 4.2, note b.

residents, 59 of the directorships in the five big banks (28 per cent of the positions), and 36 insurance directorships (25 per cent). These figures are almost identical to those of 1951, the corresponding figures being 25 per cent, 29 per cent, and 23 per cent, respectively. One difference between the "Top 100" identified in 1951 and those for 1972 is that there were 88 Canadian-born in the group for the earlier period, but only 80 now.

Of the 274 multiple directorship holders resident in Canada, adequate biographical data was available for 267, representing a coverage of 97.5 per cent. These 267 individuals constitute 28.9 per cent of the total number of elites resident in Canada. Although Porter did not use multiple directorship holders as an analytical distinction, he did report that 22 per cent of the Canadian residents had a total of 46 per cent of the dominant directorships in 1951. Multiple directorship holders in 1972, while representing only 28.9 per cent of the elite, account for 53.8 per cent of all dominant directorships, 58.6 per cent of all insurance directorships, and 68.3 per cent of the directorships in five key banks. Enormous power is concentrated in this group and represents an increased number of directorships and a greater scope over 1951. Over half the group holds a directorship in one of the key banks. Together they hold over two-thirds of these important posts.

The core of the corporate elite can be considered as the members of the "Top 100" and those who hold multiple directorships. Since only fifteen members of the "Top 100" are not overlapped with multiple directorship holders, there is a core of 282 persons who wield enormous economic power even relative to other members of the corporate elite.

There is a great similarity between the class origins of the Canadian-born members of the "Top 100" in 1951 and in 1972 in that 65 per cent of each group has upper class origins. The most important finding is that almost three-quarters of those who hold multiple directorships are from the upper class, 13.4 per cent more than the elite as a whole. Even when compared to the "Top 100," 8 per cent more of the multiple directors started in the upper class. Once again, class barriers become important within the elite. Members with upper class origins have a much stronger probability of becoming multiple directors than do those from lower classes. This confirms the value of upper class connections and the social network operating at that level. Another fact which confirms the vitality and power of the core group of indigenous capitalists is the fact that 86 per cent of those with multiple directorships are Canadian born.

EDUCATION AS TRAINING AND SOCIAL NETWORKS

Less than 10 per cent of the male population in the same age group as the corporate elite have any education past secondary school, and about 5 per cent have university degrees; the few who did have the advantage of higher education were indeed privileged. Of course, if females of the corresponding age were included, the proportions who attended university would drop even lower since only about 2 per cent of the women had the same advantage. The corporate elite, in contrast to the general population, has had two distinct advantages; it is almost exclusively male (only six women), and most of its members have graduated from university.

In 1951, 58.3 per cent of the corporate elite were university-educated, with an additional 5.4 per cent having some other higher education past the secondary level such as chartered accountancy degrees or technical training. By 1972, 80.5 per cent of the elite had university training, and an additional 4 per cent had other post-secondary education. In other words, only 104 (15.5 per cent) of the Canadian-born members of the elite do not have more than secondary education; in 1951, 36.3 per cent of the elite were in this position.

Not only is university education important, but it appears that post-graduate training and professional degrees are also rapidly becoming prerequisites of elite membership. Of the Canadian-born, 280 have additional training beyond their undergraduate degrees. This number accounts for 41.6 per cent of the entire Canadian-born elite. Of these, 183 have law degrees, including fifteen who have post-graduate degrees beyond law, with ten of them attending Harvard for MBAs. Although, 53 of those with post-graduate degrees went to the United States for their education and 34 of these to Harvard for MBAs. An additional fourteen went to the United Kingdom and two to France for their post-graduate training, with the rest obtaining their degrees in Canada.

THE PRIVATE WORLD OF POWERFUL PEOPLE

The upper levels of power in Canada are surrounded by a society very different from that experienced by most Canadians; the elite are people who become involved at the executive level in a range of philanthropic and cultural activities. From private schools to private clubs, they lead a life quite apart from, although very much affecting, the existence of the vast majority of Canadians. Through a series of elite forums and political connections, they make decisions well beyond those confined to the dominant corporations where they gain their power.

Private Schools

Attending "Dad's" old school is another form of inheritance which preserves elite continuity. The fee-paying private schools of eastern Canada are institutions that stem well back into Canada's history, with some, like Upper Canada College, founded in 1829, and Trinity College School, founded in 1865, providing common class experience for many generations of Canada's upper class.

The pervasiveness of private school attendance is on the increase in the elite. While 34.2 per cent of the Canadian-born elite attended in 1951, this figure has increased to 39.8 per cent or 267 of the elite in 1972.

It is evident why 64 per cent of the elite members who had careers in family firms attended private schools. Providing the aspiring elite with a total environment for usually eight of the most formative years, private schools teach the sons of the upper class values appropriate to their position; they have "strong characters built" and the opportunity to build lasting friendships with other upper class boys they later meet in the boardrooms of Canada's largest corporations.

Private Clubs, Bastions of the Elite

Providing more than simply status to the upper class male, the exclusive gentlemen's club is a meeting place, a social circle, where businessmen can entertain and make deals. It serves as more than a badge of "social certification" in that the club is a place where friendships are established and old relationships nourished. Especially in the six national exclusive men's clubs, there is an opportunity for the corporate elite to come together socially at the national level, thus transcending the metropolitan or regional class system. These six Canadian clubs are one of the key institutions which form an interacting, active, national upper class. [Elite membership in these clubs has remained stable from 1951 to 1972.]

CONCLUSION

It has become increasingly evident that the men who fill corporate elite positions are predominantly of upper class extraction or have become accepted into the upper class in terms of life-style and social circles. The process by which the upper class is able to maintain itself may be understood as one of co-optation and inherited advantage. Porter has argued, "Class continuity does not mean that there is no mobility. Rather it means there is sufficient continuity to maintain class institutions" (Porter 1965: 285n). As long as the upper class remains in control of dominant corporations and is able to keep its class institutions such as private schools and clubs intact, it will be able to maintain itself in Parkin's term as a "class of reproduction" and ensure conformity through "class nomination" of those members of middle class, and occasionally lower class, deemed acceptable and, conversely, excluding those who are not. This means accepting the lifestyle, attitudes, and values of the upper class. As guardian of institution of power and avenues of access, they are able to dictate that the system should operate as they see fit, that is, as a system of exclusion and monopoly for their own privileges and perogative of power. The economic elite in Canada is that section of the upper class which operates the major economic institutions of Canadian society on behalf of, and in the interest of, the upper class. As long as economic power is allowed to remain in its present concentrated state, there appears to be no hope for equality of opportunity or equality of condition in Canada.

NOTES

[1] In a recent paper, Parkin (1974) has examined two types of "social closure as exclusion." One he calls "class nomination," whereby "ruling groups claim the right to nominate their successors, but not to transmit their statuses to their own lineal descendants ... class nomination depends upon the use of exclusion rules which single out specific attributes of individuals, rather than the attributes of a particular social group." On the other hand, "classes of reproduction" are "those exclu-

Table 4.4
Class Origins of the Canadian-Born Members of the Corporate Elite, 1951 and 1972

Class Indicators	All (Cumulative)			Top 100 (Cumulative)			Multiple Directorship (Cumulative)			1951[f] (Cumulative)	
	N	N	%	N	N	%	N	N	%	Top 100	All
Upper[a]											
Father in corporate elite	192	(192)	28.5	26	(26)	32.5	86	(86)	37.4	30.3	22
Father in other elite	16	(208)	30.9	1	(27)	33.8	7	(93)	40.4	37	24
Wife from elite family	39	(247)	36.7	5	(32)	40	16	(109)	47.4	46	31
Father in substantial corporation	68	(315)	46.8	12	(44)	55	30	(139)	60.4	54.4	37.8
Upper/Middle[b]											
Attended private school	85	(400)	59.4	8	(52)	65	27	(166)	72.2	67	50
Middle											
Father in middle class occupation[c]	57	(475)	67.9	7	(59)	73.8	15	(181)	78.7		
Attended university[d]	177	(634)	94.2	16	(75)	93.8	37	(218)	94.8	85.2	82
Working[e] (left)	39	(673)	5.8	5	(80)	6.2	12	(230)	5.2	(14.8)	(18)
N	(673)			(80)			(230)			(88)	(611)

[a] Since the categories are presented as mutually exhaustive from top to bottom, some in higher categories could also be placed in lower ones.

[b] *Upper/Middle* refers to the fact that although private schools are not exclusively the preserve of the upper class, they are upper class and the values as well as life-styles are those of the upper class. It should be remembered that most current members of the elite would have attended private schools during the thirties.

[c] Middle class occupations refer to that section of the population with the advantages of high skills and income. This includes fathers who were doctors, lawyers, engineers, or managers, and also ministers, who are special cases since they have high status and advantages such as reduction in their sons' tuition fees at private schools.

[d] Since only about 8 percent of the male population in the age group of the current elite had even some university training, it is reasonable to assume that using this as an indicator of middle class origin is still confining the class of origin to fairly near the top of the class structure.

[e] Elite members in this category have none of the above attributes and are considered to be of working class origin.

[f] For a detailed breakdown of Porter's findings for 1951, see Porter (1965: 292, Table 28). Porter collapsed 'father in middle class occupation' and "attended university," while these have been reported separately here.

sion practices which *are* based upon purely group attributes — lineage, race, religion, or whatever." He goes on to say the distinction "is of course a purely notional one; in most modern societies, both sets of exclusion practices seem to operate" (Parkin 1974: 4). In the following analysis of inequality of access to the Canadian corporate elite, it is apparent that both means of exclusion operate. For example, "classes of reproduction" are evident in terms of both class and ethnicity and explain a great deal of the means of access to these elite positions, while for some others, university education and particular career patterns based on "class nomination" offer an explanation.

2 The "Top 100" were selected in this, and in Porter's study, on the basis of holding top executive positions, particularly presidencies and chairmanships, within the largest of the dominant corporations, multiple directorships which include more than one of the largest dominant corporations, or a combination of each of these.

Perspectives on the Class Origins of Canadian Elites: A Methodological Critique of the Porter/Clement Tradition
R. Ogmundson

INTRODUCTION

Porter's *Vertical Mosaic* (1965) remains the most important book written by a Canadian sociologist. In tandem with Clement's *Canadian Corporate Elite* (1975a), its images of Canadian society still dominate the academic consciousness. Central to its imagery is the notion that Canada's elites are dominated by a homogenous and exclusive group of anglophone, Protestant (especially Anglican) males of British, upper-class ancestry.

This paper will re-assess the methodology and interpretations of Porter and his student Clement (1975a). It will then briefly outline changes over time and put the social composition of Canada's elites into an international perspective.

METHODOLOGICAL CRITICISMS

Criticisms relevant to findings about the social characteristics of Canadian elites may usefully be organized under three headings — the original selection of elites, measures of class origins, and treatment of the data. In each case, a plausible argument can be made to the effect that the measurement procedures adopted systematically biased the data toward the finding of elites with exclusive social characteristics.

The Original Selection of Elites

In his work on the business elite, Clement (1975a: 127–28) failed to replicate Porter's selection methodology. As Hunter (1976: 126) noted, this change in methodology makes it impossible to infer trends over time with any confidence. Nonetheless, Clement (1975a) consistently makes the error of doing so.

MEASURES OF CLASS ORIGINS

The elite social characteristics data in this tradition used biographical information available in published sources. While it may have been impractical to use any other approach in Porter's time, the biography method comes up with findings of a much more exclusive and homogenous elite than does the more accurate survey method (Clement 1977a: 207).

Indicators of Class Origins

One of the most effective critiques of the Porter tradition was one of the earliest — that of Harvey Rich in an unjustly ignored paper in the *Journal of Canadian Studies* in 1976 (Rich 1976a). For our present purposes, the most important methodological point he made had to do with measurement of the class origins of those in elite positions. Porter and his students *assumed* that attendance at a university could be taken as an indicator of middle- (or better) class origins. In an extreme case, one semester at a university was taken as a sign of privilege.

Rich (1976a), in his study of the Ontario civil service elite, however, obtained interview data which showed that there was a spectacular difference between results using educational attainment as a measure of class origin (87 percent middle or upper) and interview data concerning father's occupation as a measure of class origin (36 percent middle or upper). Clearly, the interview data are a better indicator of class origins.[1] Just as clearly, a difference in findings like this cannot be ignored. In particular, working-class participation in our elites must have been greater than previously thought.

A more detailed inspection of the data supports this suggestion (see Table 4.5). Clement (1975a: 458–59) reports that 26.3 percent of his business elite were classified on the basis of "university attendance." Thus, about three-quarters (26.3 percent of 34.8 percent) of those classified as being of "middle-class origin" in the business elite were so placed on this basis. If the same ratio (3/4) can be applied to Porter's business elite, about 24 percent of Porter's business elite were likely classified as middle class on this basis.

It is difficult to guesstimate how many of those who had attended university were of working-class origin. Since, even in the mid-fifties, about one-half of the university students were from origins below the professional-managerial classes (Porter 1965: 184), it seems reasonable to speculate that at least one-quarter of those designated as middle class by this criterion were actually working class. A revision such as

Table 4.5
Class Origins of Canadian-Born Members of the Economic Elite, 1951 and 1972 (Percentages)

Class Indicator	1951 (Appendix)	1951 (Main Text)	1972 (Appendix)	1972 (Main Text)
Upper Class	37.8	50	46.8	59.4
Father in corporate elite	22		28.5	
Father in other elite	2		2.4	
Wife from elite family	7		5.8	
Father in substantial corporation	6.8		10.1	
Upper/Middle				
Attended private school	12.2		12.6	
Middle				
Father in middle-class occupation	32	32	8.5	34.8
Attended university			26.3	
Working				
(Left)	18	18	5.8	5.8
	100		100	
N	(611)		(673)	

Source: Adapted from Clement 1975a: 458, 192.

this changes the picture dramatically. For example, the lower-class component of Porter's business elite would be 24 percent — higher than the clearly established upper-class component (22 percent, see Table 4.5).

Thus, *the Porter tradition classified anywhere between 20 and 60 percent of the class origins of Canadian elites on the basis of an indicator which is highly inaccurate, and which has a powerful bias towards exaggerating the apparent exclusivity and class homogeneity of the elites.*

Other methodological criticisms of the measurement of class origin are possible. For example, "upper-class origin" measures include "wife from elite family," "father in other elite," and "father in substantial business" (see Table 4.5).

Marriage to someone in an elite status is an *achieved* status which does not necessarily indicate original upper-class origin. Indeed the *Encyclopedic Dictionary of Sociology* (Frank et al. 1986: 1) specifically cites "marriage" as an illustration of an achieved characteristic. Given that Rosen and Bell (1966) found that only 21 percent of upper-class marriages in Philadelphia in 1961 were within the upper class, we can be confident that some of those classified as "upper class" on this basis were less privileged. Similarly, the use of both "wife from elite family" and "father in other elite" confuses the concepts of class and elite. Someone in an elite state (e.g., union leader, member of the Royal Society, deputy minister) need not be a member of the upper class. A third criterion for "upper class" origin, "father in substantial corporation" is also unsatisfactory in that it is not clear what a "substantial" corporation is (Porter 1965: 291; Clement 1975a: 190). This allows an uncomfortable degree of subjectivity in classification.

These questionable procedures account for as much as two-thirds of those classified as "upper class" and very definitely increase the apparent class exclusivity and social homogeneity of Canadian elites. While a substantial proportion of those classified as "upper class" on these bases were probably of upper-class origin, it is equally probable that a significant proportion were not. Given the "zero-sum" nature of our calculations (i.e., every 5 percent removed from the upper-class group adds 5 percent to the middle or lower group), even modest revisions might lead to a dramatic difference in the images generated by the data.

Clement (1975a: 190, 192, 222) went further than Porter and used "private school attendance" as an indicator of upper-class origin. (Porter [1965: 292] had used this measure as an indicator of "middle or higher" class origins.)[2] This had the effect of changing Porter's original estimate of the upper-class origins of the economic elite from the 37.8 percent reported in *The Vertical Mosaic* — mentioned in a footnote (Porter 1975: 222) and in the appendix (Porter 1975: 458) — to the

50 percent reported in the main text of *The Canadian Corporate Elite* (Clement 1975a) (see Table 4.5). A similar technique was used in reports on the class origins of the media elite (Clement 1975a: 330, 459). This methodological change was important in terms of general perceptions because many are familiar with Porter's work on the class origins of the business elite mainly through Clement's work (e.g., Pakulski 1982).

TREATMENT OF THE DATA

Although the amount of missing data is substantial (see Table 4.6), this point received minimal attention and was not reported in the tables. In the case of class origins, this problem is exacerbated by exclusion of the foreign born from the analysis. This is so in every case except that of the labour elite. However reasonable the rationale, this was a significant omission. For example, if one includes the 17.2 percent of the elite who were excluded because they were foreign born, Porter's data on class origins refer to only 62 percent of his original economic elite. In this instance, as in others, even small changes can have a major impact on relative percentages in this zero-sum situation. If, following the example of Bendix and Howton (1959), the data were reported with missing data and foreign born fully acknowledged, the results in many key instances would look quite different. One illustration of this is provided by a comparison of the figures on the business elite in Table 4.6 to the figures in Table 4.5. The upper-class component of Porter's business elite declines from 37.8 percent to about 23.5 percent! Furthermore, a high degree of missing data reduces our confidence in any findings and should moderate whatever conclusions we draw from them.

Since, by definition, we do not know what missing data would tell us, all parties concerned are able to imagine what they please. Many, including Porter, believe that missing data are likely to refer disproportionately to those of humble origins (Porter 1965: 394; Baldwin 1977: 10; Pakulski 1982: 202) while others, notably Clement (1977a: 207), take the opposite view. If one is willing to make the assumption that the missing data refer disproportionately to those of humble origins or non-charter-group identities, our impression of the class and ethnic origins of Canadian elites again changes substantially.

The Porter tradition is also notable for the habit of reporting data only when it is complete for an individual. Given that the more prominent the individual, the greater the likelihood of complete data, this introduces yet another bias which would lead to an exaggeration of the exclusivity of Canadian elites. As Baldwin (1977) demonstrates, this omission can make a substantial difference in the apparent findings.

Table 4.6
Class Origins of the Economic Elites Reported with Missing Data and Foreign Born

Class Origins[a]	1951[b]	1972
Upper	23.5	42.3
Middle[c]	27.6	24.7
Lower	11.0	4.1
Foreign born	15.1	10.8
Unknown	22.9	18.1
N=	985	946

[a] Missing data on class origins were 30.2 percent for the anglophone labour elite; 28.1 percent for the CNTU elite, and 12.9 percent for Section II of the Royal Society. Foreign born for Section II of the Royal Society was 26.7 percent. In other cases, it was apparently not mentioned. (Class origins for labour were calculated with the foreign born.)

[b] The figures given for the economic elite in 1951 are those provided by Porter (1965), not those provided in the main text of Clement (1975a). The figures given for the business elite in 1972 are provided by Clement in the main text.

[c] Those classified as "middle or upper" by Porter (1965) are placed in the middle class.

Source: Adapted from Porter 1965; Clement 1975a. I am indebted to James McLaughlin for the preparation of this table.

Another flaw in this tradition is the habit of comparing the characteristics of an elite with those of the entire population and then inferring "discrimination" if the figures are not similar. This practice is unreasonably crude in that it fails to control for all manner of relevant sociological variables such as the age structure of groups, their geographic distribution, their educational qualifications, the amount of time spent in the country, and so forth (Sowell 1984: Ch. 1). If such comparisons are made, they should follow the example of Alba and Moore (1982) and be made between the elite itself and with the societal pool of people who might be "at risk" for membership in the elite — e.g., males, ages forty to sixty, with university degrees. At the mass level in Canada, Tepperman (1975) has shown that much apparent "discrimination" evaporates when such factors are taken into account (see also Berkowitz 1984: 252–53).

In sum, a number of methodological decisions served to generate data which exaggerate the social exclusivity and homogeneity of our elites. We cannot know how great the distortion is, but we can feel confident that it is sufficient to alter fundamentally our impressions of class, elites, and power in Canada.

HISTORICAL PERSPECTIVE

It is widely believed that Canadian elites have become more exclusive in their social characteristics over time. An examination of the relevant literature indicates that precisely the opposite is true. The widespread impression that Canadian elites have been becoming *more* socially exclusive over time stems mainly from the influential work of W. Clement in *The Canadian Corporate Elite* (1975a). In this book, Clement reports work on *only* two elites — the economic and the mass media elites.

Porter's research on the business elite was done in 1951, while Clement reports on the situation in 1972. Studies done subsequent to that date, while also not replications, serve to give us some sense of what the trend has been. Here the findings indicate that the trend has been towards less exclusive class origins (see Hunter 1986: 157; Niosi 1981; Williams 1989; Newman 1975, 1981; Francis 1986). To illustrate briefly, Williams (1989: 73) reports that 11.8 percent of his "large business" elite came from a "bourgeois" background, while 22.8 percent came from a "working-class" background. Newman (1989: 15) notes:

> the Canadian Establishment is becoming increasingly like Damon Runyon's crap game: anybody can join. It no longer matters very much who you are, who your father was, what school you attended, who you marry, what clubs you join, or who you know — only what you have achieved.... Instead of a pseudo-aristocracy, Canada's Establishment has become a fiscal meritocracy.

In sum, the image of inherited British wealth is becoming increasingly obsolete. Whatever the original validity of images derived from Porter and Clement, they no longer hold true for the upper echelons of Canadian society. The more heterogeneous social characteristics of Canadian elites also raise questions about the existence of a "bourgeoisie" or even of "elites" in the sense of a conscious and cohesive group. Also, the increased heterogeneity of Canadian elites overall would seem likely to reduce overall elite cohesion and unity. If it was reasonable to argue before that homogeneous elite social characteristics facilitated elite unity and thus rendered "power elite" and "ruling class" arguments more plausible, surely the findings of contemporary research must increase the plausibility of "pluralist" positions.

INTERNATIONAL PERSPECTIVE

The conventional wisdom of Porter and Clement also implies that Canadian elites are unusually non-representative of the general Canadian population. Nonetheless, an examination of the international literature indicates that virtually all elites anywhere, including those in Marxist-Leninist societies, are characterized by atypical social characteristics. This exceedingly common, if not universal, phenomenon is referred to as "the law of increasing disproportion" (Putnam 1976: 33).

Though precise comparisons are difficult to make, the social characteristics of Canadian elites appear "normal" in an international perspective (Presthus 1974; Grayson et al. 1979; Pakulski 1982; Nock 1982).

Was the Conventional Wisdom Ever Correct?

At this point, one may ask whether the conventional wisdom was ever correct. One key event in the development of contemporary Canadian sociology has been the "capture" of the Porter heritage of studies in elites and power by those in a critical tradition. Porter's work was not necessarily radical. Indeed, critics have debated his "true" orientations (Heap 1974). Furthermore, Porter was cautious in his claims and carefully noted the limitations of his empirical work (Rich 1976b). Nonetheless, our image of *The Vertical Mosaic* (Porter 1965) has been shaped by its highly popular sequel in *The Canadian Corporate Elite* (Clement 1975a). Although Porter (1975) outlined reservations about the interpretations of his student, the conventional wisdom concerning elites and power has accepted the radical version of reality.

Consequently, it is interesting to re-examine Porter's data. No precise data are provided on the mass media. Only partial data are provided for the intellectual, religious, and labour elites. This makes it difficult to assess the entire elite structure. Where data are provided, however, the picture that emerges is one of *clear numerical domination by those of middle- and lower-class origins*. This is so even in the case of the business elites. Even using Porter's measures, and even where missing data and foreign born are excluded from the analysis, a *full* 62 percent of the Canadian-born economic elite come from "middle" — or "lower" — class origins! Indeed, the proportion of those probably from working- or lower-class origins (18 percent) is almost as great as the proportion from clearly established upper-class origins (22 percent, see Table 4.5).

In sum, conventional impressions about elites and power in Canadian society have been largely based upon ignorance of the weak and incomplete data on which the broader claims of British upper-class dominance were based.

NOTES

[1] *University attendance was a highly inaccurate indicator of class origin in earlier time periods.* Rich (1976a: 30) divided his sample according to age. Of those fifty-five and over in his group: "the proportion from working class origins did not drop, and contrary to Porter's strategic methodological decision that an upper class background could be inferred from university attendance, 70 percent of those from working class background also were university graduates."

[2] It is obvious that ambitious families would send their children to private school. Consequently, attendance at a private school is not a decisive indicator of upper-class origins.

DISCUSSION QUESTIONS

1. What is the difference between equality of opportunity and equality of condition? Which of these concepts is more accepted in popular views? Why is it important that there should be equality of opportunity? What about equality of condition?

2. Based on your own personal experience, what is more important for landing a good job: who you know or what you know? List the ten most powerful and/or richest persons in your city. Trace their class background. Are they more likely to be self-made, or did they inherit their wealth and power? How easy is it for ordinary persons to acquire a job like theirs? Under what conditions?

3. Based on your own experience, do you think Canada's class system is becoming more open or closed? Is this pattern different for entry into the elite from the general population?

4. Select twenty names from the most recent issue of *Who's Who in Canada* and read their biographical information. Compare these with twenty other names from the 1971 issue. Has there been a visible change in class background of these elites? In what direction?

CANADIAN DEPENDENCY

The Canadian Corporate Elite: Financiers or Finance Capitalists?
William K. Carroll

The development of the Canadian economy presents an interesting case of capital accumulation and class formation which can be interpreted from quite divergent theoretical perspectives. One view draws on dependency theory (see Frank 1967, 1972), stressing similarities between the Canadian experience and the dependent pattern of underdevelopment in the Third World. According to this interpretation, Canada's position in the world economy has been that of a satellite to larger and more advanced metropolitan centres, first France, then Britain, and presently the United States (see Naylor 1972: 1–41; Clement 1977a; Hutcheson 1978). Evidence cited in support of this thesis includes (1) the leading role played by staple commodities such as wheat, forest products, oil and gas, and base metals in the Canadian economy; (2) the apparent dominance of merchant capital within the Canadian bourgeoisie; (3) penetration of the Canadian economy, especially since World War Two, by foreign-based multinational corporations in search of resources and markets; and (4) the resulting remittance of branch-plant profits to foreign parents, restricting opportunities for independent development.[1]

An alternative viewpoint stresses basic similarities between Canada and other advanced capitalist Societies. These similarities include (1) the monopoly farm in which a substantial bloc of indigenously controlled capital has been organized throughout this century; (2) the growth of Canadian-owned investments in the Third World; and (3) a level of labour productivity and a standard of living among the highest in the world (see Moore and Wells 1975; Piedalue 1976: 3–34; Degrass 1977; Szymanski 1977: 144–51; Sweeny 1980).

The key issue behind these divergent perspectives is whether there exists in Canada a capitalist class fraction with the means to accumulate capital independently of foreign domination. Without such a capacity, the course of Canadian capitalism would seem fixed toward a "harvest of lengthening dependency."[2] Alternatively, to the extent that a fraction of Canadian capital manifests a capacity to control its own extended reproduction, we may entertain the possibility of a national bourgeoisie with some degree of autonomy from foreign dependence, and of an independent Canadian imperialism.

Empirical assessment of these theses have relied on two types of data: (1) aggregate economic statistics describing patterns of capital accumulation, particularly the extent of foreign ownership in Canada (Watkins et al. 1968; Levitt 1971; Moore and Wells 1975), and (2) interlocking directorships among leading Canadian corporations (Park and Park 1973; Clement 1977a; Carroll et al. forthcoming). Two short-comings in these approaches motivate the present study. First, while capital accumulation has been studied on the level of the entire economy, interlock data pertain only to the largest firms, introducing a discrepancy in the data to which the two kinds of analyses refer: what may be true of the economy overall need not apply in the same way to the largest firms. Second, with two important exceptions,[3] structural analyses of interlocks in Canada have been cross-sectional, limiting the inferences which may be drawn regarding Canadian development. This study attempts to overcome these problems by longitudinally examining interlocks in a sample of large Canadian firms over a thirty-one-year period and by restricting the analysis of capital accumulation to the same sample of corporations.

MONOPOLY CAPITAL AND INTERLOCKING DIRECTORATES

Directorate interlocking is a particular form of intercorporate organization found in all advanced capitalist societies. To the empiricist, interlocks offer the appeal of being publicly documented, permitting systematic analysis using quantitative methods.

Economic motives are especially characteristic in the case of multiple directors shared between a pair of firms. While single interlocks may result merely from chance selection of directors from a small pool of candidates deemed most suitable, the sharing of several directors may be taken as an unambiguous indicator of planned liaison between firms.

It appears to be universally the case that advanced capitalist social formations are characterized by the dominance of an indigenous fraction of finance capital comprising the largest firms in industry and finance knit together by intercorporate ownership of stock, by credit relations, and by interlocking directorates.[4] In order for such a fraction to be truly dominant within a society, it must exercise control over domestic financial institutions as well as over a substantial portion of large-scale industrial capital, enabling it to directly appropriate surplus value while controlling both its home market and its own accumulation fund. To the extent that a capitalist class fraction fails to control industrial capital, it lacks control of its own home market and must ultimately depend for its revenue on whatever fraction controls industrial capital; to the extent that a fraction fails to control financial capital, its horizons for growth are limited by the availability of exogenous financing. It is only through the effective integration of control over industrial and financial capital that a capitalist class comes to occupy a relatively autonomous position in the world economy. From this formulation we may conclude that the issues of Canadian development and the character of the Canadian bourgeoisie, raised at the outset of this paper, can be fruitfully addressed in the longitudinal study of capital accumulation and directorate interlocks among large corporations in Canada. The degree to which Canada has developed as an independent, advanced capitalist society can be gauged by the extent to which an indigenous fraction of the bourgeoisie owns and controls large-scale industrial and financial capital and is integrated through interlocking directorates.

This article attempts to present a less equivocal case for the thesis that the dominant fraction of the Canadian bourgeoisie comprises a financial–industrial elite. The presence of this elite is demonstrated both in post-war patterns of capital accumulation and in the structure of directorate interlocks among leading corporations. Specifically, (1) the indigenous elite retains under its control a substantial bloc of large-scale industrial and financial capital throughout this period, and (2) the firms within this bloc are densely integrated by means of multiple shared directors, particularly between industrial and financial firms.

METHODS

Using total assets as an indicator of capital controlled, the 70 largest industrials, 20 largest financial intermediaries, and ten largest merchandizing firms were selected for the years 1946, 1951, 1961, 1966, 1971, and 1976, to produce successive "top 100s."[5]

For each year from 1946 through 1977 and for every firm in the sample, data were gathered on directors and executives and gross assets. Corporation annual reports were the primary source of this information; secondary sources included manuals such as those published by *The Financial Post, Moody's,* and *Standard and Poor's,* the Ontario Ministry of Consumer and Commercial Affairs (Company Services Branch), and the companies themselves.

RESULTS

A substantial majority of firms is controlled in Canada throughout the period of study. In 1946, 70 firms representing 87 per cent of all assets were controlled in Canada. By 1956, Canadian control had fallen to 64 firms representing 77 per cent of all assets; but by 1976, the bloc of large-scale capital under indigenous control had returned to its 1946 level (86 per cent of all assets), although the number of firms in which this capital is organized totals only 71. U.S.-controlled capital shows an interesting pattern of rapid growth between 1946 and 1956 followed by relative decline to 1976. By 1976, the proportion of large-scale capital under U.S. control had fallen to 11 per cent, especially the level in 1946 — this in spite of the fact that the assets of several U.S. controlled industrial firms are included in the 1976 figures but excluded from earlier tabulations. The only fraction of capital experiencing consistent growth relative to the others is that controlled in other countries (Europe and South Africa), which increases from one firm representing 0.6 per cent of all assets in 1946 to seven firms accounting for 2 per cent of assets in 1976.

The distribution of industrial firms and their assets shows a relative decline of utilities and an increase in the number of mining firms and the portion of big industrial capital they represent. In 1946, 17 of the top 70 industrials were utilities, acounting for 47 per cent of the total assets of the top 70. By 1976, the number of utilities and their share of industrial assets has declined to 11 and 28 per cent. Some of this relative decline is due to nationalization of electric utilities in Quebec, Manitoba, and British Columbia. For example, six utilities in the 1946 top 70 had been nationalized by 1962, five of them in Quebec. Another reason for the shifting of capital from the utilities sector is the slow growth of Canadian Pacific Limited in the years prior to its diversification into a range of commodity-producing industries (Chodos 1973: 118–21). In 1946, the CPR accounted for a remarkable 23 per cent of top industrial assets, but by 1961, its share had fallen to 9 per cent, a level maintained through 1976.

In contrast to the utilities sector, the number of mining firms and their share of industrial assets grow from 9 and 16 per cent in 1946 to 19 and 26 per cent in 1976, pointing out this sector's importance in the post-war accumulation of large-scale capital. Finally, the number of manufacturing firms in the top 70 decreases slightly from 1946 to 1976, while the proportion of industrial assets in manufacturing increases from 36 per cent to 46 per cent. This latter change reflects in part the unavailability of asset data for several large U.S.-controlled manufacturing firms in the earlier years.

It is, of course, the joint distribution, across both industrial sector and country of control, that is of key importance to the present study. In this regard, the tables show the anticipated pattern of strong Canadian control of big financial capital: virtually all the assets of financial inter- mediaries are controlled in Canada in all years. There is also evidence of an increased Canadian presence among the investment companies; 80 per cent of these firms' assets is controlled in Canada by 1976. Moreover, the investment companies claim a greater share of the total assets of financial firms over time, increasing from 0.7 per cent in 1940 to 6 per cent in 1976.

Large-scale industrial capital shows a somewhat different pattern of development. In 1946, 63 per cent of this capital (organized in 41 firms) is controlled in Canada, 32 per cent (24 firms) in the United States, and 4 per cent (four firms) in the United Kingdom. By 1976, each of these percentages shows a slight decline, while the portion of large-scale industry controlled by other foreign capitalists jumped from 2 per cent (one firm) to 7 per cent (seven firms). This relative expan- sion of big capital controlled in Europe and South Africa is the only net change over the 31-year period of any significance. It is true that the number of Canadian-controlled industrials declines by ten to 31, while the number of U.S.-controlled firms increases by four to 28, but the por- tion of big industrial capital controlled by each elite fraction in 1946 and 1976 is nearly identical.

In the decades between 1946 and 1976, however, there is consid- erable shifting in the national control of dominant industrials. Canadian control of big industry undergoes a marked decline between 1946 and 1956, coincidental with the slow growth of Canadian Pacific in these years, but then evidences a resurgence from 1956 to 1976. U.S. control shows the opposite pattern. It should be noted that even at its lowest ebb in 1956, the indigenous fraction of the corporate elite controls a large portion of the industrial capital represented by the top 70 industrials.

These same trends are evidenced for each of the three categories of industrial capital in Table 5.1. It is especially noteworthy that Canadian capitalists *increase* their share of manufacturing and mining assets between 1966 and 1976, in the latter case by a remarkable factor of 2.6. These trends are clearly not evidence of a commercial indigenous cor- porate elite, unwilling or unable to accumulate industrial capital. They do indicate that for a period of time immediately following World War Two, the rate of growth of large-scale U.S.-controlled industrial cap- ital outstripped its Canadian-controlled counterpart.

The results considered so far indicate that the indigenous fraction of the corporate elite in Canada has controlled virtually all the large-scale financial capital and a substantial portion of big industrial capital

Table 5.1
Percentage Distribution of Assets by Country of Control
for Seven Industrial Sectors, 1946–1976

Industry	Year	Canada	U.S.	U.K.	Other	Total
			Country of Control			
Mining	1946	23.6	76.4	0	0	16.5
	1956	13.2	86.8	0	0	17.4
	1966	17.7	63.1	4.5	14.7	17.6
	1976	46.4	34.8	5.9	12.9	25.9
Manufacturing	1946	58.0	31.2	10.8	0	36.5
	1956	49.2	39.1	9.5	2.2	47.8
	1966	46.2	39.5	9.5	4.9	52.1
	1976	54.4	35.7	2.5	7.5	46.1
Utilities	1946	80.0	16.2	0	3.8	47.0
	1956	62.6	37.4	0	0	34.8
	1966	85.8	14.2	0	0	30.3
	1976	83.4	16.6	0	0	28.0
Subtotal: Industrials	1946	62.7	31.6	3.9	1.8	33.6
	1956	47.6	46.8	4.5	1.1	38.8
	1966	53.1	36.0	5.7	5.1	37.0
	1976	60.4	30.1	2.7	6.8	30.6
Financial intermediaries	1946	100.0	0	0	0	99.3
	1956	98.7	1.3	0	0	96.6
	1966	98.7	1.3	0	0	92.8
	1976	98.9	1.1	0	0	94.0
Investment companies	1946	69.8	30.2	0	0	0.7
	1956	23.5	39.0	34.7	2.9	3.4
	1966	39.8	29.4	30.8	0	7.2
	1976	80.5	17.9	1.6	0	6.0
Subtotal: Financials	1946	99.8	0.2	0	0	65.5
	1956	95.9	2.8	1.2	0.1	59.0
	1966	94.5	3.3	2.2	0	60.3
	1976	97.8	2.1	0.1	0	65.9
Commercials	1946	50.7	0	49.3	0	0.7
	1956	65.6	18.9	15.4	0	2.0
	1966	60.6	26.6	12.9	0	2.5
	1976	62.1	37.9	0	0	2.1
Property development	1946	100.0	0	0	0	0.2
	1956	100.0	0	0	0	0.2
	1966	0	0	100.0	0	0.2
	1976	100.0	0	0	0	1.4
Grand total	1946	86.9	10.8	1.7	0.6	100.0
	1956	76.6	20.2	2.8	0.5	100.0
	1966	78.1	16.0	4.0	1.9	100.0
	1976	85.7	11.4	0.9	2.1	100.0

throughout the post-war era. They also suggest that the present trajectory of the indigenous fraction is not toward "silent surrender" of industrial assets, but in the direction of a net repatriation of capital.

If the indigenous capitalist fraction makes up a financial–industrial elite in the sociological sense, we should find a great deal of directorate interlocking within this fraction (particularly between financial and industrial capitals) and substantially less interlocking with other firms controlled in other countries. Alternatively, if the dominant fraction of the indigenous elite is commercial in character and closely allied to U.S. capital, we should find cleavage between Canadian financial and industrial companies, together with a great deal of interlocking between Canadian financial and U.S. industrial firms.

The percentage distributions of single and multiple interlocks in Table 5.2 indicate a pattern of interlocking very similar to the densities reported above. Fully 35 per cent of all multiple-director ties in 1946 and 38 per cent in 1976 occur between Canadian-controlled financial and Canadian-controlled industrial companies. These percentages compare with 15 and 9 per cent of interlocks between Canadian financial and U.S.-controlled industrial capital in 1946 and 1976 respectively. Thus, in the post-war period, the proportion of interlocks integrating indigenous industrial and financial capital increases as the proportion integrating indigenous financial capital with U.S.-controlled industrial capital declines. These changes occur in spite of the absolute decrease in the number of Canadian-controlled industrial firms and increase in the number of U.S.-controlled industrials. Again, we do find greater interlocking over time between financial companies controlled in Canada and industrial concerns controlled outside of North America: from an absence of multiple interlocks in 1946 to 5 per cent in 1976.

There is also a tendency over time for interlocks involving indigenously controlled financial firms to account for proportionately more of the total number of multiple-director ties, rising from 63 to 69 per cent between 1946 and 1976. But, as we have seen, this increased structural prominence of Canadian-controlled financial capital is not associated with a consolidation of ties to U.S.-controlled industrial capital. Instead, it reflects general increases in corporate interlocking among indigenous financial firms and between indigenous industrial and financial companies, combined with a dramatic decrease in the extent to which industrial corporations interlock with each other. More and more, the network comes to resemble a wheel, with indigenously controlled financial capital forming the hub, indigenously controlled industrial firms densely tied to the centre but tied less densely to each other, and foreign-controlled industry scattered along the periphery.

Table 5.2
Percentage Distributions of Single and Multiple Interlocks by Industrial Sector and Country of Control, 1946–1976

Subnetwork	1946 Single Ties	1946 Multiple Ties	1956 Single Ties	1956 Multiple Ties	1966 Single Ties	1966 Multiple Ties	1976 Single Ties	1976 Multiple Ties
Within Canadian industrial capital	15.9	17.9	9.8	14.4	7.5	8.6	11.1	11.5
Between Canadian industrial and Canadian financial capital	31.3	35.3	22.3	35.3	21.4	30.0	27.2	37.7
Within Canadian financial capital	11.2	12.2	9.8	14.0	9.1	18.0	6.0	18.0
Other Canadian	3.0	2.6	5.0	6.5	4.3	4.9	13.2	9.8
Subtotal: Interlocks among Canadian firms	60.8	68.0	46.9	70.2	42.3	61.5	57.5	77.0
Between Canadian financial and U.S. industrial capital	11.4	15.4	15.6	12.6	14.4	12.0	10.2	9.0
Between Canadian financial and other industrial capital	1.1	0	3.7	1.4	6.7	7.1	6.8	4.1
Between Canadian industrial and foreign industrial	19.3	11.5	16.0	10.2	16.0	10.5	15.9	5.3
Between Canadian other and foreign industrial	0.3	0	0.9	0	1.9	0.4	2.5	1.6
Subtotal: Interlocks between Canadian firms and foreign industrial firms	32.1	26.9	36.2	24.2	39.0	30.0	35.4	20.0
Within foreign industrial capital	3.5	1.3	4.3	1.9	9.3	3.7	4.5	1.2
Other interlocks	3.5	3.8	12.6	3.7	9.4	4.9	2.5	1.6
Total	100.0	100.0	100.0	100.0	100.0	100.0	100.0	100.0
Number of interlocks	367	156	539	215	583	267	646	244

For the sake of comparison, Table 5.2 also provides percentage distributions for interlocks that involve the sharing of only one director or executive between a pair of firms. These single ties show a pattern similar to that described above for multiple interlocks, although proportionately more of them serve to unite indigenous and foreign-controlled companies, particularly in the industrial sector. A growing proportion of single ties connects indigenous financial capital to industrial capital controlled outside of North America. Yet, significantly, the proportion of single interlocks uniting indigenous financial capital with U.S.-controlled industry is never much greater than the corresponding proportion of multiple interlocks, and by 1976, declined to 10 per cent. Although single-director interlocks are somewhat less concentrated among Canadian-controlled firms than are multiple-director ties, they in no way comprise a "continental axis" of Canadian financial and American industrial interests.

DISCUSSION

Our results may be summarized as follows. The indigenous elite fraction is found to control a substantial bloc of financial and industrial capital throughout the post-war period. Although the decade of 1946–1956 did witness a relative decline in indigenous control, the most recent trend appears to be toward increased indigenous control of large-scale mining and manufacturing — the most dynamic sectors and those which, according to Clement's (1977a) analysis, indigenous capitalists have given up to foreign interests. The preponderance of multiple-director interlocks unite indigenously controlled companies, both financial and industrial. There is certainly no cleavage between Canadian-controlled financial and industrial firms: instead, their directors interpenetrate quite extensively. Moreover, there is no evidence that Canadian financial firms tend to be densely tied to U.S.-controlled industrial corporations. Rather, these firms are interlocked at levels approximating the overall network density in each year. Further, the trend over time is toward increased ties between indigenously controlled financial and industrial firms and decreased ties between indigenously controlled financial and U.S.-controlled industrial companies.

These results seriously question the thesis that the dominant fraction of the Canadian bourgeoisie comprises a commercial elite locked into a dependent alliance with U.S. industrial capital. An interpretation more consistent with our findings is that offered in the classical concept of finance capital. Indeed, it would not be unreasonable to propose on the basis of present results that the most recent years of the post-war era have involved a consolidation of finance capital in Canada.

Such a consolidation is suggested by three secular trends: (1) the increased indigenous control of large-scale industry, especially since 1977; (2) a tendency for Canadian industrials to become relatively less interlocked with foreign capital and more tied to indigenous financial capital; and (3) the increasing importance of indigenous investment companies in holding sets of firms under common control. By 1976, 80 per cent of this capital was under Canadian control, and its share of big financial capital had increased greatly from 1946. The four most important indigenous holding companies directly controlled seven of the 24 largest Canadian-controlled manufacturing and mining companies, accounting for 37 per cent of the indigenously held assets in these sectors.

The finding that the dominant fraction of the Canadian bourgeoisie comprises not a commercial but a financial–industrial elite has important substantive implications with regard to the question of Canada's location in the world capitalist system. As an emergent feature of modern capitalism, finance capital is closely bound up with the internationalization of capitalism since high concentrations of capital in the advanced economies necessitate reinvestment of profits in the larger world market. Indeed, Lenin employed the terms "monopoly capital" and "imperialism" as virtual synonyms, descriptive of the "over-ripe" character of capitalism in the developed social formations (Lenin 1970: 716, 736).[6] The existence of an independent finance capital in a given country signals an advanced development of the productive forces under control of indigenous capitalists (Bukharin 1973), likewise, the extent to which a given capitalist economy engages in foreign investment is an important indicator of its capacity to conduct extended reproduction beyond the home market, and thus of its relative position in world economy.

The emergence of Canadian foreign investments, coincidental with the development of monopoly capital in Canada and the subsequent growth of capital exports from Canada are beyond dispute (Park and Park 1973: 122–61; Moore and Wells 1975: 65–89; Naylor 1975: 218–67), but the form and significance of those investments have been more open to question. Those who have emphasized the dependent, commercial character of the Canadian bourgeoisie have interpreted Canadian foreign investment in the same light, as a "branch plant quasi-imperialism," most of which is ultimately controlled in the United States or centred in the same non-industrial sectors that the Canadian bourgeoisie retains under its control (Naylor 1972: 34; Clement 1977a: 113–31; Drache 1977: 25–26). If, however, recent years have witnessed a consolidation of indigenous finance capital, we should expect a movement away from "go-between" foreign investments that are ultimately controlled elsewhere and a more direct assertion of an independent Canadian imperialism. Recent statistics on Canada's international investment position strongly confirm this expectation, showing a dramatic upsurge since 1970 in total Canadian direct investment abroad, accompanied by an equally dramatic decline in the portion of Canadian foreign direct investment under foreign control (Statistics Canada 1981).[7] In terms of both the internal structure of Canadian capital — the predominance of an indigenous bloc of financial capital — and the international production relations that tie Canadian interests to foreign accumulation sites, we find compelling evidence of a trajectory toward more independent imperialist status within world capitalism. At the level of the state, this movement has taken the form of an economic nationalism, as agencies such as FIRA, Crown corporations such as Canada Development Corporation and Petro-Canada, and acts of parliaments such as the National Energy Program endeavour to protect and expand the Canadian bourgeoisie's accumulation base.

The political implication of this conclusion is not, however, that progressive Canadians should accept with complacency the various economic, political, military, and cultural forms in which American Imperialism intrudes into Canada. There is a very large kernal of truth to the cliché that when Wall Street sneezes, Bay Street catches cold. The dependency perspective has gained wide appeal in Canadian studies precisely because it address important issues surrounding the limits to national autonomy imposed by a stronger imperialist power. The purpose of this study has not been to explain away those limits, nor to offer an *apologia* for the American influence in Canada, but to challenge the view that this influence is of a degree and kind that uniquely marks Canada as a dependent — yet advantaged — society.

NOTES

[1] On the predominance of staples, see Innis (1956) and Drache (1977: 15–33). On the dominance of merchant capital, see Creighton (1972), Naylor (1972), and Clement (1977a). The role of foreign direct investment is examined in Watkins et al. (1968), Levitt (1971), Clement (1977a), and Marchak (1979).

[2] The colourful phrase is Levitt's (1971: 116).

[3] Piedalue (1976) has examined the network of corporate interlocks in the formative period of Canadian monopoly capital (1900–1930), and Sweeny (1980) has recently replicated Piedalue's study for the post–World War Two years. Neither of these investigations considers directly the issue of national class fractions, which is the focus of our attention here.

4 See, for instance, Mandel (1968: Ch. 12) and Fennama and Schijf (1979). Useful analyses of finance capital in the post-war American economy are given in Perlo (1957) and in Menskikov (1969). Overbeek (1980) has recently examined the history and structure of finance capital in Britain.

5 To ensure maximal coverage, a variety of sources were consulted in compiling these ranked lists, the principal ones being the annual surveys published by *The Financial Post* and the ranked lists published in *The Fincial Post* since 1966 and in *Canadian Business* since 1973. Firms majority-owned by the state (whether federal or provincial) were excluded from the sample.

6 In 1917, Lenin distinguished four such centres of monopoly: Britain, France, Germany, and the United States.

7 In 1970, total Canadian foreign direct investment was $6,188 million, 35 per cent of which was controlled outside Canada. By 1977, Canadian foreign direct investment had grown to $13,443 million, and the portion under foreign control had fallen to 15 per cent. See Statistics Canada (1981) and previous issues.

Capital and the State in Canada: Some Critical Questions on Carroll's Finance Capitalists
Paul Stevenson

My impressions of this work [William Carroll's article] and of the evidence and argument contained in it are as follows. First, I believe that Carroll offers a useful counterweight to the left-wing nationalist position which sees Canada's economy and state as being dominated by American multinationals. Indeed, Carroll's data suggest that even the more moderate position of Wallace Clement, who tends to see Canadian capital as a kind of junior partner within the American-dominated continental corporate capital structure, is in need of some reformulation (Clement 1977a). Second, I believe, however, that Carroll goes too far beyond his data in concluding that the indigenous corporate élite in Canada has become the dominant fraction of capital in the country and that state actions accurately reflect this shift. Let me elaborate a bit.

Carroll's data show that the indigenous fraction of the corporate élite in Canada has increased its control of big industrial capital since the mid-1950s (having had a substantial level of control throughout the post–World War II period), while also controlling virtually all the large-scale financial capital over the post-war era. The data "also suggest that the present trajectory of the indigenous fraction is not toward 'silent surrender' of industrial assets, but in the direction of a net repatriation of capital" (p. 100 [p. 104 in this book]). The resurgence of the indigenous fraction relative to the comprador is also the theme of Jorge Niosi's recent work, *Canadian Capitalism*, although Niosi places the turnaround point later (in the later 1960s when the American and world capitalist economies went into stagflation) (Niosi 1981).

Why this is surprising is what puzzles me. After all, it has been known for some time that American direct foreign investment has been shifting to Europe and away from Canada and the Third World. Between 1950 and 1974, the percentage of total U.S. direct private investment assets abroad went from 31 per cent to 24 per cent for Canada, from 48 per cent to 24 per cent for the periphery, and from 15 per cent to 37 per cent for Western Europe (Edwards et al. 1978: 478). It is true that the absolute value increased in all of those areas for that time period, but these data do reflect a shift in the nature of investment flows between the United States and other regions. The capital being drained from Canada and the periphery to the U.S., of course, went up very substantially during this time period — again a rather common capitalist procedure. Given these shifts in foreign investment and capital repatriation by American multinationals, one would expect the degree of control of Canadian industry to level off (or even decline slightly) as a result of the everyday machinations in the capital accumulation process. This does not mean that American influence in the Canadian economy has undergone the radical decline that Carroll and Niosi seem to think it has. Indeed, dependency theorists could argue, especially in Niosi's case, that shifts of the 1970s substantiate the dependency argument. André Gunder Frank argued almost twenty years ago that when the metropolis is faced with an economic, political, or military crisis, the ties with the satellite will be weakened, "which may lead to more or less autonomous development or industrialization of the satellite ..." (Frank 1969: 149).[1]

Both Carroll and Niosi, having seen a resurgence in the strength of the indigenous fraction of capital in Canada to the point of dominance vis-à-vis the comprador fraction, have repeated the error of the left nationalists with regard to the actions of the Canadian state. The left nationalists have tended to see the Canadian state as the *instrument* of American multinational corporate capital and the comprador fraction of Canadian capital. Ottawa does what its American bosses tell it to, to put the matter bluntly. Now we have Carroll and Niosi viewing the Canadian state as the instrument of the indigenous fraction of capital in Canada, doing the bidding of the indigenous corporate élite. The "economic nationalism" of the Liberal government in Ottawa is explained in this manner (i.e., the actions of the state — the Canadian Development Corporation, the Foreign Investment Review Agency (FIRA), Petro-Canada, the National Energy Program (NEP) — are determined by the rise to dominance of the indigenous fraction of capital in Canada).

This perspective seems to be questionable on at least two grounds. First, the problems with an "instrumentalist" conception of the state have been rather thoroughly identified in Marxist literature. Second the "nationalistic" thrust and impact of FIRA, NEP, etc., has been grossly overestimated. The history of FIRA has been to approve the vast majority of foreign takeover applications (Clement 1977a: 300; 1977b: 238). Just recently, a story in the *Winnipeg Free Press* (hardly a proponent of economic nationalism or anti-Americanism) indicated that FIRA processed 357 applications in the four months following the June 1982 budget, which was more than double the 176 processed during the same period in 1981. "Only six per cent of those applications were rejected, fewer than half of last year's 14-per-cent rejection rate" (*Winnipeg Free Press* 1982).

Regarding Petro-Canada and the NEP, it is possible to point to other political–economic forces which have compelled the Canadian state to act in such a "nationalistic" fashion. The Liberal Party has a history of usurping the policies of the Cooperative Commonwealth Federation/New Democratic Party — with accompanying rhetoric — in a politically astute and opportunistic manner. The so-called energy crisis of the early 1970s had an important political impact in that the manipulative nature of the oil oligopolies was often exposed for what it was and that the oil industry had gained superprofits at the expense of the average consumer, both directly through price increases at the pumps and indirectly through price increase to manufacturers (who passed them on to consumers). In Canada, the behaviour of the oil companies became even more resented because much of the oil industry was owned by outsiders (mostly Americans). Thus, a poll conducted in 1975 revealed that 51 per cent of Canadians favoured nationalization of the oil industry (Douglas 1976: 207–208). This was a political development which the federal government has to take seriously, and it did so rather astutely by further developing Petro-Canada, by coming up with the National Energy Program, and by battling with the big oil producers and their representatives in the Alberta state, etc., while not really challenging the big oil giants such as Imperial/Exxon — all of this without having to go the anti-capitalist route that most Canadians seemed to want. Thus, the Liberals raised the issue of nationalism, pushed its rhetoric, and implemented a bit of actual policy — all of which quelled public opinion and enabled the Canadian state to back away from any further real changes.

The *political* and economic nature of the Liberals' "economic nationalism" is further revealed when one considers the problems of the Canadian dollar. Foreign ownership in the Canadian economy lies at the root of Canada's balance of payments problems. We end up running large deficits on our total current account and borrow heavily in U.S. money markets to offset them. A highly valued Canadian dollar meant that we were importing too much and not exporting enough since our goods were too expensive for foreigners. A depreciating dollar means higher prices for imports and enables Canadian producers of substitutes to charge higher prices as well and to remain competitive at home. A depreciating dollar also means that purchases in Canada are less and less expensive for Americans. This includes the purchase of Canadian enterprises, plant, and equipment. Without the NEP, the depreciation of the Canadian dollar would have continued and/or speeded up. The result would have been rising prices in Canada accompanied by increasing foreign ownership in oil, coal, uranium mining, etc., at the very time when Canadians were becoming more and more fed up with such developments (Pratt 1982: 47–48). In short, the NEP was an action by the state that responded to these political–economic pressures and that had little to do with the resurgence of indigenous capital.

For all Carroll's complaints about Clement's work, I believe that Clement has a more sophisticated conception of the Canadian state than does Carroll. Clement has written:

> The state's role in foreign investment in Canada is a complex one. In areas where Canadian capitalists have been strong, particularly in banking, life insurance, trust companies, transportation, utilities, and the mass media, the state has provided strong protection. In these areas, legislation prohibits foreign capitalists from owning sufficient stock to control or take over companies. But legislation to protect other areas such as retail trade, manufacturing, and resources, although recommended by many government inquiries, has only recently been enacted. (Clement 1977a: 300)

The state in capitalist Canada is viewed as a mediator of conflicting interests and pressures. The Canadian state is a pro-capitalist and patriarchal state that must mediate a contradictory reality composed of competing and/or conflicting interests and forces, including fractions

of capital, classes, regions, ethnic groups, men and women, political ideologies and events, and so forth. Thus, the state in Canada is
continually juggling these conflicting forces in order to mediate
between them in such a way that capitalist production and capitalist
patriarchal reproduction can continue to prevail within the context of
continental corporate capitalism. Niosi and Carroll fail to understand
this notion of the state (and, I would argue, "of reality") and thus fall
into the trap of one-sided instrumentalism which, in turn, leads them
away from understanding more fully and correctly Canada's political
economy.

NOTES

[1] Carroll makes critical remarks (p. 108 [of original article]) about the
usefulness of a dependency approach vis-à-vis Third World nations
themselves, referring positively to the works of Szymanski and Warren,
among others. The articles, and later the books based on those articles, have been rather thoroughly criticized. For a summary, see
Stevenson (1980: 214–31).

DISCUSSION QUESTIONS

1. Based on your experiences, to what extent does the cliché "when
   Wall Street sneezes, Bay Street catches a cold" hold true? Read
   some newspapers reports on Canada–U.S. relations. How are their
   viewpoints similar? How do they differ? Is there any difference
   between Canadian and American policies during G7 (now G8)
   meetings?

2. Study data provided in various issues of *Corporations and Labour
   Union Return Act (CLURA), Part 1: Corporations*. Update Carroll's
   data on Canadian and foreign-owned corporation assets since
   1976. What is the direction of these changes? Has foreign ownership in Canada increased or decreased, and in what sectors? What
   is the implication of your research for Carroll's thesis?

3. Evaluate the content of the Free Trade Agreement (FTA) and the
   North American Free Trade Agreement (NAFTA). What are the
   implications of these agreements for Canadian economic independence? Would you say that the FTA and NAFTA helped increase
   or decrease foreign ownership of the Canadian economy? In what
   economic sectors? Provide evidence (see *CLURA*).

4. Do you think that the Canadian state is an instrument of the capitalist class or a mediator of conflict between various groups in the
   population? Do any of these groups have more power within the
   Canadian state? Which group(s) and why?

Part Two

GENDER INEQUALITIES

INTRODUCTION

What accounts for the inequality between the sexes? Why are women paid less than men and/or are segregated in low-paying and low-status occupations? Why are men and not women often in positions of power and wealth? Why are women responsible for most household tasks? Why are they subject to abuse and violence inside and outside the home? In other words, why are most of the institutions of society controlled by men and not women? Marxists have historically subsumed women's oppression as another aspect of class exploitation and domination. They argue that development of private property facilitated the control of women's labour and bodies by men in the past. In more recent times, under capitalism, Marxists view women as workers who are involved in the reproduction of labour power in the house by performing housework tasks and by rearing and nurturing future workers. In this sense, women's work in the house is seen as necessary for capitalist production and reproduction. First, it ensures that their husbands' needs, as workers, are satisfied, making available fresh and relaxed workers for capitalist exploitation on a daily basis, and second, their labour ensures the availability of future workers. Thus, for Marxists, women's liberation is part and parcel of the working-class struggle for the elimination of capitalist exploitation and domination.

Feminists have long been dissatisfied with the Marxist explanation of women's oppression and do not accept the explanation that it is simply a part of the class struggle. Feminists argue that men and women have different positions in society, which is crucially significant in explaining women's oppression as long as sex structure remains significant in the society. They insist that they should produce a theory about women's lives that is directly relevant to challenging the oppression of women by men and thus improving women's position in society. Feminists, however, differ in their explanation of women's oppression. Liberal feminists (Wollstonecraft 1971; Frieden 1963) challenge the boundaries of gender differences by focussing on gender role socialization. Marxist feminists (Engles 1972; Rowbotham 1973) relate women's oppression to that of capitalism and exploitation of labour in general. Radical feminists (Firestone 1970; Brownmiller 1975) focus on the biological source of women's oppression and use of violence by men to control women. Lesbian feminism, an extension of radical feminism, focusses on sexuality and criticizes heterosexual marriages (Rich 1980). Socialist feminists (Mitchell 1971, 1974; Hartmann 1981a) agree with Marxists on the importance of class relations for understanding women's oppression but focus on the interconnection between sex oppression and class oppression. For them, both patriarchal and capitalist oppression needs to be eradicated. Psychoanalyst feminists focus on how women are "made," and the infant is gendered through guilt, anxiety, and experiences such as lack of penis or phallus (Hamilton 1997; Barret 1992; Lacan 1968). Poststructural feminists (Parr 1990), rooted in the work of the French poststructuralists Jacques Derrida (1967) and Lacan (1968), try to unmask binary oppositions such as masculine/feminine, public/private, and paid/unpaid work, which have made women invisible and which ignore the differences between women by race, ethnicity, and class. From this, anti-racist feminists, or feminists of people of colour, emerged. They criticize white middle-class feminists for ignoring that racism is prevalent in all aspects of society. In general, all feminists agree that gender inequality is a pervasive feature of most (if not all) societies and that gender inequality requires a distinct theoretical framework because women's oppression is distinct from other oppressions. For debates on biological versus social causes of gender inequality, see Goldberg (1986a), Epstein (1986), Abbott et al. (1986), Schlegel (1986), Gulick (1986), Reinhartz (1986), Goldberg's response (1986b), Kimura (1992), Foss (1996), Lowe (1978), and Ralls (1980). On the role of women organizations and feminist policy success, see Burt (1990) and Pross (1990). For debates on feminism and psychoanalysis, see Wilson (1981) and Sayer (1982). On sex preference attitudes, see Williamson (1976) and Rent and Rent (1977).

In a class contribution to the feminist analysis, Heidi Hartmann (1981a) argues that Marxist theory and categories are gender/sex blind. According to her, Marxist theories have failed to deal with feminist questions such as how and why women are oppressed as women, perform unpaid labour for, and are being exploited by, men, and how patriarchy is reproduced within capitalism. She also criticizes radical feminists for their biological and universal characterization of patriarchy. For her, patriarchy is a set of hierarchical social relations reproduced systematically in every aspect of the society, with its material base being in men's control of women's labour power. Hartmann uses the analytical power of Marxism to develop a (socialist) feminist theory. In this theory, both capitalism and patriarchy are seen as responsible for women's oppression. This dual system theory is criticized by Iris Young (1981). Young argues that we cannot separate patriarchy from capitalism because they are both manifested in identical social and economic structures. In fact, it is capitalism that has separated the sphere of productive activity from kinship relations and thus has produced the dual spheres of social life. For her, the dual system theory (as that of Hartmann's) maintains the Marxist domination and thus undermines feminism. She proposes that we move from a model based on class analysis to one based on gendered division of labour, which is both universal and varied across time and space. For her, the structured gendered differentiation of labour such as bearing and rearing children, caring for the sick, cleaning, cooking, and so on is, in fact, what capitalism is based on. By conceptualizing capitalism as essentially patriarchal, she concludes that feminists should part with their unhappy marriage to Marxism. This debate continues: see Ferguson and Folbre (1981), Ehrlich (1981), Vogel (1981), and Hartmann's response (1981b). For debates between Marxists and feminists on class and gender, see Hart (1985), Evans (1989), Magas (1971), Blackburn (1971), Rey (1971), Armstrong and Armstrong (1983a), Miles (1983), Connelly (1983), and Armstrong and Armstrong's response (1983b). On the domestic labour debate, see Secombe (1973) and Gardiner (1975).

The debate about the relationship between capitalism and patriarchy has not been resolved satisfactorily. In more recent times, Carol Johnson (1996) reconsidered this debate. She criticizes Pateman (1988) for arguing that the capitalist employment contract presupposes the subordination of women in the marriage contract. The implication is that if there was no such sexual contract, it would be equally plausible that females rather than males be the breadwinners (recall the family wage debate in Hartmann 1981a). In other words, the existence of the marriage contract suggests that capitalism has a patriarchal structure or that capitalism is a product of patriarchy. Johnson argues that the existing patriarchal relations, such as that of the family wage where men are paid a wage to support themselves, their wives, and their children and thus has contributed to women's exclusion from the labour market, is not to the capitalist's financial advantage. It would have been logically more advantageous if capitalists split the family wage in half and ensured that both husband and wife worked. In this way, they pay for one person and receive the labour of two persons plus any children. Why settle for cheap and flexible female labour when capitalists could have cheap and flexible male labour as well. In sum, Johnson argues that capitalism need not be patriarchal. In fact, patriarchy is counter-productive for capitalists. For her, the family wage was the outcome of a long battle by many male workers who wanted to improve their wages by excluding and marginalizing women and children as well as other minorities.

Carole Pateman (1996) criticizes Johnson for misreading her argument. Pateman insists that she did not argue that the marriage contract came before the employment contract or that patriarchy preceded capitalism. However, she still believes that the marriage contract is indispensable for an understanding of employment contract and subordination of the worker. She also emphasizes that patriarchy structured class in that both capitalist and workers had a common interest as men. This issue is important since it provides a clue as to why capitalists paid family wages to men and did not hire both husband and wife (plus any children) for the price of one, as Johnson (1996) questioned. The reason, Pateman insists, is that capitalists do not always act rationally, and that family wage was accepted by capitalists because the labour market was embedded in patriarchal relations. Because of such relations, capitalists did not choose to employ women even though their labour was cheaper than men's. Furthermore, there was also the possibility of unrest by male workers if cheap female workers were employed by capitalists. Both authors agree that there have been significant changes in the labour market in recent times: an increase in women's employment (some in non-traditional sectors) and some decrease in the gender wage gap.

In the Canadian context, Catherine Fillmore (1990) undertakes a study of census data from 1931 to 1981 in order to reveal the pattern of gender differences in earning and to provide some explanations for the gender earnings gap. She tests three specific theories: (1) The functionalist-based, human capital theory. It suggests that one's occupation and income is a function of his/her ability to contribute productively in his/her place of work. In this sense, education, skill, experience, and intelligence are types of capital that men and women may bring into work that affect their productivity and hence their occupation and income; (2) Marxist-based reserve army of labour theory suggests that the difference in the pool of available labour for work results in the over- and/or undersupply of that labour. Since women's labour is more available and/or is concentrated in a few female occupations, women's wages are lower than those of men; and, (3) dual labour market theory sees the gender earnings gap as a function of the economic sector in which one is employed. Primary economic sectors are capital intensive, unionized, and have higher wages, while secondary economic sectors are the opposite. Women are more likely to work in the secondary sectors than men and thus have lower wages. Fillmore (1990) shows that females' earnings as a percentage of males' have continually increased from 39.4 percent in 1931 to 68.9 percent in 1981 for all occupations, and from 58.5 percent to 72.1 percent for 41 matched occupations. Furthermore, she shows that the ratio of female to male earnings has risen as the proportion of female workers in an occupation has risen, and as the proportion of females in an occupation has declined, the average earnings for both men and women have increased. Her research, she suggests, tends to reject the human capital theory while providing some support for the reserve army and dual labour market theories. She concludes that equal pay legislation has been ineffective in its attempts to close the gender earnings gap.

Alice Nakamura (1990) questions Fillmore's study for misreading various theories, for deducing incorrect hypotheses from these theories, and for Fillmore's policy conclusions. For example, Nakamura argues that according to human capital theory, the gender gap may be more a function of the productivity differences due to investment utilization between males and females than simply the differences between males and females, per se, as argued by Fillmore (1990). That is to say, women are less likely to take advantage of their investment in the labour market because of the dual roles they play — as a housewife and as a paid worker. Nakamura also suggests that there is nothing in Fillmore's evidence that could be used as evidence that equal pay legislation has been ineffective. If anything, since the gender gap has declined, the evidence may support the effectiveness of equal pay legislation. For Fillmore's response, see Fillmore (1991).

However, there is much work to be done to ensure employment equity. In fact, in a recent ruling by the Canadian Human Rights Tribunal, the federal government was ordered to pay back the money it owes its 54 000 clerks, secretaries, librarians, data processors, hospital workers, and education support staff now working for the federal government, as well as 140 000 former public servants. This ruling is intended to wipe out the wage gap between female- and male-dominated jobs in the public service and could cost the federal government up to $4 billion (see May 1998: A1–A2). However, the federal government has decided to appeal the Tribunal's formula for calculating the wage gap of the affected workers.

For more debate on the male–female wage gap, see Jacobs and Steinberg (1990a), Filer (1990), Jacobs and Steinberg's response (1990b), Brenhardt et al. (1995), Cotter et al. (1997), and Brenhardt et al.'s response (1997). For debates on the reserve army of labour, see Beechey (1977) and Anthias (1980). On female labour force participation, see Ward and Pampel (1985a), Tyree (1985), and Ward and Pampel's reply (1985b).

Women not only have lower status, are relegated to lesser occupations, and are paid less than men, but they are also subject to significant violence at home, school, and work. That is to say, patriarchal relations persist in both the public and private domains. Dobash et al. (1992) reviewed the evidence from courts, police, women's shelters, divorce records, emergency room patients, hospitals, victimization, and self-report surveys and concluded that there is a clear sexual asymmetry in conjugal violence. Males are significantly more likely to engage in violent activity in conjugal relationships than females. This evidence clearly supports the feminist argument that males use violence to establish their patriarchal power within the family. Other research, however, relying on self-report surveys, has pointed to sexual symmetry in conjugal violence. Men and women equally engage in conjugal violence. This evidence moves away from a single-cause explanation and searches for the root of conjugal violence in such factors as education, income, occupation, employment status, class culture, age, alcohol, and so on. For example, Nakhaie (1998) shows that conjugal violence is age graded. It is asymmetrical among the younger couples and more symmetrical among the older ones. In the early years of marriage, males are more capable of inflicting violence on their younger and physically weaker partners than females are on their older and stronger partners. In the later years, however, males' physical strength deteriorates faster than their partners', both because of the differences in the age of marriage and the lower life expectancy for males compared with females. This deterioration results in a husband's lower capability for violence against the wife, a greater need for care, and a higher degree of physical and mental impairment. It is, therefore, important to understand that there are many reasons for sexual violence, and its dynamics are not clear.

In a large national study of undergraduate students in Canada, Walter DeKeseredy and Katharine Kelly (1993) showed that 45.1 percent of females stated that they had been victimized since leaving high school. More specifically, "during the past twelve months," 18.2 percent of women said that they had given in to sex play (without intercourse) and 11.9 percent had given into sexual intercourse that they did not want because they were "overwhelmed by a man's continual arguments and pressure." Another 3.8 percent of women said that they had given in because they were threatened or were physically forced to. These figures jumped to 31.8 percent, 20.1 percent, and 9.8 percent respectively when the time horizon was changed to "since leaving high school" as against "the past twelve months." The figures for psychological abuse were higher. This evidence points to the widespread prevalence of physical, sexual, and psychological abuse of women in courtship.

Bonnie Fox (1993) comments that sociological research should go beyond the simplistic explanations of abuse and provide the theoretical framework that maps out those relations that produce sexual abuse. She criticizes DeKeseredy and Kelly for reducing patriarchy to powerful men dominating passive, weak women. Moreover, she also questions DeKeseredy and Kelly's unstated assumption that data "speak for themselves." According to Fox, there are many explanations of woman abuse other than a simple understanding that men who are likely to abuse are those who need to be in control. In fact, research also points to the powerless men (unemployed, low income, etc.) and not men who want to be in control as the likely abusers. Furthermore, by labelling both an unwanted kiss and rape as abuse, as DeKeseredy and Kelly (1993) did, there is a tendency to trivialize serious abuse and inflate less significant matters. The dynamic and the kind of man involved in an unwanted kiss and forced intercourse are different. Fox concludes that they should have at least differentiated the types of abuse by the kind of men who abuse and kind of women who are abused by various types of abuses. For another criticism, see Gartner (1993) and responses by DeKeseredy (1994) and Kelly (1994).

Finally, we look at the economic consequence of divorce as it affects men and women. Lenore Weitzman's (1985) study of divorced individuals in Los Angeles shows that just one year after divorce, men's standard of living improved by 42 percent and women's declined by 73 percent. This is a dramatic decline for women. They must now cut back on everything that they took for granted: clothing, shelter, food, entertainment, and so on. Often they will have to apply for welfare, ask parents for help, or go to the Salvation Army for Christmas clothing. The negative psychological impact of the economic consequence of divorce is all the more severe for divorced mothers when they have to refuse the requests of their children for simple things such as ice cream. Weitzman argues that three factors account for this postdivorce disparity in the standard of living for men and women:

1. The court rarely awards alimony. This means that wives who were supported by their husbands during marriage are left to their own devices. Moreover, the child support granted by the court is always less than the cost of raising the child.
2. After divorce, household demands increase for the wife and decrease for the husband. She is now solely responsible for raising the children, which means that she will have more need for paid help and services but less income. In contrast, the ex-husband is no longer financially responsible for his ex-wife. Now, most of his income is his own.
3. In general, not only do men receive higher incomes than women, but also marriage enhances men's careers and is a liability to women's. After divorce, women are totally responsible for their children, which means they will be restricted in terms of job opportunities for career advancement.

Richard Peterson (1996a) re-analyzes Weitzman's data and concludes that her report of 73 percent decline in women's standard of living and 42 percent increase in men's is in error. He shows that the decline in standard of living (mean income/need ratio) after divorce is actually 27 percent for women and the increase is 10 percent for men. Peterson re-analyzes Weitzman's own data using several methods and assumptions and shows that nowhere are the estimates of decline and improvement in standard of living close to those reported by Weitzman (1985). Peterson concludes that Weitzman made an error in calculating those results. He discusses the policy consequences of such "scientific" errors. This debate continues: see Weitzman's response (1996) and Peterson's reply (1996b).

FEMINISM AND MARXISM

The Unhappy Marriage of Marxism and Feminism: Towards a More Progressive Union
Heidi Hartmann

The "marriage" of marxism and feminism has been like the marriage of husband and wife depicted in English common law: marxism and feminism are one, and that one is marxism.[1] Recent attempts to integrate marxism and feminism are unsatisfactory to us as feminists because they subsume the feminist struggle into the "larger" struggle against capital. To continue our simile further, either we need a healthier marriage or we need a divorce.

The inequalities in this marriage, like most social phenomena, are no accident. Many marxists typically argue that feminism is at best less important than class conflict and at worst divisive of the working class. This political stance produces an analysis that absorbs feminism into the class struggle. Moreover, the analytic power of marxism with respect to capital has obscured its limitations with respect to sexism. We will argue here that while marxist analysis provides essential insight into the laws of historical development and those of capital in particular, the categories of marxism are sex-blind. Only a specifically feminist analysis reveals the systemic character of relations between men and women. Yet feminist analysis by itself is inadequate because it has been blind to history and insufficiently materialist. Both marxist analysis, particularly its historical and materialist method, and feminist analysis, especially the identification of patriarchy as a social and historical structure, must be drawn upon if we are to understand the development of western capitalist societies and the predicament of women within them. In this essay, we suggest a new direction for marxist feminist analysis.

I. MARXISM AND THE WOMAN QUESTION

The woman question has never been the "feminist question." The feminist question is directed at the causes of sexual inequality between women and men, of male dominance over women. Most marxist analyses of women's position take as their question the relationship of women to the economic system rather than that of women to men, apparently assuming the latter will be explained in their discussion of the former. Marxist analysis of the woman question has taken three main forms. All see women's oppression in our connection (of lack of it) to production. Defining women as part of the working class, these analyses consistently subsume women's relation to men under workers' relation to capital. First, early marxists, including Marx, Engels, Kautsky, and Lenin, saw capitalism drawing all women into the wage labor force and saw this process destroying the sexual division of labor. Second, contemporary marxists have incorporated women into an analysis of everyday life in capitalism. In this view, all aspects of our lives are seen to reproduce the capitalist system, and we are all workers in the system. And third, marxist feminists have focused on housework and its relation to capital, some arguing that housework produces surplus value and that houseworkers work directly for capitalists.

While the approach of the early marxists ignored housework and stressed women's labor force participation, the two more recent approaches emphasize housework to such an extent they ignore women's current role in the labor market. Nevertheless, all three attempt to include women in the category working class and to understand women's oppression as another aspect of class oppression. In doing so, all give short shrift to the object of feminist analysis, the relations between women and men. While our "problems" have been elegantly analyzed, they have been misunderstood. The focus of marxist analysis has been class relations; the object of marxist analysis has been understanding the laws of motion of capitalist society. While we believe marxist methodology *can* be used to formulate feminist strategy, the marxist feminist approaches clearly do not do so; their marxism clearly dominates their feminism.

Marxism enables us to understand many aspects of capitalist societies: the structure of production, the generation of a particular occupational structure, and the nature of the dominant ideology. Marx's theory of the development of capitalism is a theory of the development of "empty places." Marx predicted, for example, the growth of the proletariat and the demise of the petit bourgeoisie. More precisely and in more detail, Braverman, among others, has explained the creation of the "places" clerical worker and service worker in advanced capitalist societies (Braverman 1975). Just as capital creates these places indifferent to the individuals who fill them, the categories of marxist analysis, class, reserve army of labor, wage-laborer, do not explain why particular people fill particular places. They give no clues about why *women* are subordinate to *men* inside and outside the family and why it is not the other way around. *Marxist categories, like capital itself, are sex-blind.* The categories of marxism cannot tell us who will fill the empty places. Marxist analysis of the woman question has suffered from this basic problem.

II. RADICAL FEMINISM AND PATRIARCHY

The great thrust of radical feminist writing has been directed to the documentation of the slogan "the personal is political." Women's discontent, radical feminists argued, is not the neurotic lament of the maladjusted, but a response to a social structure in which women are systematically dominated, exploited, and oppressed. Women's inferior position in the labor market, the male-centered emotional structure of middle class marriage, the use of women in advertising, the so-called understanding of women's psyche as neurotic — popularized by academic and clinical psychology — aspect after aspect of women's lives in advanced capitalist society was researched and analyzed. The radical feminist literature is enormous and defies easy summary. At the same time, its focus on psychology is consistent. The New York Radical Feminists' organizing document was "The Politics of the Ego" (Hole and Levine 1971: 440–43). "The personal is political" means, for radical feminists, that the original and basic class division is between the sexes and that the motive force of history is the striving of men for power and domination over women, the dialectic of sex.[2]

Accordingly, Firestone rewrote Freud to understand the development of boys and girls into men and women in terms of power. Her characterizations of what are "male" and "female" character traits are typical of radical feminist writing. The male seeks power and domination, he is egocentric and individualistic, competitive and pragmatic; the "technological mode," according to Firestone, is male. The female is nurturant, artistic, and philosophical; the "aesthetic mode" is female.

No doubt, the idea that the aesthetic mode is female would have come as quite a shock to the ancient Greeks. Here lies the error of radical feminist analysis: the dialectic of sex, as radical feminists present it, projects male and female characteristics as they appear in the present back into all of history. Radical feminist analysis has greatest strength in its insights into the present. Its greatest weakness is a focus on the psychological which blinds it to history.

The reason for this lies not only in radical feminist method, but also in the nature of patriarchy itself, for patriarchy is a strikingly resilient form of social organization. Radical feminists use patriarchy to refer to a social system characterized by male domination over women. Kate Millett's definition is classic:

> our society ... is a patriarchy. The fact is evident at once if one recalls that the military, industry, technology, universities, science, political offices, finances — in short, every avenue of power within the society, including the coercive force of the police, is entirely in male hands. (Millett 1971: 25)

The radical feminist definition of patriarchy applies to most societies we know of and cannot distinguish among them. The use of history by radical feminists is typically limited to providing examples of the existence of patriarchy in all times and places (e.g., Brownmiller 1975). For both marxist and mainstream social scientists before the women's movement, patriarchy referred to a system of relations between men, which formed the political and economic outlines of feudal and some pre-feudal societies, in which hierarchy followed ascribed characteristics. Capitalist societies are understood as meritocratic, bureaucratic, and impersonal by bourgeois social scientists; marxists see capitalist societies as systems of class domination.[3] For both kinds of social scientists, neither the historical patriarchal societies nor today's western capitalist societies are understood as systems of relations between men that enable them to dominate women.

Towards a Definition of Patriarchy

We can usefully define patriarchy as a set of social relations between men which have a material base and which, though hierarchical, establish or create interdependence and solidarity among men that enable them to dominate women. Though patriarchy is hierarchical, and men of different classes, races, or ethnic groups have different places in the patriarchy, they also are united in their shared relationship of dominance over their women; they are dependent on each other to maintain that domination. Hierarchies "work" at least in part because they create vested interests in the status quo. Those at the higher levels can "buy off" those at the lower levels by offering them power over those still lower. In the hierarchy of patriarchy, all men, whatever their rank in the patriarchy, are bought off by being able to control at least some women.

The material base upon which patriarchy rests lies most fundamentally in men's control over women's labor power. Men maintain this control by excluding women from access to some essential productive resources (in capitalist societies, for example, jobs that pay living wages) and by restricting women's sexuality.[4] Monogamous heterosexual marriage is one relatively recent and efficient form that seems to allow men to control both these areas. Controlling women's access to resources and their sexuality, in turn, allows men to control women's labor power, both for the purpose of serving men in many personal and sexual ways and for the purpose of rearing children.

The material base of patriarchy, then, does not rest solely on child-rearing in the family, but on all the social structures that enable men to control women's labor. The aspects of social structures that perpetuate patriarchy are theoretically identifiable, hence separable from their other aspects. Gayle Rubin has increased our ability to identify the patriarchal element of these social structures enormously by identifying "sex/gender systems":

> a "sex/gender system" is the set of arrangements by which a society transforms biological sexuality into products of human activity, and in which these transformed sexual needs are satisfied. (Rubin 1975: 159)

We are born female and male, biological sexes, but we are created woman and man, socially recognized genders. *How* we are so created is that second aspect of the *mode* of production of which Engels spoke, "the production of human beings themselves, the propagation of the species."

How people propagate the species is socially determined. If, biologically, people are sexually polymorphous and society were organized in such a way that all forms of sexual expression were equally permissible, reproduction would result only from some sexual encounters, the heterosexual ones. The strict division of labor by sex, a social invention common to all known societies, creates two very separate genders and a need to men and women to get together for economic reasons. It thus helps to direct their sexual needs towards heterosexual fulfillment and helps to ensure biological reproduction. In more imaginative societies, biological reproduction might be ensured by other techniques, but the division of labor by sex appears to be the universal solution to date. Although it is theoretically possible that a sexual division of labor not imply inequality between the sexes, in most known societies, the socially acceptable division of labor by sex is one which accords lower status to women's work. The sexual division of labor is also the underpinning of sexual subcultures in which men and women experience life differently; it is the material base of male power which is exercised (in our society) not just in not doing housework and in securing superior employment, but psychologically as well.

Economic production (what marxists are used to referring to as *the* mode of production) and the production of people in the sex/gender sphere both determine "the social organization under which the people of a particular historical epoch and a particular country live," according to Engels. The whole of society, then, can be understood by looking at both these types of production and reproduction, people and things.[5] There is no such thing as "pure capitalism," nor does "pure patriarchy" exist, for they must, of necessity, coexist. What exists is patriarchal capitalism, or patriarchal feudalism, or egalitarian hunting/gathering societies, or matriarchal horticultural societies, or patriarchal horticultural societies, and so on. There appears to be no necessary connection between *changes* in the one aspect of production and changes in the other. A society could undergo transition from capitalism to socialism, for example, and remain patriarchal.[6] Common sense, history, and our experience tell us, however, that these two aspects of production are so closely intertwined that changes in one ordinarily creates movement, tension, or contradiction in the other.

Capitalist development creates the places for a hierarchy of workers, but traditional marxist categories cannot tell us who will fill which places. Gender and racial hierarchies determine who fills the empty places. *Patriarchy is not simply hierarchical organization,* but hierarchy in which *particular* people fill *particular* places. It is in studying patriarchy that we learn why it is women who are dominated and how. While we believe that most known societies have been patriarchal, we do not view patriarchy as a universal, unchanging phenomenon. Rather, patriarchy, the set of interrelations among men that allow men to dominate women, has changed in form and intensity over time.

To recapitulate, we define patriarchy as a set of social relations which has material base and in which there are hierarchical relations between men and solidarity among them which enable them in turn to dominate women. The material base of patriarchy is men's control over women's labor power. The control is maintained by excluding women from access to necessary economically productive resources and by restricting women's sexuality. Men exercise their control in receiving personal service work from women, in not having to do housework or rear children, in having access to women's body for sex, and in feeling powerful and being powerful. The crucial elements of patriarchy as we *currently* experience them are: heterosexual marriage (and consequent homophobia), female childrearing and housework, women's economic dependence on men (enforced by arrangements in the labor market), the state, and numerous institutions based on social relations among men — clubs, sports, unions, professions, universities, churches, corporations, and armies. All these elements need to be examined if we are to understand patriarchal capitalism.

Both hierarchy and interdependence among men and the subordination of women are *integral* to the functioning of our society; that is, these relationships are *systemic.*

III. THE PARTNERSHIP OF PATRIARCHY AND CAPITAL

We argue that patriarchy as a system of relations between men and women exists in capitalism and that in capitalist societies, a healthy and strong partnership exists between patriarchy and capital. Yet if one begins with the concept of patriarchy and an understanding of the capitalist mode of production, one recognizes immediately that the partnership of patriarchy and capital was not inevitable; men and capitalists often have conflicting interests, particularly over the use of women's labor power. Here is one way in which this conflict might manifest itself: the vast majority of men might want their women at home to personally service them. A small number of men, who are capitalists, might want most women (not their own) to work in the wage labor market. In examining the tensions of this conflict over women's labor power historically, we will be able to identify the material base of patriarchal relations in capitalist societies as well as the basis for the partnership between capital and patriarchy.

Industrialization and the Development of Family Wages

Marxists made quite logical inferences from a selection of the social phenomena they witnessed in the nineteenth century. But marxists ultimately underestimated the strength of the preexisting patriarchal social forces with which fledgling capital had to contend and the need for capital to adjust to these forces. The industrial revolution was drawing all people into the labor force, including women and children; in fact, the first factories used child and female labor almost exclusively.[7] That women and children could earn wages separately from men both undermined authority relations and kept wages low for everyone.

Male workers resisted the wholesale entrance of women and children into the labor force and sought to exclude them from union membership and the labor force as well. Male unionists did not want to afford union protection to women workers; they tried to exclude them instead. In 1879, Adolph Strasser, president of the Cigarmakers International Union, said: "We cannot drive the females out of the trade, but we can restrict their daily quota labor through factory laws" (Hartmann 1976: 162–63).

While the problem of cheap competition could have been solved by organizing the wage earning women and youths, the problem of disrupting family life could not be. Men reserved union protection for men and argued for protective labor laws for women and children. Protective labor laws, while they may have ameliorated some of the worst abuses of female and child labor, also limited the participation of adult women in many "male" jobs.[8] Men sought to keep high wage jobs for themselves and to raise male wages generally. They argued for wages sufficient for their wage labor alone to support their families. This "family wage" system gradually came to be the norm for stable working class families at the end of the nineteenth century and the beginning of the twentieth. Several observers have declared the nonwage-working wife to be part of the standard of living of male workers. Instead of fighting for equal wages for men and women, male workers sought the family wage, wanting to retain their wives' services at home. In the absence of patriarchy, a unified working class might have confronted capitalism, but patriarchal social relations divided the working class, allowing one part (men) to be bought off at the expense of the other (women). Both the hierarchy between men and the solidarity among them were crucial in this process of resolution. Family wages may be understood as a resolution of the conflict over women's labor power which was occurring between patriarchal and capitalist interests at that time.

For most men, then, the development of family wages secured the material base of male domination in two ways. First, men have the better jobs in the labor market and earn higher wages than women. The lower pay women receive in the labor market both perpetuates men's material advantage over women and encourages women to choose wifery as a career. Second, then, women do housework, childcare, and perform other services at home which benefit men directly. Women's home responsibilities in turn reinforce their inferior labor market position.

The Family and the Family Wage Today

We argued above, that, with respect to capitalism and patriarchy, the adaptation or mutual accommodation took the form of the development of the family wage in the early twentieth century. The family wage cemented the partnership between patriarchy and capital. Despite women's increased labor force participation, particularly rapid since World War II, the family wage is still, we argue, the cornerstone of the present sexual division of labor — in which women are primarily responsible for housework and men primarily for wage work. Women's lower wages in the labor market (combined with the need of children to be reared by someone) assure the continued existence of the family as a necessary income pooling unit. The family, supported by the family wage, thus allows the control of women's labor by men both within and without the family.

Although the terms of the compromise between capital and patriarchy are changing as additional tasks formerly located in the family are capitalized, and the location of the deployment of women's labor power shifts, it is nevertheless true, as we have argued above, that the wage differential caused by extreme job segregation in the labor market reinforces the family and, with it, the domestic division of labor, by encouraging women to marry. The "ideal" of the family wage — that a man can earn enough to support an entire family — may be giving way to a new ideal that both men and women contribute through wage earning to the cash income of the family. The wage differential, then, will become increasingly necessary in perpetuating patriarchy, the male control of women's labor power. The wage differential will aid in *defining* women's work as secondary to men's at the same time it necessitates women's actual continued economic dependence on men. The sexual division of labor in the labor market and elsewhere should be understood as a manifestation of patriarchy which serves to perpetuate it.

Ideology in the Twentieth Century

Patriarchy, by establishing and legitimating hierarchy among men (by allowing men of all groups to control at least some women), reinforces capitalist control, and capitalist values shape the definition of patriarchal good.

If we examine the characteristics of men as radical feminists describe them — competitive, rationalistic, dominating — they are much like our description of the dominant values of capitalist society. This "coincidence" may be explained in two ways. In the first instance, men, as wage laborers, are absorbed in capitalist social relations at work, driven into the competition these relations prescribe, and absorb the corresponding values. The radical feminist description of men was not altogether out of line for capitalist societies. Secondly, even when men and women do not actually behave in the way sexual norms prescribe, men *claim for themselves* those characteristics which are valued in the dominant ideology.

A parallel argument demonstrating the partnership of patriarchy and capitalism may be made about the sexual division of labor in the work force. The sexual division of labor places women in low-paying jobs and in tasks thought to be appropriate to women's role. Women are teachers, welfare workers, and the great majority of workers in the health fields. The nurturant roles that women play in these jobs are of low status because capitalism emphasizes personal independence and the ability of private enterprise to meet social needs, emphases contradicted by the need for collectively provided social services. As long as the social importance of nurturant tasks can be denigrated because women perform them, the confrontation of capital's priority on exchange value by a demand for use values can be avoided. In this way, it is not feminism but sexism that divides and debilitates the working class.

IV. TOWARDS A MORE PROGRESSIVE UNION

Many problems remain for us to explore. Patriarchy, as we have used it here, remains more a descriptive term than an analytic one. If we think marxism alone inadequate and radical feminism itself insufficient, then we need to develop new categories. What makes our task a difficult one is that the same features, such as the division of labor, often reinforce both patriarchy and capitalism, and in a thoroughly patriarchal capitalist society, it is hard to isolate the mechanism of patriarchy. Nevertheless, this is what we must do. We have pointed to some starting places: looking at who benefits from women's labor power, uncovering the material base of patriarchy, investigating the mechanisms of hierarchy and solidarity among men. The questions we must ask are endless.

Feminism and the Class Struggle

The struggle against capital and patriarchy cannot be successful if the study and practice of the issues of feminism is abandoned. A struggle aimed only at capitalist relations of oppression will fail since their underlying supports in patriarchal relations of oppression will be overlooked. And the analysis of patriarchy is essential to a definition of the kind of socialism useful to women. While men and women share a need to overthrow capitalism, they retain interests particular to their gender group. It is not clear — from our sketch, from history, or from male socialists — that the socialism being struggled for is the same for both men and women. For a humane socialism would require not only consensus on what the new society should look like and what a healthy person should look like, but more concretely, it would require that men relinquish their privilege.

As women, we must not allow ourselves to be talked out of the urgency and importance of our tasks, as we have so many times in the past. We must fight the attempted coercion, both subtle and not so subtle, to abandon feminist objectives.

This suggests two strategic considerations. First, a struggle to establish socialism must be a struggle in which groups with different interests form an alliance. Women should not trust men to liberate them after the revolution, in part, because there is no reason to think they would know how; in part, because there is no necessity for them to do so. In fact, their immediate self-interest lies in our continued oppression. Instead, we must have our own organizations and our own power base. Second, we think the sexual division of labor within capitalism has given women a practice in which we have learned to understand what human interdependence and needs are. While men have long struggled *against* capital, women know what to struggle *for* (Vogel 1973). As a general rule, men's position in patriarchy and capitalism prevents them from recognizing both human needs for nurturance, sharing, and growth, and the potential for meeting those needs in a nonhierarchical, nonpatriarchal society. But even if we raise their consciousness, men might assess the potential gains against the potential losses and choose the status quo. Men have more to lose than their chains.

As feminist socialists, we must organize a practice which addresses both the struggle against patriarchy and the struggle against capitalism. We must insist that the society we want to create is a society in which recognition of interdependence is liberation rather than shame, nurturance is a universal, not an oppressive practice, and in which women do not continue to support the false as well as the concrete freedoms of men.

NOTES

1 Often paraphrased as "the husband and wife are one and that one is the husband," English law held the "by marriage, the husband and wife are one person in law: that is, the very being or legal existence of the women is suspended during the marriage, or at least is incorporated and consolidated into that of the Husband," W. Blackstone, *Commentaries*, 1965, pp. 442–445, cited in Kenneth M. Davison, Ruth B. Ginsburg, and Herma H. Kay, *Sex Based Discrimination* (St. Paul, Minn.: West Publishing Co., 1974), p. 117.

2 "Radical feminists" are those feminists who argue that the most fundamental dynamic of history is men's striving to dominate women. "Radical" in this context does *not* mean anti-capitalist, socialist, countercultural, etc., but has the specific meaning of this particular set of feminist beliefs or group of feminists. For additional writings of radical feminists, of whom the New York Radical Feminists are probably the most influential, see Koedt (1972).

3 For the bourgeois social science view of patriarchy, see, for example, Weber's distinction between traditional and legal authority (Parsons

1964: 328–57). These views are also discussed in Fee (1973: 23–29) and
in Nisbet (1966: Ch. 3).

[4] The particular ways in which men control women's access to important economic resources and restrict their sexuality vary enormously,
both from society to society, from subgroup to subgroup, and across
time. The examples we use to illustrate patriarchy in this section, however, are drawn primarily from the experience of whites in western
capitalist countries. The diversity is shown in Reiter (1975), Rosaldo and
Lamphere (1974), and Leibowitz (1978). The control of women's sexuality is tightly linked to the place of children. An understanding of the
demand (by men and capitalists) for children is crucial to understanding
changes in women's subordination.

Where children are needed for their present or future labor power,
women's sexuality will tend to be directed toward reproduction and
childrearing. When children are seen as superfluous, women's sexuality for other than reproductive purposes is encouraged, but men will
attempt to direct it towards satisfying male needs. The Cosmo girl is a
good example of a woman "liberated" from childrearing only to find herself turning all her energies towards attracting and satisfying men.
Capitalists can also use female sexuality to their own ends, as the success of Cosmo in advertising consumer products shows.

[5] Himmelweit and Mohun point out that both aspects of production
(people and things) are logically necessary to describe a mode of production because by definition, a mode of production must be capable
of reproducing itself. Either aspect alone is not self-sufficient. To put it
simply, the production of things requires people, and the production of
people requires things. Marx, though recognizing capitalism's need for
people, did not concern himself with how there were produced or
what the connections between the two aspects of production were.
See Himmelweit and Mohun (1977: 15–31).

[6] For an excellent discussion of one of such transition to socialism, see
Weinbaum (1976).

[7] It is important to remember that in the preindustrial period, women
contributed a large share to their families' subsistence — either by participating in a family craft or by agricultural activities. The initiation of
wage work for women both allowed and required this contribution to
take place independently from the men in the family. The new depar-
ture, then, was not that women earned income, but that they did so
beyond their husbands' or fathers' control. Clark (1969) describes
women's preindustrial economic roles and the changes that occurred as

capitalism progressed. It seems to be the case that Marx, Engels, and Kautsky were not fully aware of women's economic role before capitalism.

8 For a more complete discussion of protective labor legislation and women, see Hill (1970), parts of which have been published in Babcock et al. (1975), an excellent law text. Also see Hartmann (1976: 164–66).

Beyond the Unhappy Marriage: A Critique of the Dual Systems Theory
Iris Young

Even in its title, Hartmann's essay reflects what has been the specific project of socialist feminism: to "wed" the best aspects of the new wave of feminist theory developed in the sixties and seventies to marxian theory, thereby transforming marxian theory. Hartmann argues that this marriage has thus far not succeeded. She recommends that the marriage between marxism and feminism be put on a stronger footing by developing a theoretical account which gives as much weight to the system of patriarchy as to the system of capitalism. Rather than perceiving the particular situation of women as an effect of capitalism, as she believes Engels, Mitchell, Dalla Costa, and Zaretsky do, we should understand that the system of patriarchy is at least of equal importance for understanding the situation of women. Socialist feminist theory thus should seek the "laws of motion" of the system of patriarchy, the internal dynamic and contradictions of patriarchy, and articulate how these interact and perhaps conflict with the internal dynamic of capitalism.

Hartmann's essay is not the first to have proposed this dual systems theory for socialist feminism. On the contrary, the majority of socialist feminists espouse some version of the dual systems theory. I shall argue, however, that the dual systems theory will not patch up the unhappy marriage of marxism and feminism. There are good reasons for believing that the situation of women is not conditioned by two distinct systems of social relations which have distinct structure, movement, and histories.

Hartmann emphasizes that patriarchy has a material base in the structure of concrete relations and maintains that the system of patriarchy itself undergoes historical transformation. Precisely these strengths of Hartmann's account, however, weaken her argument for a dual systems theory which conceives of patriarchy as a system distinct from the relations of production. If, as Hartmann maintains, "the material base upon which patriarchy rests lies most fundamentally in men's control over women's labor power," and if "men maintain this control by excluding women from access to some essential productive resources," then it does not seem possible to separate patriarchy from a system of social relations of production even for analytical purposes. If, as Hartmann states, patriarchal social relations in contemporary capitalism are not confined to the family but also exist in the capitalist workplace and other institutions outside the family, it is hard to see by what principle we can separate these patriarchal relations from the social relations of capitalism. Hartmann concedes that "the same features, such as division of labor, often reinforce both patriarchy and capitalism, and in a thoroughly patriarchal capitalist society, it is hard to isolate the mechanisms of patriarchy." Yet she insists that we must separate patriarchy. It seem reasonable, however, to admit that if patriarchy and capitalism are manifest in identical social and economic structure, they belong to *one* system, not two.

Hartmann distinguishes between two different "types" or "aspects" of production: the production of people and the production of things. She does not, however, posit the "production of people" as a distinct *mode* of production, however, nor does she want to restrict this type of production to the family, though it is not clear where or how it takes place, nor how it can be distinguished from relations in which people produce things.

In order to have a dual systems theory which conceives patriarchy as a system of concrete relations as well as an ideological and psychological structure, it appears necessary to posit patriarchy in this fashion as a distinct system of production. Almost invariably, however, this approach relies on what Rosalind Petchesky calls a "model of separate spheres" which usually takes the form of distinguishing the family from the economy and in locating the specific relations of patriarchy within the family (Petchesky 1979: 373–87). There are, however, a number of problems with the model of separate spheres.

One of the defining characteristics of capitalism is the separation of productive activity from kinship relations and thereby the creation of two spheres of social life. Making this point, and showing how this separation has created a historically unique situation for women, has been one of the main achievements of socialist feminist analysis (Zaretsky 1976; Oakley 1974; Hamilton 1978). The model of separate spheres presupposed by many dual systems theorists tends to hypostasize this division between family and economy specific to capitalism into a universal form.

Because the model of separate spheres assumes the primary sphere of patriarchal relations is the family, it fails to bring into focus the character and degree of women's specific oppression as women outside the family. For example, it is difficult to view contemporary capitalism's use of women as sexual symbols to promote consumption as a function of some separate sphere distinct from the economic requirements of monopoly capitalism. More mundanely, a dual systems theory does not appear to have the theoretical equipment to identify and analyze the specific forms of sexist oppression which women suffer in the contemporary workplace. When more than half the women over sixteen in the U.S. are at work at any one time, and when over 90 percent work outside the home at some time in their lives, such a failing may serve the interests of contemporary capitalism itself.

This, more generally, is the ultimate objection to any dual systems theory. However one formulates it, the dual systems theory allows traditional marxism to maintain its theory of production relations, historical change, and analysis of the structure of capitalism in a basically unchanged form. That theory, as Hartmann points out, is completely gender-blind. The dual systems theory thus accepts this gender-blind analysis of the relations of production, wishing only to add onto it a separate conception of the relations of gender hierarchy. Thus, not unlike traditional marxism, the dual systems theory tends to see the question of women's oppression as merely an additive to the main questions of marxism.

As long as feminists are willing to cede the theory of material social relations arising out of laboring activity to traditional marxism, however, the marriage between feminism and marxism cannot be happy. If, as Hartmann claims, patriarchy's base is a control over women's labor that excludes women from access to productive resources, then patriarchal relations are internally related to production relations as a whole. Thus, traditional marxian theory will continue to dominate feminism as long as feminism does not challenge the adequacy of the traditional theory of production relations itself. If traditional marxism has no theoretical place for analysis of gender relations and the oppression of women, then that theory is an inadequate theory of production relations. Our historical research, coupled with our feminist intuitions, tells us that the labor of women occupies a central place in any system of production and that sexual hierarchy is a crucial element in any system of domination. To correspond to these intuitions, we need a theory of relations of production and the social relations which derive from and reinforce those relations which takes gender relations and the situation of women as *core* elements. Instead of marrying marxism, feminism must take over marxism and transform it into such a theory. We must develop an analytical framework which regards the material social relations of a particular historical social formation as one system in which gender differentiation is a core attribute.

DIVISION OF LABOR ANALYSIS

In this essay, I will propose that gender division of labor must be a central category for such a theory.

Traditional marxism takes class as its central category of analysis. Feminists have rightly claimed that this category does not aid the analysis of women's specific oppression or even its identification. The concept of class is indeed gender-blind. Precisely this conceptual flaw of the category class helped bring about the dual systems theory. Since class functions as the core concept of the marxian theory of social relations, and since it provides no place for analysis of gender differentiation and gender hierarchy, there appears to be no alternative but to seek another category and another system in which gender relations can appear. I suggest that there is another alternative, however. Agreeing that the category of class is gender-blind and hence incapable of exposing women's situation, we can nevertheless remain within the materialist framework by elevating the category of *division of labor* to a position as fundamental as, if not more fundamental than, that of class. This category *can* provide us with means of analyzing the social relations of laboring activity in a gender differentiated way.

The category of division of labor can not only refer to a set of phenomena broader than that of class, but also more concrete. It refers specifically to the *activity* of labor itself, and the specific social and institutional relations of that activity, rather than to a relation to the means of labor and the products of labor, as does class. The specific place of individuals in the division of labor explains their consciousness and behavior as well as the specific relations of cooperation and conflict in which different persons stand.

These attributes of division of labor as a category both more concrete in its level of analysis and broader in extension than the category class make it an indispensable element in any analysis of the social relations involved in and arising from laboring activity. Each category entails a different level of abstraction. Class analysis aims to get a vision of a system of production as a whole, and thus asks about the broadest social divisions of ownership, control, and appropriation of surplus product. At such a level of abstraction, however, much pertaining to the relations of production and the material bases of domination remains hidden. Division of labor analysis proceeds at the more concrete level of particular relations of interaction and interdependence in a society which differentiates it into a complex network. It describes the major structural divisions among the members of a society according to their position in laboring activity and assesses the effect of these divisions on the functioning of the economy, the relations of domination, political and ideological structures.

GENDER DIVISION OF LABOR

With the term "gender division of labor," I intend to refer to all structured gender differentiation of labor in a society. Such traditional women's tasks as bearing and rearing children, caring for the sick, cleaning, cooking, etc., fall under the category of labor as much as the making of objects in a factory. Using the category of production or labor to designate only the making of concrete material objects in a modern factory has been one of the unnecessary tragedies of marxian theory. "Relations of production" or "social relations arising from laboring activity" should mean the social relations involved in *any* task or activity which the society defines as necessary. Thus, in our own society, for example, the relation between female prostitutes and the pimps or organizations they work for is a relation of production in this sense. Use of the gender division of labor category provides the means for analyzing the social relations arising from the laboring activity of a whole society along the axis of gender.

Gender division of labor analysis can have a number of advantages over the approach of the dual systems theory. It brings gender relations and the position of women to the center of historical materialist analysis.

Gender division of labor analysis may provide a way of regarding gender relations as not merely a central aspect of relations of production, but as fundamental to their structure. For the gender division of labor is the first division of labor, and in so-called primitive societies, it is the only institutionalized division of labor. The development of other forms of social division of labor, such as the division between mental and manual labor, may thus be explicable only by appeal to transformations in the gender division of labor and the effect such changes have on the relations between members of each sex as well as potentialities such changes make available to them.

Gender division of labor analysis can also explain the origins and maintenance of women's subordination in social structural terms. Neither a biological account nor a psychological account, for example, can show how men in a particular society occupy an institutionalized position of superiority only if the organization of social relations arising from laboring activity gives them a level of control over, and access to, resources that women do not have. Gender division of labor can help explain this differential access to the means of labor and control, and thus can help explain how the institutions of male domination originate, are maintained, and change.[1]

Hartmann herself appears to take the division of labor by sex as the foundation of male domination, perhaps even of gender itself.

> The strict division of labor by sex, a social invention common to all known societies, creates two very separate genders and a need for men and women to get together for economic reasons.... The sexual division of labor is also the underpinning of sexual subcultures in which men and women experience life differently; it is the material base of male power which is exercised (in our society) not just in not doing housework and in securing superior employment, but psychologically as well. (Hartmann, p. 16 [p. 127 in this book])

Gender division of labor analysis allows us to do material analysis of the social relations of labor in gender specific terms without assuming that all women in general or all women in a particular society have a common and unified situation. I believe this to be one of the primary virtues of such an analysis. Because the dual systems theory posits a distinct system underlying the oppression of women, it tends to claim that *qua* women we are in an identical situation whatever our historical location or situation. Gender division of labor analysis, however, can avoid this false identification while still focusing on the gender specific situation and oppression of women. Gender division of labor analysis notices the broad axes of gender structuration of the relations of labor and distribution and notices that certain tasks and functions in a particular society are always or usually performed by members of one sex. This does not necessarily commit it to any claims about the common situation of all members of that sex. In some societies, every women must perform some tasks, but in most societies, the tasks and positions of women vary, even though they are gender specific.

Not only can gender division of labor analysis take account of specific variations in the situations of women in its descriptions, but it can better explain such variations than can the dual systems theory. In particular, explaining variations in the kind or degree of women's subordination in a society requires reference to what women concretely do in a society. For example, it is not surprising that women tend to stand in a more equal position to men when they have access to weapons and warfare than when men have a monopoly over these (Boulding 1976: 257–63). Gender division of labor analysis, moreover, may prove fruitful in giving an account of why in a few societies — the Iroquois, for example — women do not appear to occupy a subordinate position.[2]

GENDER DIVISION AND CAPITALIST PATRIARCHY

In her account of women's oppression within capitalist society, Hartmann assumes a model of the structure and dynamic of capitalism as gender-blind. In her view, nothing about the logic of capitalism itself requires differentiation among workers along lines of ascribed characteristics like sex (or race). Indeed, Hartmann shares an assumption about the nature of capitalism held by liberal and marxist theorists alike: that capitalism's inherent tendency is to homogenize the workforce, reducing the significance of ascribed statuses based on sex, race, ethnic origin, and so on. She claims that the development of capitalism from the fifteenth to the eighteenth century undermined male dominance over women and threatened to make women independent from and equal to men. "The theoretical tendency of pure capitalism would have been to eradicate all arbitrary differences of status among laborers, making all laborers equal in the marketplace" (Hartmann 1979: 207). Given that the internal dynamic of capitalism tends toward such homogenization, she argues, only the operation of a separate system of patriarchy can explain women's continued subordination and unequal status.

I believe that abandoning the assumption of a gender-blind capitalism allows one to approach the history of women's status in capitalist society in a more revealing light. A gender division of labor analysis of capitalism, which asks how the system itself is structured along gender lines, can give an account of the situation of women under capitalism as a function of the structure and dynamic of capitalism itself. *My thesis is that marginalization of women and thereby our functioning as a secondary labor force is an essential and fundamental characteristic of capitalism.*

In her book, *Women in Class Society*, Heleieth Saffioti argues that the marginalization of women's labor is necessary to capitalism and is the key to understanding women's situation under capitalism. Capitalism emerges as the first economic system whose nature dictates that not all potentially productive people be employed, and which also requires a fluctuation in the proportion of the population employed. The existence of the system thus requires, she argues, that some criteria be found to distinguish the core of primary workers from marginal or secondary workers. The preexistence of patriarchal ideology, coupled with the necessity that women be near small children, operated to make sex the most natural criterion by which to divide the workforce (Saffioti 1978: Ch. 12). Capitalism uses criteria of race and ethnicity as well, when these are present in the society, but the sex division is always the most obvious and permanent; women are not likely to be "assimilated."

Hartmann cites the indisputable fact that women's social subordination existed before capitalism as evidence that our subordination under capitalism has its source in a separate system of social relations that interacts with the capitalist system (Hartmann 1979: 209–11). We need not draw this conclusion, however. A marxist would not assert that the existence of class society prior to capitalism demonstrates that all class societies have some common structure independent of the system of capitalism. Class societies undergo systemic historical transformation. The weakness of the ahistorical view of patriarchy, which sees it as essentially the same through changes in other social relations, has already been pointed out. Once we admit, with Hartmann, that the form and character of women's oppression have undergone fundamental historical transformation, then the existence of precapitalist patriarchy need no longer count as evidence that male domination in capitalist society has its foundation in a structure of social relations independent of the system of capitalism itself.

While women in precapitalist society were by no means the social equals of men, all the evidence points to the conclusion that our situation deteriorated with the development of capitalism. In precapitalist society, women dominated a number of crucial skills, and thus their labor and their knowledge were indispensable to the family, the manor, and the village. In many craft guilds of the sixteenth and seventeenth centuries, women were members on equal terms with men and even dominated some of them. Women engaged in industry and trade. Precapitalist culture understood marriage as an economic partnership; men did not expect to "support" women. The law reflected this relative equality of women by allowing them to make contracts in their own name and retain their own property even in marriage (Ehrenreich and English 1978: 6–9; Clark 1920; Oakley 1974: Ch. 2; Case 1976: 224–49; Ryan 1975: 19–82).

By the nineteenth century, women's economic independence had been almost entirely undermined, and her legal rights were nonexistent. Capitalism thrust women, for the first time in history, to the margins of economic activity. This marginalization of women's labor by capitalism never meant that women's labor was jettisoned entirely from the socialized economy. In 1866 in France, for example, women comprised 30 percent of the total industrial workforce (Saffioti 1978: 53). Rather, women were defined as a secondary labor force which served as a reserve of cheap labor.

Throughout the history of capitalism women have served the classic functions Marx describes as those of the reserve army of labor (Marx 1967: vol. I: 631–39). They have served as a pool of workers who can be drawn into new areas of production without dislodging those already employed and as a pool which can be used to keep both the wages and militancy of all workers low. Whenever in the history of capitalism large numbers of new workers have been needed in new and expanding industries, it is women more often than not who fill the need. The early textile mills in New England, for example, actively recruited women, as did the printers (Baker 1964: Ch. 1). Many of the occupations which today are considered "women's jobs" were areas of employment which opened in huge numbers during the nineteenth century and which required relatively skilled workers. This is true of nursing, for example, as well as saleswork, telephone workers, and clerical workers (Baker 1964: Ch. 1; Kessler-Harris 1976: 335).

Employers have always tended to exaggerate divisions among workers in order to keep wages low and to maintain worker docility. Women have been used consistently for such purposes. Throughout the history of capitalism, women have served as a ready pool of strikebreakers. In the history of industrialization, capitalists consistently replaced men with women and children when they mechanized the production process. Then, once the will and expectations of the men had lowered, they rehired the men and removed the women and children (Baker 1964: Ch. 1; Kessler-Harris 1975: 217–42). A similar pattern seems to have operated during the depression of the 1930s. Employers replaced high priced men by lower priced women until the wage expectations of the men had fallen, at which point the employers once again replaced the women with men (Humphries 1975). The literature on sex segregation of the contemporary labor force often suggests that sex segregated jobs are new to the twentieth century. A close look at the history of capitalism, however, reveals that a sexually mixed occupation has been rare. Those jobs in which women have dominated at any particular time, moreover, have usually been accorded less pay and prestige than male jobs of comparable skill (Baker 1964; Kessler-Harris 1975).[3] In this way as well, women have always served as a secondary labor force.

Preexistent patriarchal ideology and the traditional location of women's labor near the home initially made possible the marginalization of women's labor, according it secondary status. Bourgeois ideology, however, greatly expanded and romanticized, at the same time that it trivialized, women's association with a domestic sphere and dissociation with work outside the home. The ideology of femininity which defined women as nonworking emerged as a consequence of, and justification for, the process of marginalization of women that had already begun. Not until well into the nineteenth century did treatises appear arguing that the true vocation of women was motherhood, that women were too frail to engage in heavy work, that women's proper activity was to nurture and create an atmosphere of shelter and comfort for her family (Ehrenreich and English 1978; Ryan 1975: Ch. 3; Gordon and Buhle 1976).

Capitalists actively promoted, and continue to promote, the ideology of domestic womanhood to justify low wages for women, arguments for their indispensability, and to keep women from organizing (Kessler-Harris 1976: 333–37). Because only the bourgeois or petty bourgeois woman could live a life that corresponded to the ideology of femininity, that ideology acted as a powerful force in the upwardly mobile desires of the working class. Women internalized the image of femininity and both men and women took the "nonworking" wife as a sign of status. One should note here that among the working class, a wife who was not a wage worker was freed to bring in income through petty commodity production or to produce food and clothing which would make buying less necessary.

Without question, male workers had sexist motivations and used sexist arguments in the struggle for the family wage which Hartmann discusses and in the struggle for protective legislation for women and children which occurred at about the same time. Given the history of capitalism up until that time, however, one can see these motives and arguments as an effect and consolidation of the capitalist gender division of labor which accorded women a marginal and secondary position. One can, that is, explain the sexism of male workers without appealing to a system of social relations independent of capitalism by seeing the essentially patriarchal character of the system of capitalism itself. One explains it by seeing how capitalism is an economic system in which a gender division of labor, having a historically specific form and structure which by marginalizing women's labor, gives men a specific kind of privilege and status.

Capitalism does not merely use or adapt to gender hierarchy, as most dual systems theorists suggest. From the beginning, it was *founded* on gender hierarchy which defined men as primary and women as secondary. The specific forms of the oppression of women which exist under capitalism are essential to its nature.[4] This does not mean, of course, that gender hierarchy did not exist prior to capitalism, nor does it mean that the development of capitalism's gender division of labor did not depend on the prior existence of sexist ideology and a feudal gender division of labor. Many other aspects of capitalism developed out of feudal society, but at a certain point, these developments took a specifically new form.

If we could find one instance of a capitalist society in which the marginalization of women's labor did not occur, we might be entitled to consider it a characteristic external to the structure of capitalism. We can find no such instance, however. In her book *Women's Role in Economic Development*, Ester Boserup documents in detail that the situation of women in third world economies seems to worsen with the introduction of capitalist and "modern" industrial methods. Even when capitalism enters a society in which women's work is the center of the economy, it tends to effect the marginalization of women's labor (Boserup 1970; Chaney and Schmink 1976). In claiming that the capitalist economy requires the marginalization of women, I am not claiming that we cannot logically conceive of a capitalism in which the marginalization of women did not occur. I am claiming, rather, that given an initial gender differentiation and a preexisting sexist ideology, a patriarchal capitalism in which women function as a secondary labor force is the only *historical* possibility.

NOTES

[1] There is much evidence, for example, that whether a society is matrifocal or patrifocal depends in large measure on the gender division of labor. See Denich (1974).

[2] Much of Judith Brown's account of Iroquois women's relatively high status depends upon looking at their role in production and the control over resources they have by virtue of that role. See Reiter (1976).

[3] Both Baker and Kessler-Harris detail the degree of sex segregation in the U.S. in the nineteenth century. For a comparable account for Europe, see McBride (1977).

[4] Ann Foreman argues that the specific type of domestic labor which is allocated to women under capitalism is a form of labor peculiar to and definitive of capitalism. Wage labor, that is to say, is not the only form of labor that capitalism creates; it also creates privatized household labor, and Foreman argues that this is an integral element of the capitalist mode of production. See Foreman (1977).

DISCUSSION QUESTIONS

1. Formulate a Marxist explanation of the way in which capitalism provides the necessary conditions for exploitation of workers. Then, situate women's position as both homemakers and paid workers in the labour force within the Marxist tradition. Finally, criticize Marxists' account of women's oppression.

2. Look at various institutions of Canadian society (economy, education, church, political organization, family, etc.). Show how each is responsible for women's oppression. Are these institutions patriarchal? How?

3. What does Young mean when she refers to Hartmann's explanation of women's oppression as a dual system theory? What are the problems (if any) with the dual system model?

4. How does gendered differentiation of labour explain women's oppression? In your opinion, which of the two writers (Hartmann or Young) is better able to explain women's oppression? Why?

PATRIARCHY OR CAPITALISM

Does Capitalism Really Need Patriarchy? Some Old Issues Reconsidered

Carol Johnson

Much of the 1970s and 1980s debate over the relationship between capitalism and patriarchy[1] arose in the context of socialist–feminist critiques of crude Marxist conceptions that saw class relations as of primary importance in explaining women's oppression (Sargent 1981). Socialist feminists sought to retain some of the insights of Marxism while rejecting class reductionism. Consequently, influential socialist feminists such as Heidi Hartmann (1981a: 21–22) argued that there was a "partnership" between the interests of capital and the interests of patriarchy in constructing modern forms of women's subordination. By the late 1980s, Anne Phillips (1987) could argue that "most contemporary feminist writing on women and work has converged on the notion that class and gender intertwine" (Phillips 1987: 21), and few feminists now associate with the position that sees the problems of women as workers as being caused predominantly by capitalists or men. Phillips went on to caution against constructing the debate in terms of "capitalism versus patriarchy," arguing that there was not "any universal priority" and that the key issues shift through context and time as "our male-structured capitalism ... poses different sets of problems to different groups of women" (Phillips 1987: 21–22). Similar perspectives that capitalism and patriarchy are indissolubly intertwined come from writers engaging with poststructuralist issues of identity and difference and arguing against establishing a hierarchy of oppression.

The issue of the relationship between capitalism and patriarchy has also been raised in somewhat new form in recent theoretical literature that questions the consensus Phillips believes exists in material dealing with women and work. Here, the intertwining of capitalism and patriarchy is also accepted but in a way that tends to privilege patriarchal explanations by depicting capitalism as just another patriarchal form. Carole Pateman's book *The Sexual Contract* (Pateman 1988) seems certain to become a modern classic of feminist political theory. In it,

Pateman provides an erudite and trenchant critique of social contractual theory, arguing that contracts not merely presuppose social relationships characterised by subordination rather than equal exchange. (Pateman 1988: 58), but that, more particularly, they presuppose the subordination of women to men in the marriage contract (Pateman 1988: 1–8, 135–36). Pateman concentrates on discussing the marriage contract, the capitalist employment contract, and the slave contract. It should be noted that Pateman claims she is not telling a new, feminist story of patriarchal origins but rather deconstructing a patriarchal story of origins (contract theory) to tell another story that reveals a prior contract (the sexual contract) based on the subordination of women (Pateman 1988: 18, 219). However, in fact, she slides uneasily between the level of myth and realism. Her story does presuppose a particular historical trajectory. So, for example, she argues that the capitalist employment contract presupposes the subordination of women in the marriage contract. In her words:

> The marriage contract is not like an employment contract; rather the employment contract presupposes the marriage contract. Or, to make this point another way, the construction of the "worker" presupposes that he is a man who has a woman, a (house)wife, to take care of his daily needs. (Pateman 1988: 131)

Consequently, capitalism is reduced to a form of patriarchy.

> Capitalism and class have been constructed as modern patriarchal categories. The social contract is about the origins of the civil sphere and capitalist relations. Without the sexual contract there is no indication that the "worker" is a masculine figure or that the "working class" is the class of men. The civil, public sphere does not come into being on its own, and the "worker," his "work" and his "working class" cannot be understood independently of the private sphere and his conjugal rights as a husband. The attributes and activities of the "worker" are constricted together with, and as the other side of, those of his feminine counterpart, the "housewife." (Pateman 1988: 135)

In such passages, Pateman (1988) is being partially influenced by some versions of radical feminism that see patriarchy as the ultimate shaper of other forms of oppression (Tong 1989: 98). Simultaneously, her arguments also reveal the influence of socialist feminist arguments that capitalism and patriarchy are highly compatible — indeed, this passage occurs in the context of a debate with Hartmann's conception of the "partnership" between the "dual systems" of capitalism and patriarchy (Pateman 1988: 133). However, Pateman specifically rejects "dual system" arguments that patriarchy predates capitalism "and now, in some way, exists alongside or within, or as an adjunct to, capitalist relations" (Pateman 1988: 37), arguing that "if capitalism is patriarchal, it is hard to see what can be gained by insisting that there are two systems" (Pateman 1988: 38). She goes on to argue that "one of the advantages of approaching the question of patriarchy through the story of the sexual contract is that it reveals that civil society, including the capitalist economy, has a patriarchal structure" (Pateman 1988: 38). By contrast, Pateman argues that in order to "understand modern patriarchy, including capitalist economic relations," one needs to keep in mind the relationship between the marriage contract and the employment contract (Pateman 1988: 37). For Pateman, capitalism is, in effect, depicted as another version of patriarchy; the question of whether capitalism need be patriarchal cannot really arise in a formulation that collapses them into one system.

This article will largely be addressing the issue of the "logic" of capitalism rather than being confined to historically existing forms. In other words, the argument does not assume that historically existing relationships between capitalism and patriarchy can be used to predict future forms. Nonetheless, since Pateman and other commentators do draw on historical material, it is worth pointing out that there is some historical basis for questioning Pateman's story of the development of contracts. Let us begin with an historical example that Pateman does use, one that is very familiar to Australian-influenced feminists such as Pateman and myself, namely the *Harvester* judgement of 1907. In this judgement, as Pateman points out, Justice Higgins of the Australian industrial arbitration court, "ruled in favour of a legally guaranteed minimum wage — and defined a living wage as sufficient to keep an unskilled worker, his wife and three children in reasonable comfort" (Pateman 1988: 138). In 1918, the same Justice Higgins went on to establish a female basic wage set effectively at 54% of the male breadwinner rate and warned employers not to employ cheaper female labour in "men's jobs." Unions subsequently succeeded in making repeated applications for jobs to be classified as "male" (Probert 1989: 98). As we shall see later, Hartmann also refers to the American example of the family wage to support her argument that there was a partnership between patriarchy and capitalism.

Pateman uses such historical examples as evidence that the sexual contract precedes the employment contract; the implication is, as stated above, that capitalism is predicated upon female subordination. However, it will be suggested here that such contracts may have no inherent benefits for capitalist employers but rather reflect a long struggle by many male workers to consolidate their own superior position, based on women's subordinate position, in respect to the wage labour relation. Their struggle was frequently aided by the patriarchal (rather than purely capitalist) allegiances of male judges, politicians, and employers. Let us consider the concept of the "family wage" purely in terms of a possible "logic" of capitalism, that is, from an imagined vantage point abstracted from actually existing historical relations but based on arguments regarding financial advantage. To begin with, it should be noted that, in Australia at least, interpretations of the "family wage" are contentious, and the employers' preferred principle tended to be "the capacity of industry to pay" (Cass 1988: 55). However, the "family wage" seems a good deal for capitalists if, for example, one assumes that the only alternative was for the employer to pay women the same as the higher rate that men were receiving. That would have been an ideal solution for feminists but does not seem a historically feasible alternative given that the higher male rate was set on the basis of a dependent spouse as well as children. *The more appropriate question to ask is why it would be to a capitalist's financial advantage to pay a wage that can support four people yet only get the labour of one?* Wouldn't it be better to split the wage amount equally between husband and wife and get the labour of two employees; or, even better, to split the wage amount between four people if child labour laws allowed? Furthermore, if the capitalist were to employ both husband and wife, why would he or she benefit financially from employing the husband at the family wage rate and the wife at, for example, 54% of that rate? The capitalist would be paying one and a half times what was necessary to support the family unit. Admittedly, capitalists employing a predominantly female work force might well benefit from paying them only 54% of the male rate, but what about those capitalists employing a predominantly male work force? Their wages bill would be much higher than if they were paying males only 50% of the family wage. Note, too, that if the family wage were split equally between male and female employees, female labour would be even cheaper.

Such examples suggest that the way in which the "family wage" developed may actually have been financially disadvantageous for capital and may have partly reflected the outcome of a long battle by many male workers to improve their wages by excluding and marginalising both women and children. (In the case of the Australian work force, it also involved a long battle by many White males to exclude Chinese and Kanak workers.) Pateman (1988) notes in passing that "the history of the labour movement leaves no doubt that the insistence on a family wage was an important strategy through which men were able to exclude women from many areas of paid work and bolster the husband's position as master in the home" (Pateman 1988: 139), but she doesn't discuss why this struggle was necessary. It was necessary because the capitalist employment contract, contrary to Pateman's view, posed a direct threat to an aspect of the marriage contract, namely who would have control over components of female labour (as well as child labour, but we'll exclude that from our subject of discussion). Was it to be the husband or the capitalist? This would have been a particularly important issue for the rural and town households in which males had controlled the female labour of "housewifery" which, as Stevi Jackson (1992: 154–55) has pointed out, involved production for both exchange and household use.

The potential conflict of "interests" between men and capitalists over the control of female labour has been acknowledged by Hartmann (1981), among others, in the American context, but Hartmann doesn't develop this insight because she then argues that capitalists "realized that housewives produced and maintained healthier workers than wage-working wives" (Hartmann 1981: 22) — a point that still begs the question of whether domestic labour could have been shared between male and female workers, possibly at the cost of a reduced working week but in a way that still enabled capitalists to benefit from employing both male and female labour for the cost of a family wage.

Indeed, the resolution of the tensions between capitalism and patriarchy were far from a foregone conclusion. Some British examples are pertinent here. As a number of feminists have pointed out, the history of the development of capitalist employment relations in Britain was particularly fraught for patriarchy, although Pateman does not refer to feminist literature on this matter when citing British evidence to support her case on the wage contract. Capitalist employment relations, in the form of factory relations, first developed in areas of female employment such as spinning — work that had been predominantly done by women in cottage industries. There was, therefore, initially a significant demand for female employment (Lewenhak 1977: 17). The numbers of women employed in factory work should not be underestimated. In his 1845 book, *Condition of the Working Class in England*, Engels (1975) cited extensive statistical evidence pointing to the disproportionate employment of women, as opposed to adult males, in the factory system. He also noted "the just wrath aroused among the working-men by this virtual castration, and the reversal of all relations within the family" and argued that there were hundreds of families in Manchester alone where "the wife supports the family, the husband sits at home, tends the children, sweeps the room and cooks." Even when men were employed in factories, women would sometimes be employed in jobs earning more than them (Engels 1975: 435). However, unlike many trade unionists of the period, Engels did conclude that "if the reign of the wife over the husband, as inevitably brought about by the factory system, is inhuman, the pristine rule of the husband over the wife must have been inhuman too" (Engels 1975: 438–39). It was their observations of the early impact of capitalism that led Marx and

Engels to their mistaken belief that capitalism would liberate women by increasing their participation in the public sphere — mistaken, partly because, given their belief that women's oppression arose from property-ownership, they underestimated working-class men's response to the challenge to patriarchal relations (Engels 1970: 245). They also underestimated the extent to which men of other classes might place patriarchal allegiances before pecuniary ones.

It was therefore far from inevitable that men rather than women would inherently benefit from the capitalist employment contract in Britain, a point that tends to undermine Pateman's assertion that the wage contract was established upon the basis of the marriage contract and that the worker was indelibly constructed as male. Indeed, as Sheila Lewenhak (1977: 6, 11) has pointed out, there was a long history of women working for paid employment, and although female labour was generally paid less than the male, this was not exclusively so. However, in the nineteenth century, male-dominated unions mobilised to exclude or marginalise women in areas as diverse as tailoring and mining (Taylor 1983: 83–117). Male labourers often explicitly argued that this strategy would force capitalists to pay a male employee the equivalent of what they'd previously paid for the labour of the man, wife, and children — an argument that has led some commentators to support the strategy as justifiable (Humphries 1977: 252). Despite Humphries' arguments, it is clear that the strategy was based upon a patriarchal division of labour. The rationale lay not only in attempting to increase male dominance in wages and employment, but also in the home. Opponents of female employment, such as the radical tailor Francis Place, noted that "It will be found universally ... where men have opposed the employment of women ... their own wages are kept up to a point equal to the maintenance of a family" (cited by Taylor 1983: 107). He urged workers in other industries to follow the lead of the tailors so that women would "become all that can be desired as companionable wives" (cited by Lewenhak 1977: 41). As Anne Phillips and Barbara Taylor (1986) point out:

> Left to its own devices, capitalism might well have fulfilled the prophecies of Engels and others, and effectively destroyed sexual divisions within the family by drawing women indiscriminately into wage labour. But patriarchy intervened, and ensured through the development of the family wage system that women's subordinate position within the family be reproduced within wage labour. (Phillips and Taylor 1986: 57)

The Phillips and Taylor (1986) analysis reveals the problems in assuming that capitalist employment contracts were inherently based on a patriarchal marriage contract since a patriarchal form of the wage relation had to be fought for rather than being a foregone conclusion. Although Phillips and Taylor do not go on to consider the extent to which capitalism per se may actually be antithetical to patriarchy, their position does draw attention to a degree of antagonism that Pateman (1988) ignores and Hartmann (1981a) glosses over in her conception of a "partnership." Unfortunately, as we have seen, Phillips also did not develop this initial insight in her later characterisations of the relationship between capitalism and patriarchy.

The issue of the early antagonism between capitalism and patriarchy has been addressed in more detail by Sylvia Walby (1990). However, Walby has suggested that the tension between capitalism and patriarchy was largely resolved when patriarchy moved from a private to a public form in which cheap, sex-segregated, and casual female labour could be exploited by capitalists. In Walby's words:

> The main basis of the tension between capitalism and patriarchy is over the exploitation of women's labour. On the one hand, capitalists have interests in the recruitment and exploitation of female labour, which is cheaper than that of men because of patriarchal structures. On the other, there is resistance to this by that patriarchal strategy which seeks to maintain the exploitation of women in the household.... Indeed there was often a strong cross-class patriarchal alliance of strong male unions. However, this cross-class alliance had weaknesses when it cut across the interests of employers to recruit the cheaper labour of women.... An alternative patriarchal strategy developed of allowing women into paid employment, but segregating them from men and paying them less. (Walby 1990: 185)

Or, as Walby sums it up, as we move from private to public labour, "women are no longer restricted to the domestic hearth but have the whole society in which to roam and be exploited" (Walby 1990: 201). Walby suggests that this compromise particularly suits modern-day capitalism which requires a flexible work force (Walby 1990: 199).

The major problem with Walby's depiction of the historical compromise between (male) labour and (male) capital is that it overlooks the implication, discussed above, that some capitalists, or often the same capitalists, were having to pay male labour more than if the "family wage" had been divided equally between the husband and wife. The family wage may no longer exist, but higher wages for male-dominated jobs do. Why settle for cheap female labour when you could have had cheap male labour as well? Why settle today for the flexibility of casual and part-time female labour if you could exploit a potential army of casual, part-time male labour as well? However, Walby's account is superior to that of Pateman's in a number of respects. One of these is that she does acknowledge tensions between earlier forms of patriarchy and capitalism, even if she believes that those tensions were largely resolved with the move from private to public patriarchy. Indeed, Walby criticises dual systems theorists such as Hartmann for assuming that there is primarily harmony between capitalist and patriarchal relations (Walby 1990: 41). Hartmann has recently reaffirmed her position, arguing that sex-segregation, low female wages, and devalorization of nonmarket work "are examples of a basic complementarity between patriarchy and capitalism that has made patriarchy quite resistant to change (Folbre and Hartmann 1989: 93). Pateman (1988: 38), as we have seen, in effect, accepts the degree of harmony proposed by these theorists at face value but criticises them for not collapsing capitalism into patriarchy.

The above arguments emphasise the fact that capitalism need not be inherently patriarchal. The fact that we currently live in a very gendered capitalist society is due to the fact that men of various classes mobilised to ensure that preexisting patriarchal conditions continued to exist and interact with capitalist relations. As Walby points out, the mobilisation frequently involved using the state to exclude, marginalise and under-value female labour — an option that has become less possible now that women are gaining political rights and representation (Walby 1990: 41–42). Not surprisingly, there were frequent attempts to preclude women from the emerging citizenship rights of liberal capitalist societies. The original draft of the People's Charter, keystone of the English Chartist movement, included a clause extending the suffrage to women, but this was dropped almost immediately (Taylor 1983: 270–71). Obviously, men of property were also involved in attempting to block female suffrage. The point is not to paint working-class men as the worst enemies of women, but simply to question whether the inequality of women is a necessary feature of capitalism. The fact that working-class men played such an important role in helping to produce the patriarchal form of capitalism does, however, lend weight to the argument that women's subordination under capitalism is not due to the operation of capitalist "interests" per se. Male capitalists also wished to sustain existing conceptions of masculinity, for example, by paying men more and women less, or sex-segregating the work force, but, if so, it was not due to any logic inherent in capitalist relations but to their own patriarchal allegiances. Indeed, the fact that most capitalists were male was due to preexisting patriarchal property relations that restricted women's ability to own wealth in their own right rather than to any inherent logic in the capitalist system which prevents women from being capitalists. As Walby puts it, "the development of capitalism opened up new sites of power, and these were colonized by men because they were strategically placed to do so" (Walby 1990: 184).

Socialist feminists have rightly pointed out that, rather than having economic benefits that "trickle down" to the disadvantaged, free-market policies generally have very bad consequences for those who are dependent on welfare benefits and/or who are in a weak economic position in the labour market, including the majority of women (Sharp and Broomhill 1988: 33–57). However, the issue is whether there is something inherent in capitalism which requires women to be in such an economically disadvantaged position or whether, as suggested here, that gendered location is due solely to patriarchal influences and mobilisations. In this scenario, it would be conceivably possible, in some future form of capitalist society, for free-market policies to be gender-neutral while still having detrimental effects on both men and women in terms of their class position. In other words, capitalists do benefit from paying particularly low wages to some workers, but gender need not be a factor in determining who those low paid workers are. Similarly, it would be conceivable to imagine a society in which welfare services were cut but the burden fell equally upon both men and women in the home. It is, therefore, important to note that even New Right policies, rather than simply revealing a complete compatibility between capitalism and patriarchy, can also reveal some real tensions.

While male capitalists, who are currently in the vast majority, may sometimes have conflicts between their perceived "interests," for example, as males wishing to reproduce masculine power in the workplace and as capitalists wishing to exploit labour irrespective of sex, female capitalists may encounter fewer personal contradictions in rushing to exploit men equally with women. Seen in this way, it is not surprising that women calling themselves feminist can be attracted to right-wing economic thought — hence, the profeminist views of the laissez-faire conservatives interviewed by Klatch (1987: 4–5, 50–51) in America or the libertarian feminists interviewed by Campbell (1987: 201, 230–31) in Britain. Their feminism is grounded in a belief that individual women should be able to advance through class hierarchies rather than an ethic of collective care or sisterhood, but it is a form of liberal feminism nonetheless. While right-wing thought is often literally constructed around conceptions of rational economic *man* (Ferber and Nelson 1993), the self-reliant individual of laissez-faire economics could conceivably be reconstructed as gender neutral. For once patriarchy is theoretically severed from capitalism, feminism will no longer be predominantly the property of the left. Nor, as Pateman (1988) mistakenly implies, does feminism, in general, necessarily presuppose a critique of capitalism, although many socialist feminists will remain critical of it. Just as class-reductionist explanations of patriarchy need to be rejected, so do gender-reductionist explanations of capitalism. Neither class relations nor the marriage contract can provide universal explanations for the complex social and political relations within which we live.

NOTES

[1] The term *patriarchy* is used here to refer to a system of male domination that involves the subordination of women. Patriarchy takes different forms in different societies and different historical periods. It interacts with other forms of oppression, such as class, race, and sexuality, in very complex ways. This article largely centres around the question of whether a particular system of class surbordination (capitalism) requires, or depends upon, female subordination. While using historical examples, the discussion here also concentrates on analysing the "logic" of both systems in terms of capitalists' financial advantage.

A Comment on Johnson's "Does Capitalism Really Need Patriarchy?"
Carole Pateman

I want, first, to say something about Johnson's discussion of *The Sexual Contract*; second, to turn to her question about capitalists and the family wage; and, third, to make some general observations about the global restructuring of capitalism.

Carol Johnson states that she is looking at the "logic" of capitalism. My book was about the "logic," or the standpoint, of contract (I paid particular attention to its strict form, contractarianism) as exhibited in theories of the original contract and contracts about property in the person, including the employment contract. Thus, I was not arguing, as Johnson claims, that the marriage contract came before or was prior to the employment contract, or that patriarchy preceded capitalism, in an historical sense. (Nor was my claim that the sexual contract came first, before the social contract; I saw it as one dimension of the original contract). Indeed, I explicitly argued — against those who see patriarchy as a "feudal relic," those who see feminist theory as the completion of leftist critiques of capitalism, or those who claim that patriarchalism had vanished by the end of the seventeenth century — that a new, specifically modern, form of patriarchy emerged. This modern form is distinctive in being contractual, and it developed along with, and helped shape, capitalism.

Johnson misunderstands my presentation of the relationship between the marriage contract and the employment contract. She mistakenly infers from passages that she quotes from *The Sexual Contract*, in which I emphasise the mutual interdependence between the marriage and employment contracts, that I "reduce" capitalism to, or "collapse" capitalism into, patriarchy, and that I treat capitalism as "another version" of patriarchy, so that my argument is "gender reductionist."

On the contrary, I emphasised that there were significant differences between the employment contract (capitalism) and the marriage contract (patriarchy). Husbands were not like capitalists, nor were wives like workers. The marriage and employment contracts both gave rise to examples of civil subordination, but the respective subordination of workers and wives took different forms. When I argued that the employment contract presupposed the marriage contract, or stressed the mutual interdependence of two contracts, I was not "collapsing" one into the other. I was drawing out the logic of the relationship.[1]

I was criticising leftist theorists who claim that the employment contract can be analysed and criticised without any reference to the marriage contract and feminist theorists who claim that the relation between capitalist and worker provides the model for the relation between husband and wife. My claim was that the marriage contract is indispensable for an understanding of the employment contract and the subordination of the worker. Some knowledge of domestic contracts is required to understand the long transformation through which masters and servants become employers and employees, husbands become worker/breadwinners and wives become housewives. I stressed the length and complexity of the process through which the housewife and worker appeared on the historical scene (somewhere around the 1840s in Britain). Workers and housewives had to be created, a process that, as both Johnson and I indicate, can be charted from historical evidence.

I am not sure precisely what point Johnson is making when she attributes to me the view that "the worker was indelibly constructed as male," because I drew attention to some aspects of women's employment. My argument was that men and women occupied a very different status and a very different place as workers. Johnson's argument that there was a tension between the marriage and employment contracts, and that the husband and the capitalist were in competition for the wife's labour, complements rather than runs counter to my analysis in *The Sexual Contract*.

When I emphasised that class was structured by patriarchy, I was making two points. One, I was agreeing with Johnson that men, whether capitalists or workers, had a common interest as men. If men were to be "workers," women had to be excluded from paid employment or confined to certain jobs (and I would add that the state assisted too, notably in the British Poor Law and the construction of the welfare state). Two, my point was that the worker was not only a man but a breadwinner. The development of employment as the means through which able bodied men would gain their livelihood involved the transformation of wives into the economic dependents of their husbands. That is, it involved the family wage.

Much of Johnson's article is concerned with the specific question of why capitalists would go along with the demand by male workers (and some of their wives) for a family wage. The result was, as Johnson emphasises, that capitalists obtained the services of only one worker while (in principle) paying for the upkeep of two, plus any children. But this is only as puzzling as Johnson suggests if the assumption is made that the "logic" of the capitalist market can always be put into practice. Or, to make this point another way, the puzzle rests on the assumption that capitalists are always rational, in the sense that they respond to price fluctuations in order to minimise their costs and maximise their profits. Therefore, they will always contract with the workers, irrespective of who that worker is, willing to sell labour power at the lowest price.

But the labour market, as Johnson's examples illustrate, has never worked exactly as its logic demands. The labour market does not exist in the abstract, but, as Polanyi (1944) showed, is embedded in social relations including, in the case under discussion, modern patriarchal relations. Workers have not been treated as interchangeable pieces of labour power. Capitalists' preferences, that is to say, do not necessarily follow prices; they may prefer not to employ certain categories of workers even though they may be cheaper than existing employees.

In the case of women, capitalists risked costly unrest among their male workforce by employing cheaper women workers. Their reluctance to employ women would be all the greater if other capitalists did not follow suit. Moreover, as men, they also shared the view that male workers should be breadwinners and so were happy to confine any women workers to "women's work." A similar argument can be made about male workers of different races and ethnic groups who have also occupied distinct sections of the labour market.

While capitalism is not patriarchal in its "logic" — consider my discussion of the standpoint of contract in Chapter 6 of *The Sexual*

Contract — the historical development of the labour market and employment is another matter. One problem about following that "logic," and I, along with other critics, have noted, is that, when taken toward its limits, contract undermines the social conditions of its own existence.

At the end of her paper, Johnson raises some important issues, and I want to expand on her discussion. Johnson remarks that I did not pursue recent economic developments. This is true; however, in the penultimate paragraph of my book, I highlighted some changes of the past 25 years. The patriarchal structures with which I was concerned have been considerably weakened, and the heyday of the worker/breadwinner was from 1840–1970. The present, vast global restructuring of capitalism has swept away many of the old industries in advanced industrialised countries. With the rapid growth of the service sector, large numbers of jobs have opened up for women, who have also entered the professions in considerable numbers.

One of the most important developments is the reappearance of mass unemployment. Loss of jobs, combined with an increasing number of low paid or casual "junk jobs," means that the family wage is fading into history. It is not clear whether unemployment can be reduced significantly; one possibility for the beginning of the twenty-first century is a labour force divided between those with employment, whether men or women, and those unemployed or in casual work, so that a large proportion of citizens remain forced to the margins of social life. Inequality has been increasing in the West and between North and South since the 1960s, and millions of women's lives have been changed and impaired by, for example, structural adjustment policies. In the former Soviet Union and Eastern Europe, women have been losing their jobs at a faster rate than men. Women and men alike are now being drawn into a global division of labour, and assessments of which women may gain or lose and whether new forms of subordination are developing are, necessarily, enormously complex and difficult when the restructuring is still gathering pace. I believe that my argument in *The Sexual Contract* can throw light on the course of some recent developments, but to examine these issues would require another, very different, book.

NOTES

[1] My exploration of this "logic" does not, as Johnson charges, mean that I "imply" that "feminism in general necessarily presuppose(s) a

critique of capitalism." My criticism of the employment contract hinges on my analysis of the fiction of property in the person. "Feminism in general" has had to be concerned with such property owing to the long sway of coverture. The growing influence of the standpoint of contract has brought property in the person to the fore in recent controversies over, for example, prostitution, but there is no agreement among feminists about such issues or about the employment contract. I argued that there was a close connection, through contract, between the different forms of civil subordination.

DISCUSSION QUESTIONS

1. What are the similarities between Hartmann's, Johnson's, and Pateman's explanations of women's oppression? What are the differences?

2. Why is "family wage" an important aspect of feminists' explanation of women's oppression? Explain how women are oppressed because of the "family wage."

3. Why have male workers asked for a "family wage"? Why have capitalists given into their demand? Did capitalists benefit financially by granting workers a "family wage"? Why?

4. Discuss the relationship between a marriage contract and an employment contract. Can you draw a conclusion from their relationship as to whether patriarchy structured capitalism or vice versa? How?

5. To what extent have the patriarchal relations in the labour market changed in Canada? In what direction? For example, do men dominate women in all employment sectors and occupations? What is the implication for patriarchy of women being in positions of authority in female-dominated occupations?

6. Read the article "Women of the Future: Alternative Scenarios" (Exhibit 2.1). What kind of change should happen in the labour market in order for any of the alternative scenarios to materialize? In your opinion, which of the scenarios is closer to reality?

Exhibit 2.1

Women of the Future: Alternative Scenarios

Women's status in Western societies has undergone dramatic changes in the past four decades. The changing status of women is not simply a lifestyle change or a minor alteration of social patterns. It is an unprecedented transformation in our social and cultural reality. And we have only seen the tip of the iceberg.

The historical subordination of women is nearing the threshold of collapse. Social, cultural, political, and technological changes are converging to eat away the structures of male dominance. Over the next millennium, women (and men) are likely to undergo enormous changes psychologically, culturally, biologically, physiologically, and even genetically. Thus, women in the future may be considerably different from what they have been in the past.

This author is the wrong gender to describe women's experience, but he has tried to overcome that handicap by studying what women have said and written about their experience and by looking through more objective evidence such as statistical data.

While women have succeeded in making some inroads into decision-making positions in business and government, they are still expected to perform traditional functions of maintaining a household, taking care of the kids, fixing the meals, and being a good spouse. Not an easy chore. And while the image of superwoman has been featured in both advertising and women's magazines, the image has, of late, come under fire for being just what it is — superhuman — and not a normal state of activity.

To understand the potential transformational power of the women's movement, we must also understand the growing social and cultural power that comes from the least understood and most maligned part of the women's movement: the radical feminist movement.

Radical feminism was always a strand of the women's movement, even as far back as the nineteenth century, but the radical feminists parted ways with the political feminists sometime during the late 1960s and early 1970s and have continued to follow a different path. Where political feminists want to be equally represented along with men, radical feminists want a totally different power structure. Where political feminists want policies and laws that assist women and families, the radicals want a totally new spiritual paradigm.

(continued)

Exhibit 2.1 *(continued)*

Beginning with the premise that the personal is political, radical feminists argue that to adopt traditional political methods would be to play into the hands of male institutions. They seek instead to re-create their own world, their own reality, and give energy to new, female-centered institutions rather than the old male ones. One segment of radical feminists has rediscovered or re-created the pagan practices of the pre-Christian world. They now actively promote Great Goddess worship and paganism or female-oriented aspects of mainstream religions. Mythic remnants of pagan mother-goddess worship can be found in nearly all patriarchal religions: Islam, Judaism, and Christianity. The importance of the Virgin Mary in Catholicism is a classic example.

This trend in women's culture is growing and not easily swept under the rug. While it is not as visible as a female nominee to the Supreme Court, the cultural implications have the potential to be seen in nearly every aspect of life over the next century or two.

Trends Suggest Potential Scenarios

There are at least three mini-trends stemming from radical feminism that could result in dramatically different futures for women — and men. One of those has been called *lesbian separatism*, a tendency for some women to reject men entirely as some sort of evolutionary mistake. This movement has less to do with sexual orientation than with the acceptance of an entirely different paradigm, one that rejects male-influenced values.

At virtually the opposite end of the spectrum is male hatred of women, or misogyny, manifesting itself as a *widespread male backlash* against women. There are already symptoms of this throughout society, and the potential for a reversal in the status of women is a growing possibility. The pressures on men are growing and thus the chances of male backlash may grow. Just as the anti-immigrant movement in Europe has been fueled by loosened immigration laws, so, too, may violence against women grow if male-dominated society feels truly threatened.

A third mini-trend that has roots in radical feminism is the push toward a *partnership model* of relations between men and women rather than the dominance of either. While the partnership model might suggest a radical redefinition of gender roles and the division of labor in society — even the end of patriarchal religions as we know them — it argues against violence toward either gender and for the growth of healthy relationships between men and women.

(continued)

composition of an occupation and earnings: human capital theory, dual labour market theory, and reserve army theory. Each model provides a different prediction regarding the trend in the gender earnings gap and the relationship between gender composition and earnings.

In the economic literature, the most common approach in explaining the gender earnings gap is human capital theory (Becker 1964). Human capital theory assumes that there are productivity differences between female and male workers. Productivity differences, such as formal education and labour force experience, are usually associated with women's withdrawal from the labour force to bear and raise children (Mincer and Polacheck 1974). Given that women have career interruptions to assume domestic responsibilities, they tend to choose occupations which have fast returns, such as a higher starting salary (Zellner 1975), or ones where the required skills do not deteriorate quickly over time (Polacheck 1979; 1981). The tradeoff for women, however, is that these occupations yield small returns to experience (Zellner 1975). Women may also choose to enter occupations where "shortages in a preferred type of labour induce rising wage rates" (Oppenheimer 1973: 957). In this case, the rising wage rate of an occupation is an important factor for women to consider in making their labour market choices.

A basic premise of human capital theory is that the labour market is perfectly competitive. According to this model, most employers do not discriminate against women in terms of hiring or pay since this would constitute an irrational practice antithetical to the rationality of an open market (Block and Walker 1982). In practice, neoclassical economists acknowledge the imperfections of the labour market, such as employer monopsonies, labour unions, and internal labour markets, but they feel that "these do not invalidate the theory in the long run" (Denton and Hunter 1984: 6–7). Since employers are seen as rational profit maximizers who tend, for the most part, not to discriminate, human capital theory predicts that the gender earnings gap will largely disappear over time. At the same time, if women are being drawn to particular occupations by rising wage rates (relative to investment), we would expect a positive correlation between occupational earnings and female composition (Treiman and Terrell 1975: 182–83).

The economists Doeringer and Piore (1971) are the principal authors of dual labour market theory. In this approach, the growth of large firms and unions facilitates the development of internal (within firm) labour markets which are weakly linked to external (between firm) labour markets (Cain 1976). The internal labour market is viewed as the major barrier to women's employment in higher paying occupations. Unlike human capital theory, the labour market in this model is a non-competitive one.

Briefly, dual labour market theory assumes that the labour market is divided into two sectors between which there is restricted mobility. In the primary sector, the better jobs are located in large firms and unionized occupations. These jobs are more likely to be characterized by higher wages, greater promotional opportunities, good working conditions, equity and due process in the administration of work rules, and stability of employment. Jobs in the secondary sector generally have the opposing traits. In dual labour market theory, a distinction is also made between the groups of workers employed in each sector. The traits which define the primary and secondary workers reflect their working environment. Workers in the secondary sector, for example, experience greater turnover rates, higher rates of absenteeism, and harsher and more capricious work discipline than workers in the primary sector (Piore 1975: 126).

The secondary sector draws a greater proportion of the less stable working population — women, minorities, and youth. As secondary workers, women are placed in a disadvantaged structural position where earnings are relatively fixed. Viewed as having unstable employment patterns, women are not considered suitable candidates for primary sector work. Moreover, applicants for jobs in the primary sector (with the exception of entry-level jobs) are generally selected from the existing (internal) work force. Dual labour market theory assumes that the gender composition of occupations and pay rates are institutionalized by customs and traditions in the administrative and bureaucratic rules of the internal labour market (Treiman and Hartmann 1981). This theory predicts that the gender earnings gap will remain relatively stable over time. As high paying occupations are strongly organized with rigidly controlled barriers to entry (internal labour markets) which enable them to exercise considerable monopoly power (Taeuber et al. 1966: 281), we would expect a negative relationship between occupational earnings and female composition. For both human capital and dual labour market theories, the level of wages in an occupation determines the gender composition of an occupation, although the posited direction of the relationship is different.

In contrast to the economic models discussed above, reserve army theory emphasizes the historical origins of women's low wages. The analytical framework of reserve army theory is from Marx's *Capital* (1954: vol. I). For Marx, the industrial reserve is an essential structural component of his theory of capital accumulation (Mandel 1975a; Yanz and Smith 1983). The reserve army is "a lever of capitalist accumulation, nay a condition of existence of the capitalist mode of production" (Marx 1954: 592). The assumptions on which Marx makes this connection are carefully worked through in Harvey's *The Limits to Capital* (1982) and will not be elaborated upon here.

Marx specifies a long-run or secular role for the industrial reserve in addition to a temporary or cyclical one (Simeral 1978; Power 1983). As the capitalist mode of production creates conditions of labour surplus and shortage, the reserve army responds to keep the accumulation process running smoothly. During short-run fluctuations of economic stagnation and recession, the reserve army helps to absorb the unemployed, while at times of rapid economic growth and recovery, it supplies a source of labour power. Over the long run, it sustains the labour supply necessary to meet the labour demands in expanding economic sectors.

Braverman (1974) adapts the reserve army concept to the analysis of women's low wage rates in his book *Labour and Monopoly Capital.* The fastest growing industrial and occupational sectors under monopoly capitalism are found in the labour-intensive areas of the economy. The labour supply which is most available to these sectors is the female reserve. Braverman argues that wage rates in these new industries and occupations are depressed by the continuous availability of surplus workers who are then discarded as the work process is mechanized. Braverman also considers, to some extent, the impact of women's domestic role on their recruitment to certain areas of work, such as consumer goods manufacturing. He explains this particular demand for female labour as a consequence of the extension of capital into the home and the displacement of domestic work.

Reserve army theory predicts an increase over time in the gender earnings gap as women's rising and more permanent labour force participation continues to coincide with a demand for labour in the growing, labour-intensive sectors of the economy. Since women provide an available, abundant, and cheap labour supply (Connelly 1978), they will tend to depress occupational earnings (Braverman 1974; Armstrong and Armstrong 1984). We would expect, therefore, a negative relationship between female composition and earnings, although in this model, gender composition of an occupation rather than wage levels is the causal factor influencing earnings attainment.

DATA ANALYSIS 1

Estimating Changes over Time in the Gender Earnings Gap

In order to create a data set for analyzing the gender earnings gap and the relationship between gender composition of an occupation and earnings, we carried out a longitudinal analysis of occupational characteristics using census occupations matched (or linked) across the period 1931 to 1981. Aggregate occupational data will be examined first in order to assess the direction of the general trend. Then non-aggregate occupational data will be inspected as they provide more detail on the nature of changes in the gender earnings gap at the level of individual occupations. The average employment earnings for females and males are computed for two sets of occupations for 1931–1981. Both sets are based on detailed occupational categories, but in the first, the calculation is based on earnings data for all occupations in each census, while in the second, it is based on a reduced set of matched female and male occupations. The results of both occupational sets indicate that there has been a decrease over time in the gender earnings gap (see Table 8.1). The following discussion will refer to the findings for data set number 1 since this set provides more complete occupational information for each census.

The long-run trend shows a substantial reduction in the disparity of earnings between female and male workers. The gender earnings gap (average female earnings calculated as a percentage of average male earnings) decreased over the five censal periods from 39.4 to 68.9 percent. There are, however, some inter-decade fluctuations. The first fluctuation occurs between 1931 and 1941, where the gender earnings gap widened from 39.4 to 34.8 percent. A second fluctuation can be observed over the next decade. Here, the earnings gap narrowed to 45.9 percent in 1951. The gender earnings gap remained relatively stable over the 1951–1961 decade, hovering around 45 percent. Over

Table 8.1
Average Annual Occupational Earnings for Full-Time, Full-Year Female Workers and Earnings Gap, for Canada, 1931–1981 [a]

| | Data Set 1 (All Current Occupations, N Varies, 117–516) | | Data Set 2 (Matched Occupations, N=41) | |
	Average Female Earnings	Earnings Gap, %	Average Female Earnings	Earnings Gap, %
	$ 505	39.4	$ 725	58.5
	444	34.8	610	50.1
1951	1,119	45.9	1,341	56.1
1961	1,911	46.9	2,201	55.2
1971	4,272	52.3	5,553	64.3
1981	14,133	68.9	15,167	72.1

[a] Earnings gap: female earnings as a percentage of male earnings.

Source: M.N. Meltz, Manpower in Canada 1931 to 1961 (Ottawa: Queen's Printer, 1969, Table C); 1971 Census of Canada, Cat. 94–767; 1981 Census of Canada, Cat. 92–917.

the following decades, the earnings gap consistently decreased, to 52.3 percent in 1971 and to 68.9 percent in 1981.

Estimating Changes over Time in the Gender Earnings Gap for Selected Occupational Categories

In order to assess the association between gender composition and occupational earnings, several sets of occupations were examined. For this discussion, two are considered: the leading female occupations and a selected set of high-wage occupations. Leading female occupations simply refers to those occupations which contain the highest percentage of all female workers and which have comparable data across censuses (Armstrong and Armstrong 1984). For brevity, the earnings data for the twelve leading female occupations for the 1931 and 1981 censuses and a selected number of (27) leading female occupations for the 1971 and 1981 censuses will be presented.

The gender earnings gap for the twelve leading female occupations (75.4 percent) is small relative to the earnings gap for all occupations (68.9 percent) (see Tables 8.1 and 8.2). Yet, both women and men earn substantially less in the leading female occupations than they do on average for all occupations ($2,116 and $4,590, respectively). While both women and men are penalized for working in female-dominated occupations (McLaughlin 1978), the earnings differential in this case is greater for men. It is not surprising that men are not attracted to female-dominated occupations. According to Gunderson, in female-dominated occupations, we could expect less discrimination both from employers "who may consider this a job best performed by women" and from coworkers who are also predominantly female (Gunderson 1976: 122).

The occupational locations which have experienced shifts in gender composition over time suggest that women's transfers do not impact favourably on their economic returns. In the largest occupation employing women, stenographers, where the percentage of female workers has continued to climb, the gender earnings gap has been widening — a percentage increase of 17.7 over 1931–1981. In the highest paying female occupation, teaching, where there has been a pronounced reduction in female employment (notably at the secondary level), the gender earnings gap has shown a substantial decrease over the past five decades of 28.6 percentage points. In low status male occupations, such as janitors, where there has been a steady influx of female workers over 1931–1981, the earnings gap has declined considerably by 23.7 percentage points; these occupations, however, are typically characterized by low wage rates.

Table 8.2
Average Annual Earnings for Full-Time, Full-Year, Female Workers and Earnings Gap[a] for the Leading Female Occupations, for Canada, 1931 and 1981[b]

	1931		1981	
Occupation	Average Female Earnings	Earnings Gap, %	Average Female Earnings	Earnings Gap, %
Stenographers,[c]	$829	85.8	$12,816	68.1
typists, clerk typists			11,788	73.3
Teachers[d]	917	58.2	20,279	83.8
secondary			23,133	86.8
Nurses				
graduate	914	—[e]	18,040	95.4
practical	421	59.5	13,711	88.3
Agricultural workers	235	72.0	6,660	50.0
Telephone operators	682	62.6	11,770	70.4
Waiters, waitresses	378	52.6	7,686	69.4
Labourers	375	76.8	11,337	68.8
Cleaners, dyers, launderers	448	58.4	10,016	77.7
Cooks	447	64.6	9,503	73.4
Barbers, hairdressers, manicurists	595	70.7	9,863	70.8
Charworkers, cleaners, janitors	391	45.6	9,638	69.3
Average total earnings	519	63.3	1,017	75.4

[a]   Earnings gap: female earnings as a percentage of male earnings.
[b]   Occupations are rank-ordered by the proportion of female workers represented in a given category, e.g., female concentration, using the 1931 census as its reference.
[c]   For the 1931 to 1961 censuses, the stenographers category combined stenographers, typists, and clerk typists; for the 1971 and 1981 censuses, this category was split into two unit groups: stenographers; and typists and clerk-typists.
[d]   For the 1931 to 1961 censuses, the school teachers category combined elementary and kindergarten teachers and secondary school teachers; for the 1971 and 1981 censuses, this category was split into two groups: elementary and kindergarten teachers; and secondary school teachers.
[e]   No males employed in this category.

Source: M.N. Meltz, *Manpower in Canada 1931 to 1961* (Ottawa: Queen's Printer, 1969: Table C); *1971 Census of Canada*, Cat. 94–767; *1981 Census of Canada*, Cat. 92–917.

The more detailed set of leading female occupations for 1971–1981 provides further evidence of female and male earnings inequality. Marked earnings disparities are found, for example, in two areas of work — sales and service — where there is a high and growing demand for female labour (see Table 8.3). In 1981, for sales, the third largest occupation employing women, the earnings gaps was 55 percent. Among the service occupations, two categories, which are virtually

Table 8.3
Average Annual Earnings for Full-Time, Full-Year, Female Workers and Earnings Gap[a] for the Leading Female Occupations, for Canada, 1971 and 1981[b]

Occupation	1971		1981	
	Average Female Earnings	Earnings Gap, %	Average Female Earnings	Earnings Gap, %
Sales clerks, commodities	$3,348	53.4	9,667	55.0
Personal service occupations, n.e.c.	2,435	52.2	6,795	58.3
Child-care occupations	1,878	43.9	5,683	50.0

[a] Earnings gap: female earnings as a percentage of male earnings
[b] Occupations are rank-ordered by the proportion of female workers represented in a given category, e.g., female concentration, using the 1971 census as its reference.

Source: 1971 Census of Canada, Cat. 94–767; 1981 Census of Canada, Cat. 92–917.

dominated by women, are particularly noteworthy. In personal service occupations, n.e.c. (not elsewhere classified), for 1981, the earnings gap was 58.3 percent. The largest differential in female and male earnings was in the service occupation of child-care. Here, women earned half of the average male earnings in 1981.

An examination of the leading female occupations demonstrates that women continue to enter occupations where they are already over-represented, such as secretaries and stenographers, cooks, hairdressers, and janitors. This trend will likely continue as employment growth is expected to rise in these occupations in the 1990s (Krahn and Lowe 1988). There is very little evidence of male entry to these occupations except in one of the two female professions — school teaching. Boulet and Lavallée (1984) report that during the 1970s, less than 7 percent of the increase in the male labour force occurred in occupations that were female-dominated in 1971. Rosenfeld (1983) suggests that employers might discourage men from entering typical female jobs, presumably to keep wage rates low in these occupations. As for the higher paying female occupations, often referred to as the "lower" or semi-professions (Etzioni 1969), Parkin claims that the boundaries to these occupations are easier for women to penetrate because they generally have not been very attractive to men and as a consequence, lack the exclusionary barriers and practices associated with the more establish professions (Parkin 1979b: 104).

Women are concentrated in a limited number of occupations, and their occupational distributions denote little diversification over time

(Nakamura et al. 1979a; 1979b; Nakamura and Nakamura 1981; 1985). Boulet and Lavallée (1984) report that women accounted for 15.9 percent of male-dominated occupations in 1971 and 22.7 percent in 1981. They predict that "even if every woman entering the labour force over the next 20 years were to choose a male occupation, the overall representation in these occupations would only reach 35 percent at best" (Boulet and Lavallée 1984: 17). The examination of the leading female occupations over time suggests further that this movement is to low wage male occupations in the service and trade sectors and to primary jobs in agriculture. It may be that women are "losing ground in occupations where the earnings gap is small and gaining where the earnings gap is large" (Gunderson 1976: 122).

In order to evaluate the gains that women have made in higher paying occupations, their representation is examined for several male professions and managerial categories. These occupations are displayed in Table 8.4. Two of the highest paying male professions, law and medicine, have experienced notable growth in female membership. Yet, women earned considerably less than men in these occupations. In law, women earned 58.3 percent of the average male earnings in 1981 — a percentage decrease in the earnings gap of 10.6 from 1971. In medicine, women earned 60.3 percent of the average male earnings in 1981 — a percentage decrease in the earnings gap of 8.6 from 1971. While this represents some improvement, the disparities are considerable in terms of absolute dollars. Taking lawyers as an example, men earned on average $17,055 more than women in 1981. Regarding the managerial occupations, two of the highest paying categories for women were in financial management ($18,469) and in sales and advertising ($16,483). However, women were more highly represented in the lower paying management categories such as food and beverage preparation ($11,356) and apparel and furnishing service ($11,163).

These results suggest that women do not reap the expected benefits of working in a high wage occupation. Krahn and Lowe (1988) substantiate this finding in an examination of female and male earnings for the fifteen highest paying occupations for males in 1980. For these occupations, the gender earnings gap was larger among the highest paying occupations such as sales and security trading (39 percent) and management (mines and oil wells — 47.7 percent) and smaller among the lower paying occupations in the education field such as university teaching (74.0 percent) (Krahn and Lowe 1988: 135–37).

In summary, the analysis of aggregate occupational data shows a narrowing of the gender earnings gap over 1931–1981, although an earnings differential of 68.9 percent remains. Despite this finding, the persistence of a sizable earnings gap for the past 50 years cannot be explained by human capital theory. An inspection of non-aggregate

Table 8.4
Average Annual Earnings for Full-Time, Full-Year, Female
Workers in Selected High Wage Male Occupations and
Earnings Gap,[a] for Canada, 1971 and 1981[b]

	1971		1981	
Occupation	Average Female Earnings	Earnings Gap, %	Average Female Earnings	Earnings Gap, %
Professions				
Lawyers, notaries	$10,469	47.7	$23,935	58.3
Physicians, surgeons	14,965	51.7	36,115	60.3
Dentists	13,873	57.9	40,510	69.6
Actuaries, statisticians	7,319	63.3	20,337	71.4
Professors, college principals	11,402	72.5	26,585	73.9
Management				
Sales and advertising management	7,427	42.2	16,483	54.9
Financial management	7,582	46.7	18,469	61.4
Supervisors: food and beverage preparation	4,313	60.6	11,356	67.4
Supervisors: apparel and furnishing	4,114	56.1	11,163	67.8

[a] Earnings gap: female earnings as a percentage of male earnings.
[b] The professional and managerial categories are rank-ordered by the size of the gender earnings gap.

Source: 1971 Census of Canada, Cat. 94–767; 1981 Census of Canada, Cat. 92–917.

occupational data reveals, moreover, that the general trend obscures gender differences at a more detailed level of analysis. The economic rewards of working in predominantly female occupations are low for both women and men, particularly for women employed in the "growth" occupations of sales and service. This finding is consistent with reserve army theory. Finally, the discrepancy between female and male earnings was significantly greater in the high wage (male) occupations than in the leading female occupations. This exclusion from higher paying occupations may reflect the duality of the labour market — a market that confines women for the most part to secondary, low paying occupations.

DISCUSSION AND CONCLUSION

The results of this study have important implications for women's earning potential in the 1990s. It is important then that we consider recent

projections of women's labour force participation and the areas of expected employment growth over the next decade. Women are expected to
constitute around one-half of all workers and to reach a female labour
force participation rate of 75 percent by the year 2000 (Neiman 1984).
The increased participation of women, particularly married women,
underscores the economic necessity of a dual income. Just over one-
half of all husband–wife families were dual earners in 1977, while more
than two-thirds were dual earners in 1987. The average income of dual
earner families was roughly $10,000 higher than a family where the
husband was sole earner (Statistics Canada 1987: 8). Women with
preschool children are a growing segment of the labour force population.
In 1985, around 53.9 percent of all mothers with children under three
years of age were in the labour force (Statistics Canada 1986: 95). With
the increased participation of women with preschool children, any legislation or policy directed toward reducing the gender earnings gap is
severely limited without addressing the issue of child-care.

The earnings data for the 1980s and the projection of demand for
female labour in the 1990s suggest that women will see little, if any,
improvement in their earnings attainment in the 1990s. They also point
to the failure of employment legislation and government policies in
reducing the gender earnings gap. The paper will conclude therefore
with a critique of current laws and policies governing their enforcement.

Since 1918, equal pay for equal work has been a policy of the federal government. It was legislated at the federal level in 1956 in the
form of the Female Employees Equal Pay Act, although this Act was
revoked and equal pay provisions were consolidated in the Canada
Labour Code in 1956 (Neiman 1984). Legislation specifically enacting
"equal pay for equal work" provisions is found in all jurisdictions in
Canada (*Canadian Labour Law Reporter* 1989).

Equal pay legislation has evolved through four distinct phases:

1. equal pay for equal (identical) work,
2. equal pay for similar or substantially similar work,
3. equal pay for work of equal value, and
4. proactive pay equity (*Canadian Labour Law Reporter* 1989).

In the development from phase one to phase two, the application of
equal pay legislation was broadened to a certain extent. In phase one,
equal pay for equal work (waitress and waiter) is based on the principle that female and male employees are to be paid the same wage for
doing identical work. In the second phase, the principle underlying
the legislation is that female and male employees are to be paid the
same wage if they perform similar or substantially similar work (female
cleaners and male janitors) when measured in terms of the job, duties,
responsibilities, or services performed in the same establishment

(*Canadian Labour Law Reporter* 1989). This definition continued to be problematic, however, since it was "held that relatively slight variation in duties and services permitted the employer to use different wage rates for employees" (Arthurs et al. 1988: 97).

The concept of equal pay for work of equal value differs radically from the concepts of equal pay for equal work or substantially similar work as it does not compare work but the value of work (*Canadian Labour Law Reporter* 1989). When the Canadian Human Rights Act went into force in 1977, the antidiscrimination provisions of the Canada Labour Code were repealed. At the same time, the equal pay provisions for doing the same or similar work were also repealed and a new clause was substituted which endorsed the principle of equal value (Neiman 1984). The Canadian Human Rights Commission (CHRC) and Labour Canada are the authorized bodies to administer antidiscrimination and fair employment practices legislation at the federal level. Under the Canadian Human Rights Act, it is a discriminatory practice for an employer to establish or maintain differences in wages between female and male workers in the same establishment if the work being performed is of equal value. The criterion to be applied is a composite of skill, effort, responsibility, and working conditions (*Canadian Labour Law Reporter* 1989). This allows the employer to compare positions which are dissimilar, such as maintenance fitter and company nurse, and to assess their relative worth within the company. Discrimination in wage rates, however, is still permitted when the employer can justify differences in pay between jobs of equal value on "reasonable" grounds which include a seniority or merit system, a payment by quantity system, and where the discrimination is not found to be based on the criterion of sex (Arthurs et al. 1988).

Equal value legislation, which is not proactive in its enforcement, has a number of limitations. One limiting factor is its complaints system of enforcement which assumes that violations are the exception and not the rule, thereby placing the onus on disadvantaged individuals to trigger enforcement of the legislation's general prohibitions (*Canadian Labour Law Reporter* 1989). Another limitation concerns the permitted comparisons under the legislation which requires that the complaining employees must show that they work for the same employer as the comparison group (Arthurs et al. 1988). Finally, the investigation of complaints tends to emphasize education and conciliation rather than active enforcement and monitoring of employers. Labour Canada, for example, feels that it is more desirable if employers implement equal pay for work of equal value on their own initiative rather than in response to complaints (Labour Canada 1987). Field officers of Labour Canada, who work directly with employers, try to help them "understand" and identify pay discrimination in their establishments and "recommend" ways to correct the situation (Labour Canada 1987). The ineffectiveness of equal value legislation is reflected in the number of resolved cases. By 1984, the CHRC had received only 68 complaints of which 30 were dismissed or withdrawn and eighteen were settled (Arthurs et al. 1988: 214). The federal government and its agencies have been extremely passive in the enforcement of equal value legislation. For example, neither the CHRC nor Labour Canada, both of which have the power to initiate complaints, had done so in the first eight years (Neiman 1984; Arthurs et al. 1988).

Proactive pay equity legislation differs from the preceding phases as it introduces a regulatory model of enforcement. This is an improvement over the complaints system of enforcement as it assumes that "wage discrimination is systemic and pervasive throughout the economy" (*Canadian Labour Law Reporter* 1989: 812). Pay equity legislation places an obligation on employers to evaluate their pay practices and to ensure that they comply with the legislation. In 1985, Manitoba was the first jurisdiction in Canada to pass proactive pay equity legislation. Since then, four provinces have proclaimed proactive legislation in varying degrees of application (Ontario, Nova Scotia, Prince Edward Island, and New Brunswick). While the CHRC has recommended that the federal government amend the Canadian Human Rights Act to incorporate a proactive pay equity approach, the federal government has not moved from its complaint-based model (Manitoba Labour 1989).

One important limitation in pay equity (and equal value) legislation is that comparisons are to be made within one employer's establishment. For some occupations, there are no male/female comparison groups, and in these cases, the legislation has no application. In other occupations, women will find it difficult to identify a comparable male category in their establishment (Arthurs et al. 1988). Another limitation, specific to proactive pay equity legislation, is that it is narrow in terms of jurisdiction. Pay equity laws typically cover only the public sector. Ontario is one exception, having proclaimed pay equity legislation in both the public and private sectors in 1988. Ontario's legislation is restrictive, nonetheless, as it applies to all private sector employers except those with fewer than ten employees. The Ontario Pay Equity Commission has observed that one-half of the 1.7 million women within its jurisdictions would not be entitled to benefits. The Ontario Commission found that the jobs most commonly found outside the legislation were traditional female jobs, notably those in child and health care, libraries, clothing manufacture, retail sales, and tourism (*Canadian Human Rights Advocate* 1989c).

Another important form of legislation is the right of equal opportunity in employment which is contained in the federal and provincial Human Rights Acts. It prohibits discriminatory practices on the part of employers, trade unions, employer or employee associations, and employment agencies. Discriminatory practices include refusal to employ, advance, or promote an employee on the grounds prohibited by the Human Rights Code. The prohibited grounds are fundamentally the same in all jurisdictions: sex, race, national/ethnic/place of origin, colour, religion/creed, marital status, and physical disability (*Canadian Labour Law Reporter* 1989).

Sex-based employment discrimination includes both unequal pay and unequal opportunity (Neiman 1984: 65). Despite the federal government's intentions to remedy these sources of discrimination, its commitment has faltered. This is reflected both at the federal (Lacoste 1989) and provincial levels (Gordon 1987).

Evidence from the *Brief Presented to the Task Force on Barriers to Women in the Public Service of Canada* (Lacoste 1989) demonstrates that women face many barriers to career advancement. Four examples which clearly document women's barriers to equality of opportunity in the public service are:

1. the percentage of women in the scientific and professional category of the federal public sector has not changed since 1971 (24 percent in 1971 and 1988);
2. the percentage of women in predominantly male professions in the federal public service is lower (with the exception of law) than in the Canadian labour force as a whole;
3. women are concentrated at the lower levels of the scientific and professional category despite having similar levels of experience and equal or higher levels of education as compared to their male colleagues;
4. women in the federal public service are in a less favourable position than men in relation to promotions, transfers, resignations, layoffs, and term positions (Lacoste 1989).

The report observes that "while equality exists in principle, evidence suggests that women are not equals in the federal public service" (Lacoste 1989: 1).

Finally, we will examine the federal Employment Equity Act which was proclaimed in 1986. This legislation was implemented to: (1) achieve equality in the workplace so that no person shall be denied employment opportunities or benefits for reasons unrelated to ability; and (2) ameliorate the conditions of disadvantage in employment experienced by women, aboriginal peoples, persons with disabilities, and visible minorities (*Canadian Labour Law Reporter* 1989: 637). While equal value legislation attempts to address women's earnings inequality by raising wage rates to comparable male-dominated occupations, it does not address the pervasive problem of women's ghettoized work.

Employment equity legislation is designed to deal with this problem. Federally regulated employers and Crown corporations (with at least one hundred full- or part-time employees) are required to "eliminate employment practices creating barriers and to take positive steps to ensure that the designated groups receive a proportionate degree of representation" (*Canadian Labour Law Reporter* 1989: 637). Employers are obliged to file reports with the Minister of Employment and Immigration. The reports are to include work force statistics on such factors as the number of persons in the designated groups employed, position held by employees, and salaries.

The first federal review by the CHRC was based on nineteen major employers which covered almost one-half of nearly one million employees under the federal program of employment equity. The CHRC found that the four designated groups were underrepresented in the work forces of eleven employers (*Canadian Human Rights Advocate* 1989a: 1). Furthermore, the federal review indicates that the legislation has had little impact on women's wage rates. For example, in the banking sector in Canada, for the female majority of 72.5 percent, women's average annual salary was 55.9 percent of the average male salary; and only 3 percent of the women but 44 percent of the men earned more than $40,000 a year (*Canadian Human Rights Advocate* 1989a: 7).

The basic approach for ensuring compliance is to use the employment equity data to identify employers who have discriminatory policies against one of the four groups and "then seek meetings to encourage voluntary compliance" (*Canadian Human Rights Advocate* 1988: 130). It has been this approach which has weakened the enforcement of the Employment Equity Act. Initially, the Mulroney government stated that enforcement would come through the CHRC's power to initiate "complaints." This shift in enforcement was largely a consequence of the pressure from management. Employers were "far more aggressive and successful" (than community groups or representatives of the four groups covered in the legislation) "in influencing policy" (*Canadian Human Rights Advocate* 1988: 12). The increasing pro-management trend has been noted in other Canadian Human Rights decisions (*Canadian Human Rights Advocate* 1989b: 5).

The Chief Commissioner of the CHRC believes that the voluntary approach is the "quickest way to get the job done," although he states that "we will not hesitate for a moment to initiate complaints when that is the only way to get action" (*Canadian Human Rights Advocate* 1988: 12). Yet, the CHRC has only initiated a "handful" of complaints since it was established in 1978 (*Canadian Human Rights Advocate* 1988: 12). Despite employment equity legislation, a study of Canadian employers shows that they are slow in adopting effective affirmative action programs (Jain and Hackett, cited in *Canadian Human Rights Advocate* 1989d: 12) and will undoubtedly resist compliance unless there is more rigorous enforcement and stronger penalties for violation.

In conclusion, it is clear from this review that current legislation has been ineffective in bringing about significant changes in women's wage rates. Until the federal and provincial governments recognize women as an integral part of the primary work force (Neiman 1984), the prognosis for Canadian women in the 1990s is not a favourable one.

Gender Differences in Earnings: A Comment
Alice Nakamura

INTRODUCTION

Catherine Fillmore's paper, "Gender Differences in Earnings: A Re-Analysis and Prognosis for Canadian Women," is a mixture of useful descriptive information on earnings in Canada for 1931–1981; a poorly conceived and executed attempt to test three economic theories of labour market behaviour; and a useful review of the development of equal pay legislation in Canada. It is commendable when a sociologist tries, as Fillmore obviously has, to understand the research of economists. Nevertheless, it would be unfortunate if other sociologists came to accept the ways in which Fillmore uses and attempts to differentiate the economic theories examined in her paper.

THE ECONOMICS OF LABOUR MARKETS

The problem of concern in Fillmore's paper is long-standing gender differences in earnings. Fillmore explores three bodies of economic theory in seeking to understand this problem: human capital theory, dual labour market theory, and reserve army theory. My remarks concerning Fillmore's analysis of these labour market theories deal solely with the adequacy of the hypotheses she tests. This is the fundamental difficulty.

HUMAN CAPITAL THEORY

It is instructive to compare Fillmore's assertions about human capital theory with the views of an important contributor to the literature on human capital theory, Sherwin Rosen. In his article in *The New Palgrave: A Dictionary of Economics*, Rosen provides an overview of human capital theory and its development and describes the application of human capital theory to the analysis of selected problems, including the gender earnings gap. Rosen writes:

> A final important recent development proceeds on somewhat more conventional theoretical grounds. It addresses the role of human capital in observed wage differences between men and women.... The main fact to be explained is that women earn less than men, even after adjusting for differences in occupational status and hours worked. Labour market discrimination against women is one possible interpretation. However, there may be more subtle forces at work.... The value of an investment increases with its rate of utilization. Compare two persons: one who expects to utilize an acquired skill very intensively and one expects to utilize it less intensively. Suppose further that the costs of acquiring the skill are approximately independent of its subsequent utilization. Then the rate of return on investment is larger for the intensive user and that person will tend to invest more.... In so far as married women play dual roles in the market and in the household, there is a tendency to invest less in labour market skills and more in non-market skills. The opposite is true of men, given prevailing marriage institutions. (Rosen 1987: 689)

Note that, according to Rosen, human capital theory posits productivity differences among individuals who have made different levels of job-related skills, not between female and male workers per se. This result from human capital theory and supporting empirical research has helped spur the development and adoption of public policies to eliminate both formal and informal gender barriers to training programs and public campaigns to make girls and young women more aware of the probable earnings consequences of schooling and other training choices.

Both Fillmore and Rosen note that human capital theory attributes gender differences in job-related training and experience to the household activities of women. However, Fillmore does not tie this behaviour in with the utility maximization perspective on family decision making postulated in human capital theory. Certain aspects of public policy have been motivated, in part, by this theorized tie-in. For instance, one argument in favour of expanding day care facilities is that this would allow women to have and plan for careers with less time out for children.

Fillmore also claims that "human capital theory predicts that the gender earnings gap will largely disappear over time" (p. 4 [p. 165 in this book]). In fact, however, human capital theory only predicts, as Rosen notes, that discrimination based on gender (or other factors not directly related to productivity) will largely disappear as a result of competitive forces. (Discrimination is defined as pay or hiring differences that are not justified by productivity differences.) Many human capital advocates, including Rosen, see gender productivity differences as persisting for as long as traditional practices persist concerning the division of labour in families.

A final point of difference concerns the implications (or lack thereof) of human capital theory for the relationship between occupation-specific earnings and the proportion of workers who are female. Fillmore claims that human capital theory implies that women will be "drawn to particular occupations by rising wage rates (relative to investment)" and hence that there will be a "positive correlation between occupational earnings and female composition" (p. 4 [p. 165 in this book]).

In his Palgrave review article, Rosen notes that "a central finding in this literature is that current market conditions have large effects on occupational choice" (Rosen 1987: 687). Suppose it were true that both male and female labour force participants were drawn toward occupations with rising wage rates. According to human capital theory, women would be expected to be less well prepared, on average, to compete for the desired jobs. It seems clear, therefore, that human capital theory does *not* imply "a positive correlation between occupational earnings and female composition," as Fillmore asserts. Failure to find evidence in support of this hypothesis is *not* a rejection of human capital theory, whatever the merits may be of this theory.

DUAL LABOUR MARKET THEORY

Dual labour market theory has made an important contribution to mainstream economics and the formulation of public policies by reminding economists of the importance of institutions and habits often ignored in simplified theories. Institutions and habits may persist beyond the timer period or scope within which these practices could be justified on economic or social grounds. These practices may become enshrined in hiring and admissions procedures and regulations, or vested interest groups may seek to protect practices they benefit from through political and other power structures.

Higher wages and better conditions may be offered in the primary sector in order to hold workers with relatively scarce abilities or training or in whom employers have made (or plan to make) substantial special-ized training investments. Fillmore notes that women have often been perceived to be too loosely committed to the workforce to be good prospects for jobs in the primary sector. Many economists would agree that this is an appropriate description of a dual labour market outlook. This does not imply, however, that higher earnings or wage rates in an occupation *lead* to the formation of barriers to keep out women (though this sort of behaviour is not ruled out). Thus the validity of dual labour market theory cannot be assessed, as Fillmore attempts to do, by testing whether the casual path from average earnings to percentage female is neg-ative. Nor can dual labour market theory be differentiated from human capital theory by the sign of this path since, as already noted, human capital theory does not provide a clear sign prediction for this path.

RESERVE ARMY THEORY

The key implication which Fillmore draws from reserve army theory is that "Since women provide an available, abundant and cheap labour supply ..., they will tend to depress occupational earnings.... We would expect, therefore, a negative relationship between female composition and earnings" (p. 7 [p. 167 in this book]). When she comes to specifying hypotheses, Fillmore asserts that the reserve army theory predicts a negative sign for the relationship between the average earnings and the percentage female in occupations, as she claims is also the case for dual labour market theory, but that the causal path "is from percentage female to average earnings" instead of the other way around.

In the economics literature, the *direction* of causation is usually *asserted* as an implication of economic theory or on other logical grounds. The magnitudes of hypothesized effects are then estimated sub-ject to the specified model, with the direction(s) of causation included in the maintained hypothesis. This practice persists, in part at least, because of the unsatisfactory nature of statistical tests for the direc-tion of causation. This is a difficult econometric problem. If the hypotheses Fillmore offers were the only, or the best, way of testing the validity of reserve army theory or of comparing it with the dual labour market and human capital theories, the prospects for credibly dif-ferentiating these theories would be poor.

EVIDENCE VERSUS POLICY CONCLUSIONS

The policy conclusions Fillmore draws are poorly related to her empir-ical findings. Fillmore summarizes her policy views as follows:

In conclusion, it is clear from this review that current legislation has been ineffective in bringing about significant changes in women's wage rates. Until the federal and provincial governments recognize women as an integral part of the primary labour force, the prognosis for Canadian women in the 1990s is not a favourable one. (Fillmore 1990: 295 [p. 179 in this book])

Lack of enforcement of equal pay legislation in Canada is what she singles out as a key reason for the claimed ineffectiveness of this legislation.

At several points in the paper, Fillmore juxtaposes her remarks about the ineffectiveness of Canadian equal pay legislation with assertions that the gender earnings gap cannot be fully accounted for by any of the leading economic theories of labour market behaviour. In particular, she emphasizes that the gender earnings gap cannot be fully explained by variables such as years of schooling, age, and marital status that economists often use as proxies for human capital and other productivity-related attributes of workers.

It is important to note, however, that understanding the causal basis of a problem is a helpful — but not a necessary — precondition for having effective public policies for dealing with the problem. All available evidence, including Fillmore's, shows that the gender earnings gap did decrease substantially from 1971 to 1981, both in aggregate and for most occupations. This is true whether the 1971–1981 changes are viewed relative to the size of the gap in 1971 or in a longer historical context. Moreover, women experienced substantial gains in earnings. (As Fillmore's analysis makes clear, occupation-specific improvements in the ratio of female to male earnings do not necessarily imply a rise in earnings for the average working woman.) No one has presented conclusive evidence that the lessening of the gender earnings gap since 1941, and particularly since 1971, was *caused* by the equal pay legislation enacted in Canada; but the timing is suggestive. Furthermore, there is no evidence in Fillmore's paper demonstrating that the legislation was *not* a causal factor.

One final observation on Fillmore's descriptive statistics concerns the role of work experience. Workers with more experience generally have higher earnings. Occupations that have traditionally been male dominated, and where the proportion of workers who are women has been rising, are precisely those where female workers are likely to be at the greatest disadvantage relative to male workers in terms of experience. Without controlling for work experience, there is no way of concluding that equally experienced (and qualified) women are being paid poorly compared with men.

Fillmore refers to Canadian studies of the gender earnings gap, such as Gunderson's, which do control for "labour force experience." However, information on years of work experience has *never* been collected in the Canadian censuses of population for those for whom earnings data are available. What is termed "experience" in the cited empirical studies is actually a "potential experience" variable computed as age minus years of schooling minus 6, where 6 is subtracted to allow for the (nonworking) years prior to grade one. Needless to say, such an experience variable does *not* control for differences between women and men in actual work experience. Moreover, even "potential experience" is not controlled for in the figures Fillmore presents.

Fillmore might still be correct in asserting that more vigorous enforcement of the provisions of Canada's equal pay legislation would have resulted in more rapid closure of the gender earnings gap and may be crucial in achieving progress on this problem in the 1990s. However, she offers no empirical *evidence* relating the level of enforcement, or any other aspect of equal pay legislation, to the rate of change in the ratio of female to male earnings. It is important to be clear about which generalizations and recommendations are, and which are not, supported by empirical evidence.

DISCUSSION QUESTIONS

1. What is the most recent gender earnings gap ratio in Canada? In what occupations do you think the gender earnings gap is lowest?

2. Does female composition of an occupation effect the gender earnings gap? Why?

3. What hypothesis can you deduce from the reserve army of labour theory? What about the dual labour market theory? Why? What hypotheses does Fillmore's study support? Give examples. Does Fillmore correctly hypothesize based on the human capital theory, reserve army of labour thesis, or dual labour market thesis? Why? If she is incorrect, what should be the correct hypotheses?

4. What is the key policy implication of Fillmore's findings? Are Fillmore's policy suggestions related to her empirical evidence? How?

5. In your opinion, what can be done to reduce the gender earnings gap? What has been done to reduce the gender earnings gap?

6. Read the article "Filling a Non-Existent Wage Gap" (Exhibit 2.2). Do you agree with Walter Block that discrimination is not the source of the gender wage gap? Why?

Exhibit 2.2

Filling a Non-Existent Gap

Contemporary feminism has more than its share of enduring myths. One of the most powerful is the notion that sex-based differences in earnings stem from patriarchal discrimination against women in the marketplace. Two weeks ago, Women's Equality Minister Sue Hammell cited this "gender wage gap" myth while threatening state intervention into the private marketplace. If the current disparity between male and female earnings doesn't shrink, Ms. Hammell warned, the NDP government will consider mandating private-sector "pay equity" programs.

Like other feminist ideologues, Ms. Hammell ignored a pertinent point: Statistical analysis doesn't support the existence of any anti-female earning bias. But as her comments confirm, the provincial New Democrats aren't letting the absence of empirical evidence interfere with their pursuit of politically correct social objectives.

Ms. Hammell's pay equity musings were prompted by last month's release of 1994 income data. Statistics Canada reported that Canadian males had a median income of $25,400 that year, compared to $15,800 for women. That meant the median female income was 62% of the comparable male figure. While median earnings for B.C. men and women both exceeded the national average, at $27,700 and $16,300 respectively, the percentage difference was even wider; the female median was only 59% of the male median.

If that discrepancy persists, Ms. Hammell told the *Vancouver Sun*, the NDP might pass legislation forcing private-sector companies to eradicate the wage differential. Nothing is currently "being planned or prepared," she said, but "we want to close the gap and we will work on all fronts."

Economist Walter Block, editor of *Discrimination, Affirmative Action, and Equal Opportunity*, counters that Ms. Hammell's underlying premise is unsound. There is no income disparity arising from discrimination against women, he insists. The real determinant of the difference is marriage. Prof. Block says that an analysis of Statistics Canada's own income data conducted by the Fraser Institute several years ago confirmed that fact. Comparison of never-married men and women revealed that they had virtually identical incomes, as would be expected if the income differential was due not to sex but rather to marital status. Prof. Block says this "marriage gap" merely reflects the fact that most couples choose to adopt different roles. Women assume more of the housekeeping and

(continued)

Exhibit 2.2 *(continued)*

childrearing duties, particularly when kids are young. As a result, they tend to be absent for long periods of time from the workplace, a fact that permanently suppresses average incomes because experience is a powerful determinant of earning capacity.

So cherished is the gender-wage-gap myth, however, that Statistics Canada's analysts rejected the Fraser Institute's number-crunching of its own data, Prof. Block recalls. But by 1994, the evidence was too compelling for the federal agency to deny. An October 1994 Statscan study reported that hourly earnings among the most recently graduated females in the study actually slightly exceeded those of men.

Given these findings, Prof. Block jokingly suggests feminists like Ms. Hammell should shift their sights. "Marriage is the causal agent," he notes. "So let's ban marriage."

Strident feminists might privately support that prescription, but the NDP has settled for less contentious measures. NDPers have been staunch backers of pay equity, which many people mistakenly assume means equal pay for men and women who perform the same work. Since widespread discrimination of that sort is notably difficult to document, feminists instead define pay equity as "equal pay for work of equal value." That definition allows them to arbitrarily assert that female-dominated job sectors, such as clerical work, should be regarded as having equal value with unrelated but higher-paid male-dominated fields.

In pursuit of the "equal pay for work of equal value" concept, the New Democrats have furthered the implementation of a public-sector pay equity program implemented by their Socred predecessors. That initiative has resulted in female-dominated bureaucratic classifications receiving bonuses.

Economists say that while such bonuses impose an additional burden to taxpayers, the economic damage is somewhat mitigated by the fact that government operations are relatively immune to market discipline. Much more serious dislocations would inevitably ensue should the province carry through on Ms. Hammell's threat to foist pay equity on the private sector, Prof. Block warns.

Ironically, the biggest effect may be to boost female unemployment. If forced to pay women working in so-called "pink ghetto" jobs more than they are worth, employers will have no choice but to discard them. "It's identical to the deleterious effect of minimum-wage laws," Prof. Block says. "If you artificially boost anyone's wage, you render them less employable."

(continued)

Exhibit 2.2 *(continued)*

Indeed, the fact that male and female rates of unemployment have remained roughly equal in Canada is further proof that women haven't been discriminated against, Prof. Block adds. If their wages had been unfairly suppressed, they would have displaced higher-priced men.

The absence of valid economic arguments hasn't deterred feminist-minded Canadian governments, however. Ontario was the first jurisdiction in North America to pass private-sector pay-equity legislation, and Saskatchewan's NDP government is considering its own initiative. As well, the Parti Québécois plans to introduce pay-equity legislation this fall. Quebec business spokesmen estimate that the legislation will drive up provincial wage costs by between $2 billion and $5 billion annually, precipitating a massive flight of investment and jobs.

The economic damage will be worsened, Quebec employers warn, by the fact that the Ontario Conservative government of Mike Harris has already begun eliminating the pay-equity package it inherited when it succeeded the NDP last year.

Source: Tom McFeely, "Filling a Non-Existent Gap," *British Columbia Report*, August 5, 1996, p. 8. Reprinted by permission.

SEXUAL VIOLENCE

The Incidence and Prevalence of Woman Abuse in Canadian University and College Dating Relationships
Walter DeKeseredy and Katharine Kelly

Research shows that men who physically assault their spouses do so because their partners have violated, or are perceived as violating, the ideals of familial patriarchy (Dobash and Dobash 1979; Smith 1990a, 1993). According to Smith (1990a), relevant themes of this ideology are an insistence upon womens' obedience, respect, loyalty, dependency, sexual access, and sexual fidelity. Some scholars contend that many men in college and university dating relationships also espouse a set of attitudes and beliefs supportive of familial patriarchy (DiIorio 1989; Lamanna and Reidman 1985; Lanar and Thompson 1982). When their partners either reject or fail to live up to these "ideals" and "expectations" (Smith 1990a), men experience stress which motivates them to abuse women for the purpose of maintaining their dominance and control (DeKeseredy 1988; DeKeseredy and Schwartz 1993). While this feminist account of courtship abuse has not yet been directly tested, it is a promising interpretation of the large body of survey data which demonstrate that male-to-female physical, sexual, and psychological assaults are endemic to American university and college dating relationships.

This study attempts to fill a major research gap by providing estimates of the incidence and prevalence of woman abuse in Canadian university/college dating relationships which are derived from the first national representative sample survey of men and women. Incidence refers here to the percentage of women who stated that they were abused and the percentage of men who indicated that they were abusive in the past twelve months. Prevalence is, since they left high school, the percentage of men who reported having been abusive and the percentage of women who indicated having been abused.

METHOD

[The sample consists of 3142 people, including 1835 women and 1307 men representative of undergraduate and community college students in Canada.]

Abuse Measures

Any intentional physical, sexual, or psychological assault on a female by a male dating partner was defined as woman abuse. Following Okun (1986) and DeKeseredy and Hinch (1991), the term abuse was chosen over terms such as "battering" and "violence" because its connotation addresses the fact that women are victims of a wide range of assaultive behaviours in a variety of social contexts. Indeed, a large body of research shows that male-to-female victimization in intimate relationships is "multidimensional in nature" (DeKeseredy and Hinch 1991).

To measure psychological and physical abuse, a modified version of Straus and Gelles' (1986) rendition of the Conflict Tactics Scale (CTS) was used. The CTS consists of at least 18 items and measures three different ways of handling interpersonal conflict in intimate relationships: reasoning, verbal aggression, and physical violence. The items are categorized on a continuum with the first ten describing non-violent tactics and the last eight describing violent strategies.

Two new items were added to the CTS. They were employed by Statistics Canada in their pretest for a national Canadian telephone study on violence against women. These measures are: "put her (you) down in front of family" and "accused her (you) of having affairs or flirting with other men." Previous research shows that these items are related to physical violence in marital relationships (e.g., Smith 1990a).

The CTS has been extensively criticized as a simple count of abuse with no sense of the context, meaning, or motives for being violent (Breines and Gordon 1983; DeKeseredy and MacLean 1990; Dobash et al. 1992). These criticisms are generally in response to some researchers who use sexually symmetrical CTS data to justify their claims that intimate, heterosexual violence is a "two-way street" and that there is a "battered man syndrome" (e.g., McNeely and Robinson-Simpson 1987; Steinmetz 1977–78). While their data do show that women hit men as often as men hit women, these findings do not demonstrate "sexually symmetrical motivation" (Dobash et al. 1992). For example, as Schwartz and DeKeseredy (1993) point out, there has never been any doubt that *some* women strike their partners with the intent to injure. However, research specifically on the context, meanings, and motives of intimate violence shows that most female-to-male assaults are acts of self-defence (Berk et al. 1983; Browne 1987; DeKeseredy 1992; Dobash and Dobash 1988; Dobash et al. 1992; Makepeace 1986; Saunders 1986, 1988, 1989; Schwartz and DeKeseredy 1993).

In response to the above criticisms, also included in our version of the CTS were three questions asking male and female participants to explain why they engaged in dating violence since they left high school. The following measures are modified versions of those developed by Saunders (1988). The responses to them, however, have not yet been analyzed:

> On items ... what percentage of these times overall do you estimate that in doing these actions ... you were primarily motivated by acting in self-defence, that is, protecting yourself from immediate physical harm?
> you were trying to fight back in a situation where you were not the first to use these or similar tactics?
> you used these actions on your dating partners before they actually attacked you or threatened to attack you?

A slightly reworded version of Koss et al.'s (1987) Sexual Experience Survey (SES) was employed to operationalize various forms of sexual assault. It covers a range of unwanted sexual experiences. Both the CTS and SES are widely used, and they are reliable and valid measures (Koss and Gidycz 1985; Smith 1987; Straus et al. 1981). The texts of all of the items used are presented in Tables 9.1, 9.2, 9.3, and 9.4, and different wording was used for male and female respondents.

FINDINGS

The Incidence and Prevalence of Sexual Abuse

The items used in the SES are presented in Tables 9.1 and 9.2. These measures range from unwanted sexual contact, to sexual coercion, attempted rape, and rape. In this study, the SES global incidence rate for female victims was 27.8 percent. Approximately 11 percent of the males reported having victimized a female dating partner in this way in the past year. The prevalence figures are considerably higher, with 45.1 percent of the women stating that they had been victimized since leaving high school and 19.5 percent of the men reported at least one abusive incident in the same time period. Within the margin of error, except for the male prevalence figure, these results are similar to those reported in pretest (DeKeseredy et al. 1992).

Caution, however, must be used in interpreting these figures since they represent a composite of several items which vary in both the amount of violence used and in whether they actually constitute a

Table 9.1
Sexual Abuse Incidence Rates

Type of Abuse	Men (N=1307)		Women (N=1835)	
	%	N	%	N
1. Have you given in to sex play (fondling, kissing, or petting, but not intercourse) when you didn't want to because you were overwhelmed by a man's continual arguments and pressure?	7.8	95	18.2	318
2. Have you engaged in sex play (fondling, kissing, or petting, but not intercourse) when you didn't want to because a man used his position of authority (boss, supervisor, etc.) to make you?	.9	10	1.3	21
3. Have you had sex play (fondling, kissing, or petting, but not intercourse) when you didn't want to because a man threatened or used some degree of physical force (twisting your arm, holding you down, etc.) to make you?	1.1	13	3.3	54
4. Has a man attempted sexual intercourse (getting on top of you, attempting to insert his penis) when you didn't want to by threatening or using some degree of physical force (twisting your arm, holding you down, etc.), but intercourse did not occur?	.6	7	3.9	67
5. Has a man attempted sexual intercourse (getting on top of you, attempting to insert his penis) when you didn't want to because you were drunk or high, but intercourse did not occur?	2.5	29	6.6	121
6. Have you given in to sexual intercourse when you didn't want to because you were overwhelmed by a man's continual arguments and pressure?	4.8	55	11.9	198
7. Have you had sexual intercourse when you didn't want to because a man used his position of authority (boss, supervisor, etc.) to make you?	.8	9	.5	8
8. Have you had sexual intercourse when you didn't want to because you were drunk or high?	2.2	25	7.6	129
9. Have you had sexual intercourse when you didn't want to because a man threatened or used some degree of physical force (twisting your arm, holding you down, etc.) to make you?	.7	8	2.0	34
10. Have you engaged in sex acts (anal or oral intercourse or penetration by objects other than the penis) when you didn't want to because a man threatened or used some degree of physical force (twisting your arm, holding you down, etc.) to make you?	.3	3	.8	29

Table 9.2
Sexual Abuse Prevalence Rates

Type of Abuse	Men (N=1307)		Women (N=1835)	
	%	N	%	N
1. Have you given in to sex play (fondling, kissing, or petting, but not intercourse) when you didn't want to because you were overwhelmed by a man's continual arguments and pressure?	14.9	172	31.8	553
2. Have you engaged in sex play (fondling, kissing, or petting, but not intercourse) when you didn't want to because a man used his position of authority (boss, supervisor, etc.) to make you?	1.8	24	4.0	66
3. Have you had sex play (fondling, kissing, or petting, but not intercourse) when you didn't want to because a man threatened or used some degree of physical force (twisting your arm, holding you down, etc.) to make you?	2.2	25	9.4	154
4. Has a man attempted sexual intercourse (getting on top of you, attempting to insert his penis) when you didn't want to by threatening or using some degree of physical force (twisting your arm, holding you down, etc.), but intercourse did not occur?	1.6	19	8.5	151
5. Has a man attempted sexual intercourse (getting on top of you, attempting to insert his penis) when you didn't want to because you were drunk or high, but intercourse did not occur?	5.5	63	13.6	244
6. Have you given in to sexual intercourse when you didn't want to because you were overwhelmed by a man's continual arguments and pressure?	8.3	96	20.2	349
7. Have you had sexual intercourse when you didn't want to because a man used his position of authority (boss, supervisor, etc.) to make you?	1.4	17	1.5	24
8. Have you had sexual intercourse when you didn't want to because you were drunk or high?	4.7	55	14.6	257
9. Have you had sexual intercourse when you didn't want to because a man threatened or used some degree of physical force (twisting your arm, holding you down, etc.) to make you?	1.5	18	6.6	112
10. Have you engaged in sex acts (anal or oral intercourse or penetration by objects other than the penis) when you didn't want to because a man threatened or used some degree of physical force (twisting your arm, holding you down, etc.) to make you?	1.4	16	3.2	51

violation of the *Canadian Criminal Code*. Even so, all the items reflect experiences that many survivors identify both traumatic and damaging (Kelly 1988). Furthermore, using the SES allows us to replicate previous work and to compare Canadian results with American data.

It is difficult to compare the incidence findings with other Canadian studies. For example, though Finkleman (1992) used the same measures and time period, he does not provide data on gender variations in victimization. Instead, he reports the total number of students (both men and women) who were sexually abused. Moreover, for male reports of their behaviour, there are no comparable statistics (that is figures based on the SES). DeKeseredy (1988) asked men whether they had threatened to use force or actually used force "to make a woman engage in sexual activities" in the past 12 months. This might have been narrowly defined by respondents to refer to actual or attempted intercourse or to include forced fondling or petting. Because of these problems in interpretation, comparisons are meaningless.

Comparing prevalence findings is also problematic. For example, Elliot et al. (1992) used slightly different measures and combined male and female figures. Methodological differences also make it hard to compare our findings with those produced by Koss et al.'s (1987) national American study. Although these researchers used the same sexual abuse items to determine prevalence rates, they used a broader time period — since age 14.

Despite some methodological differences, the findings presented in Tables 9.1 and 9.2 are consistent with Koss et al.'s American national data. They show that male respondents were more likely to report using less severe forms of coercion to get women to engage in sexual activities. These included arguments and pressure and the use of alcohol. Women's reports concur with male responses in terms of the types of coercion used to engage in sexual activities. There are, however, large gender differences in reporting the incidence of abuse, and the reporting gaps widen for the prevalence data.

Interpreting these reporting differences is a complex process. Researchers argue that socially desirable reporting is more common among perpetrators than victims (Arias and Beach 1987; Dutton and Hemphill 1992). The greatest differences[1] between men and women were on the most socially undesirable items: sex play, attempted intercourse, and sexual intercourse involving some degree of force. The findings indicate that women were seven to eight times more likely to report these behaviours than men when response differences were standardized using women's figures as the base. This suggests that social desirability is probably shaping responses. However, the response differences on four other items were also large.

On these items, women were 6 to 6.5 times more likely to have reported abuse than men. These items included: giving in to sex play or to sexual intercourse due to continual arguements and pressure and attempted sexual intercourse or actual sexual intercourse when you were too drunk or high to resist. These four items focus on the negotiations between men and women over sexual activity. The differences in reporting rates on these items, most of which are lower in social undesirability, suggest that there may be considerable miscommunication between men and women. The exact nature of this miscommunication cannot be determined from these data. But, given the proposed changes to Canadian laws on consent and sexual assault, they suggest the need for further investigation.

The Incidence and Prevalence of Physical Abuse

The male physical abuse incidence figure of 13.7 percent approximates statistics reported in previous Canadian and American incidence studies which used similar methods (DeKeseredy 1988; DeKeseredy et al. 1992; Makepeace 1983). Though Table 9.3 shows that every type of physical violence was used by at least one respondent, less lethal forms

Table 9.3
Psychological and Physical Abuse Incidence Rates

Type of Abuse	Men (N=1307)		Women (N=1835)	
	%	N	%	N
Psychological				
Insults or swearing	52.7	623	52.5	857
Put her (you) down in front of friends or family	18.9	233	30.7	491
Accused her (you) of having affairs or flirting with other men	29.3	350	37.2	614
Did or said something to spite her (you)	57.7	670	61.7	989
Threatened to hit or throw something at her (you)	6.1	71	10.6	174
Threw, smashed, or kicked something	25.4	304	25.5	433
Physical				
Threw something at her (you)	3.5	40	5.1	85
Pushed, grabbed, or shoved her (you)	11.7	132	19.6	319
Slapped her (you)	2.9	30	5.5	85
Kicked, bit, or hit her (you) with your (his) fist	1.7	16	3.9	61
Hit or tried to hit her (you) with something	1.9	20	3.3	54
Beat her (you) up	.9	7	1.4	21
Choked you (her)	1.0	10	2.1	32
Threatened her (you) with a knife or a gun	.9	9	.5	9
Used a knife or a gun on her (you)	1.0	8	.1	2

of assault were reported more often. This is consistent with most of the earlier North American research (Sugarman and Hotaling 1989). Expectations of socially desirable reporting are further supported when female incidence rates are calculated. These are higher than male figures with 22.3 percent of the female participants reporting victimization. Again, there are more reports of less lethal forms of abuse, and reporting differences are largest for the most socially undesirable variants of abuse.

Table 9.4 shows that there are also gender differences in responses to the physical abuse prevalence items. Almost 35 percent of the women reported having been physically assaulted and 17.8 percent of the men stated ever having used physical abuse since leaving high school. Both the male and female prevalence figures are similar to the pretest results (DeKeseredy et al. 1992). But the male figure is considerably lower than Barnes et al.'s (1991) rate (42 percent). This inconsistency probably reflects differences between the specific renditions of the CTS employed by the two studies. Barnes et al.'s version included a sexual assault item, and several other items were distinct from those used in our modified version.

Table 9.4
Psychological and Physical Abuse Prevalence Rates

Type of Abuse	Men (N=1307) %	N	Women (N=1835) %	N
Psychological				
Insults or swearing	62.4	747	65.1	1105
Put her (you) down in front of friends or family	25.9	322	44.2	742
Accused her (you) of having affairs or flirting with other men	40.9	495	52.6	901
Did or said something to spite her (you)	65.2	773	72.2	1216
Threatened to hit or throw something at her (you)	8.0	97	20.6	346
Threw, smashed, or kicked something	30.6	373	37.3	652
Physical				
Threw some thing at her (you)	4.3	50	10.6	185
Pushed, grabbed, or shoved her (you)	15.8	182	31.3	529
Slapped her (you)	4.9	53	11.1	186
Kicked, bit, or hit her (you) with your (his) fist	2.8	28	8.0	135
Hit or tried to hit her (you) with something	2.9	33	8.0	136
Beat her (you) up	1.0	8	3.9	63
Choked you (her)	1.0	9	4.6	80
Threatened her (you) with a knife or a gun	.9	9	2.4	41
Used a knife or a gun on her (you)	1.0	9	.5	8

Tables 9.3 and 9.4 include some notable features. For example, on both the incidence and prevalence scales, men were more likely to indicate having used a weapon than women were to state having been subjected to this form of abuse. Moreover, Table 9.4 reveals that more men reported threatening a date with a weapon than women reported being threatened. These are considered socially undesirable acts, and men's higher rates of reporting suggest that, not surprisingly, social desirability alone does not account for reporting.

The Incidence and Prevalence of Psychological Abuse

Similar accounts of psychological abuse were provided by both men and women. For example, the proportion of men who reported having been psychologically abusive is 74.1 percent, and 79.1 percent of the female respondents indicated having been a victim of such mistreatment. As anticipated, the prevalence figures were higher at 86.2 percent for women and 80.8 percent for men.

The male incidence figure is higher than those reported by DeKeseredy (1988) and DeKeseredy et al. (1992). The women's incidence figure is also higher than the DeKeseredy et al. estimate. The male prevalence statistic is about 12 percent lower than that reported by Barnes et al. (92.6 percent). This difference probably reflects the use of different measures.

An examination of the psychological abuse items presented in Tables 9.3 and 9.4 indicates that there is considerable congruency in reporting. This suggests that there is a perception on the part of abusers that these occurrences are part of the "common currency" of dating relationships. This is particularly true of insults or swearing, throwing, smashing or kicking something, and doing something to spite a partner. There was less reporting agreement on threatening to throw something at her, putting her down in front of friends and family, and accusing her of having affairs or flirting with other men. These three items are less likely to be equal exchanges and are more likely to be unvaryingly threatening or psychologically damaging.

CONCLUSION

Surveys on the extent of woman abuse in Canadian university/college dating relationships are in short supply. The few which have been conducted clearly demonstrate that many women are at great risk of being physically, sexually, and psychologically attacked in courtship. They also intimate that many male dating partners may be attempting to mirror the dynamics of patriarchal marriages in which men have superior power and privilege (DeKeseredy and Schwartz 1993). However, since the data presented in these studies are gleaned from nonprobability samples, they are only suggestive of the incidence and prevalence of woman abuse in the Canadian post-secondary student population at large. Such data are clearly necessary to "provide a surer footing than presently exists for the development of social policies and programs needed to ameliorate the problem" (Smith 1987: 144).

In preparing to conduct this national study, substantial effort was devoted to considering the various measures used by researchers in this field in the past (Kelly and DeKeseredy 1993). Our intention was to balance the need to replicate previous studies with the necessity of avoiding their methodological problems. The best available measures were selected and where necessary, modifications were made to address known difficulties. One of the major controversies in the woman abuse literature involves the use of composite scales to measure abuse. Such scales include the full range of potentially abusive items, that is psychological, physical, and sexual abuse. Interpreting the data derived from these items is extremely problematic given the range of activities covered. There is, for example, considerable debate about whether certain items in the sub-scales constitute abuse. This paper has presented the abuse figures for sexual, physical, and psychological abuse separately. Consistent with existing research in this area, composite measures (global incidence and prevalence figures) were computed but are not reported here since it is our position that they tend to be so large that they obscure and trivialize the more serious and less controversial abuse figures reported by the respondents.

The results of this nationally representative sample survey provide more accurate and reliable data on the abuse of college and university women by male dating partners. The findings suggest that very serious forms of abuse are quite common in campus dating. A comparison of our global prevalence findings with those reviewed by Sugarman and Hotaling (1989) show that the problem of dating abuse is just as serious in Canada as it is in the U.S.

Although these figures are high, as is the case with all survey statistics on woman abuse, they should be read as underestimates for the following reasons. First, many people do not report incidents because of fear of reprisal, embarrassment, or because they perceive some acts as too trivial to mention. Second, some people forget abusive experiences, especially if they took place long ago and were relatively "minor" (Kennedy and Dutton 1989; Smith 1987). Third, because of social desirability factors, men are less likely than women to provide reliable accounts of their behaviour. Finally, many women may not want to recall the pain and suffering they endured in their dating relationships (Smith 1987).

In order to advance a better understanding of woman abuse in post-secondary school dating relationships and to both prevent and control it, more than just accurate incidence and prevalence data are required. We need to empirically discern the major "risk markers" (Hotaling and Sugarman 1986) associated with assaults on female university/college students, such as level of intimacy, ethnicity, and educational status. This type of analysis will provide information on who is at the greatest risk of being abused or of being abusive. Such correlational research will also assist in the development of theories, such as the one offered at the beginning of this article.

Research on the links, if any, between psychological abuse and physical and sexual abuse is also necessary for providing us with more direct interactional warnings. For example, strong correlations between accusations of flirting or having affairs (jealousy) and later physical or sexual abuse could be used to warn people to "get help" or "get out" when confronted with such abusive situations.

Another important issue is the possible difference between men and women in their interpretations of consent for sexual activities. As noted above, reporting differences between men and women on the items about sexual negotiations or consent were large and very similar to the gaps between men and women in their reporting of the most socially undesirable activities. These preliminary findings raise important questions of a social and legal nature regarding the interpretations that men and women have of consent within dating relationships. These bear directly on current discussions about whether consent has been given or one partner has simply complied because they felt pressure to do so or were unable to refuse — the "no means no" debate. Subsequent articles on the national survey will address this and other issues, such as the influence of familial patriarchy on male violence; the context, meanings, and motives assigned to dating violence; the influence of male peer group dynamics on abusive behaviour; and the effectiveness of various social support services for women.

NOTES

[1] The gap in reporting was calculated by subtracting the percentage of men who stated that they abused a date from the percentage of women who reported having been abused and then dividing this difference by the percentage of women reporting that type of abuse.

On Violent Men and Female Victims:
A Comment on DeKeseredy and Kelly
Bonnie J. Fox

In collecting representative data on the abuse of women by male
dating partners, DeKeseredy and Kelly have done us a service. We
have known for some time that it is not rare for men living with
women to hurt them seriously, and that it is extremely unusual for
women to do so to their male partners. There is little research on
more casual relationships, however. Nonetheless, despite the clearly competent sampling and interviewing done by York's Institute
for Social Research, I have misgivings about the project after reading
this initial summary.

As feminist researchers and educators working in an environment
that is still generally hostile to our analyses and indifferent to women's
particular concerns, it is crucial that we make strong arguments
involving claims we can support (although no amount of reason and
evidence will persuade everyone). At the same time, as sociologists, our
conceptualization of social structure and our sensitivity to the complexity of the relationship between the individual and society should
lend sophistication to any arguments we make about gender inequality. Thus, long ago, most feminist social science left behind the notion
that "patriarchy" is reducible to powerful men dominating passive,
weak women.

This paper is disappointing because it rests implicitly on that
argument. Related to this implicit theory are methodological weaknesses that I will try to elaborate. But first a general comment.
Devoid of any explicit analysis — statistical or theoretical — the
article indicates that DeKeseredy and Kelly assume that the data
"speak for themselves." That too is a position I thought we had
abandoned long ago.

To be fair to these researchers, the issue of violence against women
is perhaps the most poorly theorized of all aspects of gender inequality. The argument that men who are powerful victimize women, as a
prerogative of their more privileged position and in order to bolster
it (by controlling women), is common in the literature. Yet both the
empirical research and various feminist insight and arguments suggest
a far more complex interpretation.

For instance, the evidence on "wife battering" indicates that the
type of man who is likely to abuse is one who needs to be in control
and one who believes men are entitled to women's services (Dobash

and Dobash 1979; Straus and Gelles 1990). As well, though, the kind of objective material situation that promotes abuse is one that leaves a man feeling powerless — involving unemployment, perpetual low income, etc. (Straus and Gelles 1990). With respect to sexuality, some writers have discussed the feelings of vulnerability, not potency, evoked by men's desire for women (Hollway 1983; Kaufman 1987; Segal 1990). The point I am trying to make is that the dynamics of violence and abuse are complicated; what is going on is not obvious.

Given that the behaviour in question is so complex and our understanding so primitive, it is disappointing to see DeKeseredy and Kelly opt for "global" estimation, of global categories (i.e., "abuse"), rather than detailed analysis. Their global measures of abuse combine the least with the worst offences (e.g., rape with an unwanted kiss). Their objective seems to be to support the argument that "female students' lives rest upon a continuum of violence" by men. Instead, by combining what is debatably abusive with what everyone agrees to be seriously abusive, they stand to trivialize the latter. That 2 percent of women in Canadian universities and colleges may be forced into sexual intercourse every year is more obviously significant than the "global" figures DeKeseredy and Kelly highlight. Not only is forced intercourse different from an unwanted kiss in terms of damage, the questions we need to ask about an unwanted kiss are of a different nature. For example, we are probably much more concerned to determine the meaning attached to the act by both the woman and the man in the case of unwanted "sex play"; we cannot assume it constitutes abuse, much less intentional abuse.

The argument is, of course, that soft-core abuse leads to hard-core abuse — that we are discussing a continuum. But is there evidence of that? That there are far more instances of the soft-core behaviour than the serious stuff raises the possibility than some men will not move beyond pressure to force. Are there not different types of men and, more generally, wholly different contexts and causal factors behind the use of force than pressure — or, at least, a larger variety of causes and contexts with respect to the latter? We do not know until we investigate.

Similarly, despite their separation of sexual, physical, and psychological forms of abuse, DeKeseredy and Kelly clearly classify them all under the same general category. They all represent "intentional assault on a female by a male dating partner" (p. 146 [p. 189 in this book]). Again, implicit is that the minor abuse (e.g., swearing at someone) is a mild version of the major abuse (e.g., rape). But slippage occurs in other ways: "intention" refers to one set of possibilities with respect to rape (e.g., inflicting pain, forcing submission, achieving a sense of power, etc.) but likely a very different set of things with respect to a forced kiss (e.g., from desiring sex to wanting to humiliate), or swearing, or an accusation of flirting (which are more likely displays of anger, hurt, etc.). In short, it is not clear what "intentional" means here when applied to all these phenomena — unless you *assume* that all men aim primarily to use or abuse women.

In the case of "psychological abuse," DeKeseredy and Kelly's discussion (pp. 153–54 [p. 196 in this book]) is less than clear, but it involves reference to "equal exchanges" between dating partners. It is indeed possible that women are in a less vulnerable position in psychological and verbal battles with men. In other words, this seems a different phenomenon than the other two. But the framework adopted here precludes an exploration of this possibility. This is not to suggest that men are sometimes victims in the ways women can be. It is to suggest that we need to investigate the dynamics of each of these types of aggressive behaviour before we lump them together and cast women solely in the role of victim — or, at least, passive victim.

A final instance of agglomeration in lieu of disentangling — or analyzing — is DeKeseredy and Kelly's frame of reference: dating. Surely "dating" includes a range of different types of relationships, from serious involvement and commitment to brief encounters between near strangers. Again, my general point is about method: combining what is qualitatively different undercuts any search for understanding.

At minimum, DeKeseredy and Kelly owed themselves and us a look at the statistical relationships in the data they collected: differences between age cohorts, university and college students, fields of study, etc., would at least provide some clues; data on type of relationship, type of man, and both parties' perception of what went on would be more revealing. Are the relationships with key independent variables the same for the different kinds of abuse? Shouldn't DeKeseredy and Kelly have established that before talking of all types of abuse in the same breath? Similarly, that DeKeseredy and Kelly present these figures before looking at their data on why the man used violence/force/pressure is puzzling and supports my sense that they thought the data would speak for themselves and that all these types of abuse are the same.

In sum, I think that DeKeseredy and Kelly have not shown that "very serious forms of abuse are quite common in campus dating" (p. 155 [p. 197 in this book]). What do they hold to be "very serious"? Where have they argued that percentages of a particular size indicate commonplace events? Aside from the methodological problems with this article and this project, to suggest the above is politically irresponsible. As many have argued already, conclusions like these instil fear in young women, which serves to control them rather than to help to empower them. Moreover, weak arguments undercut the campaign to raise people's consciousness.

Clearly women face risks in close relationships with men that men need not fear. But before we can assume that aggressive and abusive behaviour is of the same nature and arising from the same sources, we need to investigate. Focus groups and in-depth interviews using various approaches and questions would probably be extremely helpful in developing a sense of how women experience different kinds of incidents, what is going through men's heads, etc. Moreover, different questions need to be asked of men than women. We need both symmetry and asymmetry in our questioning: we should determine what women do as well as what men do, but because women and men are in different positions, we should also ask them different questions, especially about intent or motive (e.g., questions about self-defence are critical for female but not male respondents). Most importantly, we need to remember that social science is about asking why and trying to explain — not counting.

DISCUSSION QUESTIONS

1. Are women helpless victims in violent dating relationships with men, or are they responsible for such relationships? Why?

2. Why do you think that police reports, hospital reports, and shelter data show sexual asymmetry of conjugal violence, while self-report data tend to show sexual symmetry in conjugal violence?

3. Based on your personal experiences, what are the factors that have, or could have, contributed to sexual abuse in a dating relationship? If possible, share your personal experiences with your class. How similar or different are your experiences from theirs?

4. Do you think that men have a tendency to want to dominate women by using force? Do you think that women would tend to dominate men by using force if they could? Explain.

5. Read the article "Going over the Edge" (Exhibit 2.3). What are the factors that can cause family violence? Explain how each of these factors affect family violence specifically?

6. What would be your policy suggestions in order to reduce conjugal and/or dating relationship violence?

Exhibit 2.3

Going over the Edge

For most people, the family is a place of safety, nurturing, and positive values. For others, violence turns family life into a nightmare.

Family violence is a serious social and criminal problem. It can involve killing, physical, and sexual assault. It also involves other forms of harmful behaviour such as emotional abuse, financial exploitation, and neglect. Family violence has long-lasting psychological effects on its victims who are primarily women, children, and seniors. In most cases, the offenders are male.

According to 1993 Statistics Canada figures, one out of every four women is being assaulted by a husband or live-in partner.

It is estimated that:

- family violence accounts for more than 60% of female homicides;
- 25% of girls and 10% of boys are sexually abused before age 16;
- at least 4% of elderly persons are victims of some form of significant abuse.

Research also indicates that people with disabilities, especially women and girls, are frequently victims of abuse; 40% of respondents in a survey of adult women with disabilities reported being abused sometime in their lives.

The results of family violence are severe and far-reaching. Family violence experienced during childhood may be linked to alcohol and drug abuse, delinquency, suicide, juvenile prostitution, running away from home, mental health problems, and violent crime later in life. Studies have shown that men who abuse their wives were often themselves abused as children or witnessed the abuse of other family members. Similarly, women who are victims of wife assault often report that they were abused as children or witnessed other family members being abused.

It seems to be a never-ending cycle with tragic results. An Ottawa study in 1991 and 1992 chronicles intentional injuries to children who were treated at three urban hospitals in different provinces. It uncovered 951 cases of children treated for intentional injury, including neglect, physical abuse, and sexual abuse, over the two years.

Source: Abridged from "Going over the Edge," *Canada and the World Backgrounder*, Waterloo, ON: Taylor Publishing Consultants Ltd., Vol. 62, No. 5 (March 1997), pp. 26–27. Reprinted by permission.

POVERTY AFTER DIVORCE

The Divorce Revolution: The Unexpected Social and Economic Consequences for Women and Children in America
Lenore J. Weitzman

POSTDIVORCE STANDARDS OF LIVING: IMPOVERISHMENT OF WOMEN AND CHILDREN

The income disparity between men and women after divorce profoundly affects their relative standards of living.

To examine this effect, we rely on an index of economic well-being developed by the U.S. government. The model for our analysis was constructed by Michigan researchers who followed a sample of 5,000 American families, weighted to be representative of the U.S. population (Hoffman and Holmes 1976: 24). Economists Saul Hoffman and John Holmes compared the incomes of men and women who stayed in intact families with the incomes of divorced men and divorced women over a seven-year period.[1]

A comparison of the married and divorced couples yielded two major findings. First, as might be expected, the dollar income of both divorced men and divorced women declined, while the income of married couples rose. Divorced men lost 19 percent in income, while divorced women lost 29 percent (Hoffman and Holmes 1976: 27, Table 2.1 and 31, Table 2.2).[2] In contrast, married men and women experienced a 22 percent rise in income (Hoffman and Holmes 1976: 27, Table 2.1). These data confirm our common-sense belief that both parties suffer after a divorce. They also confirm that women experience a greater loss than their former husbands.

The second finding of the Michigan research is surprising. To see what the income loss meant in terms of family purchasing power, Hoffman and Holmes constructed an index of family income in relation to family needs.[3] Since this income/need comparison is adjusted for family size, as well as for each member's age and sex, it provides an individually tailored measure of a family's economic well-being in the context of marital status changes.

The Michigan researchers found that the experiences of divorced men and women were strikingly different when this measure was used. Over the seven-year period, the economic position of divorced men actually improved by 17 percent (Hoffman and Holmes 1976: 27, Table 2.1).[4] In contrast, over the same period, divorced women experienced a 29 percent decline in terms of what their income could provide in relation to their needs (Hoffman and Holmes 1976: 31, Table 2.2).

To compare the experiences of divorced men and women in California to those in Michigan, we devised a similar procedure to calculate the basic needs of each of the families in our interview sample. This procedure used the living standards for urban families constructed by the Bureau of Labor Statistics of the U.S. Department of Labor.[5] First, the standard budget level for each family in the interview sample was calculated in three different ways: once for the predivorce family, once for the wife's postdivorce family, and once for the husband's postdivorce family. Then the income in relation to needs was computed for each family. (Membership in postdivorce families of husbands and wives included any new spouse or cohabitor and any children whose custody was assigned to that spouse.) These data are presented in Figure 10.1.

Figure 10.1 reveals the radical change in the standards of living to which we alluded earlier. Just one year after legal divorce, *Men experience a 42 percent improvement in their postdivorce standard of living, while women experience a 73 percent decline.*

These data indicate that *divorce is a financial catastrophe for most women:* in just one year, they experience a dramatic decline in income and a calamitous drop in their standard of living. It is hard to imagine how they deal with such severe deprivation: every single expenditure that one takes for granted — clothing, food, housing, heat — must be cut to one-half or one-third of what one is accustomed to.

It is difficult to absorb the full implications of these statistics. What does it mean to have a 73 percent decline in one's standard of living? When asked how they coped with this drastic decline in income, many of the divorced women said that they themselves were not sure. It meant "living on the edge" and "living without." As some of them described it:

> We ate macaroni and cheese five nights a week. There was a Safeway special for 39 cents a box. We could eat seven dinners for $3.00 a week ...
> I think that's all we ate for months.

Figure 10.1
Change in Standards of Living[a] of Divorced Men and Women (Approximately One Year after Divorce)

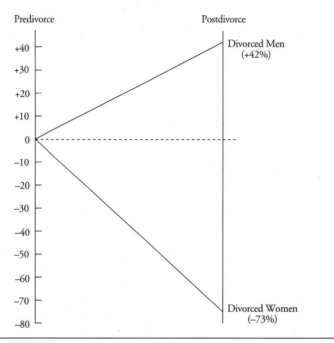

^a Income in relation to needs with needs based on U.S. Department of Agriculture's low standard budget.

Source: Based on weighted sample of interviews with divorced persons, Los Angeles County, California, 1978.

I applied for welfare.... It was the worst experience of my life.... I never dreamed that I, a middle-class housewife, would ever be in a position like that. It was humiliating ... they make you feel it.... But we were desperate, and I *had* to feed my kids.

You name, I tried it — food stamps, soup kitchens, shelters. It just about killed me to have the kids live like that.... I finally called my parents and said we were coming ... we couldn't have survived without them.

Even those who had relatively affluent life-styles before the divorce experienced a sharp reduction in their standard of living and faced hardships they had not anticipated. For example, the wife of a dentist sold her car "because I had no cash at all, and we lived on that money — barely — for close to a year." And an engineer's wife:

> I didn't buy my daughter any clothes for a year — even when she graduated from high school, we sewed together two old dresses to make an outfit.

The wife of a policeman told an especially poignant story about "not being able to buy my twelve-year-old son Adidas sneakers." The boy's father had been ordered to pay $100 a month child support but had not been paying. To make up that gap in her already bare-bone budget, she had been using credit cards to buy food and other household necessities. She had exceeded all her credit limits and felt the family just could not afford to pay $25 for a new pair of Adidas sneakers. But, as she said a year later,

> Sometimes when you are so tense about money you go crazy ... and you forget what it's like to be twelve years old and to think you can't live without Adidas sneakers ... and to feel the whole world has deserted you along with your father.

Others spoke of cutting out all the nonessentials. For one woman, it meant "no movies, no ice cream cones for the kids." For another, it meant no replacing tires on her son's bike "because there just wasn't the money." For another women, it meant not using her car — a real handicap in Los Angeles — and waiting for two buses in order to save the money she would have had to spend for gas. In addition to scaled-down budgets for food ("We learned to love chicken backs") and clothing ("At Christmas, I splurged at the Salvation Army — the only "new" clothes they got all year"), many spoke of cutting down on their children's school lunches ("I used to plan a nourishing lunch with fruit and juice; now she's lucky if we have a slice of ham for a sandwich") and school supplies and after-school activities ("he had to quit the Little League and get a job as a delivery boy").

Still, some of the women were not able to "make it." Fourteen percent of them moved onto the welfare rolls during the first year after the divorce, and a number of others moved back into their parents' homes when they had "no money left and nowhere to go and three children to feed."

EXPLAINING THE DISPARITY BETWEEN HUSBANDS' AND WIVES' STANDARDS OF LIVING

How can we explain the strikingly different economic consequences of divorce for men and women? How could a law that aimed at fairness create such disparities between divorced men and their former wives and children?

The explanation lies first in the inadequacy of the court's awards, second in the expanded demands on the wife's resources after divorce, and third in the husband's greater earning capacity and ability to supplement his income.

Consider first the court awards for child support (and in rarer cases, alimony). Since judges do not require men to support either their children or their former wives as they did during marriage, they allow the husband to keep most of his income for himself. Since only a few wives are awarded alimony, the only supplementary income they are awarded is child support, and the average child support award covers less than half of the costs of raising a child. Thus, the average support award is simply inadequate: even if the husband pays it, it often leaves the wife and children in relative poverty. The custodial mother is expected to somehow make up the deficit alone even though she typically earns much less than her former husband.

In this regard, it is also important to note the role that property awards play in contributing to — rather than alleviating — the financial disparities between divorced women and men. Under the old law, when the wife with minor children was typically awarded the family home, she started her postdivorce life on a more equal footing because the home provided some stability and security and reduced the impact of the income loss suffered at divorce. Today, when the family home is more commonly sold to allow an "equal" division of property, there is no cushion to soften the financial devastations that low support awards create for women and children. Rather, the disruptive costs of moving and establishing a new household further strain their limited income — often to the breaking point.

The second explanation for the disparity between former husbands and wives lies in the greater demands on the wife's household after divorce and the diminished demands on the husband's. Since the wife typically assumes the responsibility for raising the couple's children, her need for help and services increases as a direct result of her becoming a single parent. Yet at the very time that her need for more income and more financial support is greatest, the courts have drastically reduced her income. Thus the gap between her income and her needs is wider after divorce.

In contrast, the gap between the husband's income and needs narrows. Although he now has fewer absolute dollars, the demands on his income have diminished: he often lives alone, and he is no longer financially responsible for the needs of his ex-wife and children. While he loses the benefits of economies of scale, and while he may have to purchase some services (such as laundry and cooking) that he did not have to buy during marriage, he is nevertheless much better off because he has so much more money to spend on himself. Since he has been allowed to retain most of his income for himself, he can afford these extra expenses and still have more surplus income than he enjoyed during marriage.

The final explanation for the large income discrepancy between former husbands and wives lies in the different earning capacities and starting points of the two adults at the time of the divorce. Not only do men in our society command higher salaries to begin with, they also benefit from the common marital pattern that gives priority to their careers. Marriage gives men the opportunity, support, and time to invest in their own careers. Thus marriage itself builds and enhances the husband's earning capacity. For women, in contrast, marriage is more likely to act as a career liability. Even though family roles are changing, and even though married women are increasingly working for pay during marriage, most of them nevertheless subordinate their careers to their husbands' and to their family responsibilities. This is especially true if they have children. Thus women are often doubly disadvantaged at the point of divorce. Not only do they face the "normal" 60 percent male/female income gap that affects all working women, they also suffer from the toll the marital years have taken on their earning capacity.

Thus marriage — and then divorce — impose a differential disadvantage on women's employment prospects, and this is especially severe for women who have custody of minor children. The responsibility for children inevitably restricts the mother's job opportunities by limiting her work schedule and location, her availability for overtime, and her freedom to take advantage of special training, travel assignments, and other opportunities for career advancement.

Although the combined income of the former spouses typically increases after divorce, most of the rise is a result of the husband's increased income. Even though women who have not been employed during marriage seek jobs after divorce, and part-time workers take full-time jobs, neither of these factors accounts for as much as the rise in male wages in the first year after divorce.

It is, in fact, surprising to see how many divorced men receive salary increases (and bonuses) immediately after divorce. While some of these are probably routine raises, and others may be the result of more intense work efforts or overtime work, it is also evident that some men manage to delay a bonus or commission or raise until after the divorce is final. This allows them to minimize the income they have to report to the court when child support (or alimony) awards are being made.

While the courts have long been aware of the control that self-employed men can exercise over the amount and timing of the income they receive, our data suggest that many salaried employees may exercise similar control over their income since many of them manage to obtain salary increases soon after their divorces become final. Whether or not this is coincidence, the fact remains that the income of divorced men often increases substantially in the first year after the divorce.

During the same period, the obligations that these men have for alimony and child support typically remain fixed or diminish: some support obligations have been reduced or terminated by terms of the divorce settlement (and others have been reduced or stopped without the courts' permission). The result, once again, is that divorced men have more "surplus income" for themselves.

The discrepancy between divorced men and women has been corroborated by other research. Sociologist Robert Weiss and economist Thomas Espenshade found parallel disparities in the standards of living of former husbands and wives after divorce, and Weiss corroborates the finding that the greatest reduction in postdivorce income is experienced by women who shared higher family incomes before the divorce (Weiss 1984; Espenshade 1979; see also Little 1983 and Brandwein et al. 1974). Census Bureau data also document the disparities in both income and standards of living of men and women after divorce. In 1979, the median per capita income of divorced women who had not remarried was $4,152, just over half of the $7,886 income of divorced men who had not remarried (Bureau of the Census 1981: 23).

The situation of divorced women with young children is even more grim. The median income in families headed by women with children under six years of age was only 30 percent of the median income for all families whose children were under six (Bureau of the Census 1980: 36). Thus, for the United States as a whole, the "income of families headed by women is at best half that of other families; the income of families headed by women with young children is even less, one-third of that of other families (National Center on Women and Family Law 1983: 1132).

CONCLUSION: THE TWO-TIER SOCIETY

The economic consequences of the present system of divorce reverberate throughout our society. Divorce awards not only contribute heavily to the well-documented income disparity between men and women, they also lead to the widespread impoverishment of children and enlarge the ever-widening gap between the economic well-being of men and women in the larger society. Indeed, if current conditions continue unabated, we may well arrive at a two-tier society with an underclass of women and children.

Thrust into a spiral of downward mobility by the present system of divorce, a multitude of middle-class women and the children in their charge are increasingly cut off from sharing the income and wealth of former husbands and fathers. Hampered by restricted employment opportunities and sharply diminished income, these divorced women are increasingly expected to shoulder alone the burden of providing for both themselves and their children.

Most of the children of divorce share their mother's financial hardships. Their presence in her household increases the strains on her meager income at the same time that they add to her expenses and restrict her opportunities for economic betterment.

Meanwhile, divorced men increasingly are freed of the major financial responsibility for supporting their children and former wives. Moreover, these men retain more than higher incomes. They experience less day-to-day stress than their ex-wives, they enjoy relatively greater mental, physical, and emotional well-being, and have greater freedom to build new lives and new families after divorce.

The economic disparities between men and women after divorce illuminate the long-standing economic disparities between the incomes of men and women during marriage. In theory, those differences did not matter in marriage since they were partners in the enterprise and shared the husband's income. As Christopher Jencks observes, "As long as most American men and women married and pooled their economic resources, as they traditionally did, the fact that men received 70 percent of the nation's income had little effect on women's material well being" (Jencks 1982). But with today's high divorce rate, the ranks of unmarried women are vastly increased, and the relative numbers of women who share a man's income are greatly diminished.

The result is that the economic gulf between the sexes in the larger society is increasing. Some of this would have occurred even if the traditional divorce law remained everywhere in force. But the new divorce laws — and the way these laws are being applied — have exacerbated the effects of the high divorce rate by assuring that ever greater numbers of women and children are being shunted out of the economic mainstream.

The data on the increase in female poverty, child poverty, and the comparative deprivation of middle-class women and children suggest that we are moving toward a two-tier society in which the upper economic tier is dominated by men (and the women and children who live with them). The former wives of many of these men, the mothers of their children, and the children themselves are increasingly found in the lower economic tier. Those in the first tier enjoy a comfortable standard of living; those in the lower tier are confined to lives of economic deprivation and hardship.

Obviously the two tiers are not totally segregated by sex: professional women, for example, whether married or divorced, are more likely to
be found in the first tier, and members of many minority groups, both
men and women, are more likely to fall into the second. Yet among
these groups and among all families at the lower income levels, divorce
brings a better economic future for men than for their former wives.

The concept of a two-tier society does not imply a static model.
There is movement between the two tiers. But the structural conditions
of the lives of women in the lower tier make it extremely difficult for
them to improve their economic fortunes by hard work or any of the
other traditional routes to economic mobility. The divorced women in
the lower tier face not merely the sex-segregated job market and the
male–female wage gap that confront all women, but also the responsibilities and restrictions that devolve upon heads of one-parent families.
For these women, the discrepancy between earnings and need is typically too large to allow them to provide even the bare necessities of
life for themselves and their families.

Obviously, membership in the second tier is not necessarily permanent. Some women will find jobs or return to school or obtain
training that will enable them to improve their status. Many of those
who are under thirty and some of those who are under forty will accomplish the same result by remarrying. But even those women who manage
eventually to improve their financial situation will typically spend their
early postdivorce years in acute economic hardship. The fact that they
are poor only temporarily does not mean that they and their children
suffer any the less (Jencks 1982) or that they can ever recapture the
losses of those wasted years.

NOTES

[1] Detailed information from the interviews provided the researchers with
precise income data, including income from employment, intra-fam-
ily transfers, welfare, and other government programs. Alimony and/or
child support paid by the husband was subtracted from his income
and added to the wife's postdivorce income. Finally, to facilitate direct
comparisons, all income was calculated in constant 1968 dollars so
that changes in real income could be examined without the com-
pounding effect of inflation.

[2] Hoffman and Holmes are frequently cited as showing that divorced
men have only a 10 percent decline in real money income. While this
figure is shown in Table 2.1 [in Hoffman and Holmes 1976], it is based
on the husband's total postdivorce income before alimony and/or child

support is paid. Once these support payments are deducted from the husband's income, husbands experience a 19 percent decline in real income.

[3] This index, which is based on the Department of Agriculture's "Low-Cost Food Budget," adjusted for the size, age, and sex composition of the family, is described in note 5 below.

[4] This is closer to the rate of improvement of married couples who improved their standard of living by 21 percent. (Note that their income rose 22 percent, but their income in relation to needs rose 21 percent.)

[5] We assumed that the basic needs level for each family was the Lower Standard Budget devised by the Bureau of Labor Statistics (1967). This budget is computed for a four-person urban family (husband and wife and two children) and kept current by frequent adjustments. See, for example, McCraw (1978). A Labor Department report devised a method for adjusting this standard budget to other types of families, depending on family size, age of oldest child, and age of head of household (Bureau of Labor Statistics 1968). For example, the needs of a family of two persons (husband and wife) with the head of household of age thirty-five was calculated at 60 percent of the base figure for a Lower Standard Budget.

A Lower Standard Budget was calculated for each family in our interview sample three different ways: once for the predivorce family, once for the wife's postdivorce family, and once for the husband's postdivorce family. The income over needs for each family was then computed. Membership in postdivorce families of husbands and wives included a new spouse or cohabitor (where applicable) and any children whose custody was assigned to that spouse. I am indebted to my research assistant, David Lineweber, for programming this analysis.

A Re-Evaluation of the Economic Consequences of Divorce
Richard R. Peterson

Over the last 20 years, researchers and policymakers have focused considerable attention on the economic consequences of divorce. Interest in this issue has been driven by several concerns. The number of people affected by divorce has increased dramatically — the divorce rate has risen and the economic well-being of women and children after divorce has become a significant problem. Most states have enacted no-fault divorce legislation, and some also have established new guidelines for dividing property, awarding alimony, and assigning custody of children. As these reforms were introduced, researchers and policymakers became interested in evaluating their effects. Also, scholars began to examine the differential economic consequences of divorce for men and women.

For several reasons, one book, Weitzman's *The Divorce Revolution* (1985), stands out among studies of the economic consequences of divorce. First, Weitzman reported that the decline in women's standard of living after divorce was much worse than was previously thought. Prior studies have reported an average decline for women of between 13 percent and 35 percent. Weitzman reported that the average standard of living for women who divorced in Los Angeles in 1977 declined by 73 percent after divorce, which is particularly striking when one considers that the *maximum* possible decline is 100 percent. Second, the gender gap in standards of living after divorce was much greater than previously thought. While the average decline for women was 73 percent, Weitzman reported that men's standard of living improved 42 percent. Finally, she argued that these economic consequences of divorce are due to no-fault divorce and other reforms introduced in California in 1970. These reforms eliminated fault-based grounds for divorce, based alimony awards on financial need, required equal division of marital property, and included new procedures to reduce hostility and conflict. Because those supporting reform had claimed that no-fault divorces would place men and women on an equal footing, Weitzman's book has raised serious questions about no-fault legislation.

The Divorce Revolution received considerable attention in academic, legal, and popular publications. It was reviewed in at least 22 social science journals, 12 law reviews, and 10 national magazines and newspapers. The book received the American Sociological Association's 1986 Book Award for "Distinguished Contribution to Scholarship" (Weitzman 1986). From 1986 to 1993, it was cited in 348 social science articles (based on a search of the Social Science Citation Index) and in more than 250 law review articles (based on a search of legal periodicals indexed in Westlaw). *The Divorce Revolution* was also discussed widely in the popular press: It was cited over 85 time in newspapers and over 25 times in national magazines from 1985 to 1993. Remarkably, *The Divorce Revolution* has also been cited in at least 24 legal cases in state Appellate and Supreme courts (based on a search of legal cases indexed in Westlaw) and was cited once by the U.S. Supreme Court (Abraham 1989).

Much of the attention received by *The Divorce Revolution* focused on the contrast between the 73 percent *decline* in women's standards of living and the 42 percent *rise* in the standard of living of men. Most reviews reported this as a major finding, describing is as staggering, startling, or dramatic. A legal history of American women cited Weitzman's results and concluded "... it is difficult to exaggerate the economic problems created by no-fault reform of divorce" (Hoff 1991; see also Hewlett 1986). A review by Polikoff (1986) concluded "... the serious research in this book should form the basis for moving forward with much heeded legal reforms" (Polikoff 1986: 116). In fact, the findings on the economic consequences of divorce did affect subsequent divorce law reforms and debates about those reforms. For example, the California State Senate Task Force on Family Equity was formed in response to *The Divorce Revolution*, and some of its recommendations were enacted in 1987 and 1988 (Weitzman 1992).

The most cited statistic from *The Divorce Revolution* is the finding that women's average standard of living declines by 73 percent in the first year after divorce. While this finding continues to be cited, some scholars began to question it soon after the book was published (Thornton 1986; Furstenberg 1987; Sugarman 1990). Some raised questions about the sample, which consisted of 228 individuals who received a divorce in Los Angeles in 1977. Among the criticisms were assertions that the sample was too small (Furstenberg 1987; Abraham 1989), that the sample was not representative of Los Angeles because of the low response rate (42 percent) (Thornton 1986; Hoffman and Duncan 1988; Abraham 1989), and that California is not representative of the U.S. because few states have similar divorce legislation (Jacob 1988). Others noted that the findings were inconsistent with results based on representative national samples (Thornton 1986; Peterson 1989; Morgan 1991). Analyses based on such samples found that women's standards of living declines between 13 percent and 35 percent in the first year after marital disruption (Nestel et al. 1983; Duncan and Hoffman 1985; David and Flory 1989; Peterson 1989; Stirling 1989; see Holden and Smock 1991 and Sørenson 1992 for reviews). Similarly, estimates based on national samples showed that men's standard of living increases by 11 to 13 percent after marital disruption (Duncan and Hoffman 1985; David and Flory 1989). These percentages are not nearly as large as those reported by Weitzman.

One of the most serious critiques of Weitzman's book was whether the 73 percent decline reported for women in Figure 10.1 (Weitzman 1985: 338) is consistent with other data Weitzman presented. Using income data for subsets of the sample presented in other tables in the book, Hoffman and Duncan (1988) estimated that the decline in the standard of living for divorced women in the sample is about 33 percent. They concluded that if the data in the other tables were accurate, Weitzman's estimate of a 73 percent decline for women is probably in error. Faludi (1991) highlighted and defended Hoffman and Duncan's findings. However, considerably more attention has been given to the findings in *The Divorce Revolution* than to critiques of those findings.

In spite of numerous questions and critiques, many still accept Weitzman's estimates. The findings continue to be cited without question in some social science articles (e.g., Lonsdorf 1991; Seiling and Harris 1991; Butler and Weatherly 1992; Haffey and Cohen 1992), law review articles (e.g., Fineman 1986; Melli 1986; Woodhouse 1990; Allen 1992), and newspapers and magazines (e.g., Mansnerus 1995; Thurow 1995). Okin (1991) defends the findings, arguing that they "are far less surprising than is the fact that people have been so surprised by them" (Okin 1991: 384). Critics of no-fault legislation cite the 73 percent decline reported for women as evidence that no-fault has had disastrous economic consequences for women and children (e.g., Hewlett 1986; Okin 1991; Parkman 1992).

Why have some scholars and journalists continued to cite Weitzman's findings on the economic consequences of divorce? Some may not be aware that the accuracy of the findings has been questioned. Others may continue to believe that the controversy is unresolved since no one has reanalyzed Weitzman's data. Sørenson (1992), after reviewing questions about the data, concludes there is "no clear and simple answer to the question of the magnitude of the economic consequences of marital separation" (Sørenson 1992: 280). While Hoffman and Duncan (1988) demonstrated that a 73 percent decline for women appears to be inconsistent with other data presented in the book, this conclusion is based on unweighted income data reported for selected subsamples. Furthermore, Hoffman and Duncan did not evaluate the estimate of a 42 percent rise in men's standard of living. The latter figure is particularly important because it provides evidence of a large gender gap in the economic consequences of divorce.

I reanalyze Weitzman's data and demonstrate that the results reported in *The Divorce Revolution* are in error. I also find that the erroneous results cannot be attributed to weaknesses of the sample or to errors in the dataset.

DATA

I analyze the dataset used by Weitzman (1985) in *The Divorce Revolution*. The original sample was drawn from the court dockets of divorces recorded in Los Angeles County between May and July 1977. Interviews were conducted in 1977 and 1978 with respondents from

228 of these couples. Only one member of each couple was selected for interviewing. Respondents were selected to yield a final sample with equal numbers of men and women (114 each). Long-married couples and high-SES couples were oversampled and weights were used to correct for this oversampling.

The data I analyze are derived from the computer files and paper records of the original interviews as provided by Weitzman to the Murray Research Center at Radcliffe College. Two computer files are available: one is an SPSS system file, and the other file contains the raw data. Weitzman (personal communication) and the staff of the Murray Research Center reported that each computer file contained inaccurately transcribed data, and that there were numerous inaccuracies in the data for the income variables. I compared data for selected variables from each computer file to the original paper records to determine which computer file most accurately duplicated the data in the paper records. I found that the raw data file contained fewer discrepancies than did the SPSS system file. Because the raw data file was more accurate, I used it to create a third data file, corrected using the information from the paper records.

To create this corrected file of raw data, I compared the raw data in the computer file to the responses from the paper records of the original interviews. Coding from the paper records focused on the approximately 100 variables needed to analyze the economic consequences of divorce. Whenever data in the computer file differed from information in the paper records, I corrected the data in the computer file. Errors were found in one or more income variables for 27 cases. Except where otherwise noted, all analyses in this paper are based on the corrected raw data file I created.

MEASURES

Measures were created to replicate the original analysis as described in Weitzman (1985, Ch. 10). However, because Weitzman did not explain how she handled a variety of measurement problems, I describe in detail the procedures I used to create the measures.

Like Weitzman, I use the *ratio of income to needs* as a measure of the standard of living. Respondents were asked to report their own and their spouse's income in the year before their separation, as well as their own and their ex-spouse's income at the time of the interview (i.e., within one year of the divorce). Weitzman's findings are based on three measures of the income/needs ratio for each divorced couple: one for the couple's household in the year before separation, one for the husband's post-divorce household, and one for the wife's post-divorce household. Although only one member of each couple was interviewed, each respondent was asked to report information about his or her ex-spouse as well as for him- or herself. Therefore, data on husbands' post-divorce households are based on reports from the male respondents for 114 couples plus reports from the female respondents about their ex-husbands for the other 114. Data for women's post-divorce households were similarly derived.

RESULTS

Weitzman (1985) reports results on the change in the average income/needs ratio from the time of separation to one year after a legal divorce was granted (Weitzman 1985: 323). Although she does not specify whether the "average" she uses is the median or the mean, she describes her analysis (Weitzman 1985: 337) as following the method used by Hoffman and Holmes (1976). As they report changes in the mean income/needs ratio, I present my results based on the mean.

Results based on the corrected raw data file using the measures of the income/needs ratio described above show that the effects of divorce are not nearly as large as those reported by Weitzman (1985) (see Table 10.1, Panel A). The mean income/needs ratio is 10 percent higher for men in the year after divorce than it was in the year before separation; for women, the mean income/needs ratio was 27 percent lower.

These findings represent as exact a replication of the original analysis as possible. They are based on data coded from the original interviews, the results are weighted, and the analysis replicates all the key methodological decisions described by Weitzman in *The Divorce Revolution*. The measures of post-divorce income exclude income of new spouses or new partners. New spouses or partners, however, are counted as members of the post-divorce household and therefore increase economic need. Post-divorce income measures assume full compliance with alimony and child support awards. Based on the findings reported here, it is clear that the results reported in *The Divorce Revolution* for the change in the average standard of living are in error. They could not have been derived from the data and methods described in the book.

The results presented here for both men and women are within the range of results reported from analyses of representative national samples. Thus, while the quality and representativeness of the Los Angeles sample are still open to question, the differences between Weitzman's results and those of other studies cannot be attributed to problems with the sample. The result for women reported here (–27 percent) is also reasonably close to the –33 percent estimated by Hoffman and Duncan (1988) who used the incomplete income tables presented in Weitzman's book.

Table 10.1
Changes in Income/Needs Ratio for Men and Women:
Divorced Individuals Sample, Los Angeles, 1977–1978

Variable	Men	Women
PANEL A		
Income/Needs Ratio and		
Percent Change Based on		
Corrected Raw Data File		
Mean income/needs ratio		
in year prior to separation	4.42	4.58
Mean income/needs ratio		
in year after divorce	4.88	3.34
Percent change	+10%	–27%
Number of cases	161	161
PANEL B		
Percent Change Based on		
Uncorrected Raw Data File		
Percent change	+7%	–28%
Number of cases	155	157
PANEL C		
Percent Change Based on		
Uncorrected SPSS System File		
Percent change	+7%	–20%
Number of cases	135	140

Note: See text for a description of the three data files. Means and percentages are weighted; unweighted Ns are reported to reflect true sample size.

To explore the likelihood that the data could have produced Weitzman's reported results, I examined changes experienced by individuals in the sample. Approximately 10 percent of the weighted sample of women experienced a decline in their standard of living of 73 percent or more. While this suggests that a subgroup of women do experience the severe economic consequences Weitzman described, the small size of this group indicates that the *average* decline cannot be 73 percent.[1]

To determine whether Weitzman's findings on changes in standard of living were affected by her methodological decisions (which I have replicated here), I re-estimated the results under a variety of assumptions using the corrected raw data file (results not shown). Results for the median income/needs ratio differ only slightly from results based on the mean. Because respondents' reports of post-divorce data for their ex-spouses are likely to reflect some guessing and errors, I also examined results based solely on respondents' reports of their own income and household composition. Results based on respondents' self-reports shows that the mean standard of living increased by 11 percent for men after divorce and declined by 34 percent for women. Because adjusting post-divorce income to reflect alimony and child support *awards* may overstate the amount of income actually transferred, I adjusted the post-divorce income of men and women based on the reported amounts of alimony and child support *actually paid.* This analysis produces little change in the results.[2] Since data on the income of new spouses and cohabitors were not available in the dataset, I also conducted an analysis to determine the consequences of excluding these household members from the estimation of economic need. If new spouses and cohabitors are not counted as contributing to post-divorce economic need, the mean standard of living for men increases by 20 percent after divorce, while the mean for women declines by 25 percent.

I also attempted to assess the effects of alternative ways of handling missing income data (results not shown). If cases with imputed estimates of annual income based on weekly, bimonthly, or monthly income data are removed, men's standard of living increases by 15 percent, while women's declines by 28 percent. To determine whether having income data for all cases in the dataset could substantially change the results, I made some radical assumptions. For men, I imputed $0 of income to all those for whom pre-divorce was missing. For women, I imputed $0 of post-divorce income to all those for whom post-divorce income was missing. This approach maximizes the gender disparity in results. Under these extreme (and unrealistic) assumptions, men's standard of living increases by 23 percent, while women's declines by 34 percent. These results suggest that even having complete income data from all respondents would not produce substantially different results.

Taken together, all of these alternative analyses suggest that the findings I report are stable across different estimation methods. In other words, analyses based on a variety of different assumptions do not produce results substantially different from those I report in Table 10.1, Panel A.

As described above, examining the paper records from Weitzman's study revealed that both the raw data file and the SPSS system file contained inaccurately transcribed data. Since an analysis of one of these uncorrected data files may have produced the erroneous results reported in Weitzman (1985), I conducted analyses using each of the uncorrected data files. Estimates of changes of living based on the uncorrected raw data file (Table 10.1, Panel B) are similar to those based on the corrected raw data file (Table 10.1, Panel A). The mean standard of living increases by 7 percent for men after divorce, while the mean for women declines by 28 percent. Estimates based on an analysis of the SPSS system file, which contained more errors than the uncorrected raw data file, actually show a *smaller* decline for women (Table 10.1, Panel C). The mean standard of living increases by 7 percent for men after divorce, and declines by 20 percent for women. These analyses indicate that the data errors in the two computer files do *not* account for the incorrect results reported by Weitzman.

I tried to replicate Weitzman's analysis as closely as possible with the information she presented in her book. I also examined reasonable alternative approaches for analyzing the corrected data file, and I examined the two uncorrected data files. I have been unable to discover how Weitzman's results could have been obtained. The most likely explanation is that errors in her analysis of the data were responsible for producing her results.

CONCLUSION

I have used the same data analyzed in Weitzman's (1985) *The Divorce Revolution*, have replicated the procedures she reported as closely as possible, and have demonstrated that her reported results are in error. Weitzman's much-cited estimate of a 73 percent decline in women's standard of living after divorce is inaccurate, and the estimate of a 42 percent increase for men is inaccurate as well. The figures based on the corrected data are –27 percent and +10 percent, respectively, for women and men.

Although I have shown that the economic consequences of divorce are not as severe as those described by Weitzman, this reanalysis is not intended to minimize the significance of a 27 percent decline in women's standard of living after divorce. The gender gap in economic outcomes after divorce is a significant problem and must be addressed through legal reforms and public policy. However, as Weitzman acknowledges, others reported the gender gap in economic outcomes after divorce long before she did (Hoffman and Holmes 1976; Espenshade 1979). Yet others' estimates of the economic consequences of divorce did not receive much attention, while the inaccurately large estimates reported by Weitzman were widely publicized.

The estimates I report, as well as estimates from previous research, provide a more solid basis for considering policy remedies to address the serious economic problems women face after divorce. For example, the severe economic consequences of divorce described in *The Divorce Revolution* have been used to campaign against no-fault divorce in the United States (see Faludi 1991: 19). The inaccurate findings have distorted the debate over no-fault legislation because some critics attributed differences between Weitzman's results, based on a California sample, and those of other studies to California's no-fault divorce laws. These critics argued that the economic consequences of divorce for women were much more severe in California than elsewhere in the United States because of California's no-fault divorce legislation. In fact, I have demonstrated that the findings reported by Weitzman were inaccurate. The corrected findings reported here do not support the argument that the economic consequences of divorce for women were more severe in California than elsewhere.

Clearly, Weitzman is not responsible for all the arguments made by those who cite here data — she did not argue in *The Divorce Revolution* that states should return to fault-based divorce laws. However, extreme findings are likely to be noticed and to be used to support extreme points of view. When extreme results are in error, they distort discussions of public policy and social issues (Cherlin 1990).

Social scientists must draw conclusions and develop new research projects based on reliable results from prior studies. Weitzman's findings have unnecessarily raised questions about the results of other studies and have diverted attention from more reliable estimates of the economic consequences of divorce. I hope the corrected results I report here resolve these questions and redirect our attention to more reliable data for developing policy recommendations.

NOTES

[1] Interestingly, about 9 percent of men also experienced a decline in standard of living of 73 percent or more after divorce. Weitzman did not address this finding.

[2] That little change was observed can be explained by three factors: First, in many divorces, alimony or child support was not awarded. Second, when alimony and child support were awarded, many ex-husbands were paying the full amount of the award or more. Finally, when ex-husbands paid less than the amount of the award, the difference was not usually large.

DISCUSSION QUESTIONS

1. What are the economic consequences of divorce? Place yourself in the position of a single mother, and assume that your standard of living has declined by 30 percent. How would you go about dealing with this? What kind of expenses will you have to cut? What about children's expenses?

2. What are the specific consequences of Canadian divorce laws for husbands, wives, and children?

3. What are various social policies that you would recommend in order to deal with the postdivorce gender gap?

4. Based on the Weitzman and Peterson articles, what are your perceptions of other scientific research? Do you think this kind of error is frequent? Can you think of any other "scientific mistake"?

Exhibit 2.4

Redefining Deadbeats: Ottawa's New Divorce Law Is Called Anti-Male

Allan Rock's Justice Department has written 30 pages of amendments to the Divorce Act and other federal statutes to solve the "deadbeat dads" problem — the non-custodial father who lets his kids languish in poverty with the ex-wife. Bill C-41 had first reading in Parliament last May (almost unnoticed) and is now making its way out of the standing committee on justice and legal affairs. If fathers are the source of all evil and mothers the font of all good, then C-41 will make just law.

The amendments obliges judges to set child support payments based solely upon the non-custodial parent's (read "father's") income. It ignores the possible misuse of child support by the custodial parent (read "mother"), pays no attention to her possible remarriage or future income, and does nothing to encourage her co-operation with access orders. By assuming an adversarial situation, Bill C-41 ignores the current movement toward the "presumption of joint custody" and mandatory mediation in child-custody disputes. Though it does nothing to ensure a father's access to his children, should he miss three payments or fall $3000 in arrears, he could lose his passport, see his public service pension raided, or have his aviation or maritime licences yanked — and thus be thrown out of work.

"Mr. Rock puts a black hat on men and white hat on women," says REAL Women national vice-president Gwen Landolt. "He treats fathers as nothing more than wallets." A REAL Women delegation presented its objections to C-41 to the justice committee October 24. Liberal

(continued)

Exhibit 2.4 *(continued)*

committee member and feminist Mary Clancy objected to REAL Women's contention that mothers, too, might act irresponsibly. "Show me a woman who has frittered away her child support payment and I'll show you a bald-headed sheep," she fumed. To this, Mrs. Landolt later replied that Ms. Clancy "is unmarried and doesn't have a clue" about the eventual impact of the legislation she's pushing.

"The worst thing about the bill is the mandatory nature of its child-support guidelines," says lawyer Landolt. "It gives the appearance of consistency and fairness, but since every case is so unique, it'll have exactly the opposite effect. It's typical Allan Rock: long-winded, badly written, one-sided, and absurd."

The fact that the children of divorce have problems is unquestionable. The week that C-41 was being studied in the justice committee, Statscan released the first results of its National Longitudinal Survey of Children and Youth. Much to the dismay of social engineers, 83% of kids still live in ordinary two-parent families — 78% with both their biological parents.

But kids in single-mom families have problems, running almost twice the normal risk of anxiety, depression, or aggression. It's unclear, however, whether these problems result from mom's poverty or the absence of dad. "If what's really important is a good standard of living, we're wrong to bias child custody in favour of mothers," says lawyer Karen Selick of Belleville, Ontario, a columnist with *Canadian Lawyer* magazine. "A visitor from Mars would tell us to give the kids to dad; he's the one who can best support them. And if we gave the kids to dad, a lot of women would think twice about walking out on their husbands."

Stewart Buroker, vice-president of the Men's Educational Support Association (MESA) in Calgary, finds Ms. Selick's answer simplistic. "In early childhood, kids need their mothers, while later on, the single biggest contributor to juvenile crime is the absence of fathering," he says. Basically, income-earning and childcare are competing activities, and neither partner — or ex-partner — can do both well. The trick, he says, is keeping the productive parent devoted to providing for the nurturing parent when they no longer share their income. For this reason, support can't be divorced from access issues, and C-41 is fatally flawed in looking at only half the problem.

Pro-family Liberal MP Tom Wappel (Scarborough West) believes there's nothing wrong with C-41 either in the mandatory support guidelines or in its ignoring access. "Judges will still do whatever they think fair, regardless of government guidelines," says the lawyer, formerly in

(continued)

Exhibit 2.4 *(continued)*

divorce practice. "There shouldn't be any linkage between support and access because kids need support regardless of whether mothers co-operate or not. You have to look after the kids. Neither parent should use them as levers, withholding access to get a payment or withholding payment for access."

For MESA's Buroker, that sort of thinking simply flies in the face of human experience. "The typical sequence of events is like this," he says. "Dad gets to see kids a lot and happily pays support. Then, after a while, mom wants to see less of dad, so she starts obstructing access. Then mom gets a new boyfriend, and dad figures he's not needed any more. The only thing he knows for sure: he's not seeing his kids anymore."

Reform family-policy critic Sharon Hayes (Port Moody–Coquitlam) thinks the whole problem has to be rethought. "Canadian governments have put no value on the traditional family, marriage, and parenting, but they talk about 'the best interests of the child' as if the legal system were the only way of achieving it," she says. "If we really want the best interests of the child, we have to get away from this adversarial system and institute mandatory mediation. We have to ensure that the children have access to both parents."

Source: Joseph K. Woodard, "Redefining Deadbeats: Ottawa's New Divorce Law Is Called Anti-Male," *British Columbia Report,* November 11, 1996, p. 23. Reprinted by permission.

Part Three

ETHNIC INEQUALITIES

INTRODUCTION

In addition to class and gender, race and ethnicity are important dividing characteristics of most societies. Individuals from various ethnic and racial groups have access to different resources and are evaluated differently by other groups in the society. For example, in Canada, the colonization of Canada by the French, along with the conquest of New France by the British, and finally the later arrival of non-French and non-British helped produce what is often referred to as the vertical mosaic (Porter 1965; Clement 1975). People of British origins have historically had more power and privilege than the French who, in turn, were higher in the hierarchical order than the colonized Native Canadians and the non-British or non-French immigrants. Some have argued and have provided some evidence that, at least among the masses of Canadians, this vertical division of cultural groups is not and never was as pronounced as it has been made to believe (Darroch 1979; Darroch and Ornstein 1980). Others insist that such a structure is even questionable among the most powerful elites in Canada (Ogmundson 1990). Nevertheless, in a multiethnic society such as Canada, ethnic divisions, inequality, prejudice, and racism have been and still are a part of the society. Native Canadians have historically experienced cultural and physical genocides. Blacks have experienced slavery, although not to the same extent as in the United States. Some groups have been prevented from immigrating to Canada and have been or still are the target of significant immigration obstacles (e.g., Oriental Exclusion Act 1923–1947, Chinese Head Tax, the Immigration Point System, and $1000 application fee), while others were prevented from voting and/or being involved in specific business activities such as law and pharmacy (East Indians). All of these groups are still the target of prejudice and racism. In sum, ethnic and racial divisions, similar to class and gender divisions, tend to structure inequality. For debates on immigration, see Veugelers and Klassen (1994a), Foot (1994), Simmons (1994), and Veugelers and Klassen's response (1994b). For debates on anti-Semitism, see Brym and Lenton (1991), Langlois (1992), and Brym and Lenton's response (1992).

In this light, it is of little surprise that feminists who have made a significant contribution to the understanding of women's oppression have

228

themselves encountered substantial criticism from people of colour. The critics argue that contrary to the white feminists' assertion that the family is the site of oppression, for people of colour, it is a haven that protects women from the racism they encounter in everyday life. Moreover, they insist that women of colour have more power in the family, are more likely to have a job, and work for a longer period of time than white women. The resulting socio-economic resources increase the power of these women within the family and diminish the power of their husband/partner. Criticisms such as these have persuaded Michèle Barrett and Mary McIntosh (1985) to come to terms with racial and ethnic divisions among women. They recognized their earlier ethnocentrism, which fed into the stereotypes about women of colour and ignored the extent to which those women were oppressed by white men *and* women. They acknowledged that the concept of patriarchy as a universal domination of men over women *is* defendable but inadequate. For example, under slavery, black men were systematically barred from positions of power in the social hierarchy. In such a situation, most black men were subordinate to all white men *and* women. Caroline Ramazanoglu (1986) responds that such a self-criticism does not address the systematic racism embedded in all institutions of (white) society. "What is missing in this article is the pain, the passion, and the power of racism which is beyond anything Barrett and McIntosh seem to have imagined." She argues that privileged white feminists who have secure jobs, control over their own bodies, and who can avoid establishing a (patriarchal) family if they choose to are removed from the experience of most other women and cannot understand the complexity of women's oppression. That is to say, the problem has less to do with ethnocentrism and more with institutional racism. The political implication of the criticism by people of colour is that a common front to eliminate patriarchy is perhaps not possible and that the struggle should take into account the diversity of women's experiences. They suggest that "The politics of black feminism cannot then be the same as the politics of white feminism except in specific struggle." For more criticism of Barrett and McIntosh, see Kazi (1986), Lees (1986), and Mirza (1986). For debates on fractured feminism, see Harris (1989) and Briskin (1990). For cross-cultural differences in gender inequality, see Okin (1994), Flax (1995), and Okin's response (1995).

As suggested earlier, the imagery of the vertical mosaic in Canada may differ whether the focus is on the masses or on the most powerful individuals and institutions. Ethnic inequality among the elites is significantly more resistant to change than that among the masses. In Canada, given its history of conquest, colonialism, and domination, Porter (1965) has long argued that the British have institutionalized avenues of upward mobility based on their own values, attitudes, and behaviours, thus limiting the access of the conquered and the newly arrived to positions of power. Such a view of Canada has generated many debates, such as the recent empirical criticism directed at the vertical mosaic by Ogmundson and McLaughlin (1992). They provide evidence that for each category of elites, the British proportion has declined from 1935 onward, and that of the French and "other" ethnic groups has increased. Nakhaie (1995) questions such a generalization on the grounds that Ogmundson and McLaughlin fail to take into account the changes in the ethnic composition of the Canadian population. That is, when we factor in the declining portion of the population of British ancestry and the increasing proportion of the other ethnic groups, the evidence suggests that the British have maintained their elite domination, particularly among the directors of the largest corporations. Nevertheless, there has been a modest increase in the French and other ethnic group representation among the elites. However, this increase has not been at the expense of the British, but it is more likely that the French and other groups have established parallel institutions of upward mobility. For more debates on the vertical mosaic see Ogmundson and McLaughlin (1994), Ogmundson (1993, 1992, 1990), Li (1978, 1988), Nakhaie (1995), Clement (1990), Darroch (1979), Darroch and Ornstein (1980), Winn (1985), Lautard and Guppy (1990), and Lautard and Loree (1984).

The conflict between the British and the French has been and still is the centerpiece of Canadian history. From the conquest of New France to the present, French Quebeckers have resisted Anglo-American domination culturally, politically, and economically. Such a conflict is often identified as French nationalism manifesting itself in events such as the rebellion of 1837. In more recent times, the birth of modern Quebec nationalism can be attributed to the 1960s, when Quebeckers proclaimed that they were "*maitres chez nous.*" They also passed legislation to promote the French language, and they underwent demographic changes such as low fertility rates and new immigration patterns. The Quiet Revolution was important to the nationalist tendencies in that it helped fuel the expansion of the new francophone middle class and the organized labour movement, of which the political loyalty and economic interests rested in Quebec and not in Canada. Camille Laurin's (1978) article presents us with the history of British–French relations and the importance of the French Language Charter (Bill 101) for the survival of the French Quebeckers. Laurin argues that French Canada continues to exist because of the ability of French collectivity to resist British domination, and that the language charter is essential to the endurance of this collectivity. It is important for us to remember that the persistence of a cultural group is strongly related to its ability to maintain its language. It is through language that a nation's identity is shaped according to its historical myths and realities. In the case of Canada, the maintenance of the French language and culture becomes crucial. If immigrants to Quebec were to learn a language other than French, the French portion of the overall population of the province would decline and jeopardize French culture. This decline would crystalize itself in the political arena, leading to a corresponding deterioration in French power. It is therefore not surprising that Quebec governments have legislated language bills, and the Supreme Court of Canada has approved much of this legislation. The court has argued that although such legislation violates individual rights, it is necessary to protect the collective rights of French Quebeckers.

Bernard Blishen (1978) uses 1977 data to challenge Laurin's argument for a homogenous French-Canadian nationalism. True, compared to most other provinces, the French in Quebec are more likely to identify with their province first rather than with Canada, but a large proportion of the French Canadians identify with their province and with Canada equally. Among French Canadians, identification with Quebec is the highest among the younger age groups, educated individuals, and middle-income groups. The data did not point to the strong Quebec nationalism portrayed by Laurin (1978). Of course, we know now that the first Quebec referendum (1980) supported Blishen's view as well. However, the last Quebec referendum (1995), with almost half of those voting supporting some type of change in Quebec's association with Canada, suggests a growing nationalism in that province. Perhaps the increasing educational attainment of the French Quebeckers, as well as the aging of the young nationalists at the time of Blishen's study, have contributed to a new surge in nationalist sentiment. Mobilization of French Canadians by their political elites (René Lévèsque and Lucien Bouchard), political party (Parti Québécois), and recent language legislation (Bill 8 and Bill 178) should also be taken into account. For more debates on the Quebec question, see Griffin (1984), Lubin (1985), Gould (1990/91), McRoberts (1991/92), Edwards (1985, 1994), Cummins (1994), MacMillan (1990), Sniderman et al. (1989, 1990), Usher (1995a, 1995b), and Watson (1995).

Colonization of Canada, first by the French and then by the British, has had a lasting impact on the aboriginal peoples. No other group in Canada has experienced as much cultural and physical genocide as people of the First Nations. Aboriginal peoples, on average, have lower education, income, and occupation, and are poorer in terms of housing, health, and other qualities of life. These inequalities are attributed to both the history of colonization and to a "culture of poverty," which itself may have been produced by the European domination of the First Nations.

One of the most persistent threats of the European domination of the aboriginal peoples has been the assimilationary practices of the dominant Europeans. According to Peter Kulchyski (1995), capitalism and the Canadian government are both responsible for this assimilation because of what he terms their hegemonic domination of aboriginal peoples. The capitalist structure has expanded into every aspect of the aboriginals' lives, destroying their traditional ways of life. Similarly, official government policy, such as the British North America Act (1867), was intended to regulate the transition of aboriginal peoples into the mainstream way of life. Aboriginal peoples, however, have continuously resisted these assimilation attempts. They have responded with resistance mechanisms such as maintenance of aboriginal language or using radio and television to strengthen their own culture. The most important aspects of this resistance have been the aboriginals' demands for self-government and land claims. The question of identity is also the crucial aspect of this struggle.

D.A. West (1996) agrees that the dominant Europeans have tried and are trying to assimilate aboriginal peoples. However, West argues that the very "theoretical map" adopted by Kulchyski for explaining the relationship between the aboriginal and the Canadian state is Eurocentric. According to West, it is misleading to adopt the theoretical framework developed by Europeans and interpret the actions of the aboriginal peoples through that structure. In fact, West considers aboriginal politics as a type of resistance to the theoretical framework that is imposed on the aboriginal ways of life. Moreover, it is misleading to argue, as does Kulchyski, that, for example, the Inuit Broadcasting Corporation (IBC) is a tool of resistance used by the Inuit people against their masters. For West, IBC is simply another mechanism to assimilate the Inuit people into the dominant society. He questions how five or six hours of Inuit television could counter the effect of thousands of hours of North American television broadcast for the Inuit. Television itself is a source of domination of aboriginal life. He sums up that instead of using Eurocentric theoretical maps to understand the Canadian aboriginals, we should "listen carefully to what aboriginal people are saying about land and spirit and *what we look and sound like to them.*" For more debates on the aboriginal issues, see Flanagan (1989), Griffin (1989), Janes (1994), West (1994a, 1994b), Bourgeault (1983), and Russell (1984).

Canadian society is composed of many ethnic groups. In addition to the two Canadian Charter groups (British and French) and the aboriginal peoples, Canada is inhabited by the new immigrants to whom Porter (1965) referred as the "entrance groups." In his terminology, these are the diverse group of newcomers who are placed at the bottom of the mosaic after those of British and French origin. Partly because of the socio-economic status of entrance groups, their experience of alienation and rootlessness, and as a political ideology against Québécois nationalism, the government of Canada enacted a multicultural policy. The official position, however, has been that this policy is intended to help all Canadian ethnic groups maintain their cultural heritage. Lance Roberts and Rodney Clifton (1982) suggest that this policy is doomed. For them, ethnic cultural maintenance requires relevant supporting institutions and organizations such as schools, churches, social service organizations, clubs, and media. Similarly, Breton (1964) has previously argued that "institutional completeness" is the necessary precondition for cultural maintenance. Lack of such structures will result in assimilation of the minority ethnic groups into that of the dominant culture. Only a few ethnic groups possess such structures and institutions that will enable them to maintain their language and marry among themselves, thus experiencing cultural persistence (e.g., Hutterites). According to Roberts and Clifton, most of the Canadian ethnic groups lack such institutions. Under such conditions, Canada's diverse ethnic groups face the dilemma of assimilating into the dominant group's culture and thus benefiting from dominant structures, or retaining their own cultural heritage. Often, this dilemma has been resolved in the form of "symbolic ethnicity." They "feel" their culture but do not "live" in it. This is a type of structural assimilation with a feeling that they are part of their own ethnic culture. Thus, according to Roberts and Clifton, since ethnic groups lack such structural prerequisites for cultural maintenance, the multicultural policy is doomed and the government should stop funding it.

Don Dawson (1982) criticizes Roberts and Clifton for underestimating the degree of institutional completeness of Canadian ethnic groups as well as the degree of their compatibility with the mainstream society. He argues that one should not use Hutterites as an example of institutionally complete ethnic groups (as used by Roberts and Clifton) since they are isolationist secessionists whose very social structure is antithetical to modern social order. There are many institutionally complete ethnic groups in Canada (Hebrews, Ukrainians, Chinese, Italians, etc.), and many Canadian ethnic groups desire to participate fully within the Canadian society. As well, to the extent that members of an ethnic group make it within the dominant institutions they may feel safe to re-assert their ethnicity. That is to say, structural assimilation may result in the re-emergence of ethnic identity. Thus, he insists that the Canadian multiculturalism policy is not without a basis in social reality. For more debate on multiculturalism, see Brotz (1980), Lupul (1982, 1983), Isajiw (1983), Liu (1991), Rothstein (1993), Mitchell (1993), Gitlin (1994), Roper (1994), Spencer (1994), and Brand (1994).

The final debate in Part Three deals with the all-too-familiar issue of social versus genetic causes of racial inequalities. Capitalists' quest for cheap labour, strong European and weak African military institutions and government, combined with a belief in Manifest Destiny, may have all contributed to the African blacks being chosen as the targets of slavery. Once in the United States, blacks experienced one of the worst suffering ever endured by a group of people. They had little control over their lives, children, and well-being; they were considered little more than "talking animals." With the abolition of slavery, inequities experienced by blacks continued in the form of racism, discrimination, segregation, and prejudice. Although the civil rights movement attempted to eliminate these injustices, many remain. African Americans have lower educational and occupational attainment, lower income and wealth, are in poor-quality housing, are more likely to experience health problems, and have a higher mortality rate than their white counterparts. They are also more likely to be sent to prison or become victims of crime than whites.

There are two broad theoretical models that account for the racial inequities in America. Some suggest that slavery and past and present discrimination and prejudice are the source of inequalities between the races. The focus here is on the social forces that have helped produce racial inequalities. Others suggest that characteristics such as cognitive ability, intelligence, and other individual traits are responsible for these inequalities. The Committee on the Status of Black Americans emphasizes the discrimination model and suggests policies to equalize the playing field between blacks and whites. R.J. Herrnstein (1990a) questions the committee's explanation of the source of the black–white socio-economic differences as well as the suggested policy of affirmative action. He points to a large body of research that suggests that the source of black and white differences is due to the disparity in their cognitive ability. For example, in America, on the average, blacks score lower in IQ tests than whites. He insists that, in fact, the source of a lower socio-economic status for blacks is their lower cognitive abilities and not the other way around. The implication of his suggestion is that affirmative action policies are misguided and will not have the desired effect. How could such policies change individual traits such as intelligence?

Robert Hauser, Gerald Jaynes, and Robin Williams, Jr. (1990), who were a part of the National Research Council's Committee on the Status of Black Americans, agree that racial discrimination (past and present) is not entirely responsible for the black and white differences in socio-economic attainment. However, they object to Herrnstein's suggestion that cognitive ability may be the sole cause of these differences. They correctly argue that we cannot explain the last 40 years of observed *changes* in socio-economic status of blacks by a *constant*. The black gene pool has not changed in this period. Furthermore, any genetic or sociobiological explanation is useless because it has little policy implication. It is simply not possible to make policies that will change the genetic make-up of a population in order to ameliorate racial inequalities. Finally, they insist that since the differential ability hypothesis cannot account entirely for the racial differences and that many social forces have contributed to such inequalities, therefore, the suggested affirmative action policy is sound. These policies will address the social causes of black and white inequities (see also Herrnstein's response, 1990). For debates on affirmative action, see Wilson (1990), Skocpol (1990), Tollett (1991), Fraiman (1997a, 1997b), Lauter (1997), Samantrai (1997), Hill (1987a, 1987b), Salvatore (1987), Brooks (1987), Womack (1987), Arnowitz (1987), Ezorsky (1987), Brody (1987), Waltzer (1987), Roediger (1987), Weir (1987), Lichtenstein (1987), Schwarzschild (1987), and Glaberman (1987). On genetic and sociobiological explanations of racial inequalities, see Rushton (1988a, 1988b), Zuckerman and Brody (1988), Van den Berghe (1978, 1980), Reynolds (1978, 1980a, 1980b), Klein (1985), Eller and Coughlan (1993), and Grosby (1994). On racism, see D'Souza (1996a, 1996b), Williams (1996), Meyers (1996), Jaffa (1996), Burlingame (1996), and Sniderman and Tetlock (1986a, 1986b). On racial conflict, see Stone (1980) and Dubois (1980).

ble labour and that some women workers (particularly married women) may form an industrial reserve army of dispensable labour to cushion the boom and slump of capitalist production. These analyses can then be tied in with an emphasis on the state and welfare policy as an instrument for regulating the labour supply through altering the level of benefits relative to wages. In our previous work, we have argued this line of analysis, or adapted the arguments of other socialist-feminists on these topics, without considering the degree to which the data we cited or the illustrations we used would apply to the distinctive household and wage labour patterns of different ethnic groups.

Taking first the idea of the male breadwinner/dependent wife couple as the model or norm on which the household is typically based in contemporary Britain, we can see that the picture changes substantially if we look at the evidence for black households. 26% of white households in the PSI survey fitted the family model of adults living with their children, compared with 36% of West Indian and 56% of Asian households (Brown 1984: 51). The explanation of these figures, however, is quite straightforward and has more to do with age-structure than with different cultural patterns. The pattern of immigration has meant that far fewer ethnic minority households, particularly Asian ones, consist of single pensioners. (If we exclude pensioners, the white figure rises to about 38%.) More interesting, perhaps, is the question of whether these relatively conventional family-households contain the male breadwinner and full-time housewife couple. We can look at this by examining the "economic activity" rates for adult women of different ethnic groups. The 1981 *Labour Force Survey* showed that 23% of white women, 42% of West Indian women and 25% of Asian women were in full-time work; 17% of white, 14% of West Indian and 5% of Asian women were in part-time work (Central Statistical Office 1983: 183). (Unfortunately, the figures are not available in this form for later years, but the ratios of full- to part-time work have not changed much.) It is worth noting, against the usual stereotype of the Asian woman as confined to the home, that *more* Asian women work full-time outside the home than white women do — as a proportion of the group — and this is true even if you allow for the fact that there are more older and retired women among the whites. It is also worth noting that the tendency for women to work part-time — the supposedly ideal combination, in western family ideology, of employment and responsibility for children — is shown much more strongly by white women than by either of these ethnic minorities. So at first glance, perhaps it looks as if this model of family is one that is characteristic of the white family-household but less so of West Indian and Asian households.

If we look at women's employment and household situation in more detail, a number of features can be seen. The most striking differences are probably those that concern West Indian women: they show most clearly the injustice and irrationality of a "male family wage" system. 18% of all West Indian households are headed by single parents, the vast majority of whom are women, and 31% of West Indian households with children are single-parent units. The corresponding figures for white households are 3% and 10%; for Asian households, they are 4% and 5% (Brown 1984: 49, 51). West Indian women with responsibilities for dependants are much less likely than white women to receive any financial help, such as maintenance for children, from outside the household and are much more likely to be single rather than divorced or separated (Brown 1984: 232). These figures point to the fact that a higher proportion of West Indian women than of white or Asian women shoulder financial responsibilities, especially for children. In general, there are far more West Indian female "heads of household" than there are in the white or Asian samples (32% as against 6.5% Asian and 14% white, using figures that exclude single pensioner households (Brown 1984: 51)). These facts put into perspective some otherwise surprising features of West Indian women's employment — not only are they more likely to work full-time than white or Asian women, but when they do, their average weekly earnings are better. The PSI survey found that whereas the median wages of black men were substantially less than those of white men — as widespread evidence has confirmed — the median wage for women of West Indian origin was £4 a week higher than for white women and £8 a week higher than for Asian women (Brown 1984: 212). This pattern is weakened if you look only at women in the age range 25–54, so it may be that older white women are pulling down the white average (Brown 1984: 181).

There can be little doubt that a male "family wage" system is particularly iniquitous when considered in relation to this information about the household responsibilities and dependants of West Indian women. If we turn to some of the features of Asian women's employment, further differences emerge. The traditional stereotype here is that Asian women are immured in the home through religious and family customs, unable to speak the language, kept in purdah or allowed only to work in small family businesses. Parita Trivedi (1984) suggests that we abandon this stereotype and look at the facts.

It is, perhaps, a tribute to the force of this stereotype that feminists such as ourselves have failed to see the operation of a myth in the Asian context that we have unmasked in the white family. It is the myth of female dependence. It is true that on a world scale the official labour-force participation rates of women in Islamic countries are markedly lower than in other comparable countries, and this must represent some difference in the position of women. It is probably as much due to the distinctive patterns of social control and economic obligation in the kinship institutions as to simple differences in cultural beliefs about women's role (Haggag Youssef 1974). It is also probably true that such figures mask the fact that women do huge amounts of productive work, including work that brings in money. White socialist-feminists such as ourselves realize that British white women "have always worked," that the family wage system has never existed except for among a tiny group of the labour aristocracy in Britain; we recognize the ideological character of the belief that men can support women and that their status rises as a result of this ability. Yet Pratibha Parmar gives many examples of academics and policy makers reinforcing beliefs or assumptions about Asian women's passivity and exclusive home orientation; she argues that these errors rest on a complete misapprehension of the roles of women in the Indian sub-continent. Even among Islamic peoples, where purdah is practised, women principally work outside the home in the farming economy; their labour is described as "unorganized," but it is central to the household economy and recognized by all but those who choose not to see it (Parmar 1982: 254ff). Whilst it is true that the labour force participation rates in Britain are lower for Muslim women (principally from Pakistan and Bangla Desh) than for Asian women of Hindu or Sikh background (and Asian rates are lower than white or West Indian ones), the interpretation of these facts is complex. Sheila Allen observes that followers of Islam *aspire* to the ideal of women not working outside the home but that this is not the case in actuality; however the belief that women should not work outside the home leads to a serious under-representation of women in the enumeration of workers (Allen 1982: 134–35).

Information about the employment of black women adds a further dimension to the picture that white socialist-feminists such as ourselves have drawn of job segregation. Asian women are over-represented in the textile and clothing industries in repetitive assembly work; they are numerous among Britain's hyper-exploited category of homeworkers. West Indian women figure disproportionately in low-grade professional work and in the service industries generally (Brown 1984: 203).

These patterns are as yet inadequately theorized, but there can be no doubt that discussions of job segregation and a gendered division of labour in employment that simply ignored them (for instance Chapter 5 of *Women's Oppression Today* [1980]) are profoundly unsatisfactory. Equally and classically ethnocentric are statements such as "... the parallel between the married woman worker and the semi-proletarianized migrant worker cannot be pushed too far ..." (Barrett 1980: 159). Such a sentence can only be written on the assumption that the married woman is white and the migrant worker is male; it falls with all four feet into the ethnocentrism identified in the acute book title *All the Women Are White, All the Blacks Are Men, But Some of Us Are Brave*

(Hull et al. 1982). The phrase "Ain't I A Woman?" coined by Sojourner Truth in the 1850s and revived in Bell Hooks's book of that title (Hooks 1982), may not be as redolent of one historical moment as we might think. On the left and within feminism, and as part of the daily work of socialist-feminism, white people slide into ways of expressing things that systematically negate the existence and experience of black women. It is only comparatively recently that the voices of female migrant labourers have been heard above the academic and political arguments that ignored them (see *Migrant Women Speak* 1978; Phizacklea 1983).

SOME CONCEPTUAL QUESTIONS

Socialist-feminists have tended to argue that an analysis of patriarchy as universal dominance of men over women is too simple (see the extended discussion of these issues in Beechey 1979). We have tended to argue (see, for example, Barrett 1980: 10–19) that we need a more precise definition of patriarchy — if the term is to be retained — that will encompass differences between men in hierarchical situations.[2] If we look at slavery, colonialism and their legacies, it is easy to see that black men are systematically barred from positions of power in the social hierarchy. In colonial situations, some black men may be appointed by the colonial authorities to positions of relative power over their own people, though always needing the continued blessing of the white rulers. But most are subordinate to all white people, whether men or women. White women's social power in slave, colonial and racist societies may be restricted to the home, the locality, to the interpersonal relations of mistress and servant and the ritual forms of inter-racial deference, but it is nevertheless an undeniable fact that white women can dominate black men. Radical feminists have sometimes claimed that in such situations, white women are really only pawns in a white man's game. But we would argue that the interplay between white power and male power is more complex. A legal provision like the White Women's Protection Ordinance (enacting the death penalty for even the attempted rape of a white woman) in Papua New Guinea under British rule did, in a sense, posit white women as mere symbols of white "civilization," protected as part of white men's ruling strategy. On the other hand, it did give white women, as women, a measure of power over black men, as men. It is not simply a question of the racial hierarchy overriding the sexual: it can actually reverse it in a specifically sexual sphere.

An even more striking instance is the much debated "Scottsboro Boys" case in Alabama in the early 1930s. Eight of a group of nine black youths were sentenced to death in 1931 for the rape of two poor white women riding a freight train to Chattanooga. They were later reprieved after a campaign led by the Communist Party. It became clear that the women had been bullied or persuaded by a posse of white men to give perjured evidence against the youths. The campaign for reprieve exposed the white women, in all the familiar terms of rape trials, as "po' white trash," vagrants and prostitutes. Over forty years later, Susan Brownmiller (1976: 230–35) comes to the defence of the white women. She knows that they made a false accusation of rape, but it was, she claims, understandable in terms of their oppression as women. Angela Davis criticizes her: "In choosing to take sides with white women, regardless of the circumstances, Brownmiller herself capitulates to racism. Her failure to alert white women about the urgency of combining a fierce challenge to racism with the necessary battle against sexism is an important plus for the forces of racism today" (Davis 1981: 199). The reprieve campaign focused only on racism; the radical feminist position risks leaving it out altogether. At the time, it was necessary to take sides, but now it should be possible to see a complex situation in which racism was the dominant theme. The Scottsboro Nine were total victims. Nothing they did or said could save them; only a campaign from outside could get them a second, then a third, trial and eventual long prison sentences instead of death. The two white women, on the other hand, were bullied, they were disbelieved and their reputations were besmirched; they were kept in jail for a while before they gave evidence. But the younger one did recant in the second trial: they had some choices.

Examples such as the White Women's Protection Ordinance and the case of the "Scottsboro Boys" serve to emphasize the complex interrelations of class, race and gender power structures. The bulk of this article is an attempt to demonstrate how difficult it remains to theorize the relations of race and gender, but this is not the only problem involved. Socialists are currently divided as to whether the social divisions associated with ethnicity and racism should be seen as absolutely autonomous of social class, as reducible to social class, or as having different historical origins but articulating now with the divisions of class in capitalist society. Obviously it is true that racism, like women's oppression, existed long before capitalism, cannot be reduced to arguments about the supposed needs of capitalism, bedevils socialist societies and so on and so on. Yet it is also true that, unlike gender divisions which have to accommodate the fact that women are distributed across the whole of the class structure, the social divisions of race correlate closely, in a society like contemporary Britain, with class divisions. The fact that racial status (unlike gender) is inherited makes possible an association with class, which is also largely inherited. Black workers are clustered in easily identified sectors of the labour force, distinctive patterns apply to particular ethnic minorities, predictions can be made about labour migration and the relative costs of labour in different geographical areas. In these and other ways, it is possible to see a correspondence of some kind between class and race, and, of course, many black activists and writers take a "class position" on racism and imperialism.

Leaving aside these unresolved questions about the theorization of the race and class relation, we would argue that the definition of patriarchy as unambiguous male dominance found in many versions of feminist theory is less able, potentially, to cope with the question of race as a cross-cutting division to the social divisions of gender than a more complex socialist-feminist approach. Socialist-feminists have tended to reject the idea that male dominance is the principal, or only, line of power and exploitation in our society because we see the power and exploitation of social class as irrefutable. Without claiming to see much progress on this question so far, we do nevertheless think that in general, the socialist-feminist critique of the concept of patriarchy offers a better way forward to the understanding of race divisions than do the standard feminist definitions that pose men as universally powerful.

We would like briefly to mention two further concepts whose uses we believe should be examined in a new light. These are the concepts of *ideology* and of *reproduction*. The use of both of these terms should, we think, be reconsidered from two points of view. The first is that of their capacity for description. For example, it is widely stated that an important component of the way in which gender divisions are re-created over time is an "ideology of femininity" (and masculinity) which has been analysed in many contexts. Yet we know enough to say that the construction of femininity and masculinity at an ideological level differs in different ethnic groups as does the specification of acceptable behaviour in relation to sexuality and so on. If it is difficult, as we suspect, for white women to attempt to summarize these differences without running the risk of stereotyping on the basis of ethnic community, it is still possible for us to familiarize ourselves with the many accounts and analyses of these socialization processes that have been written from a basis of experience. Also, we need to be more aware of the ways in which white femininity has been constructed ideologically through negative and offensive stereotypes and myths about black sexuality and femininity. It is now widely recognized that class prejudice, and myths about working-class female sexuality such as were fostered in the nineteenth century, have played an important role in the historical definition of bourgeois feminine respectability and notions of passive feminine sexuality. Perhaps we need to pay more attention to the ways in which a specifically white construction of femininity has been formed through what Trivedi calls "racist imaginings." An example of this can be seen in the dramatic representation of the myth of black nymphomania in the treatment of Antoinette Crosby in *Wide Sargasso Sea* by

Jean Rhys. And Lucy Bland and Frank Mort comment that there is an equally racist trade-off in relation to white femininity and black masculinity: "The image of women as passive, white, civilized victims worked to intensify notions of its opposite — primitive, animal masculinity, seen as non-white, non-European and non-civilized" (Bland and Mort 1984: 145).

The question of "reproduction," seen in terms of the politics of biological reproduction, is one that has received considerable attention in the light of the issue of race. The move from an emphasis on women's right to abortion to one on women's reproductive rights in general represented a move from white feminists' priorities towards a less ethnically specific campaign. While the right to abortion remains a demand that can unite women across race and class lines, we are all now more aware of the extent to which compulsory sterilization and the use of depo-provera, for example, form part of a long-term global picture of the reproductive abuse of women from the Third World and from ethnic minorities. There can be no doubt that the politics of biological reproduction have been decisively shifted and rendered far more complex by the attempt to rid existing campaigns of an ethnocentric and class bias. Casting the term in the light of social rather than biological reproduction also generates difficulties, as Hazel Carby has pointed out, since we have as yet no means of dealing with the ways in which black female labour reproduces racialized relations of production through domestic service work (Carby 1982: 218).

With both of these concepts, however, the question is not restricted to the substance of the material that they can be used to describe and analyse. It is not only a question of what content you include when you decide to write about the ideology of femininity or about feminism and biological reproduction. For both of these concepts have been developed, at times with some difficulty, in a dialogue with the Marxist analysis of society that they ultimately stem from. For both of these concepts, it has been a problem to clarify where their use by socialist-feminists follows or departs from the meaning they carry in Marxist theory in general. From this point of view, the question of race as an independent social division is an extremely pressing theoretical one. Do we take the view that the introduction of a third system must necessarily fragment the analysis that was already creaking at the seams over feminism? Or should we regard race as easier to incorporate into a classic Marxist analysis than feminism proved to be? Or should we concentrate on the relations between race and gender and ignore for the moment the consequences of this for a class analysis? Or should we apparently back down from these academic debates and adopt a more pragmatic political approach by identifying areas of common and progressive struggle? Can we argue that racism, like women's oppression, has independent origins but is now irretrievably embedded in capitalist social relations? These questions remain as unresolved as the debate around the concept of patriarchy that we discussed earlier, but they set the agenda for further work.

THE CRITIQUE OF THE FAMILY

In *The Anti-social Family*, we argued for a sweepingly critical stance on the family, although one that rested on an appreciation of the reasons underlying the commitment people felt towards it. Various lines of criticism could be, or have been, levelled against our argument. Hazel Carby (1982) argues (in response to Barrett 1980), that the family can operate as a prime source of political and cultural resistance to racism; that the degradation of black female sexuality has come about through white racism and not within the black family; that the denial of career opportunities to Asian girls comes about through white assumptions about their family ideology rather than through those families themselves (Parmar 1982); that white feminists assume western romantic marriage to be better than models of the family with which they are unfamiliar; that the British state's pathologizing of the black family has influenced progressive opinion; that these attitudes all betray a patronizing (imperialist) approach towards so-called underdeveloped societies and their family customs (Carby 1982: 214–17). These points could be complemented by the terse remark of Floya Anthias and Nira Yuval-Davis that "the family may *not* be the major site for women's oppression when families are kept apart by occupying or colonizing forces (as in Lebanon or South Africa)" (Anthias and Yuval-Davis 1983: 73).

In conclusion, we want merely to summarize briefly what we have tried to deal with in this piece. We have recognized elements of ethnocentrism in our previous work and have pointed to important issues where the analysis we have presented has been seriously marred by a failure to consider ethnicity and racism. We have also looked at the ways in which debates about race, class and gender might alter the ways in which theoretical concepts have been used in socialist-feminist work. We have given almost exclusive emphasis to a comparison between white women and black, focusing on women of West Indian and Asian origin in Britain. We are aware that these communities are not themselves homogeneous (particularly the Asian communities here lumped together) and that we have completely excluded consideration of many other forms of racism and ethnic disadvantage. We believe that there are issues on which women can work together and hope that, at least, this article might contribute to an atmosphere of more constructive dialogue.

NOTES

[1] A recent example of such accusations would be those made by Valerie Amos and Pratibha Parmar (1984). Maxine Molyneux's carefully qualified comment that "... the changes brought by imperialism to Third World societies may, in some circumstances, have been historically progressive," which was accompanied by a discussion highly critical of the impact of imperialism on women (Molyneux 1981: 4), has been traduced in their statement that "Black and Third World women are being told that imperialism is good for us" (Amos and Parmar 1984: 7). This reaction assumes that the only politically correct position on the Third World is that of dependency theory, rejects the possibility of comparative work on women's subordination, implies that white women have no right to views on these questions, and amounts to a militant cultural relativism. Equally to write of the "racial chauvinism" of Bujra and Caplan (p. 6) or of Lewis's patronizing and condescending understanding of Black women (p. 7) in the same article, reads more as an objection in principle to white women being engaged in such work than as an argument against the substance of what is said or the status of the evidence used.

[2] "I would not, however, want to argue that the concept of patriarchy should be jettisoned. I would favour retaining it for use in contexts where male domination is expressed through the power of the father over women and over younger men. Clearly some societies have been organized around this principle, although not capitalist ones" (Barrett 1980: 250).

Ethnocentrism and Socialist-Feminist Theory: A Response to Barrett and McIntosh
Caroline Ramazanoglu

The recent article by Michèle Barrett and Mary McIntosh (1985) is difficult to respond to and yet so disturbing in its impact that some response seems called for.

Barrett and McIntosh are respected feminist authors, experienced academics, well skilled in presenting their arguments and in anticipating criticisms, particularly:

... the danger of a public breast-beating exercise that enables white women to carry on as before but with the added reassurance of having articulated some fashionable guilt. (Barrett and McIntosh 1985: 20)

They are cautious in presenting their conclusions where they hope that recognizing "elements of ethnocentrism" in their previous work, their previous failure to consider ethnicity and racism, and the importance of reconsidering concepts such as patriarchy, ideology and reproduction will contribute to "an atmosphere of more constructive dialogue" (Barrett and McIntosh 1985: 44 [p. 248 in this book]).

It is not an easy task to try to come to terms with one's own ethnocentrism. It is not easy to take personally, as Barrett and McIntosh have done, black criticisms of white feminism. Nevertheless, my response to this article was one of deep disappointment that reasoned self-criticism could come to no more than a vehicle for defensive arguments pitched at a level of academic debate which is far removed from the daily reality of racism, and which can be intimidating in its impact.

This level of tightly defended "autocritique" seems too complacent to be appropriate in a feminist journal as a means of opening up the dialogue that they seek between the exponents of white feminism and the anger and frustration which have been widely expressed by black women. If we are going to beat our breasts in public, shouldn't we unbuckle the armour plating first? By concentrating on defending themselves so carefully, Barrett and McIntosh seem to lose sight of the seriousness of the divisions between women which black women have brought to light.

The positive contribution of this article lies in the authors' attempt to open up the issue of how (or perhaps whether) feminism in its present forms can take the deep divisions between women properly into account. Feminism, as they make clear by defining their stance as socialist-feminist, is a social theory that is inseparable from political practice. A critical practical problem for feminists, therefore, has always been how to agree on what it is in society that needs to be changed. Feminist politics cannot be effective in transforming society if women have different experiences of oppression and so different priorities for transformation.

Barrett and McIntosh examine their ethnocentrism explicitly as socialist-feminists, but purging socialist-feminism of racism or ethnocentrism will not resolve the problems of a politically divided feminism. While they have given an honest attempt to identify ethnocentrism in their previous work, Barrett and McIntosh do not give any clear indication of the relation between this self-criticism and a feminist politics which is more effective than before in taking the diversity of women's oppression and struggles into account.

What is missing in this article is the pain, the passion and the power of a racism which is beyond anything that Barrett and McIntosh seem to have imagined. We cannot confront ethnocentrism in ourselves without at least some sense of the atrocities of colonial history/herstory. If socialist-feminists are to retain what is of value in Marx's theory, they should also retain Marx's sense of moral outrage and his ability to incorporate the struggles and sufferings of diverse individuals into his general theory.

Feminist theory must necessarily be general if we are to understand in general how women come to be, and to stay, oppressed, but a general theory is impracticable if it loses sight of the diversity of women's experience. The recognition of ethnocentrism in our work does not in itself render black women's experiences visible. It is only when we try to take black women's experiences into account that the extremely problematic relationship between general *ideas* of oppression and women's *experiences* of oppression becomes visible.

Perhaps the core of the problem in Barrett and McIntosh's conception of how socialist-feminists should respond to black criticisms is that while they think the political issue is one of race rather than of ethnicity (Barrett and McIntosh 1985: 26–27 [p. 239 in this book]), they have presented their self-criticisms as an article on their ethnocentrism (Barrett and McIntosh 1985: 28 [p. 240 in this book]). It seems to me that black women are not accusing white feminists so much of ethnocentrism, which could perhaps be corrected by extending the field of vision, but of a crushing, institutionalized racism which is so totally and deeply entrenched in our ways of thinking and being that we cannot see clearly how we help to justify and perpetuate it.

Barrett and McIntosh see their own ethnocentrism as stemming from an "ethnically specific" position (Barrett and McIntosh 1985: 25 [p. 238 in this book]) rather than taking up Carby's argument that there is a power relationship between black and white women in Britain since these relationships are historically structured by racism (Carby 1982: 214). Racism divides feminists not because our attitudes, statistics or concepts need correcting (although, of course, they do), but because black women have real political interests in common with black men. The test of the validity of Barrett and McIntosh's self-criticism is whether it generates an adequate political practice for women against the complexities of their oppression.

The weakness of Barrett and McIntosh's over-generalized approach is shown in the passage where they argue that racial status is inherited, and that since class is also largely inherited, there is a rough correspondence in Britain between race and class (Barrett and McIntosh 1985: 38 [pp. 245–46 in this book]) — a view which overlooks the extreme complexity of women's experience of labour migration and its colonial roots.

This is not so much an ethnically specific view of class seen from inside Britain, but an apparent failure to see a need to account for the contradictory situations and experiences of black women.

The question of how to take black women's experiences into account cannot simply be resolved into one of *either* racism *or* ethnicity. We cannot understand the diversity of women's experience without taking race and ethnicity and class into account. Women who are politically "black" in British society are very obviously divided by class, culture and political priorities. The experiences of black women cannot, then, be incorporated into feminist analysis simply by adding on Asian or West Indian families. The oppression of black women must be seen as *contradictory* in that the common interests of all women in patriarchal societies are cut across in *variable* ways by class, race and ethnicity. Black women do have interests in common with each other and in common with white women, but they also have interests — for example, of class, sexuality and ethnicity — which cut across these common ones. The politics of black feminism cannot then be the same as the politics of white feminism except in specific struggles (for example, a strike, the closure of a nursery or a hospital, etc.), and it is these differences and common points which need to be aired if society is to be transformed.

In a comparable argument, the politics of white feminism can be seen to be contradictory, although Barrett and McIntosh circumvent this issue by situating themselves in the politics of socialist-feminism. This leaves the problem of how a serious political dialogue can be started between black and white women when white feminists do not agree among themselves on the causes of their oppression and on their political priorities in struggling against it. These real contradictions undermine the search by feminists for general causes of women's oppression since the emphasis on generality has the effect of reducing the significance of the diversity of women's experiences.

White academic women who can live in communities where marriage is unnecessary, who can choose to avoid families, who have the power to counter some of the effects of patriarchy, and who exercise considerable control over reproduction and their own bodies are far removed from the experiences of the majority of women. They are unusual in the extent of the choices they can exercise and in the lack of contradictions in their personal lives — in short, they are highly privileged. This privilege has perhaps led to an under-rating of the complexity of the contradictions in which most women are embroiled and to the development of over-simple political solutions to women's oppression. Whether the key to oppression is located in marriage, the family, men, patriarchy, class, capitalism or reproduction, the excessive emphasis on general concepts and causes diminishes the vitality of feminist politics and the effectiveness of feminist practices by leaving many women's daily struggles out. Black women's emphasis on specific interests which they share *with* their men, in spite of their oppression *by* men, needs to be incorporated into any feminist politics.

Feminism has a long way to go in coming to terms with the complexity of divisions between women and the necessity of varied political solutions to oppression, but if white women are really to listen to black women, the dialogue must surely let the pain of racism, and the diversity of experience, come through. If we want to take race into account, we need a clearer sense than Barrett and McIntosh have given of the real and contradictory differences of interest between women generated by ethnicity and race. We need to take account of the strengths some women can draw from marriage, the family and heterosexual relationships, as well as of their inherent problems. We cannot build bridges if we do not know what we are building between. Only when we can hear the complexity and differences in each other's experiences can we hope to begin to create new forms of co-operation, drawing on the common interests which do exist between deeply divided women.

DISCUSSION QUESTIONS

1. What are the key components of the concept of race? What about ethnicity? How do they overlap or differ? Are there races in Canada or ethnic groups?

2. Read the article "Anything but Racism" (Exhibit 3.1). How is the tension between feminism and racism presented in the media? Can you provide other examples of racism in the media?

3. Study Canada's Immigration Act of 1976 and the recent changes to it. Are there any racist elements to it? In what ways is this act any more or less racist than previous immigration acts?

4. Check with the census of Canada. Compare employment status, occupation, and income of individuals from the British Isles with those of people of colour (blacks, Native Canadians, Chinese, etc.) for both men and women. Describe the emerging pattern. Based on these findings, do you think that there should be a common "feminist" front to overcome gender inequality? Should there also be a common ethnic/racial front among men of colour against British males? Finally, what kind of support is there for a common front among men and women of colour against those of British origins?

Exhibit 3.1

Anything but Racism

I'm going to say it again. There are profound problems of racism in the media in this country. The first time I made this statement was a few months after I stepped down as President of the National Action Committee on the Status of Women. Invited to speak about the media at McMaster University, I mentioned that while the media was both sexist and racist, in my experience, it was a great deal more racist than sexist. This quote made the next morning's Hamilton *Spectator*, ran on Canadian Press and was picked up all across the country. Coast to coast I was pilloried by various and sundry columnists for having the audacity to call the media racist. Now, after seeing the coverage of the recent NAC elections, I am going to say it again.

"Don't elect white woman NAC head," was the headline in the Winnipeg *Free Press* accompanying an article by Canadian Press reporter Diane Rinehart. This article on remarks by departing President Sunera Thobani fuelled the media fury and turned reporting on the election into a question of race.

Concerned about the continuing problems inside and outside NAC in accepting leadership of women of colour, Thobani felt it was important that a woman of colour succeed her, especially as she was stepping down in mid-term. The problem with the media coverage is not that it debated or disagreed with Thobani's comments, but rather that it took her remarks and distorted them. Thobani didn't say that a white woman should not lead NAC, but the media created that impression and, even worse, created the fiction that NAC delegates were divided on racial lines in their support for two candidates for president, one of whom was white and one black.

The story had no foundation in fact. Yet a front page *Globe and Mail* story on Friday, June 14 also suggested racial divisions. Worse, the *Globe* didn't even mention the name of Joan Grant-Cummings until the inside page, while her opponent Catherine Laidlaw was described in great detail on the front page. Laidlaw was not on the NAC Executive and was a virtual unknown to the delegates. Grant-Cummings, the NAC treasurer, went on to win the election with 90 per cent of the vote. The most cursory look at the election would show Grant-Cummings as the front runner. Even alphabetically, her name comes first. The only reason to put Laidlaw first was that she is white and Grant-Cummings is black.

(continued)

Exhibit 3.1 *(continued)*

Coverage of the annual general meeting focused primarily on the manufactured racial division in the election. Even *As It Happens*, a usually progressive program, interviewed a white delegate and a black delegate, and when they found that both delegates had similar views, the interview was dropped. They later interviewed me after complaints. Reporters from at least two newspapers filed stories either focusing on the Women's March Against Poverty or saying there was no evidence of racial division in the election then saw their articles rewritten by editors to include wire copy about the fabricated racial divisions.

Joan Grant-Cummings' overwhelming victory was described sneeringly in a *Globe and Mail* editorial as "a litmus test of NAC's level of anti-racism," and the editorial suggested that the words "white" and "middle class" have taken on a "decidedly pejorative odour" in NAC.

Joan Grant-Cummings was the best-qualified and best-known candidate, and race was not an issue in this election. But if there had been a well-known and well-qualified white candidate for president, then the race of the candidates might have weighed heavily on the delegates. The changes needed to make NAC an anti-racist organization are still in very initial stages, and there remains a lot of work to do. In my experience, a woman of colour president is essential to really break down racism. NAC supports employment equity legislation, so why wouldn't it support affirmative action in its own elections? Affirmative action is not racism.

The backlash to affirmative action and employment equity no doubt accounted for some of the media furor over Thobani's remarks. The reaction was certainly in keeping with the way in which the media has tried to marginalize NAC since Thobani's election. Both politics and race are factors here.

But I believe that the media reaction was mostly a furious response to a woman of colour who had the chutzpah to stand up to all of them and say loud and clear that she had done a good job as president, that she had accomplished a lot and that she wanted a woman of colour to continue her work.

Nothing is worse than an uppity woman, unless it's an uppity woman of colour.

Source: Judy Rebick, "Anything but Racism," *Canadian Forum*, September 1996, p. 27. Reprinted by permission.

BRITISH ELITE DOMINANCE

Trends in the Ethnic Origins of Canadian Elites: The Decline of the BRITS?

R. Ogmundson and J. McLaughlin

The conventional wisdom concerning ethnicity in the Canadian case has been dominated by the imagery of *The Vertical Mosaic* (Porter 1965). This conventional wisdom maintains that Canada is characterized by pronounced ethnic stratification, especially at the level of elites which are thought to be dominated overwhelmingly by those of British origin.

Subsequent research at the level of the general population, some of it done by Porter, has generally indicated that overall ethnic stratification in Canada is minimal and is declining. The findings indicate that those of British origin no longer enjoy an especially favoured position.

If ethnic stratification has decreased at the mass level, the question naturally arises as to whether it has waned at the elite level as well. Appointments such as those of Schreyer, a German Catholic, and Hnatyshyn, a Ukrainian, to the post of Governor-General might lead us to believe that it has. Furthermore, it might seem probable that the evolving ethnic composition of the general population would eventually — though perhaps only in a generation or two — be reflected at the highest levels of our society, and that some initial indications of this trend may already be evident.

Conversely, however, virtually all historical and international experience tells us that any inequalities found in a stratification system are typically most pronounced at the level of elites (Putnam 1976). This has been found to be true even when the more powerful ethnic group is in a numerical minority. Thus, notwithstanding diminished ethnic stratification at the mass level, it is possible that an entrenched British upper class continues to dominate the key decision-making positions at the elite level of Canadian society. It cannot be assumed, without investigation, that a decline in the role of the British has actually taken place. This paper explores that question.

THE LITERATURE

The imagery of the "vertical mosaic" at the elite level begins with Porter's studies of seven elites at a variety of times ranging from 1940 to 1961.[1] These were the political elite, the public service elite, the mass media elite, the intellectual elite, the religious elite, the labour elite and the business elite. Four of the seven (labour, media, intellectual and religious) were analysed separately as predominantly anglophone and predominantly francophone elites. The national elites and the anglophone elites were then found to be dominated by those of British origin. It is this finding which seems to have indelibly impressed itself on the intellectual consciousness of Canada.

Only four of the seven elites, the political (1961–73), public service (1973), business (1972) and media (1972), have been studied again by scholars consciously attempting to work in the Porter tradition. Unfortunately, the replications were not precise. Hence, even in these cases, inferences about trends can only be made with caution (Ogmundson 1990). Furthermore, even the most recent of these attempted replications is now almost 20 years old.

Subsequent research in other traditions has been done at a variety of times and places on a variety of elites utilizing different definitions of elites and different measures of ethnic origin. However, to our knowledge, no systematic overall examination of trends in the ethnic origins of Canadian elites has been reported since the publication of *The Vertical Mosaic* in 1965. The 1977 study done at York University (Williams 1989) would come the closest, but the definition of elite is radically different.

DATA AND METHODS

Porter's original data are used as a benchmark. Subsequent findings, notably those of Clement (1975) and Olsen (1980), are employed to help reveal trends. In most cases, new data on the ethnic origins of the elites in question will also be reported. Relevant observations in the literature will be discussed as well.

FINDINGS

Let us begin with the political elite (1940–60), which Porter defined as including both legislative and judicial figures. Olsen's replication (1961–73) indicated a decline of those of British ancestry from 75.1 to 67.1 per cent. Our approximate replication for the years 1974–87 indicates a further decline to 58.6 per cent (see Table 12.1). Further

Table 12.1
Trends in the Ethnic Origins of a Political Elite

	1940–60(a)	1961–73(b)	1974–87(c)
British	75.1%	67.1%	58.6%
French	21.7	24.2	23.6
Other	3.2	7.5	16.3
Unknown	–	1.2	1.5
N =	157	161	203

Source:
(a) The political elite includes all those who, between 1940 and 1960, were federal cabinet ministers, all provincial premiers, all justices of the Supreme Court of Canada, presidents of the Exchequer Court and the provincial chief justices (Porter 1965: 604). On the ethnic origins data, see Porter 1965: 389 and Olsen 1980: 22.
(b) A replication of Porter, see Olsen 1980: 127. Missing data were additionally calculated and added to the table by James McLaughlin.
(c) The third column includes all supreme court justices, federal cabinet ministers, provincial premiers and provincial chief justices over the years 1974–87. This elite omits the presidents of the Exchequer Court (now Federal Court), a very small group. Information was drawn from the *Canadian Parliamentary Guide* and the *Canadian Almanac and Directory*, various years. It should be noted that ethnic origin is measured differently in each of these studies.

confirmation of this trend is provided by data on the ethnic origins of federal and provincial cabinet ministers since 1935. Here the British proportion declines from 73.7 per cent of federal cabinet ministers in 1935 to 51.3 per cent in 1985. For provincial cabinet ministers, the proportion falls from 85.2 per cent in 1935 to 57.5 per cent in 1985 (see Table 12.2). Examination of the ethnic origins of Members of Parliament indicates a similar trend from 59.6 per cent British in 1965 to 52.1 per cent in 1985 (see Table 12.3).

More specific study of the political elite over this time period confirms the impression given by these numbers. Few would deny that much of the post-1965 era was largely dominated by Pierre Trudeau and his French-Canadian colleagues such as Marchand, Lalonde and Chrétien. Similarly, the growing importance of the provinces, especially Quebec, during this time period has also emphasized the centrality of the French-Canadian role in Canadian politics. What the Trudeau era did for French Canadians may have almost been matched by what the Mulroney era has done for "third ethnics," in which names like Mazankowski, Paproski, Epp, Jellinek and Hnatyshyn have become prominent. In the judiciary, a Jewish Canadian, Bora Laskin, was probably the leading jurist of his generation.

In the case of the public service/bureaucratic elite, the findings are similar. Once again, the data reported by Olsen (1980: 78) indicate a

Table 12.2
Trends in the Ethnic Origins of Federal and Provincial Cabinet Ministers and Deputy Ministers (or Equivalent), 1935 to 1985

	1935	1945	1955	1965	1975	1985
Cabinet Ministers(a)						
Federal						
British	73.7%	68.4%	65.0%	57.7%	58.6%	51.3%
French	15.8	31.6	35.0	42.3	34.5	23.1
Other	5.3	–	–	–	6.9	25.6
Unknown	5.3	–	–	–	–	–
Column *N* =	19	19	20	26	29	39
Provincial						
British	85.2	70.2	70.6	72.5	62.8	57.5
French	12.3	22.6	18.5	16.2	18.6	21.2
Other	2.5	3.6	7.6	9.2	16.5	18.9
Unknown	–	–	3.4	2.1	2.1	2.4
Column *N* =	81	84	119	142	188	212
Deputy Ministers(b)						
Federal						
British	93.8	86.7	72.2	58.8	54.5	47.8
French	–	6.7	22.2	23.5	13.6	34.8
Other	6.2	–	5.6	17.6	31.8	17.4
Unknown	–	6.7	–	–	–	–
Column *N* =	16	15	18	17	22	23
Provincial						
British	86.7	75.3	81.7	71.9	70.0	62.7
French	12.0	15.3	12.5	18.0	14.7	12.4
Other	1.2	7.1	5.0	7.0	14.1	21.5
Unknown	–	2.4	0.8	3.1	1.2	3.4
Column *N* =	83	85	120	128	170	177

Source: (a) *Canadian Parliamentary Guide*, various years.
(b) *Canadian Almanac and Directory*, various years.

decline of participation in the elite by those of British origin from 84 per cent in 1953 to 65 per cent in 1973. Further confirmation of this trend is provided by data on the ethnic origins of federal and provincial deputy ministers since 1935. Here the British proportion declines from 93.8 per cent of federal deputy ministers in 1935 to 47.8 per cent in 1985. For provincial deputy ministers, the proportion falls from 86.7 per cent in 1935 to 62.7 per cent in 1985 (see Table 12.2, bottom panel). Similar patterns are found in the case of the military elite

Table 12.3
Trends in the Ethnic Origins of Members of Parliament (Federal), Supreme Court, Military Elite, Broadcast Media Elite, Educational Elite and Labour Elite — 1965 to 1985

	1965	1975	1985
Members of Parliament(a)			
British	59.6%	53.4%	52.1%
French	25.0	29.5	24.5
Other	15.4	14.8	21.3
Unknown	3.1	2.3	2.5
Column *N* =	260	264	282
Supreme Court(a)			
British	77.8	55.6	44.2
French	22.2	22.2	33.3
Other	–	22.2	22.2
Unknown	–	–	–
Column *N* =	9	9	9
Military(b)			
British	64.8	64.7	58.6
French	24.1	17.6	20.7
Other	7.4	11.8	13.8
Unknown	3.7	5.9	6.9
Column *N* =	54	34	29
Education(b,c)			
British	75.8	71.9	58.8
French	11.3	10.9	13.2
Other	9.7	14.0	23.5
Unknown	3.2	3.2	4.4
Column *N* =	62	64	68
Labour(d)			
British	72.4	50.0	58.8
French	17.2	25.0	35.3
Other	6.9	25.0	5.9
Unknown	3.4	–	–
Column *N* =	29	24	17

Source:
(a) *Canadian Parliamentary Guide,* various years.
(b) *Canadian Almanac and Directory,* various years.
(c) *Corpus Almanac & Canadian Sourcebook* (Sova 1988), all university presidents; and Ministers of Education and Deputy Ministers (from b above).
(d) *Directory of Labour Organization in Canada,* various years, President of National Unions or Canadian Vice-Presidents of International Unions. Largest unions only (in 1965 and 1975 one international, with no Canadian director, excluded).

(1965–75–85) and in the Supreme Court (1965–75–85) (see Table 12.3). This confirms the trend noted by political scientists Van Loon and Whittington (1976: 326). More recently, Campbell and Szablowski (1979) have reported similar findings. Indeed, they found that: "… central agents' socio-economic backgrounds resemble those of the general populace much more closely than do the backgrounds of bureaucratic elites in other advantaged liberal democracies for which we have comparable data" (Campbell and Szablowski 1979: 165).

In the case of the mass media, Porter (1965) separated the anglophone and francophone organizations. The francophone media were found to be controlled by independent francophones, while the anglophone media were found to be controlled by upper class British families. Unfortunately, however, Porter did not report percentages of ethnic origins in the manner adopted for other elites. He did, however, give the impression of overwhelming (99%–?) British dominance of the anglophone media in 1961. Clement (1975), in a somewhat differently defined elite, found a reduction in the British proportion to 81.9 per cent by 1972 (but see Baldwin 1977a, 1977b; and Clement 1977c). More recently, an analysis of the ancestry of the directors of newspaper chains in 1980 found that 69.1 per cent were of British origin. Though the three elites discussed here are comparable only in a crude sense, the data would seem to indicate that the role of individuals of British origin in the media elite may well have been decreasing over time.

More comparable data were collected for the broadcast media elites, and here a clear trend is apparent. If one looks at the ethnic origins of commissioners, directors and executive officers of the CRTC, CBC, CTV and Global networks in 1975, 1985 and 1989, one finds that the proportion of British origin drops from 60.3 per cent in 1975 to 49.4 per cent in 1989 (see Table 12.4).

In the case of the intellectual elite, Porter (1965) selected the more "ideological" sections of the Royal Society. In 1961, he studied both Section I (French language and civilization) and Section II (English language and civilization). He found the first to be overwhelmingly dominated by those of French origin and the second to be overwhelmingly dominated by those of British origin. Our examination in 1987 of Section I indicates that it continues to be dominated by those of French origin (94.1%), while Section II shows a decline in those of British origin from 92 to 72.3 per cent (the 1987 data come from the Royal Society calendar for that year). Perhaps it is significant that the francophone section remained highly exclusive. As Porter (1970: 166) himself notes, his choice of the Royal Society as an elite in the educational system has been subject to some criticism. However, other categories which might well have been designated as educational elites — university presidents and ministers/deputy ministers of

Table 12.4
Trends in the Ethnic Origins of a Broadcast Media Elite[a]
— 1975, 1985 and 1989

	1975	1985	1989
British	60.3%	55.7%	49.4%
French	17.2	26.1	21.2
Other	13.8	10.2	24.7
Unknown	8.7	8.0	4.7
N =	58	88	85

[a] See text for elite definition.

Source: *Financial Post Directory of Directors*, various years.

education — display a similar pattern. The British component falls from 75.8 per cent in 1965 to 58.8 per cent in 1985 (see Table 12.3).

In the case of the labour elite, Porter (1965) again divided his study into a mainly anglophone labour elite and an overwhelmingly francophone one. In the case of the more national, mainly anglophone group, he found that about 69.4 per cent were of British origin; 14.6 per cent of French origin; and 16 per cent of "third ethnic" origin, whereas virtually all of the francophone elite were of French origin. We were unable to replicate Porter's procedures but did find that if one looks at leadership of major unions in Canada, the British proportion falls from 72.4 per cent in 1965 to 58.8 per cent in 1985 (see Table 12.3). However, this was one case in which there was no clear increase in "third ethnic" proportions.

Finally, there is the case of the business elite. Porter (1965) found virtually complete domination by those of British origin (92.3%) in 1951. Clement (1975), in a somewhat differently defined elite, found a slight reduction in the British proportion to 86.2 per cent by 1972. Williams (1989), in another somewhat differently defined business elite, reports a further reduction in the British proportion to 77.9 per cent by 1977. An analysis of the origins of the directors of the 20 largest Canadian companies in 1985, as ranked by total assets, indicates a further decline to 67.8 per cent British origins (see Table 12.5).

FINAL COMMENTS

The overall contour of the findings indicates that the days of domination of Canadian elites by those of British ancestry are coming to a close, and that the original imagery of the "vertical mosaic" needs revision. This finding indicates that the changes at the mass level reported

Table 12.5
Trends in the Ethnic Origins of Various Business Elites

	1951(a)	1972(b)	1977(c)	1985(d)
British	92.3%	86.2%	77.9%	67.8%
French	6.7	8.4	7.9	14.8
Other	1.0	5.4	14.3	14.8
Unknown	–	–	–	2.7
$N =$	760	775	142	264

It must be emphasized that these elites have been chosen in very different manners and are not comparable in any rigorous sense.

Source:
(a) This elite is drawn mainly from the directors of firms with 500 or more employees. See Porter 1965: 233; Appendix II. For the ethnic origins data, see Porter 1965: 286. Also Clement 1975: 232.
(b) See Clement 1975: 128, 232. This elite is drawn mainly from directors of "dominant" corporations. "... a corporation was defined as dominant if it had assets of greater than $250 million and income of over $50 million ..." (Clement 1975: 128).
(c) See Williams 1989: 73, 74, 76. This "large business" elite included "chief executive officers of the largest Canadian corporations in key areas of the economy" (Williams 1984: 74).
(d) This elite consists of the directors of the 20 largest Canadian companies by total assets as listed in the *Financial Post Survey of Industrials* (Pattison 1985).

by Pineo and Porter (1985) and many others now seem to be reaching the highest levels of our society.

Assuming that the findings reported here stand up under scrutiny, a number of interesting thoughts present themselves. This overall picture may obscure important variations in the relevance of ethnic origins by region, institution and generation. A given ethnic origin could be a major advantage in one situation, irrelevant in another and a distinct handicap in a third. Furthermore, one cannot help but note the fact that a remarkably high proportion of the "third ethnics" are, in fact, of Jewish origin. Their aggregate success in expanding the size of the "other" category may obscure difficulties still experienced by individuals with names like Eymundsen, Pajekowski, Taglianetti and Singh.

Nonetheless, the findings also encourage the pleasant thought that the sociological anomalies that characterize the Canadian case may be unusual openness and a high degree of social justice rather than the reverse. As Taylor (1991) notes in his discussion of the apparent reduction of racism in Canadian immigration policy, such anomalies are sufficiently rare as to demand study.

Possibly the findings are best understood as indicating a "circulation of elites." Perhaps another implication of these findings is that liberal capitalist democracy has once again demonstrated a capacity for meaningful social change. Porter would presumably be pleased (Porter 1979; Rich, forthcoming).

NOTES

[1] Little attention has been paid to the fact that the elites in *The Vertical Mosaic* were studied at quite different times. The dates seem to be 1951 for the business elite, 1952 for the religious elite, 1953 for the public service elite, 1958 for the labour elite and 1961 for the media and intellectual elites. Furthermore, Porter (1965) reports data on the political elite which summarize events covering a period of several years (1940–60). This also applies to Olsen's (1980) research (1961–73) and to the research reported here (1974–87). A stable, central individual of one ethnic category in the elite for a long period of time is counted only once, while a series of peripheral figures of another ethnic category may be counted several times. This might influence the findings. This methodology went unchallenged when Porter used it in *The Vertical Mosaic* and when Olsen used it in *The State Elite*. In order to compare our results to theirs, which is crucial for comparative purposes, we replicate their methodological practice.

Vertical Mosaic among the Elites: The New Imagery Revisited
M. Reza Nakhaie

This paper demonstrates that Ogmundson and McLaughlin's (1992) conclusions are misleading because they ignore changes in the ethnic composition of the Canadian population. This is an important omission, given the Canadian population dynamic in which the British share of the total population has continually declined and that of the "third" ethnic group has increased. The shift in the ethnic composition of the Canadian population has been particularly drastic since the Immigration Acts of 1967 and 1976.

The Vertical Mosaic (Porter 1965) has become the single most influential book published in Canada since World War II. By 1974, more than 70,000 copies had been sold (Black 1974: 640). Porter himself received the MacIver Award in 1966 for an outstanding contribution to the social sciences (Rich 1976a: 14). Nevertheless, many scholars have come to criticize him for his measurement of elites, his indiscriminate use of statistical data and his biased interpretations. Rich (1976a: 15) suggested that the book was "distorted" and a "caricature" of Canadian society. Later, he called the vertical mosaic image of Canada a "myth" (Rich 1991: 419). Tepperman (1975: 156) argued that "[i]t is patently false that ethnicity and social class are interchangeable in Canada." Berkowitz (1984: 252) called Porter and Clement "good" journalists but "bad" sociologists. Brym (Brym and Fox 1989: 99, 112) also questioned the *Vertical Mosaic* imagery as being "seriously deficient."

Perhaps the most persistent and systematic criticism has come from Ogmundson (1990, 1992, 1993) and Ogmundson and McLaughlin (1992, 1994). In his 1990 article, Ogmundson argued that Porter was biased in his selection of the elites and that Clement failed to replicate Porter's selection methodology; thus, "it is impossible to infer trends over time with any confidence" (see also Hunter 1976: 126). He argued that Clement and Olsen used quite different measures of ethnic origin, and therefore that Canadian elites couldn't be compared between periods (Ogmundson 1990: 170–71). In addition, measures of ethnic origin by last name over-estimate British origins because many of the "other" ethnic groups have Anglicized their names. Finally, he argued that missing cases are likely to refer to those of the third ethnic groups and by excluding them from the analysis, Clement and Porter under-estimated the "other" ethnic origins' representation in the elites (see also Ogmundson 1993). He concluded that the traditional imagery is "obsolete" (Ogmundson 1990: 165) and should be "abandoned" (Ogmundson 1993: 383). In his subsequent paper, which was a reply to Clement (1990), Ogmundson (1992: 314) presented a measured critique and suggested that his earlier paper was intended to "bring ... back in" the critical observations of the mid-1970s against Porter and Clement. He emphasized that "Canadian elites are becoming *less exclusive*" (emphasis in original).

Rich suggested that Ogmundson's (1990) paper delivered "the coup de grace to the myth that institutional elites in Canada have been exceptionally exclusive in terms of their social origins" (Rich 1991: 419). However, it was Ogmundson and McLaughlin's (1992) paper that aimed to deliver the final blow to the prevailing Canadian academic consciousness.

Porter, Clement and Olsen have argued that, according to the dominant "meritocratic" ideological assumption, the assignment of social tasks should be based on ability and talent, and that social characteristics such as ethnicity should not be impediments to achieving positions at the top of institutional hierarchies because social justice demands the equalization of opportunities to compete for the privileged positions (see also Parkin 1971: 13). However, contrary to this ideology, if it is found that ethnicity is an important factor for recruitment to elite positions, then inequality of opportunity and not "meritocracy" should be considered as the hallmark of the society (Porter 1965: 265, 217; Clement 1975a: 2, 7). In this regard, they have shown that there is little randomness in the representation of the ethnic groups at the elite level and that, in fact, elites tend to be exclusive by establishing patterns of selection — patterns of preference based on the attitudes and values of those already at the top, "because the selection of successors is one of the prerogatives of power" (Porter 1965: 265; Clement 1975a: 250; Michels 1962: 34). Thus, these scholars have argued that the established patterns of selection and access to elite positions demonstrate inequality of opportunity, which reproduces the dominant ethnic group at the highest level of power and privileges, pointing to class continuity for this group. This type of reproduction does not mean that there is no mobility: "Rather it means that there is sufficient continuity to maintain class institutions" (Porter 1965: 285n; Clement 1975b: 50; Olsen 1980: 82).

In contrast, Ogmundson and McLaughlin have suggested the "end of the British dominance," the "abandoning" of the vertical mosaic imagery, and thus implied equality of access to elite positions because *they did not standardize the proportion of each ethnic group in the elite to that of their respective general population.* It is not that they were unaware of this methodology. In fact, Ogmundson and McLaughlin argue that "it is tempting ... to make a systematic comparison between elite ethnic origins and the census reports on ethnic origins of the general population for various decades." They leave this task aside, though, because it "is beyond the scope of the ... paper" (Ogmundson and McLaughlin 1992: 230). But why? Weren't the focus and scope of the paper a revision and re-evaluation of Porter's, Clement's and Olsen's empirical analyses and theory?

To standardize the ethnic groups' elite participation across time, the conventional Index of Dissimilarity is calculated (a measure first introduced by Clement (1975a: 234, Table 35)). This index represents the ratio of the ethnic proportion in the elite to the corresponding proportion of the Canadian population in the census. A figure above 1.00 denotes over-representation, and a figure below 1.00 suggests under-representation.

We calculated five indices of dissimilarity for each elite category. The first index is based on the general population. This is the index that is directly comparable to that of Porter, Clement and Olsen. The second index is based on the population of ethnic groups over 35 years of age, the third for those between 35 and 65, the fourth for males between 35 and 64 years of age, and the fifth for Canadian-born males. Indices two to four are based on the reality that elites are not selected from the younger population (Clement 1975a: 203) and that some elites are constrained by mandatory retirement. The fourth index is also based on the fact that women are still rarely found among the elites. Clement (1975a: 266n; see also 191, 332) wrote that "women are probably the most under-represented social type in the economic elite. Of the total of 946 persons holding elite positions, only 6 or .6 per cent of the total are women." Williams (1989: 72) surveyed 588 elites in 1977 and showed that only 17 were women, mainly in the local political arena. In 1990, Clement (1990: 184n) wrote that according to the *Financial Post* (June 5, 1989: 35), "only 7 of the 1,169 chief executive officers in the 1990 *Directory of Directors* are women." The final index is based on the expectation that those who are born in Canada have a better chance for the inheritance of ownership, a higher access to networks for occupational mobility, and often a superior command of the official languages than immigrants (see, for example, Porter 1965: 79; Pineo and Porter 1985: 376; Boyd 1985: 441; Boyd 1990: 279; Winn 1985: 692–93; and Beaujot and Rappak 1990: 130). In addition, we constructed an index for the Québec-born French males based on the expectation that the French Canadians in Québec may have a higher chance of elite recruitment than French Canadians outside Québec (Clement 1975a: 236).

FINDINGS

The ethnic composition of the Canadian population from 1931 to 1986 is assembled in Table 12.6, apparently for the first time. Clearly, the British proportion of the population continually declined, and that of other groups (and to a lesser extent the French) increased from 1931 to 1986. This trend persisted, whether we use the total population or the age- and sex-specific portions of the total population. The largest decline for the British and increase for "other" ethnic groups was registered in the 35–64 age group. In contrast, the smallest decline for the British population is among the Canadian-born males, followed by that of the total population. The smallest increase for the "other" ethnic groups, as expected, is among the Canadian-born males. Overall, the French portion of the total population has slightly increased from 1931 to 1986, but among the Canadian- and Québec-borns, their population has been basically stable. Excluding the question of nativity, it seems that Porter, Clement and Olsen actually used a conservative index to show British dominance among the elites.

Tables 12.7 through 12.11 present the indices for various elites based on the percentages provided by Ogmundson and McLaughlin

Table 12.6
Percent Distribution of Canadian Ethnic Groups, 1931–1986

Year	1931	1941	1951	1961	1971	1981	1986
Total Population							
British	54.5	49.7	47.9	44.4	45.0	43.7	35.2
French	26.7	30.3	30.8	30.7	28.9	29.1	33.9
Others	18.8	20.0	21.3	24.9	26.1	27.2	30.8
Population 35+							
British	59.5	56.5	53.5	48.8	47.1	42.7	37.2
French	22.7	24.3	25.2	26.0	26.3	26.3	31.9
Others	17.8	19.2	21.3	25.2	26.6	31.0	30.9
Population 35–64							
British	58.9	55.1	51.3	47.2	44.3	40.8	34.6
French	23.2	24.5	26.3	27.4	26.4	27.3	33.3
Others	17.9	20.3	22.4	25.4	29.3	31.9	32.1
Population 35–64 Males							
British	56.1	53.3	50.2	46.4	43.5	40.1	34.4
French	22.0	23.7	25.6	26.8	25.9	26.8	32.5
Others	21.9	23.0	24.2	26.8	30.6	33.1	33.1
Population Canadian-Born Males							
British	50.2	48.5	47.8	45.8	47.6	42.3	38.0
French	35.3	36.0	36.0	36.3	34.1	31.3	40.4
Others	14.5	15.5	16.2	19.9	18.3	26.4	21.6
Québec French	28.3	28.4	28.0	28.1	26.6	24.8	33.3

*   Ethnic groups in 1981 and 1986 are based on the single-ethnic-origin responses.
**   1981 population is based on Census Metropolitan Areas and Census Agglomerations of 50,000 population and greater.
***   1986 population is based on 20% sample data.

Source: Census of Canada, 1931, 1941, 1951, 1961, 1971, 1981 and 1986.

(1992) and the census population reported above. These tables all indicate a vertical ethnic mosaic at the elite level as demonstrated previously by Porter, Clement and Olsen.

We start with the ethnic representation in the most dominant institution in the Canadian capitalist structure (Table 12.7). The dominant positions in this institution include the board of directors, which makes the most important decisions "about the expansion of the economy, its direction, scope and level of technology. With these decisions, they determine rates of employment and the types of occupation that will exist in ... [Canadian] society" (Clement 1975a: 24). Table 12.7 shows

Table 12.7
Index of Ethnic Representation in the Business Elite, 1951–1985

Elite year Census year*	1951[a] 1951	1972[b] 1971	1977[c] 1981	1985[d] 1986
British				
1. Total population	1.93	1.92	1.79	1.98
2. Population aged 35+	1.72	1.83	1.83	1.87
3. Population aged 35–64	1.80	1.95	1.92	2.01
4. Male pop. aged 35–64	1.84	1.98	1.94	2.02
5. Can.-born male	1.93	1.81	1.85	1.83
French				
1. Total population	0.22	0.29	0.26	0.45
2. Population aged 35+	0.26	0.32	0.29	0.48
3. Population aged 35–64	0.25	0.32	0.28	0.46
4. Male pop. aged 35–64	0.26	0.32	0.29	0.47
5. Can.-born male	0.19	0.25	0.25	0.38
6. Québec-born male	0.24	0.32	0.31	0.46
Others				
1. Total population	0.05	0.21	0.52	0.49
2. Population aged 35+	0.05	0.20	0.45	0.49
3. Population aged 35–64	0.06	0.18	0.44	0.47
4. Male pop. aged 35–64	0.05	0.18	0.43	0.46
5. Can.-born male	0.07	0.29	0.53	0.70
N =	760	775	142	257
Unknown	–	–	–	7

[a] This elite is drawn mainly from the directors of firms with 500 or more employees (see Porter 1965: 233 and Appendix II; Clement 1975a: 232).

[b] This elite is drawn mainly from directors of "dominant" corporations with assets of greater than $250 million and income of over $50 million (Clement 1975a: 128, 232).

[c] This elite included chief executives of the largest Canadian corporations in key areas of the economy (see Williams 1989: 73–75).

[d] This elite included the directors of the 20 largest Canadian corporations by total assets, as listed in the *Financial Post Survey of Industries* (see Pattison 1985).

* The Index represents the ratio of the ethnic proportion in the elite to the corresponding proportion of the Canadian population for the closest census time. A figure above 1.00 denotes over-representation, and a figure below 1.00 suggests under-representation (see Clement 1975a: 234, Table 35).

Source: Notes and proportion of ethnic groups in the elites are based on Ogmundson and McLaughlin (1992: 235).

that from 1951 to 1985, British elites dominated the economic arena, or what Clement has called the "big bourgeoisie" (Clement 1975a: 6).[1] In fact, using the more stringent indices, the British increased their economic elite participation from 1.84 in 1951 to 2.02 in 1985.

Understandably, the index of British representation among the business elites shows a slight sign of decline if compared to the Canadian-born population. However, this index fails to take into account the foreign-born members of the economic elites in the numerator. Consistent with Clement (1975a: 234), French and "other" ethnic groups registered gains among the economic elites in this period but were still under-represented relative to their populations. Thus, in 1985, French and "others" were almost equally under-represented in relation to their populations, while the British were over-represented. In other words, to reach an ethnic economic elite parity in more recent years, French and "other" ethnic groups would have had to double their economic elite participation and the British to decrease it by half. The Canadian-born male index, however, shows a lower elite representation for the French than for "other" ethnic groups. In general, with respect to inequalities that stem from the concentration of economic power, there has been little (if any) decline in the British index of elite representation in the boardrooms of the major Canadian corporations. French and other ethnic groups have improved their elite representation, but the process of change over the last 35 years seems to be slow.

Table 12.8 illustrates the index of ethnic representation in the political elite for the period 1940 to 1987. The index, based on the general population, shows a slight decline for the British in this elite category and more so for the index based on the Canadian-born population; the other stringent indices, however, point to the stability or increase of British political elite representation. Here, the image is again very close to the conventional picture in which French and "others" are under-represented and the British are over-represented. The indices for the British stood around 1.50, for the French around 0.80, and for "other" ethnic origins, below 0.60. Again, the exception is in the flawed index based on the male Canadian- and/or Québec-born French. Nevertheless, the image is still a vertical one.

The image in Table 12.9 is basically the same as Table 12.8. British stability among the federal and provincial cabinet elites, as well as among deputy ministers (but see the Canadian-born index), supports the traditional imagery; so do the junior positions of the French and "others." This table, however, has two distinctive features. First, the change in French participation among cabinet ministers is more pronounced than French representation in the political elites in general. For a brief moment in 50 years of politics (1945), they reached their true share of the cabinet ministers without being under-represented relative to their population, a pattern that is negated once we control for place of birth both in Canada and in Québec. Second, the "other" ethnic groups gained more "elite" representation in the lower ranks of the deputy ministers than cabinet ministers, particularly if they were

Table 12.8
Index of Ethnic Representation in the Political Elite, 1940–1987

Elite year Census year*	1940–1960[a] 1941–1961	1960–1973[b] 1961–1971	1974–1987[c] 1971–1986
British			
1.	1.60	1.79	1.48
2.	1.43	1.67	1.41
3.	1.47	1.74	1.51
4.	1.51	1.78	1.53
5.	1.60	1.71	1.32
French			
1.	0.71	0.82	0.76
2.	0.86	0.94	0.82
3.	0.83	0.85	0.80
4.	0.79	0.93	0.82
5.	0.60	0.70	0.73
6.	0.77	0.90	0.93
Others			
1.	0.14	0.30	0.58
2.	0.14	0.29	0.57
3.	0.14	0.28	0.54
4.	0.13	0.26	0.52
5.	0.19	0.42	0.74
N =	157	159	200
Unknown	–	–	3

[a] Includes all those who were federal cabinet ministers, all provincial premiers, all justices of the Supreme Court of Canada, presidents of the Exchequer Court and the provincial chief justices (see Porter 1965: 604).

[b] As above (see Olsen 1980: 127).

[c] All Supreme Court justices, federal cabinet ministers, provincial premiers and provincial chief justices for the years 1974–1987.

* The percentage of ethnic groups are calculated at the mean level of the two years.

Source: See Table 12.7 (see also Ogmundson and McLaughlin 1992: 230).

born in Canada. Thus, by 1985, the British scored around 1.50 for both cabinet and deputy ministers, the French scored slightly better than 0.80 among the cabinet ministers and below 0.60 among the deputy ministers, while "other" ethnic origins scored just over 0.50 among the cabinet ministers and around 0.70 among the deputy ministers.

Table 12.10 presents the indices for ethnic representation for members of parliament and for military, education and labour elites. The conventional imagery and the stability of British dominance are more apparent among the first two types of elite than the last two. Although

Table 12.9
Index of Ethnic Representation among Federal and Provincial Cabinet Ministers and Deputy Ministers, 1935–1985

Elite year	1935	1945	1955	1965	1975	1985
Census year	1931	1941	1951	1961	1971	1981
Provincial and Federal Cabinet Ministers						
British						
1.	1.55	1.44	1.50	1.61	1.41	1.38
2.	1.42	1.27	1.34	1.46	1.35	1.41
3.	1.44	1.30	1.40	1.51	1.43	1.47
4.	1.51	1.35	1.43	1.54	1.46	1.50
5.	1.69	1.48	1.50	1.56	1.33	1.42
French						
1.	0.50	0.83	0.70	0.67	0.73	0.79
2.	0.58	1.04	0.85	0.79	0.80	0.87
3.	0.57	1.03	0.82	0.75	0.80	0.84
4.	0.60	1.06	0.84	0.77	0.81	0.85
5.	0.38	0.70	0.60	0.57	0.67	0.73
6.	0.47	0.89	0.77	0.73	0.79	0.92
Others						
1.	0.11	0.15	0.31	0.32	0.59	0.62
2.	0.11	0.16	0.31	0.31	0.58	0.54
3.	0.11	0.15	0.30	0.31	0.53	0.53
4.	0.09	0.13	0.28	0.29	0.51	0.51
5.	0.14	0.19	0.41	0.44	0.85	0.64
N =	34	33	38	43	41	62
Unknown	1	1	–	–	–	–
Federal and Provincial Deputy Ministers						
British						
1.	1.61	1.60	1.69	1.63	1.58	1.44
2.	1.48	1.40	1.51	1.48	1.46	1.47
3	1.49	1.44	1.58	1.53	1.55	1.54
4.	1.57	1.49	1.61	1.56	1.58	1.57
5.	1.75	1.64	1.69	1.58	1.45	1.49
French						
1.	0.38	0.47	0.45	0.62	0.51	0.46
2.	0.44	0.59	0.55	0.74	0.56	0.59
3.	0.44	0.59	0.53	0.72	0.56	0.57
4.	0.46	0.63	0.57	0.72	0.57	0.58
5.	0.29	0.40	0.39	0.53	0.43	0.49
6.	0.36	0.51	0.50	0.68	0.55	0.62
Others						
1.	0.11	0.31	0.24	0.34	0.62	0.79
2.	0.11	0.32	0.24	0.34	0.61	0.70
3.	0.11	0.31	0.23	0.33	0.56	0.68
4.	0.09	0.27	0.21	0.32	0.53	0.65
5.	0.14	0.40	0.31	0.43	0.89	0.87
N =	164	167	234	263	352	378
Unknown	–	2	5	7	6	11

Source: See Table 12.7 (see also Ogmundson and McLaughlin 1992: 231). For cabinet ministers: *Canadian Parliamentary Guide;* for deputy ministers: *Canadian Almanac and Directory.*

Table 12.10
Index of Ethnic Representation in the Various Elites, 1965–1985

Elite year	1965	1975	1985	1965	1975	1985
Census year	1961	1971	1981	1961	1971	1981
	Members of Parliament[a]			Military Elites[b]		
British						
1.	1.34	1.21	1.22	1.52	1.53	1.44
2.	1.22	1.16	1.25	1.38	1.46	1.47
3.	1.26	1.23	1.31	1.42	1.55	1.54
4.	1.28	1.25	1.33	1.45	1.58	1.57
5.	1.30	1.15	1.26	1.47	1.44	1.49
French						
1.	0.81	1.04	0.86	0.81	0.65	0.76
2.	0.96	1.15	0.95	0.96	0.71	0.84
3.	0.91	1.14	0.92	0.91	0.71	0.81
4.	0.93	1.17	0.97	0.93	0.72	0.83
5.	0.69	0.88	0.80	0.69	0.55	0.71
6.	0.89	1.13	1.01	0.89	0.70	0.89
Others						
1.	0.62	0.58	0.78	0.31	0.48	0.54
2.	0.61	0.57	0.70	0.30	0.47	0.48
3.	0.61	0.51	0.68	0.30	0.43	0.46
4.	0.57	0.49	0.65	0.29	0.41	0.45
5.	0.77	0.82	0.82	0.39	0.68	0.56
N =	268	262	276	51	32	27
Unknown	8	2	6	3	2	2
	Education Elites[b,c]			Labour Elites[d]		
British						
1.	1.76	1.65	1.41	1.70	1.11	1.34
2.	1.60	1.57	1.44	1.54	1.06	1.38
3.	1.66	1.67	1.51	1.59	1.13	1.44
4.	1.69	1.70	1.53	1.62	1.15	1.47
5.	1.71	1.56	1.49	1.63	1.05	1.39
French						
1.	0.38	0.39	0.47	0.58	0.86	1.21
2.	0.45	0.43	0.52	0.69	0.95	1.34
3.	0.43	0.43	0.51	0.65	0.95	1.29
4.	0.44	0.44	0.51	0.67	0.96	1.32
5.	0.32	0.33	0.44	0.49	0.73	1.13
6.	0.42	0.42	0.56	0.63	0.94	1.42
Others						
1.	0.40	0.56	0.90	0.28	0.96	0.32
2.	0.40	0.54	0.79	0.28	0.94	0.19
3.	0.39	0.49	0.77	0.28	0.85	0.18
4.	0.37	0.47	0.74	0.26	0.82	0.18
5.	0.50	0.79	0.93	0.36	1.36	0.22
N =	60	62	65	28	24	17
Unknown	2	2	3	2	–	–

[a] *Canadian Parliamentary Guide.*
[b] *Canadian Almanac and Directory.*
[c] *Corpus Almanac & Canadian Sourcebook* (Sova 1988), all university presidents; and ministers of education and deputy ministers (from b above).
[d] *Directory of Labour Organization in Canada.* President of national unions or Canadian vice-president of international union. Largest unions only (in 1965 and 1975); one international, with no Canadian directors excluded.

Source: See Table 12.7 (see also Ogmundson and McLaughlin 1992: 232).

the vertical ethnic mosaic imagery is intact, there are some indications that British elite participation in education and labour, as a proportion of their population, has declined and that that of the non-British has increased. Interestingly, the highest gain among the labour elite is for the French. By 1985, the French, with a score of about 1.30, and the British, with a score of about 1.40, were both over-represented, while "others," with a score of around 0.20, were under-represented. The French were, nevertheless, still the junior partner here. This table also shows that being Canadian-born is generally inconsequential to the British but slightly more beneficial to the French and "other" ethnic groups.

Finally, Table 12.11 illustrates once again the traditional vertical ethnic mosaic imagery, this time for media elites. The British dominance,

Table 12.11
Index of Ethnic Representation in the Media Elite, 1975–1989 (Broadcast Elite)[a]

Elite year	1975	1985	1989
Census year	1971	1981	1986
British			
1.	1.47	1.38	1.47
2.	1.39	1.42	1.39
3.	1.49	1.48	1.50
4.	1.52	1.51	1.50
5.	1.39	1.43	1.36
French			
1.	0.65	0.98	0.65
2.	0.72	1.08	0.69
3.	0.71	1.04	0.66
4.	0.73	1.06	0.68
5.	0.55	0.91	0.55
6.	0.71	1.14	0.67
Others			
1.	0.58	0.41	0.84
2.	0.57	0.36	0.83
3.	0.51	0.35	0.80
4.	0.49	0.33	0.78
5.	0.82	0.42	1.20
N =	53	81	81
Unknown	5	7	4

[a] Based on *Financial Post Directory of Directors*.

Source: See Table 12.7 (see also Ogmundson and McLaughlin 1992: 234).

with a score of around 1.50 in the broadcast elites, is clear. The French, with a score of just under 0.70, are for the first time not even a junior partner. By 1989, they are replaced by "other" ethnic groups, with a score of over 0.80, in second place. The Canadian place of birth was particularly beneficial to the "third" ethnic groups' elite media representation in 1975 and 1985.

CONCLUSION AND DISCUSSION

A correct conclusion from the data provided by Ogmundson and McLaughlin (1992) is *not* to "abandon" the traditional imagery at the *elite level,* or even to suggest a noticeable decline in British participation among the elites as a proportion of their population. Such a conclusion points to the "verisimilitude" of the data. The more accurate conclusion — and this is consistent with Clement (1975a: 234; 1975b: 46) — is that British elite participation and dominance have basically been stable and that, consistent with Porter (1965: 285n), there is a clear ethnic vertical mosaic among the Canadian elites. The findings presented here also echo conclusions reached by Olsen (1980: 82). For the bureaucratic elite, he found some marginal change in the position of French and "other" ethnic groups since the time of the Porter study, which points to a "more open, more heterogeneous and probably more meritocratic, than the old" elite. But, he continues, the "overall pattern is one of the marked persistence of ethnic preference in recruitment." Similarly, we have shown that there is a clear pattern of preference for recruitment to elite positions for people of British origin.

On the other hand, consistent with the traditional imagery as well as with the views held by Brym and Fox (1989: 112), Hunter (1986), Berkowitz (1984), Rich (1991), Ogmundson (1990, 1992, 1993), and Ogmundson and McLaughlin (1992, 1994), the French and "other" ethnic groups have increased their elite participation. However, since the decline of the British in elite positions has equalled their relative decline in the Canadian population, one can conclude that the increase in the French and "other" ethnic group elite participation has not necessarily been at the expense of the British. To put it somewhat differently, there has been an absolute decline in the British elite position but, relative to their population, there has been little, if any, decline. The French and "other" ethnic groups, on the other hand, have increased their elite participation in both absolute and relative terms.

On a conceptual level, Ogmundson and McLaughlin (1992: 237) relied only on the changes in the proportion of ethnic groups among the elites and ignored the ethnic composition of the population. Therefore, they suggested that their findings indicate a "circulation of elites." This is a doubtful conclusion. In Pareto's words, the British "foxes" still dominate Canadian power structures, and the French and "other" ethnic "lions" are still subordinate (see Pareto's *Treatise* in Lopreato 1965).

Even if we accept Ogmundson and McLaughlin's (1992) data based on the percent distribution of ethnic elites, the British proportion of elites never fell below the 50% level except in one case — the broadcast media elites in 1989, at 49.4%. Assuming that, at the elite levels, decisions are made collectively and democratically, the balance of power is still overwhelmingly in favour of the British. This is because the French and "other" ethnic groups do not share a similar type of ethnic consciousness, a fact which causes disunity among the non-British; the "other" groups are further divided among themselves by ethnic origin, with little ethnic consciousness. In fact, research has shown that members of "other" ethnic groups frequently lose their "ethnicity" in Canada (see Reitz 1985; Isajiw 1990; Breton et al. 1990).

The findings presented here on the extent of continuity of ethnic homogeneity in elite positions show that it seems to be rooted in Canadian history, which is built on conquest and immigration (Clement 1975a: 231). The conquerors have institutionalized avenues of upward mobility, understandably based on their own preferred values, attitudes and behaviours, thus limiting the access of the conquered and the newly arrived to positions of power. Those who dominate the boardrooms of the major Canadian institutions make decisions and establish rules of recruitment based on the cultural values of their own British ethnic affiliation and "preferred" social background. The conquered and the newly arrived, on the other hand, have established "parallel" social networks and institutions for upward mobility that, for the most part, are distinct from what is available to the British (see Clement 1975a: 239; Breton 1978). Similarly, since earlier British dominance among Canadian institutions has established the frame of reference for future incumbents, one of the requirements of becoming a member of elite institutions is perhaps now to be "non-ethnic" (see Clement 1975b: 50; Williams 1989: 83; Berkowitz 1980; Kanter 1977). As Porter (1965: 218) has shown, the process of "like recruiting" is widespread in all of the dominant Canadian institutions.

In sum, these changing positions over 50 years can be judged in two ways. They may indicate the extent to which the British have kept their elite over-representation intact, or they may suggest a substantial intrusion of other cultural elements (see Porter 1965: 64).

The findings, however, do not support Ogmundson and McLaughlin's (1992: 237) conclusions that "the days of domination of Canadian elites by those of British ancestry are coming to a close" and that the original imagery of "vertical mosaic" at the *elite level* needs revision. What prevails in Canada is a British ruling class that has had and still has effective instrumental control in each category of elites and that has structurally dominated and continues to dominate the basic institutions of society *despite* a rapidly declining share of the general population. The inequality of access to elite positions remains the hallmark of Canadian society, and the new "balance" of the population, into a third each of British, French and "other," is *not* reflected in the positions of power. Nevertheless, there are strong indications that, in recent years, the French and "other" ethnic groups' access to elite positions has increased compared to their share of the general population.

NOTES

[1] It is worth noting that the assets of the 33 major Canadian-owned industries have continually increased in recent years. In 1970, there were 265 corporations, each with an asset of over $25 million controlling $50.9 billion in total assets (i.e., with an average of $191.4 million per corporation). These corporations increased in number to 949 in 1981 and to 1129 in 1984. Similarly, their assets increased to $260.8 billion and $344.2 billion, respectively. Thus, the average asset of each corporation amounted to $274.8 million in 1981 and to $304.9 million in 1984 (CLURA, 1972, 1981, 1985). These figures attest to an increasing concentration of capital in the major Canadian industries as well as to the increasing power of the elites in these corporations.

DISCUSSION QUESTIONS

1. What is the implication of the existence of a dominant British elite for the argument of equality of opportunity or of condition? What are the implications if we find that the British share of elites (economic, political, etc.) is declining or increasing over time?

2. Why should the ethnic composition of the Canadian population be taken into account when we deal with the trend in ethnic representation in the elites?

3. Discuss the possibility of writing a paper on economic elites in Canada with your professor. If agreed, study the directors of the twenty largest Canadian corporations by their total assets as listed in the *National Post Survey of Industries* (most recent issue). Use name dictionaries listed in the Ogmundson and McLaughlin bibliography, and identify the ethnicity of the directors. Calculate percentages as well as indices of dissimilarity using Nakhaie's Table

12.6. How do your figures compare with those of Ogmundson and McLaughlin and with Nakhaie's findings? Do they support Porter's view of the vertical mosaic? You can extend this research by looking at the biographies of these directors in *Who's Who in Canada* or other sources (check their age, education, parents' occupation, place of birth).

Another similar project would be to study the recent political elites using sources such as the *Canadian Parliamentary Guide.*

4. According to the data presented by Ogmundson and McLaughlin, among which of the elites is ethnic inequality the highest? What are the major implications of such inequality for inter-ethnic relations among various Canadian institutions?

5. Why is ethnic inequality more persistent among elites than among the masses?

6. In your opinion, why are citizens of French origin junior partners compared with those of British origin? Why are the "other" ethnic groups subordinated to the British and French?

FRENCH LANGUAGE AND NATIONALISM

French Language Charter
Camille Laurin

The building of a French Québec, officially announced to the world with this bill, has been a work of patience, of courage, and of pride. It bears witness to the strength of the human spirit and to the qualities of the people of Québec.

This has astonished and won the admiration of all the authorities in the social sciences who have studied this bill. They find it hard to understand how this people, who form a tiny enclave in the immensity of English-speaking North America, have managed to survive and to hold their own, let alone develop and thrive, in the face of — and even in the teeth of — all the laws of politics, economics, demography, and sociology. They have talked about anachronisms, accidents of history, chance, luck, and even miracles. For this was a people who should, logically, have vanished; who came close to vanishing on several occasions, and who from one point of view, would have profited from vanishing like those millions of immigrants who have sold their identity for a new allegiance to satisfy their dreams of wealth and power.

But the people of Québec turned their backs on this choice. They took advantage both of their inner dynamism and of historical circumstances to impose on their successive masters or adversaries their determination to remain themselves. Even before 1760, they were restive under the control of Paris and demanded a larger share of autonomy. Although deprived of their elite in 1763, they managed in 1774 to obtain from London an explicit guarantee of Québec's Frenchness and their right to live there according to their own laws and customs. In return, they promised to support Britain in its looming struggle with the American colonies. True, from then on, they abandoned to their British conquerors an economic and commercial hegemony that was to expand unceasingly. But for a time, they were content to occupy sectors and a place that could be developed along the lines of their own character. In 1791, they obtained limited political power and sent their first representatives to the Legislative Assembly.

In 1832, they demanded full responsible government in the face of the autocracy of the governor, who represented and defended the interests of the English-speaking minority. The demand was premature: the people lacked the strength to back it up, and it was crushed by force.

It was during this period that Durham described the situation as "two nations warring in a single state" and recommended the union of Lower and Upper Canada, convinced that the latter would absorb the former. And yet the trap was evaded. Aided by popular support, the French-speaking statesmen artfully contrived to preserve the identity and administrative structure of Lower Canada. At the same time, the Catholic Church set up a network of exclusively French-language educational and social institutions under her own control. By 1864, it was obvious that the Act of Union had failed to achieve its objectives. But the English Canadians had become a majority, and they dreamed of developing the country from sea to sea, for their exclusive profit, in the name of an industrial capitalism that was then coming into bloom. Lower Canada, to which they were constitutionally and politically tied, was a ball and chain from which they had to free themselves.

For the sake of freedom of action, they agreed to a few necessary sacrifices. Québec became a province, keeping control of its own administration and its French identity. Nevertheless, it was the only province forced into legislative and judicial bilingualism and into maintaining a Protestant school system. The new central government, for its part, claimed the only powers that mattered for economic and industrial development in addition to spending and residual powers.

The new régime was not slow to bear fruit. Thanks to a considerable influx of immigrants which increased the English majority, new provinces were created, linked from the Atlantic to the Pacific by two great railways. Everywhere the French minorities were squeezed out. Ontario controlled the new central government for its own ends. During this period, Québec reached the limits of settlement on its arable land and had to spill its extra population over into neighbouring provinces and American states. Urbanization began for the same reason. Since Québec had no say, or virtually none, in the running of the economy, all it could do was supply the new industrial and commercial establishments with the cheap unskilled labour they needed. The relative poverty of the French population grew continually, and they now ran a new risk: that of alienation and assimilation in a work world where English was omnipresent, dominant, and prestigious.

The two world wars favoured Canada's industrial growth and English Canada's economic hegemony. With the support of the latter, Ottawa took over provincial income tax and assumed the right to draw up broad policies — first social, then scientific, then cultural — all of which had been given to the provinces by the constitution.

This rapid and dynamic evolution meant wealth and prosperity for all Canadians. Québec, like all the other provinces, might have been expected to understand this, pat itself on the back, and even take a swan dive into the melting pot from which this wonderful new Canada was to emerge.

In fact, there were some French Canadians who rejoiced and more or less gave up their identities. But for the majority, doubts, reservations, and objections continued to matter more than self-satisfaction: loyalty and resistance did not die away. As a counterweight to the anglicizing influence in work, trade, business, the communications media and advertising, the working class re-created inside the cities its parishes and neighbourhoods and largely maintained its habits, customs, lifestyles, family ties, and institutions, as well as its ways of thinking and its values. In this they were encouraged, as was the whole French-speaking population, by the leadership, for a long time undisputed, of a clergy who saw the French language as a bulwark of the faith. Politicians talked tirelessly of autonomy and exalted Québec's uniqueness. Rising standards of living and education, and the resultant ever-sharpening consciousness of social problems and economic disparities in our surroundings, made it possible for church leaders, economists, professionals, and new popular elites to spark the creation of a trade-union movement, credit unions, agricultural cooperatives, family businesses, youth groups, and organizations that bore the distinctive stamp of the French-language culture.

But while the French-speaking majority was learning to stand on its own feet in the economic world, the English minority was taking giant strides ahead, thanks to the momentum it had already gained, to its position of strength, to its capital, to support from the federal government, to the American multinationals, and to the influx of immigrants that it was able to integrate or assimilate almost totally. By being made to repeat over and over to themselves that the gap was due to their own deficiencies and could only grow wider as long as Québec continued to live in the Middle Ages, "in a backward and priest-ridden province" with an outmoded school system where education was available only to the elite, the French population ended up convinced. And the Quiet Revolution began. At a cost of billions, the government modernized all levels of the educational system and made it open to everyone. The same was done for hospitals and social services. The government also nationalized the hydro-electric companies with great success and set up several government corporations in primary and secondary economic sectors.

The economic, social, and cultural development of the French-speaking community proceeded by leaps and bounds, but in the private sector, the work world remained obstinately English speaking, with all the old cultural and social inequalities, the same language barriers to promotion, and the same gap between incomes: unilingual English at the top, French at the bottom, and, at the tail end of all, the various categories of immigrants.

Obliged despite everything to recognize that it had reached the limit of its power and its resources, Québec nonetheless continued to assert vigorously its desire to be master in its own house. For that, it needed to regain the powers and resources that Ottawa had assumed and possessed in abundance. And from that time on, it has never ceased to demand them, more or less greedily, with all kinds of formulas and techniques, openly or secretly, sometimes like a lion, sometimes like a paper tiger, sometimes like a spaniel, but always vainly, and even, since the arrival on the scene of Pierre Elliott Trudeau, forced to give ground.

This cursory glance at our history leads to two major conclusions that indicate the path Québec must follow. The Canadian nation extends from coast to coast, to the profound satisfaction of its English-speaking population who derive benefit and pride from this fact. The creation of this country was the exploit of a central power that has been continually gaining in strength, and for English-Canadians, including those of Québec, this is a strength which must be maintained. The federal government must remain the "senior government" before which the provincial governments, which are basically its branch offices or administrative subdivisions, will naturally bow down. The feeling of being Canadian takes precedence over that of being a Westerner, an Ontarian, or a Quebecer, above all in times of danger or crisis. A Canadian feels at home anywhere between the Atlantic and the Pacific, and he can move to different parts of the country, according to inclination or necessity, for as long as he has to, without losing his sense of orientation. This in no way prevents the Manitoban or the Quebecer from having, especially when the sky is blue, a particular preference for his own corner, the one he has decorated or furnished himself. He feels he must at all costs preserve this delightful situation, hand it on to his children, and above all, protect it from any threat of autonomism that could alter it or overturn it.

The second conclusion is equally self-evident. French-speaking people could have found their place in this idyllic world and profited from it if they had been willing to give up their identity and adopt, on a more or less long-term basis, that of the Canadians; this is what those outside Québec are doing in increasing numbers, with the exception perhaps of those in New Brunswick and some parts of Ontario. Outside Québec, the country is so massively English that it seems to them impossible and pointless to try to fight when they have so much more to lose than to gain for themselves and above all for their children on the economic and social scale. But the same does not hold true for the French-speaking population of Québec. Once, almost all of Canada and some of the United States belonged to them, and they have retained a nostalgic pride that is a part of their collective soul. Though dispossessed of the land they had explored and of the name they had given it, they have kept their starting place, where after three hundred years of trials and struggle, they still form a very strong majority. Now there is nothing left to them but Québec. Rightly or wrongly, they have apparently decided to hold on to it and develop it according to their own history, their own culture, and their own spirit, whatever price must be paid and whatever sacrifices are required, to permit themselves this desire, this fidelity, and this determination. Here is a fact more stubborn than all the functional theories that try to prove to them that on the contrary, it would be to their great advantage to opt for federalism brought up to date, profitable, reasonably decentralized, and modelled on the huge American or European communities. Their instinct tells them this is a mirage, a confidence trick, a squared circle, and they continue, indefatigably, confusedly, clumsily, to insist on a larger and larger portion of sovereignty.

To the English provinces that ask, "What does Québec want?" Québec's French-speaking population now replies, "a homeland." By a series of amputations, that homeland — which has always existed — is now limited to Québec. Québec is a nation and has a better claim to be a nation than many other countries, including Canada, for it has long possessed all the attributes of nationhood: a territory, a language, a culture, institutions, a history, and, above all, a collective purpose and desire to exist.

The French-speaking Quebecer — the Québécois — is attached to that nation by all the fibres of his being. He was Canadian when Canada meant the territory of Québec or its extension. Since being dispossessed of Canada and shut out, he has become primarily Québécois and after that, vaguely, a bit Canadian by force of habit. The government to which he feels closest is the government of Québec, and in any conflicts that pit the federal government against the Québec government, he is by instinct always on the side of the latter, whatever his political leanings may be and whatever the admiration he may have for men like Laurier, St. Laurent, or Trudeau.

If he has behaved like a Québécois throughout his history, he will inevitably do so more and more in the future. For he is increasingly proud of his country, of the language he speaks (which is that of one of the great civilizations of the world), of his culture whose vitality and dynamism are bursting out at last in many fields, of the institutions he has created and which bear his stamp, of the uniformly accelerated rhythm of his evolution, of his humanism, and of his openness to the rest of the world. His self-esteem, his self-confidence, and his hope can only continue to grow — which does not prevent him from recognizing his weaknesses and deficiencies and especially the gap between himself and the goal he has set.

So the die is cast. Québec wishes to remain itself. It will never play second fiddle to a federal government that will always be too levelling and too centralizing for Québec's taste. It cannot help being the imbalance that endangers the health and even the life of the Canadian constitutional system. This being so, why not draw the conclusions and do what the situation logically demands? Québec owes it to itself to bring into being, on every level, the nation it in fact is; to acquire the powers and the resources it needs for this end; and then to seek the best possible relations and accord with its neighbour on the basis of interest and friendship.

It is in this perspective that the government's language policy is situated. This policy was a priority since language is the very ground under a people's feet: by it, they know themselves and are known; it is rooted in their hearts and allows them to express their identity. It was a priority also because the quality of our language is threatened by the decay resulting from the colonization of the people of Québec and because their rights must be restored to those who have suffered discrimination and injustice simply for speaking the language of their country.

Here we must reject the federal attitudes, suggestions, and solutions. Ottawa's efforts have not prevented massive anglicization of French-speaking Canadians outside Québec. We have paid hundreds of millions of dollars to increase the number of French-speaking federal civil servants, and still they are markedly in the minority. Through the fault of a central power that is either without influence or an accomplice, the *Gens de l'air* may not use French on the job in Québec, and French-speaking employees of Air Canada, Canadian National, the National Harbours Board, and so on are only too often obliged to work in English in their own country. In the same way, Ottawa has tried to bilingualize all corners of Québec where the population is 10% English-speaking — it even wanted to make the whole of Québec a bilingual district! We denounce and reject all these policies and also the free choice of language of instruction that Mr Trudeau is trying in every possible way to impose on us.

We also reject the philosophy of Bill 22, which sought to attain two conflicting and irreconcilable goals by trying to make French the official language of the State of Québec and then bilingualizing Québec at every level and considering it as the provincial branch office of a centralized unitary federal system.

In the last analysis, a choice must be made, and for us the choice is clear. Despite the minorities with which Québec has over the centuries become associated, minorities it respects and whose contributions it seeks, Québec has always been and intends to remain essentially French. Its first name was Nouvelle-France. Later, the British conquerors acknowledged that Québec had inherited the tradition of New France, and as such was a separate country with a special status within the Empire. Neither the historical continuity nor the juridical and political unity of this separate country have ever been fragmented by that arrival in Québec of immigrants from many other lands. From the beginning, French has been the language of the people of Québec, taken overall as a collective entity — which does not mean that many other mother tongues cannot exist or be used in private life and in the activities of individual ethnic groups. But the Amerindians and the Inuit are the only ones who, from a certain point of view, can consider themselves as peoples separate from the totality of Québécois and in consequence, insist on special treatment under the law. All other groups are the descendants of immigrants of full right and duty and thus co-heirs to the juridico-political and socio-cultural tradition common to the people of Québec.

This means that for Québec, there can no longer be any question of bilingualism on the official and institutional levels. Dominated economically at home and politically in Ottawa by English Canadians, to say nothing of the cultural pressure exerted on it by a massively English-speaking continent, progressive bilingualization could only push Québec sooner or later into cultural fragmentation and anglicization. Furthermore, Québec has a right to its national language, and it is only to be expected that it will use that language to express itself and assert itself in all areas of its collective life, as all other countries have always done, including English Canada. Québec also needs a common language to ensure the cohesion of its community and the normal, smooth, and efficient functioning of its institutions. In a country with a large French-speaking majority, what can that common language be but French? Finally, to ensure the democratic participation of all Québécois in Québec's economic and political life, the state must make sure that this economic and political life is essentially carried on in the language of the majority; it must also make sure that this language is taught as well as possible to all Québécois, without exception. The use of the expression "official language" has all these connotations, which necessitate the use of French on the institutional level as the language of the state and the law and as the normal and usual language of work, education, and communications.

In parliamentary committees in Ottawa and in certain editorials, the objection has been raised that we were attacking Québec's bi-cultural nature and the assured rights of the large English-language community in Québec. It could quite easily be shown, for example by quoting the speeches of Pitt, Burke, and other parliamentarians in the British House of Commons in 1774, that the British conquerors themselves never accorded distinct rights to the English in Québec but, on the contrary, insisted on submission to the laws of the French country where the English had chosen to live. Clearly, then, the Anglo-Quebecers have no separate rights as a community distinct from the people of Québec.

This is perhaps the moment to say that in legislating on the rights of French in Québec, the government has absolutely no intention of putting the French-language cultural group in a position of superiority, even in the name of the majority. French-language culture is neither better nor worse than any other. The theme has been repeated over and over again, in the White Paper and elsewhere: it is as a result of the inferior position of the French language in the Canadian and American context and of the economic subordination of those who speak it that the law must in simple justice reinforce its status. Far from denying the right of equality to different cultures, the law in this case wishes to make a small contribution to re-establishing this equality. In doing so, it draws its inspiration, in the most concrete fashion possible, from the very principles that lie at the heart of human rights. If, under the guise of equality, it had been necessary for the law to give its blessing to the existing situation, it would simultaneously have been blessing existing inequalities. The law does not stand out clearly in a universe of abstractions: rather, in the real world, it is an attempt, continually renewed, to introduce justice and equality.

In closing this analysis, we can say with pleasure that the government's language policy was drawn up with constant participation by the public. We first presented a White Paper, which the newspapers reprinted and which was widely commented on. Subsequently, I was able to talk with hundreds of individuals and groups. Each of the 265 briefs received by the parliamentary commission was read and analysed. Many substantial amendments were made. In fact, this has been a fruitful exercise in democracy in action.

It did however make us sadly aware of a deep division separating the English minority from the French majority. This gap was not caused by the election of November 15, 1976, but the election expressed it, widened it, and accentuated it even further. This may be because the government against which the minority voted, in which it is not represented, and over which it has no hold, remains completely foreign to it. But instead of trying to get to know it and the people of Québec whom it represents, this minority is up in arms, denouncing, refusing, combatting, even seeking a confrontation. Its leaders, at any event, have left no stone unthrown. They make a great fuss about free choice for parents and immigrants while actually defending an eminently profitable status quo. They pose as the champions of individual liberties even while the Charter of Human Rights and Freedoms continues to take precedence over every other law. They try to make us believe that they are on the road to second-class citizenhood when this very Charter guarantees them all their basic rights, and Bill 101 accords them a respectful and generous treatment that would certainly be endorsed under international law. They vaunt our cultural dynamism and our progress as if the French speakers did not know better than they what inadequacies, inequities, and underdevelopment they are concealing, that must as soon as possible be remedied. They even play down their strength so that we will not see them as a threat. Because the systematic gallicization of Québec seems to us to be normal, realistic, and urgent, they see it as a regression and a moral failure of which we should feel ashamed and guilty. And when they have used up all these arguments, they brandish that weapon which they wield so well — the economy — and evoke the spectre of the flight of capital, head offices, and businesses when they are not evoking that of destabilization and economic reprisals.

They are doing all this at a time when they should be seeing themselves as a minority and not as the Québec wing of the English-Canadian majority, at a time when what is required is a mature and positive reaction to a necessary loss of privileges that no normal and healthy society could uphold.

And it is precisely for this inverse reason that the French-speaking majority, with the exception of a few notables who have lost touch with it during their overly long association with English-language centres of power, is giving whole-hearted support to a liberating policy for which it has been waiting with secret hope for two hundred years. This bill seems to it to be just, for itself and for the various minorities. It comes at the right time to give the people of Québec the pride, the self-confidence, the dignity, the maturity, and the impetus they need and deserve. It will motivate them to go further still and, in the near future, to take over the control of their own destiny, having proved to them that this can be done and that they can do it. Obviously they hope to be joined in this splendid destiny by the different minorities, and in particular by the English minority, who will in the end recognize them and appreciate them for what they are.

The Québec that this bill prepares and heralds will be French, educated, modern — a country that will take its place side by side with countries of comparable size that have already set their mark on the world scene. It, too, will be able to reach the universal by and through the particularities of its own culture. In this way, it will shoulder its moral obligation to make its unique contribution to the international community.

Perceptions of National Identity
Bernard Blishen

On reading Dr Laurin's history of Quebec, one is struck by the confidence with which he places Quebec society in its historical framework. There appears to be no doubt in his mind that sequential historical events have produced a society with all the attributes of a nation, including a distinctive collective consciousness or self-awareness of the ways in which that society or nation and its members differ from the rest of Canada, and indeed North America. It is this collective consciousness and awareness of their uniqueness that provide the basis of the Québécois identity.

The past few decades have witnessed a spate of published material dealing with the idea of a Canadian identity. Perhaps the most original of these is the attempt by Morton (1961) to show how historical events have produced a unique Canadian institutional structure. Unfortunately, he fails to come to grips with the problem of the effect of these developments on the emergence of a national identification. One of the most recent attempts to examine this problem is the report by T.H.B. Symons (1975) on the state of Canadian studies in Canadian universities. Symons tries to rationalize the need for more studies of all aspects of Canadian society by claiming that we know too little about ourselves. One can have little objection to the quest for self-knowledge, but when the author suggests that a consciousness of being Canadian, of a distinctive national identity, is a necessary prerequisite to that quest, he fails to see the interplay between a knowledge of the development of institutional structure and the way in which that knowledge becomes invested with feelings of belonging to the milieu created by this structure. This feeling results in an identification with that milieu which can be regional or national. For this reason, he fails to portray the distinctive features of the Canadian identity to which we refer. In particular, he cannot tell us if what he calls a Canadian identity has a regional as well as a national component despite his stress on the importance of regional studies in Canadian universities. Symons seems to be saying that a sense of identity must exist in order to stimulate the search for those features of Canadian society to which the individual feels a sense of belonging and with which he identifies. His assumption seems to be that we must search for these features in order to identify with them. In other words, Canadians', presumably Anglophone Canadians', identification with Canada needs to be stronger.

For his part, Dr Laurin is in no doubt about the reciprocal relationship between the development of social institutions and the emergence of an awareness of belonging to that milieu. He draws upon this relationship to delineate the features of the Québécois national identity. For him, Quebec has all the attributes of a nation, " a territory, a language, a culture, institutions, a history, and most of all, a collective will to live and a goal." Laurin assumes that group consciousness or sense of belonging exists among the Québécois, and this enables them to point to features of Québécois society with which they can identify. Both Laurin and Symons are talking about what Weber calls national solidarity or national sentiment when he refers to the concept of nation. As he says, "in the sense of those using the term at a given time, the concept undoubtedly means, above all, that one may exact from certain groups of men a specific sentiment of solidarity in the face of other groups. Thus, the concept belongs in the sphere of values, yet there is no agreement on how these groups should be delimited or about what concerted action should result from such solidarity" (Gerth and Mills 1958: 172). It would appear that Laurin is much clearer than Symons not only about the delimiting features of Québécois society, but about what action should follow from the feeling of solidarity. Weber suggests that the idea of a nation "is usually anchored in the superiority, or at least the irreplaceability, of the cultural values that are to be preserved and developed only through the cultivation of the peculiarity of the group" (Gerth and Mills 1958: 176). Here, again, Laurin is on surer ground than Symons because he is quite specific about what cultural values he would like to see preserved. Symons, on the other hand, says we should develop Canadian studies so that we can become aware of Canadian values. Weber sees these common cultural values providing "a unifying national bond. But for this, the objective quality of the cultural values does not matter at all, and therefore, one must not conceive of the 'nation' as a culture community" (Gerth and Mills 1958: 178).

Laurin's claim about the strength of the Québécois' identification with their society and Symons' assumption of the relative weakness of anglophones' identification with anglophone Canada can be tested with data obtained from a national survey conducted in June 1977 consisting of a national sample of about 3200 respondents representing the Canadian population and a national sample of approximately 600 members of various institutional elites such as business, political, civil service, and university. The aim of this study, which continues over a five-year period, is to measure the level of respondents' satisfaction with the quality of life in a number of life domains and life as a whole, as well as to ascertain attitudes concerning a number of current national issues. As part of the latter aspect of the study, two questions were asked dealing with respondents' identification with province or nation. The first of these was asked in the following manner: "Some people say they are (name of province of residence) first, and Canadian second, while others say they are Canadian first and (name of province of residence) second. How would you describe yourself? Canadian first, provincial first, both equally, neither, other (specify), don't know." The second question which only French-speaking Quebec respondents were asked was worded as follows: "Comment vous définissez-vous *en tout premier lieu:* comme un Canadien-français, un Québécois, un Canadien tout simplement, ou autrement?"[1] Table 13.1 shows the answers to the first question on identification with nation or province according to provincial or regional language group. It appears that there is less identification with Canada among the francophones in Quebec than among the non-French in Quebec, Ontario, or any other region of Canada. This lack of national identification among Quebec francophones, with only 46 per cent of respondents indicating they identify themselves as Canadians first, is not much lower than the proportion with a similar identification in the Maritimes where only 52 per cent of the non-French see themselves as Canadians first. It would appear from these data that the highest proportion of people identifying themselves as Canadians is found among the non-French in Ontario and British Columbia where over four-fifths of each of these populations identify themselves in this way.

The low proportions of the French in Quebec and the non-French in the Maritimes who identify themselves as Canadians first is offset by the high proportions in both populations who identify with their province first. Surprisingly, almost 35 per cent of the non-French in the Maritimes identify with the province rather than with Canada. Other data, not presented here, indicate that this provincial identification is located mainly in Newfoundland where over one-half of the respondents expressed themselves in this fashion. It is possible that, in view of their relatively recent entry into the Canadian confederation, the people of Newfoundland still retain a strong provincial identification.

Table 13.1
Identification with Canada or Province by Provincial or Regional Language Group

| | Provincial or Regional Language Group | | | | | | | |
Identification	Fr. in Quebec	Non-Fr. in Quebec	Fr. outside Quebec	Non-Fr. in Ontario	Non-Fr. in Prairies	Non-Fr. in B.C.	Non-Fr. in Maritimes	Total
Canadian first	46.2%	71.4%	75.7%	86.1%	76.8%	81.1%	52.4%	69.6%
Both equally	22.5	13.2	6.5	3.0	10.0	6.8	10.9	10.8
Province first	30.4	9.0	11.2	6.3	10.3	9.0	34.7	16.4
Neither	0.7	2.3	1.2	2.4	1.8	1.6	1.5	1.7
Other	0.1	4.1	5.3	2.2	1.2	1.6	0.6	1.7
N	803	266	169	1018	340	322	340	3258

These data also indicate that a high proportion, around 42 per cent, of the respondents in Prince Edward Island express a provincial identification. In Nova Scotia and New Brunswick, this proportion falls to slightly more than one-quarter, which is still much higher than the proportion in Ontario or the western provinces. Table 13.1 shows that, of the French in Quebec, 30 per cent identify with that province first, but a further 22 per cent of that population claim that they identify equally with Canada and the province. This is double the proportion of non-French in the Maritimes who claim this identification. Does this mean that there is a sharper division between national and regional or provincial identification in the Maritimes than in Quebec? It is among the non-French in the former area that the individual identifies with either Canada or the region, only 11 per cent identifying themselves as both. The French in Quebec are not so clear-cut in their identification compared to the non-French in the Maritimes; smaller proportions identify themselves as Canadians first or provincial first, but more than double the Maritime proportion identify themselves as both.

It is evident that most of the French in Quebec do not identify themselves with the Québécois nation of Dr Laurin. If we can assume that the proportion of French in Quebec who identify with the province first is an indication of national sentiment, we must conclude that national sentiment for a Québécois nation, to which Dr Laurin refers, is not very prevalent. These data do provide some evidence that among the non-French in the Maritimes, there exists a fair amount of regional identification with over one-third of the population so identifying themselves. Whether this group has the national attributes Dr Laurin sees as the elements of nationhood is doubtful if only because national independence has not emerged as an issue in that area. However, a fair amount of regional sentiment appears to exist.

These data do not appear to support Dr Symons' assumption that there is a relative weakness in anglophone Canadians' identification with their country. If the proportion of non-French outside Quebec who identify with Canada first is an indication of the prevalence of national sentiment, then the large proportions who so identify themselves suggests that among anglophone Canadians, national sentiment is very prevalent except in the Maritimes.

Having described the prevalence of national and regional identification across Canada, we now focus our attention on the responses to the question on national identification which only French-speaking Quebec respondents were asked. These responses indicate that less than one-fifth of the French in Quebec see themselves as Canadian, and less than one-third identify themselves as Québécois as described by Dr Laurin, and the remaining 51.3 per cent see themselves as Canadien français.

What is the social background of these three groups who identify themselves differently? We attempt only a limited answer to this question by examining age, education, and income characteristics of these individuals. Table 13.2 shows that well over half of the 18 to 24 age group identify themselves as Québécois. As age increases, this proportion tends to decrease, and the proportion of those who identify themselves as Canadien français tends to increase. In fact, our data show that well over two-thirds of the 45 to 54 age group identify themselves as Canadien français, and in the oldest age group, this proportion is over 78 per cent. It will be interesting to see if the high proportion of those with Québécois identification who are now in the 18 to 24 age group retain that self image as they get older. Table 13.2 seems to indicate that they might change their identification to Canadien français, but the test of this assumption will require a longitudinal study of the 18 to 24 cohort.

Table 13.3 shows that as educational level rises, the proportion of those identifying themselves as Québécois tends to increase to a high of over 50 per cent among those who have technical training beyond high school. The proportion is almost as high among those with some university background but drops off to just over one-third in the most highly educated group. The opposite pattern is evident for those who identify themselves as Canadien français. Nearly two-thirds of those with no high school have this view of themselves, and this proportion declines as the level of education increases. Among those with high school plus technical education, it declines to just under 30 per cent, but in each of the two highest educational levels, the proportion increases somewhat.

When we examine the distribution of our respondents at various income levels, Table 13.4 shows that no clear-cut pattern is evident except that at each income level, those individuals who see themselves as Canadien français have the highest proportion, which never falls below 45 per cent. The pattern that emerges for those who identify themselves as Québécois is that they form between 30 and 40 per cent

Table 13.2
National Identification of Francophone Respondents in Quebec by Age[a]

Identification	Age						
	18–24	*25–34*	*35–44*	*45–54*	*55–64*	*65 or More*	**Total**
Canadien français	30.5%	41.7%	54.4%	69.8%	66.0%	78.7%	51.3%
Canadien tout simplement	14.1	21.4	20.4	16.4	19.4	17.0	18.1
Québécois	55.4	36.8	24.5	13.8	14.6	4.2	30.5
N	174	157	118	97	81	64	691

[a] Excludes "other."

of the second, third, and fourth income quintiles. They fall below 25 per cent of the poorest and richest quintiles.

In summary, our data show that a fairly high proportion of anglophones outside Quebec identify themselves as Canadian first except in the Maritimes. Among the francophones in Quebec, this proportion drops substantially; the proportion who identify equally with Canada and their province increases, but not so much as the proportion who identify with the province, which increases to just over 30 per cent. Presumably, it is this group of individuals who also identify themselves as Québécois. The two proportions are about the same. Among the anglophones in the Maritimes, an even higher proportion than among the francophones in Quebec identify with the province first. The highest proportions of Québécois are found in the youngest age groups and at the highest edu-

Table 13.3
National Identification of Francophone Respondents in Quebec by Education[a]

Identification	No High School	Some High School	High School Grad	High School Plus Tech.	Some Univ.	Univ. & Prof.	Total
Canadien français	63.8%	56.6%	50.0%	28.7%	39.4%	36.1%	51.3%
Canadien tout simplement	21.3	17.8	15.2	19.2	10.8	29.3	18.1
Québécois	14.9	25.6	34.8	52.1	48.9	34.5	30.5
N	182	149	172	44	95	50	691

[a] Excludes "other."

Table 13.4
National Identification of Francophone Respondents in Quebec by Income[a]

Identification	First	Second	Third	Fourth	Fifth	Total
Canadien français	59.9%	45.2%	55.1%	46.2%	49.9%	51.8%
Canadien tout simplement	16.4	20.8	13.2	13.3	26.3	17.5
Québécois	23.7	34.0	31.1	40.5	23.8	30.6
N	133	121	160	109	98	620

[a] Excludes "other."

cational levels. The highest proportions of Canadien français are located in the older age groups and the lower educational levels. It is from the young educated Québécois that support for an independent Quebec state will come. For that situation to become a reality via a referendum will require a switch in identification of substantial numbers of French in Quebec who now see themselves as Canadien français.

NOTES

[1] The responses contained in Tables 13.2 to 13.4 include some from respondents who did not identify themselves as of French descent but who were interviewed in French. The definition of French ethnicity, using the standard Census question, produced substantially the same results.

DISCUSSION QUESTIONS

1. Looking at French–English relations, describe the ways in which the French elite has helped the politicization of French Canadians.

2. Read newspaper articles and discuss English–French relations with your family and friends. Describe how French Canadians view their relationship with the rest of Canada. How do English Canadians view French Canadians? What do these groups want from each other?

3. Why do the Quebec government and French Canadians see language legislation as the key to their cultural survival?

4. After reading Blishen's study, what do you think is the hallmark of Canadian identity? Is it regional or national?

5. What would you do if Quebec decided to separate from Canada?

6. Recently, French–English relations came to a head in the Meech Lake Accord. Read various newspaper articles about this issue (e.g., *The Globe and Mail,* March 29, 1988; December 9, 1988). What is the Distinct Society Clause, and why did the Quebec government of the day insist on it?

7. Read "B.C. Alienation Hits Quebec Levels" (Exhibit 3.2). Is there any noticeable change in B.C.'s view towards Canada since Blishen's study? Why are these two provinces unhappy with their lot in Canada?

Exhibit 3.2

B.C. Alienation Hits Quebec Levels

Half of British Columbians think their province is getting a raw deal from Confederation and a quarter believe the province would be better off if it separated from Canada.

The remarkable results of the year-end Southam–Global poll show the level of dissatisfaction on the West Coast now rivals that found in Quebec.

The survey, conducted by national polling firm POLLARA, follows a salmon dispute this summer between B.C. and the United States during which Premier Glen Clark lashed out at the federal government for what he said was a lack of support.

POLLARA president Michael Marzolini said the country's fixation on reducing the threat of Quebec secession seems to have fuelled the alienation in B.C.

For Pat Carney, the poll results are a vindication. The Tory senator has been denounced by federal officials and media commentators, primarily those in Central Canada, since she warned last summer that British Columbians are profoundly unhappy with the federation and suggested they use the threat of secession to negotiate a better deal.

"I'm not surprised (at the poll findings) because I have been reporting on this level of frustration," Carney says.

Based on the hundreds of letters and faxes she's received since the summer, Carney believes British Columbians love Canada but are increasingly frustrated by their geographic isolation from federal institutions, chronic under-representation in Parliament and the "myopic" obsession with Quebec.

If British Columbians' concerns are taken seriously, she's convinced there's time to nip separatist sentiment in the bud.

"B.C. wants in," she said. "Everybody says we love Canada, we love to be part of Canada, but they're not paying attention ... Ottawa doesn't listen to our priorities."

The poll found 50 per cent of Quebecers and British Columbians are unhappy with their lot in Confederation. And the numbers are not far apart when respondents in both provinces are asked whether their provinces would be better off outside Canada — 31 per cent in Quebec and 25 per cent in B.C.

However, a higher 66 per cent of British Columbians think a separated B.C. would be worse off compared with 50 per cent of Quebecers.

(continued)

Exhibit 3.2 *(continued)*

Elsewhere in the country, there is more contentment.

Fully 78 per cent of Ontarians and a majority in Alberta, the Prairies and Atlantic Canada think their province gets a fair deal in Confederation.

The poll of 1,410 Canadians was conducted Nov. 28–Dec. 2 and is considered accurate within 3.4 percentage points 19 times in 20. The margin of error is larger for regional breakdowns.

The poll found Canadians everywhere, including Quebec, are more confident about the province staying in Canada than they've been since Quebecers came within a whisker of voting to separate in the 1995 referendum.

Source: Joan Bryden, "B.C. Alienation Hits Quebec Levels," *The Windsor Star*, December 20, 1997, p. A12. Reprinted by permission.

ABORIGINAL STRUGGLES

Aboriginal Peoples and Hegemony in Canada
Peter Kulchyski

Canada has increasingly come to be identified with what was, for much of this century, among the most marginal of the political and cultural issues it faced: the struggle around Aboriginal rights. Increasingly, Canadians visiting other countries are asked about James Bay, or the Innu, or Native women's issues by those who take an interest in our home. The concept of Aboriginal rights marks a shift — the significance of which has yet to be felt — in the universalist discourse of human rights towards culturally specific rights. Hence, the discourse of Aboriginal rights in Canada may come to mark something new in the world, a new phase or modality of accommodation between liberal-democratic nation-states and cultural minorities. Aboriginal politics in Canada are a specific terrain of struggle, one that demands its own theoretical maps whose links with broader theoretical reflections and, indeed, with broader struggles themselves, must be carefully worked through and cannot be assumed. What follows emerged from a working paper that attempted to sketch out such a map around the questions of hegemony, resistance, and identity.

HEGEMONY

A few comments about the terms "Aboriginal" and "hegemony" are in order. In this article, the term "Aboriginal" is deployed in the sense that the Canada Act (1982) adopts the term. That is, it applies to Indians, Métis, and Inuit. Each of these has a different legal status in Canada and would define hegemony in somewhat different ways. It is also worth noting that Indians tend now to refer to themselves as First Nations. There are Indians who have legal status in accordance with the Indian Act and those who consider themselves Indians but do not have legal status. As well, there are First Nations with treaties and those

298 PART THREE ETHNIC INEQUALITIES

without. Finally, in each of these groups, the concerns of women may differ significantly from those of men. At the outset, then, it is crucial to recognize that Aboriginal peoples describe the processes and effects of what I am here calling "hegemony" in very different ways depending on these differing contexts.

Nevertheless, some things *can* be said about hegemony in general, with specifications and qualifications duly noted and outlined. Aboriginal politics are largely about the continued assertion of difference; they are in great measure a politics of identity concerned to ensure that distinctive Aboriginal cultures find a respected place in Canadian society. The concern is to ensure that Aboriginal ways of life — which include ties to a land-based subsistence economy as well as to languages, spiritualities, and cultures — continue to have relevance in the lives of Aboriginal peoples. This means that Aboriginal politics are cultural politics.

Hegemony may be provisionally defined as any attempt on the part of the dominant society to assimilate Aboriginal peoples. Assimilation to Aboriginal leaders means the process of making Aboriginal culture irrelevant in the lives of Aboriginal peoples. The expression "apple" — red on the outside, white on the inside — is used in a derogatory fashion by some Aboriginal peoples to designate those who accept the values and practices of the dominant culture.

Assimilation takes many forms, several of which I will outline before discussing some forms of resistance to it. The normal processes of commodification or the expansion of the commodity form — that is, the restructuring of social life so that every sphere is governed by the logic of the market — have as much impact on the lives of Aboriginal peoples as they do elsewhere and can be seen as a powerful tool of the dominant culture. Thus, an implicit process of assimilation takes place because the driving force of the dominant culture is assimilatory in nature; the commodity form continues to expand as long as capital accumulation is a necessary precondition for Canada. Commodified popular culture reaches to the far corners of Canada, including isolated reserves, and acts in a powerful manner to attract Aboriginal peoples away from what they might recognize as a traditional way of life.

As well, assimilation has been in official government policy towards Aboriginal peoples for much of Canada's history; although it is no longer an official policy, many Aboriginal leaders would characterize it as a "hidden agenda" on the part of the State. The federal government was given powers over "Indians and lands reserved for Indians" in the BNA Act (1867) and therefore became the level of government most often associated with Indian policy. In the last 10 years, there has been an increasing level of provincial involvement in Aboriginal affairs, but the federal government remains the locus of struggle. The Indian Act (1876) was originally based on a piece of legislation called the

Enfranchisement Act (1869), whose purpose was to regulate the orderly transition of Aboriginal peoples into the mainstream of Canadian society. The major revision of the Indian Act in 1951 continued to assert enfranchisement as a goal (in fact, Indian Affairs was housed in the Department of Citizenship and Immigration through much of the 1950s), but it made the procedure voluntary except for women who married non-status men.

After Aboriginal peoples obtained the federal vote in the late 1950s, formal enfranchisement was no longer the cornerstone of assimilation, but assimilation remained the cornerstone of Indian policy. In fact, it was felt that providing Aboriginal peoples with voting rights would help to integrate them into the dominant cultural values. Canada was one of the last countries in the western world to have full adult enfranchisement because Aboriginal adults did not gain the right to vote while maintaining their Indian status until 1959. Most western countries reached full adult enfranchisement when women got the vote in the first few decades of this century. Canada and South Africa have the dubious distinction of being relative latecomers.

The Trudeau government in 1969 formally announced a policy of wholesale assimilation that appropriately became known as the White Paper. The struggle over the White Paper, which the federal government was forced to withdraw in 1970, became a formative event for a generation of Aboriginal political leaders. Consequently, it was after 1970 that assimilation shifted from an explicit to an implicit government policy concerning Aboriginal peoples. The State now pays lip service to the maintenance of Aboriginal cultural difference, while deploying a series of policies and programs which, in effect, work in the opposite direction.

My own theoretical position is that hegemony towards Aboriginal peoples may be characterized by "totalization." The State, in attempting to create conditions conducive to the accumulation of capital, attempts to construct a set of spatial and temporal matrices which work to marginalize and then absorb those whose material preconditions contradict the accumulation of capital. The State has become a totalizing instrument in the lives of Aboriginal peoples and is experienced by them as being totalitarian in nature. Again, it is worth noting that this attempt to totalize is hotly contested; clearly, the State does not get and has not gotten its way at every turn.

Effectively, then, unlike those members of ethnic minorities who are struggling for equality and an end to discrimination, many Aboriginal peoples are struggling for the maintenance of difference and the establishment of forms of positive "discrimination." This was called "citizens plus" in the late sixties and is now generally referred to as "Aboriginal rights." It is only with this presupposition that we can understand why the defining struggle of our era in this terrain was the struggle against a formal government policy whose explicit aim was to end discrimination against Aboriginal peoples through the 1969 White Paper. Similarly, the official State endorsement of multiculturalism in Canada can be characterized as a mechanism of totalizing power in that it positions the particular cultural claims of Aboriginal peoples as one in a series of unspecified claims by Ukrainians, Japanese, Québécois, Cree, and so on. This serves to decentre the historically and culturally specific claims of Aboriginal peoples (and, not incidentally, of Québécois and other Franco Canadians), submerging them in a vast, abstract, undifferentiated, multicultural mosaic. The struggle for Aboriginal rights — which cannot be claimed by any other cultural minority — against those who attempt to limit, regulate, or extinguish them is one of the basic features of Aboriginal peoples' struggle in contemporary Canada.

Nevertheless, Aboriginal peoples do experience negative discrimination, including racism. Two groups in particular have made the struggle against racism a priority: the Métis often are primarily concerned with establishing equal opportunities, as are non-status Indians, particularly those living in urban settings. Both groups sometimes find themselves opposed to the status Indian and Inuit groups in terms of the discourse of their struggles.

Aboriginal women, depending on their circumstances, may be primarily concerned with gender bias or sex-based discrimination, often (but not only) within their own communities. Indian women who lost legal status as Indians because of discriminatory provisions in the Indian Act sometimes have bitter memories of male Aboriginal leaders' attempts to block their struggle against sexual discrimination. Inuit and Métis women have been less concerned with this specific issue, but it remains a vital concern for many other First Nations women.

Finally, in characterizing hegemony as it is articulated in the struggles of Aboriginal peoples, it is important to recognize that capital directly has a place, but not in the same way that it does in relation to the working class. While workers more immediately experience capital as the theft of time (the theory of surplus value), Aboriginal peoples experience capital as an invasion of their space. The most notable struggles of Aboriginal peoples against capital have been over the exploitation of non-renewable resources in the Canadian hinterland and the resulting environmental impact such exploitation has, including the negative consequences for those whose material livelihood depends upon a subsistence economy directly linked to the land as the means of subsistence. It is usually the State that is on the front line of these struggles, either as the developer (as in the case of hydro-electric projects) or as a "mediator" working in the interest of transnational corporations seeking access to a particular resource (as was the case with, for example, the Mackenzie Valley pipeline construction project). At a more abstract level, however, the process of dispossessing Aboriginal peoples by separating them from their means of subsistence so that they will be forced to sell their labour on the restricted wage-labour market remains an incomplete project.

In sum, while I would describe the hegemony that Aboriginal peoples face as a totalization primarily located around the State, but also present in the cultural forms of the dominant society, I would qualify this by noting that some groups of Aboriginal peoples — such as urban Indians, Indian women, and Métis — also have concerns such as ending gender or racial discrimination.

RESISTANCE

Resistance takes place on many levels. I will begin by discussing an implicit level and then turn to organized struggle. Implicit resistance tends not to be self-reflective or self-conscious, but nevertheless moves against the workings of totalizing power. For example, in the struggle against totalization, teaching your children an Aboriginal language can be a form of resistance. Implicit resistance of this sort takes place on an everyday level and most often involves some form of subversion.

This approach to implicit resistance forms part of my own theoretical work. Subversion involves taking structures, signs, technologies, and so on that have been deployed by the established order and reversing them, deploying them in a manner that works against their intended effects. It can be characterized as a strategy of semiotic reversal. For example, Inuit have been able to take television, a powerful carrier of commodity culture, and partially remake it to reflect Inuit experience and Inuit ways of seeing. The Inuit Broadcasting Corporation uses television to strengthen aspects of Inuit culture.

Another kind of subversion can be found in an historical reading of the Indian Act. When Indians were defined by the Enfranchisement Act (1869), this was done on the assumption that Indians would want the franchise, would want to be "full" citizens of Canada, and would be prepared to "apply" to gain this status. Indians voted with their feet to remain Indians by not applying in significant numbers for enfranchisement (hence the State moved to a system of involuntary enfranchisement) and effectively created the category "Indian status" as something desirable, as a legal ground on which to assert their difference. The State-imposed definition of Indian as a tool of totalization was subverted and redeployed by Aboriginal peoples as a legal mechanism for maintaining difference. Such forms of implicit resistance or subversion continue on the level of everyday experience and must be acknowledged in any accounting of the struggles of Aboriginal peoples.

Explicitly and organizationally, each of the different fragments of the Aboriginal reality has a political voice. Most prominent of these is the Assembly of First Nations (AFN) (formerly the National Indian Brotherhood), which represents status Indians, primarily those on reserves. The chiefs of the various bands come together in the annual assembly to set policy and elect representatives. Since the federal government has constitutional authority for Indians, the AFN most frequently attempts to deal with Ottawa on a nation-to-nation basis, struggling for the recognition and assertion of collective Aboriginal rights. The Native Women's Association of Canada (NWAC) represents all Aboriginal women, whether or not they have legal status. It has had a fractious relationship with the AFN, at times supporting it and attacking it on other occasions. It is primarily but not exclusively concerned with ensuring that Aboriginal women's individual equality rights are protected.

The Native Council of Canada represents non-status Indians. Its membership has diminished somewhat as many First Nations people have regained their legal status due to Bill C-31, which attempted to reinstate people who lost status for a variety of reasons including the sexually discriminatory provisions around Indian women marrying non-Indians. The National Association of Indian Friendship Centres, while not a formal political organization, is the only organization that provides a forum for urban, status Indians. It also represents any Aboriginal person — Métis, Inuit, treaty, etc. — who may be a member of the friendship centre movement. The Métis National Council represents Métis at a national level. The inclusion of Métis in the definition of Aboriginal in the Canada Act (1982) was a significant victory for the Métis and allows them to define their struggle in terms of Aboriginal rights. The Inuit Tapirisat of Canada represents Inuit in Quebec, the Northwest Territories and Labrador. It is a member of the Inuit Circumpolar Conference, which represents Inuit in Canada, Greenland, Alaska, and Siberia. Pauktuutit represents Inuit women in Canada. Both of these organizations insist on the specificity of the Inuit struggle for Aboriginal rights.

These national organizations all have provincial and territorial counterparts. Most of the status Indian counterparts are named as a First Nation, Nation, Treaty Nations Alliance, or Tribal Council. The foundation of the status Indian organizations are band councils, established in accordance with provisions of the Indian Act. Interestingly, the government established band councils in the late nineteenth century in order to undercut the authority of traditional leaders and women. Nevertheless, band councils have become an order of government in Canada and for the most part reflect the democratic aspirations of their communities. Technically, band councils have limited powers resembling those of municipalities; however, they also act as a focus for politics in rural Aboriginal communities, frequently dealing with issues far beyond the narrow scope specified for them in the Indian Act. Some band councils are organized regionally into tribal councils, which pool resources and act as administrative and lobbying supports.

Two crucial concepts now inform the organized struggle against totalization — self-government and land claims, both subsumed by the umbrella of Aboriginal rights, itself a legal mark of positive difference in Canadian society. A few words on each is appropriate.

Self-government is an explicitly political response to a struggle whose major terms are political but not always understood as such outside Aboriginal communities. For the most part, earlier interaction between Aboriginal peoples and non-Natives in what became Canada was economic, organized around the exigencies of the fur trade. In the period between roughly 1850 and 1920, a transition look place as the fur trade became less important economically to Canada. While the fur trade remained — and continues to remain — disproportionately important to Aboriginal economies, the line of contact between Native and non-Native people changed. It became primarily political rather than economic in nature. The State replaced fur-trading companies as the non-Native institution most associated with the lives of Aboriginal peoples. Thus, the Indian Act and the treaties were both established in this period, and political control became the locus of Aboriginal peoples' struggles. As Cinday Gilday, a Dene woman from the NWT, puts it, "when an Indian breathes, it's politics."

Self-government, as a recognized right and in practice, is a response to this situation. At a minimum, self-government implies taking over the administrative responsibilities of the federal government regarding Aboriginal peoples. It implies giving band and tribal councils more government-like powers so that Aboriginal peoples themselves have greater control over their daily lives. In my own theoretical terms, it implies attacking the root source of explicit totalization by removing its legal controls and shattering its legitimating foundations.

Land claims are more directly related to ensuring that Aboriginal peoples have an economic basis for their subsistence economies. Comprehensive land claims refer to claims where no previous treaty has been signed. They usually involve very large sums of money, extinguishing Aboriginal title, establishing smaller land areas that the First Nation in question has ownership over, forms of joint management for "surrendered" land, and other more minor types of provisions. Specific land claims refer to those claims where a treaty promise has been broken or not kept. While there are very few comprehensive claims (about 20 in total in Canada), there are hundreds of specific claims. These usually involve lesser sums of money and are comparatively less complex cases.

Both the self-government and land claims processes are hotly contested — not in the least because the State and Aboriginal peoples often approach the negotiating table with a very different sense of what constitutes a desirable process and outcome — and can serve as tools of totalization. The federal government has attempted in the last decade to constrain self-government so that it is a form of delegated authority with municipal-like powers and western forms of politics. Effectively, it wants bands to administer themselves in the manner that the Department of Indian Affairs administers them, replacing State bureaucrats with Indian bureaucrats. This form of self-government would do nothing to maintain cultural difference — and would in fact erode it. The government's current model of self-government strongly resembles the Indian Advancement Act of 1884, which was developed precisely as a tool of assimilation. Most Aboriginal leaders argue that the powers of self-governing First Nations should be roughly provincial in level and that Aboriginal forms of decision making and accountability must be reflected in the self-governing bodies.

Similarly, on land claims, the government continues to assert that extinguishing Aboriginal title is a basis of the land claims process and, effectively, seeks to use the land claims process to turn the affected First Nation into little more than an indigenous capital accumulation centre. The State envisages and promotes land claims that would make First Nations stakeholders in non-renewable development processes. Again, the First Nations themselves seek to use land claims to assert Aboriginal title, to broaden the scope of negotiations to include self-government, and to protect the environment as a basis for subsistence economic activities associated with a traditional way of life.

In sum, Aboriginal resistance takes place both in institutional forums and through established processes, such as land claims or self-government negotiations, with different organizations reflecting the particular demands of different groups. Resistance also takes place on an implicit level, usually involving forms of subversion, in the sphere of everyday life.

SELF-DEFINITIONS

Collective identity for most Aboriginal peoples is associated with the particular First Nation culture to which an individual belongs. For example, someone might identify themselves as a member of the Git'san Nation, or the Nis'gaa, or as Dene, or Inuit, or Métis. Another source of identity is with the home community or region of an individual: this is particularly important for Inuit, who might identify themselves as from Baffin Island, or the Keewatin region, or Pangnirtung, and so on. Non-status Indians might identify more broadly with their culture, as in Cree, or Ojibwe, or Blackfoot. Non-status Indians who have long family histories in urban settings might not know or identify with their culture and might therefore call themselves Aboriginal, indigenous, or First Nations people.

Clearly, the question of identity is a complex and crucial one in this terrain of struggle. Legal definitions have worked to set parameters and separate Aboriginal peoples, but cultural differences remain important. The variety of potlatch cultures are very distinct from sun dance cultures, as they are from sweat lodge cultures; these are themselves distinct from longhouse cultures, as are northern drum dance cultures or Inuit from all of the above. Métis may be associated with the historic Red River Métis or as the result of more recent intermarriages that cross cultural boundaries. Métis itself means "mixed blood" and was originally used to distinguish new peoples of English-speaking and Aboriginal descent, called "half-breeds," from new peoples of French-speaking and Aboriginal descent. When we add to this the urban/rural split and the fact that gender and sexual orientation are clearly identity-defining characteristics, the complexity is apparent.

Furthermore, the question of identity converges with the struggle for self-government: citizenship is seen as a crucial area of control for First Nations in their struggle for self-government. This is only partly due to the fact that State control of citizenship through a definition of Indian via the Indian Act has had such disastrous consequences. Within Aboriginal communities, women are concerned that First Nations control over citizenship could be deployed in such a way as to deprive them of a political voice in a manner that further entrenches the patriarchy that the Indian Act attempted to establish. That is, First Nations women have a strong cultural argument, relating to traditional egalitarianism in gender relations, which distinguishes their struggle from those oriented exclusively around a liberal discourse of equality rights.

Urban Aboriginal peoples, in particular, are often sensitive to the question of identity and are frequently determined to maintain fairly rigid boundaries. They have often led the charge around issues such as cultural appropriation in the arts and the politics of representation. Rural peoples have tended to be more secure in their sense of identity and have a different source of identity concerns (such as, for example, preoccupation with museum policies and appropriation). Clearly, I would be remiss if I did not note that there are many who would challenge my right to what I am saying in this document. While I have tried to present an analysis without speaking for anyone, this too is a slippery slope.

There *is* a solidarity, which sometimes goes under the name of "pan-Indianism," which crosses the cultural and legal boundaries asserted by Aboriginal peoples — the reaction to the Oka crises demonstrated this. It is also the case that the term "Aboriginal" is by and large not meaningful in an everyday sense to most Aboriginal peoples, reflecting a constitutional category, not a collective identity. Thus, primary identification tends to be with a specific First Nation or community. And, of course, there are times when the differences between First Nations do act to divide them from each other. The politics of identity is a crucial aspect of the Aboriginal terrain of struggle.

It should be clear by now that the discussion of Aboriginal politics in Canada is not illuminated by adhering to a framework of theoretical concepts drawn to understand the struggles of dominated races, classes, or genders. Each of these frameworks provides some insight into the struggles of Aboriginal peoples, but none offers a sufficient analytical paradigm. Furthermore, combining the three in some fashion is equally insufficient. The philosopher Jacques Derrida has suggested that "each advance in politicization obliges one to reconsider, and so reinterpret, the very foundations of law such as they had previously been calculated or delimited" (Derrida 1992: 28). The call of Aboriginal peoples in Canada, which must be inscribed at the centre of any meaningful vision of social justice or human rights in this country, demands a "reconsideration" of this (foundational) magnitude and perhaps the invention of a new theoretical language and new conceptual approach if it is to be adequately addressed.

Hegemony and the Representation of Aboriginal Politics in Canada
D.A. West

In his article "Aboriginal Peoples and Hegemony in Canada" (Kulchyski 1995), Peter Kulchyski identifies, once again, the conditions under which Aboriginal peoples have been forced to play their political cards. I value his contribution to the description of this struggle for recognition by Aboriginal peoples, but I question some of his assumptions.

In commenting on the shift from universalist human rights to specific cultural rights, he identifies "a new phase or modality or accommodation between liberal democratic nation-states and cultural minorities" (Kulchyski 1995: 60 [p. 297 in this book]). I do not view Aboriginal peoples as "cultural minorities," and I think that it is entirely misleading to do so. "Cultural minority" is a term invented by a dominant society for the very purposes of intellectual hegemony. When Kulchyski remarks that Aboriginal politics in this country "demands its own theoretical maps" (Kulchyski 1995: 60 [p. 297 in this book]), he assumes two very important and sometimes dangerous positions. The first, and perhaps more quibbling of the two, is that he groups all First Nations, Aboriginal, Métis and Indian peoples under the Canada Act umbrella of "Aboriginal." The second, more serious problem is the assumption, made by all Euro-Canadian academics, that there exist "theoretical maps" that are applied by Aboriginal peoples to this new terrain of political struggle. There is no evidence that Aboriginal peoples use "theoretical maps," whatever they may be. Moreover, as Kulchyski goes on to explain *his* theoretical map "around the questions of hegemony, resistance, and identity," he clearly positions Aboriginal peoples on well-trodden terrain. Perhaps a good clue to Kulchyski's intentions comes in the quote from Dominick LaCapra's *History and Criticism* (1987). The negotiation of "proximity and distance in the relation to the 'other' that is both outside and inside ourselves," belies another, time-honoured Eurocentric position — that of the historical judge taking stock and systematically arguing the terrain of political struggle. In other words, we Euro-people are constantly at war with "ourselves," searching for the correct interpretation of our actions in analysis. The limits of analysis always come when we are confronted by the profoundly confusing reference points of Aboriginal peoples.

Kulchyski plays another telling hand when he insists that "Aboriginal politics are largely about the continued assertion of difference; they are in great measure a politics of identity concerned to ensure that distinctive Aboriginal cultures find a respected place in *Canadian* society" (Kulchyski 1995: 61 [p. 298 in this book]) (my emphasis). I believe that it will one day be possible to say without hesitation that Canadian politics are in a great measure a politics of identity concerned to ensure that distinctive Canadian cultures find a respected place among the Inuit, Dene, Nishnawbe, Cree, Chippewa, Micmac, etc. In the end, hegemony, as Gramsci taught us, is about theoretical positions in reaction to the world.

Kulchyski is correct when he argues that assimilation remains the centrepiece of the Canadian hegemonic discourse which describes the variety of aboriginal conditions. But what, we must ask, does he mean by "cultural politics" (Kulchyski 1995: 61 [p. 298 in this book])? Aboriginal politics is about resistance to theoretical maps themselves, to ways-of-life that are imposed, to the language of cultural specificity that is now championed everywhere in the decentring university.

Kulchyski's "own theoretical position" is that the hegemony practised by the Canadian State is of the "totalizing" variety. His general statement about the creation of matrices of power that subject Aboriginal peoples to the whims of capitalist enterprise, sanctioned and directed by the State, should be pointed back at himself when he argues that, "For example, Inuit have been able to take television, a powerful carrier of commodity culture, and partially remake it to reflect Inuit experience and Inuit ways of seeing. The Inuit Broadcasting Corporation uses the television to strengthen aspects of Inuit culture" (Kulchyski 1995: 64 [p. 301 in this book]). To the average reader, this counts as a significant form of resistance to hegemony — turn the tools against the masters. Kulchyski could have argued that the IBC represents a further assimilation of Inuit peoples into the dominant society because the funding for programming (in recent years and reaction to the political gains of the Inuit Tapirisat) has always been controlled from Ottawa. More to the point, four or five hours of television per week in the dominant Inuit dialect can hardly match the thousand of "dominant society" hours, as it were, that come on before and after the IBC broadcasts. Perhaps the hegemony and the totalization have been expressed best by Chief Gordon Peters of the Pikangikum Reserve when, in reaction to the mounting suicide crisis in Nishnawbe communities, he advised everyone to just turn off the television itself. It is the addictive quality of the television that is hegemonic and totalizing.

Another problem I found in the section on resistance was where Kulchyski makes the misleading generalist assumption that aboriginal organizations "represent" the interests of their constituents, a very Eurocentric assumption to say the least. That these organizations are suffering from "identity crises" is an understatement, but Kulchyski's "top ten" list of these organizations and their abbreviated mandates leads the average reader down the theoretic path that states that resistance to hegemonic power comes in the form of some enlightened mimicry. Could it be that the "representation" of Aboriginal peoples, whether through Indian Act elections or Robert's Rules of Order, is disintegrating and losing its elitist pretensions because it is based on a bad (Eurocentric) theoretical map? At times, Kulchyski's discourse sounds more like a well-travelled history lesson than a discussion of theoretical options. Where are the aboriginal voices in all this?

In his brief discussion of land claims and self-government, Kulchyski is clear and concise about the impact that the process of negotiation has had on Aboriginal peoples. The assimilation of aboriginal leadership into the complex world of land claims negotiations is itself one of the most horrendous acts of successive Crown governments in Canada. The framing of the negotiations is a very good example of an imposed theoretical map, complete with extinguishment, and the creation of what Kulchyski correctly identifies — each "successful" First Nation a new "indigenous capital accumulation centre" (Kulchyski 1995: 66 [p. 304 in this book]).

In conclusion, Professor Kulchyski's article familiarizes the reader with a partial list of the substantive issues on the negotiating table which stands between Euro-Canadian and Aboriginal peoples. However, if he wants to begin a new dialogue in earnest, he should heed Jacques Derrida's advice and avoid the well-travelled theoretical map of the hegemony of specific analytical paradigms. We do not need "new theoretical language" and a "new conceptual approach." What we need is to listen very carefully to what aboriginal peoples are saying to us about land and spirit and about *what we look and sound like to them.* We must challenge *all* of our foundations, everything from technological advances and theoretical maps to the ideas of analytical problem-solving and history.

DISCUSSION QUESTIONS

1. Use library sources and compare the extent of inequality between the Canadian aboriginal peoples and other groups. Where would you place the aboriginals in the hierarchy of inequality in terms of health, wealth, income, occupation, education, mortality, housing, and so on?

2. In your opinion, what are the causes of a lower socio-economic status of aboriginal peoples compared with other Canadians? Is the "aboriginal culture" responsible for aboriginal people's situation? If yes, how is the "culture" itself shaped by the history of colonization? How does colonization and cultural genocide play a role in their socio-economic status?

3. How is the struggle of female aboriginals different from that of their male counterparts? Have they been successful? Give examples.

4. After reading newspapers and talking to your friends and family members, describe how they perceive the First Nations' struggle for self-government or land claims. How do the media portray these things? Are they supportive? What are their reasons?

5. What are various assimilationary practices of the Canadian state? Have these been successful? Why or why not?

6. Talk to a few aboriginal people or ask an aboriginal to speak to your class. What do they say about Europeans, self-government, and land claims? How do they explain their relationship with the dominant institutions?

7. Read Exhibit 3.3, "To Aboriginal Canadians: 'Our Profound Regret.'" Do you think it addresses all aboriginal concerns? What are some other issues that are left out of the "regret." Is the regret enough? What else should the government of Canada do in order to reconcile past wrongdoings?

Exhibit 3.3

To Aboriginal Canadians: "Our Profound Regret"

The text of a document titled Statement of Reconciliation: Learning from the Past, read out January 7, 1998, in Ottawa by Jane Stewart, federal Minister of Indian Affairs:

As Aboriginal and non-Aboriginal Canadians seek to move forward together in a process of renewal, it is essential that we deal with the legacies of the past affecting the Aboriginal peoples of Canada, including the First Nations, Inuit and Métis. Our purpose is not to rewrite history but, rather, to learn from our past and to find ways to deal with the negative impacts that certain historical decisions continue to have in our society today.

The ancestors of First Nations, Inuit and Métis peoples lived on this continent long before explorers from other continents first came to North America. For thousands of years before this country was founded, they enjoyed their own forms of government. Diverse, vibrant Aboriginal nations had ways of life rooted in fundamental values concerning their relationships to the Creator, the environment and each other, in the role of Elders as the living memory of their ancestors, and in their responsibilities as custodians of the lands, waters and resources of their homelands.

The assistance and spiritual values of the Aboriginal peoples who welcomed the newcomers to this continent too often have been forgotten. The contributions made by all Aboriginal peoples to Canada's development, and the contributions that they continue to make to our society today, have not been properly acknowledged. The Government of Canada today, on behalf of all Canadians, acknowledges those contributions.

Sadly, our history with respect to the treatment of Aboriginal people is not something in which we can take pride. Attitudes of racial and cultural superiority led to a suppression of Aboriginal culture and values. As a country, we are burdened by past actions that resulted in weakening the identity of Aboriginal peoples, suppressing their languages and cultures, and outlawing spiritual practices. We must recognize the impact of these actions on the once self-sustaining nations that were disaggregated, disrupted, limited or even destroyed by the dispossession of traditional territory, by the relocation of Aboriginal people, and by some provisions of the Indian Act. We must acknowledge that the result of these actions was the erosion of the political, economic and social systems of Aboriginal people and nations.

Against the backdrop of these historical legacies, it is a remarkable tribute to the strength and endurance of Aboriginal people that they have

(continued)

Exhibit 3.3 *(continued)*

maintained their historic diversity and identity. The Government of Canada today formally expresses to all Aboriginal people in Canada our profound regret for past actions of the federal government which have contributed to these difficult pages in the history of our relationship together.

One aspect of our relationship with Aboriginal people over this period that requires particular attention is the Residential School system. This system separated many children from their families and communities and prevented them from speaking their own languages and from learning about their heritage and cultures. In the worst cases, it left legacies of personal pain and distress that continue to reverberate in Aboriginal communities to this day. Tragically, some children were the victims of physical and sexual abuse.

The Government of Canada acknowledges the role it played in the development and administration of these schools. Particularly to those individuals who experienced the tragedy of sexual and physical abuse at residential schools, and who have carried this burden believing that in some way they must be responsible, we wish to emphasize that what you experienced was not your fault and should never have happened. To those of you who suffered this tragedy at residential schools, we are deeply sorry.

In dealing with the legacies of the Residential School system, the Government of Canada proposes to work with First Nations, Inuit and Métis people, the Churches and other interested parties to resolve the long-standing issues that must be addressed. We need to work together on a healing strategy to assist individuals and communities in dealing with the consequences of this sad era of our history.

No attempt at reconciliation with Aboriginal people can be complete without reference to the sad events culminating in the death of Métis leader Louis Riel. These events cannot be undone; however, we can and will continue to look for ways of affirming the contributions of Métis people in Canada and of reflecting Louis Riel's proper place in Canada's history.

Reconciliation is an ongoing process. In renewing our partnership, we must ensure that the mistakes which marked our past relationship are not repeated. The Government of Canada recognizes that policies that sought to assimilate Aboriginal people, women and men, were not the way to build a strong country. We must instead continue to find ways in which Aboriginal people can participate fully in the economic, political, cultural and social life of Canada in a manner which preserves and enhances the collective identities of Aboriginal communities and allows them to evolve and flourish in the future. Working together to achieve our shared goals will benefit all Canadians, Aboriginal and non-Aboriginal alike.

Source: Statement of Reconciliation: Learning from the Past, Ottawa: Indian and Northern Affairs Canada, 1998, as reprinted in *The Globe and Mail,* January 8, 1998, p. A17. Reproduced by permission of the Minister of Public Works and Government Services Canada, 1998.

MULTICULTURALISM OR SYMBOLIC ETHNICITY

Exploring the Ideology of Canadian Multiculturalism

Lance W. Roberts
and Rodney A. Clifton

Ideologies are ill-founded beliefs which are often uncritically held by those whose interests are furthered by such justifications. For reasonable people, ideologies are stifling because they discourage what is essential for a balanced view — the judicious consideration of alternative ideas and evidence. In this context, Howard Brotz's (1980) refreshing article on the muddled state of Canadian multiculturalism policy is a welcome contrast to the usual tributes. Following Brotz, we wish to introduce some ideas which suggest that the Canadian policy of multiculturalism is not only muddled but misconceived.

Brotz's central point, that the ambiguous use of "culture" confuses rather than clarifies discussions of multiculturalism, is well taken. Unfortunately, by juxtaposing "culture" and "civilization," he does not focus on a more important distinction between "culture" and "social structure." Though most human behaviour is influenced by both cultural and structural forces, separation of these components is necessary for an appraisal of the multiculturalism policy.

Kornauser (1978) identifies the essence of these two concepts: "Culture ... is restricted to the realm of meaning; it refers to the *shared meanings* by which a people give order, expression, and value to common experiences.... In the grand tradition of cultural analysis, the distinctively cultural refers to those symbols by which a people apprehend and endow experience with *ultimate human significance*.... If culture is manifested in those aspects of behaviour enjoined by ideal patterns of belief, social structure is manifested in those aspects of behaviour enjoined by *patterns of interrelationship among social positions*. Social structure refers to the stabilization of cooperative efforts to achieve goals, by means of the differentiation of a social unit according to positions characterized by a set of activities, resources, and links to other positions and collectivities" (Kornhauser 1978: 6–7, emphasis added). Culture, then, represents a shared symbolic blueprint which guides action on an ideal course and gives life meaning. In contrast, social structure signifies the constraints on the individual action arising from the connections and dependencies existing in all organized systems.

Within this context, it is important to note that culture and social structure are variables, not constants; moreover, they are interdependent variables. Mankind's multiple schemes for defining ideal behaviour and providing life with meaning are well documented in philosophy and anthropology. We also recognize that there are many ways to co-ordinate collective action. Since culture and social structure are interdependent variables changes in one often result in changes in the other. Changing mental maps can direct our behaviour to alternative courses, while finding ourselves in new situations can affect the justifications we use for our actions.

These preliminary distinctions provide a framework for understanding the process of "assimilation," the force that the Canadian multiculturalism policy is designed to mitigate (Canada 1971: 8546). Assimilation is the process of "becoming alike" symbolized by the phrase "melting pot." Since the dissolution of ethnic groups is marked by their inability to perpetuate distinctive cultural and structural patterns, students of ethnic relations, following Gordon (1964), usually distinguish between "cultural assimilation" and "structural assimilation." Cultural assimilation designates the disintegration of an ethnic group's system of shared values and norms resulting from cross-cultural contact. Structural assimilation, on the other hand, indicates the decline in traditional group affiliations due to expanding contact with outside individuals and organizations.

As such, a largely unexamined but critical question for understanding the merits of a multiculturalism policy becomes: What is the relationship between cultural and structural assimilation? This question requires a two part answer. First, cultural assimilation can occur without structural assimilation. That is, members of ethnic groups can share the beliefs, norms, and values of the dominant group yet remain excluded from participating in this group's organizations and institutions. Brotz's (1980) example of South African apartheid illustrates this possibility. Second, the possibility of structural assimilation without cultural assimilation is much less likely. As Gordon (1964: 81) notes: "... structural assimilation inevitably produces acculturation (cultural assimilation). The price of such (structural) assimilation, however, is the disappearance of the ethnic group as a separate entity and the evaporation of its distinctive values." To argue that structural assimilation is not a precursor of cultural assimilation is to make a case for what Scott (1971) would label a "sociological anomaly."

These fundamental notions about social reality are generally disregarded in discussions of the Canadian policy of multiculturalism, which persists in assuming that a variety of cultures can exist without separate social structures. In fact, very few Canadian ethnic groups have social structures that can effectively restrict their members' exposure to alternative norms, values, and behaviours. Nor can most ethnic groups restrain their members should they choose to follow the lures of non-traditional ways of life. Without the organizational capacity to govern interaction in these ways, uncontrolled change becomes probable, and an ethnic group's capacity to perpetuate its cultural heritage decreases.

The exceptional case of the Hutterites illustrates the rigorous structural requirements that are needed to ensure that a coherent cultural tradition is transmitted from generation to generation in a complex society. To argue that it is possible to preserve a truly multicultural mosaic in Canada would require that other groups maintain similar standards of structural tightness. This is an unrealistic expectation.

Lieberson (1970: 30) illustrates the inapplicability of the Hutterite case as a model multiculturalism by noting that endogamy and language maintenance are two structural features that must be maintained if distinctive ethnic cultures are to be preserved. Among Canadian ethnic groups, however, these requirements are not widespread. For example, from a random sample of the 1971 Canadian census, we examined the ethnic origin of heads of households and compared these with the ethnic origin of their spouses; we also related these findings to the languages spoken at home. Two important trends were observed in these analyses.

First, considerable exogenous marriage between ethnic groups existed, especially among European groups. For instance, over 50 per cent of German men, 48 per cent of Dutch men, 57 per cent of Polish men, and 70 per cent of Scandinavian men married outside their ethnic group. Second, in marriages where *both* partners had the same mother tongue, many did not use this language at home. This was true for 53 per cent of German couples and 47 per cent of Ukrainian couples. Many similar examples could be presented (Burnet 1975: 211; Darroch 1981), but these are sufficient to make the point that structural association among Canadian ethnic groups is extensive.

If many ethnic groups lack the structural base to support their cultures, what is it that the policy of multiculturalism supports? The answer lies in the concept of "symbolic ethnicity," which Gans (1979) describes as a "... *nostalgic allegiance* to the culture of the immigrant generation ... ; a love for and pride in a tradition that *can be felt without having to be incorporated in everyday behaviour*" (Gans 1979: 9, emphasis added).

As Brotz (1980) and others observe, Canadians generally support "bourgeois-democratic" habits and values. Hardly anyone wishes to disqualify himself from the social and economic advantages offered by a modern society. However, participation in such a society often undercuts the traditional supports provided by integration within an ethnic community. Thus, Canadians of diverse ethnic origins face the dilemma of retaining a link with their heritage while remaining free to share in the benefits of a modern society. The adoption of a symbolic ethnicity is one means of managing this predicament.

Those who possess a "symbolic ethnicity" command the flexibility necessary to participate and benefit as members of a complex industrialized society while also feeling that they belong to a smaller community. Thus, flexibility exists because symbolic ethnicity is a psychological rather than a social construct; it services individual rather than community needs and, as such, is less subject to forces beyond an individual's control. To have a symbolic ethnicity, one need not belong to a genuine ethnic group — one which possesses a social structure capable of applying effective, systematic pressure for conformity to community standards. Indeed, belonging to such a community would defeat the purpose of having a symbolic ethnicity which allows an individual to "feel ethnic" but to act without traditional inhibitions and sanctions.

The important feature of symbolic ethnicity is its voluntary quality; it can be donned or discarded as preference dictates. This adaptability, which exists because the identity it fosters is not firmly grounded in a social structure, distinguishes the "new" symbolic ethnicity from the "old fashioned," traditional type of association individuals had to an ethnic group. This characteristic fluidity does not mean that symbolic ethnicity is unimportant; as part of an individual's psychological profile, it can affect one's behaviour. However, since such behaviour is not embedded in a social structure, it may not be consistently portrayed or displayed.

The transitory quality of symbolic ethnicity is evident in the unreliability of government figures on self-reported ethnic membership, variation which cannot be accounted for by immigration, natural increase, or sampling variation (Miller 1981; Kalbach 1970). In addition, if symbolic ethnicity was not voluntary, negotiated, and transitory, one would have great difficulty explaining the large proportion of people who come from mixed ethnic ancestry and "feel an affinity to two or even more groups" (Miller 1981: 29) — an extremely improbable feat if one were entirely committed to competing cultural systems.

Symbolic ethnicity involves a very different sort of individual involvement than that required by more traditional forms of ethnic commitment. The constraints of symbolic ethnicity are subject to personal selection, interpretation, and enactment, while traditional forms of attachment to an ethnic group are more collectively oriented, instituted, and enforced. Distinguishing these forms of ethnicity and asserting that the resurgence of ethnic interest among Canadians is primarily symbolic carries implications for the assessment of multiculturalism policy. However, judgements must be contingent upon how the ambiguous objectives of multiculturalism policy are interpreted.

Jean Burnet (1975: 211–12) has clearly outlined the competing interpretations concerning the goals of our multiculturalism policy. These include a policy "encouraging those members of ethnic groups who want to do so to maintain a proud sense of the contribution of their group to Canadian society" or, alternately, a policy "enabling various peoples to transfer foreign cultures and languages as living wholes into a new place and time." These alternate interpretations correspond to what we have called the "new" (symbolic) and "old" (traditional) forms of ethnicity.

It is argued here that the traditional vision of a Canadian "mosaic" composed of viable ethnic groups and communities is not credible. With very few exceptions, ethnic groups in this country cannot perpetuate coherent cultural traditions because they lack the relevant social structures. Moreover, even though the federal government may say they wish to maintain and encourage genuine ethnic communities, their actions suggest otherwise. Examples like the restrictions on Hutterite land acquisition, the reluctance to settle Native land claims, and the resistance to Francophones who want more institutional control all point out the government's general interest in institutional commonality rather than diversity. There are, of course, good sociological and economic reasons for such a position, given the great expense parallel institutions would involve (Findlay 1975: 219–20) and the potential for civil discord present where integrated groups of different cultures come into contact. In any case, whatever one's judgement of the government's position, it appears that "multiculturalism is doomed" (Burnet 1975: 212) if the policy is interpreted as perpetuating a mosaic of coherent cultural traditions.

What multiculturalism policy does support, with its sponsorship of ethnic conferences, presses, festivals, and the like is "symbolic ethnicity." Under these conditions, individuals can voluntarily choose if, when, where, and how they will express an interest in one or more ethnic traditions. Ethnicity becomes one of many characteristics that individuals may use to anchor their identity and gain a measure of psychic satisfaction. At the collective level, "ethnic groups" actually appear as loosely structured *aggregates* who share a label and an unknown degree of interest in and commitment to an ethnic heritage.

Although many observers (especially among the so-called "professional ethnics") remain committed to the idea that multiculturalism policy should create a mosaic of institutionally complete groups capable of transferring their cultures, others recognize that symbolic ethnicity is a more realistic goal. Burnet (1975: 212) and Anderson and Frideres (1981: 99) have even suggested that the term "multiculturalism" is a misnomer and that the policy would be better labelled "polyethnic" since what is being encouraged is diversity of ethnic expression rather than cultural maintenance. This revised interpretation of the goal of multiculturalism involves a fundamentally different vision from that pictured by the traditional "mosaic" version since symbolic ethnicity emphasizes social psychological attitudes, while the perpetuation of ethnic cultures stresses *institutional structures* (Findlay 1975: 215–16). The notion of "pluralism" shifts from the traditional picture of a mosaic of internally integrated ethnic groups toward a collection of individuals who use ethnic characteristics when and if it suits their psychological needs. Burnet (1975: 212) sums up the essential difference between these competing interpretations: "The resources made available by the government should not be used to impose upon the young the notions of the old; they should assist the young to solve in their own fashion the problem of their ethnic identity."

So far, it has been argued that the traditional interpretation of multiculturalism as creating a cultural mosaic is sociologically untenable. Moreover, it has been suggested that the notion of "symbolic ethnicity" provides a more adequate description of "ethnic experience" in Canada. Although symbolic ethnicity may better describe what multiculturalism policy promotes, this does not mean that the policy is immune from critical evaluation.

In conclusion, we mention a few points that deserve consideration before multiculturalism is endorsed. First is an empirical question which queries the importance of symbolic ethnicity for individual identities and behaviour. This question remains unanswered, yet some preliminary evidence suggests that ethnicity may not be a salient aspect of the identity of most Canadians. For example, when our undergraduates answered and ranked their responses to the question "Who am I?", only 10 per cent identified themselves as Canadians and only 8 per cent reported another ethnicity. Furthermore, of those reporting any ethnicity, only 3 per cent ranked this attribute first or second in importance. In a more representative sample, Peter Li (1978) notes that 45 per cent of *immigrants* in Toronto did not report an ethnicity or answered either "Canadian" or "American." Evidence of this type led John Porter to a conclusion that deserves serious consideration by those interested in any brand of multiculturalism: "I am coming increasingly to feel that ethnicity may well be an artifact of the census rather than the social reality it is claimed to be" (quoted in Ogmundson 1980b: 148). If this is the case, it can be argued that much energy and expense is being committed to a policy of little general relevance.

Aside from the empirical issue, it is legitimate to question whether the concerns of multiculturalism are matters that deserve federal government attention. Almost everyone at one time or another wrestles with the problems of personal identity, of which ethnicity may be one component. By providing public funds to support the resolution of ethnic identity problems, the government opens itself to supporting a potentially limitless pool of claims since ethnic identity issues are not more salient than the identity problems associated with other attributes like age, gender, and appearance.

Besides questioning the pragmatic involvement of government in such minute and personal concerns as those of identity, there is the broader question of whether the government should do so. Given the continuing credibility problems Western governments have (Nisbet 1975), it is worth asking whether their resources would be better spent on more efficiently performing those functions which are widely perceived as legitimate and crucial. In a society which professes a commitment to traditional liberal-democratic virtues, policies based on government intervention, especially in areas of private concern, are questionable.

After pondering the issues and evidence, our conclusion is the government should not be involved in promoting symbolic ethnicity. In our judgement, the nature of symbolic ethnicity and the association it spawns are not fundamentally different from that of other voluntary organizations and, as such, should be supported by private rather than public funds. We are confident that many social scientists, bureaucrats, and "professional ethnics" who have large vested interests in present multiculturalism policies will resist this conclusion. This is understandable. For now, what is important is that the nature and implications of multiculturalism policy come under more careful scrutiny. In this regard, Jean Burnet's (1978: 112) conclusion deserves reiteration: "If the policy is to remain vital, it must not be based on untested assumptions and political pressures. It must be based on a growing body of sound research and sophisticated theory." To date, multiculturalism policy has been taken for granted. Brotz (1980) has done a service by adopting a more critical posture toward the policy; we hope to have followed this lead and taken the argument a step further.

The Structural Realities of Canadian Multiculturalism: A Response to Roberts and Clifton

Don Dawson

Lance Roberts and Rodney Clifton (1981), in their article "Exploring the Ideology of Canadian Multiculturalism," correctly point out that Howard Brotz's (1980) juxtaposition of "culture" and "civilization," while novel, misses the important distinction between "culture" and "social structure." However, Roberts and Clifton themselves do not adequately portray the structural realities of Canadian multiculturalism which they hold to be so crucial.

Critical treatises on the concept and policy of multiculturalism, such as those by Roberts and Clifton (1981) and Brotz (1980), are long overdue. The Canadian policy on multiculturalism is indeed muddled, and it is so because it was born of political expediency, not clear thinking. While agreeing somewhat with the general thrust of the Roberts and Clifton critique of Canadian multicultural policy (e.g., that it disregards the structural components of ethnicity), it appears to me that they may have underestimated the degree of "structural completeness" of Canadian ethnic communities as well as their compatibility with mainstream modern industrial society.

Elsewhere, one of the authors (Roberts and Boldt 1979), in a refreshing treatment of the issue of social structure, has pointed out that merely counting the *number* of so-called ethnic institutions which an ethnic community can boast ignores the fact that to serve as effective instruments of boundary maintenance, these institutions must be of a certain *quality*. The idea is that structural completeness is dependent not only upon the number of ethnic institutions which exist, but upon the "tightness" of these structures as well. The argument, which is repeated in the Roberts and Clifton (1981) article, is that whatever ethnic institutions exist in Canada tolerate such a range of behavior in their members (i.e., they are "loose") that they are ineffective guides to individual conduct and cannot prevent cultural assimilation. This conclusion is unconvincing, however, in that characteristically, institutions in modern pluralist societies such as Canada are "loose" in the sense that they do not define the precise content of behavior but rather provide general behavioral guidelines. That ethnic institutions should also be "loose" in the same way is not surprising. Furthermore, one should expect that ethnic institutions would function as well as any other institutional structures in a pluralistic society. Exactly "how" these institutions work to ensure the maintenance of ethnic cultural distinctiveness is beyond the scope of this discussion, but one is referred to Breton (1964) for explication of the processes involved. In any event, the personal choice allowed to individuals in these circumstances does not serve to somehow eliminate the collective identity of the groups involved.

At this point it should be noted that Roberts and Clifton's (1981) references to Francophones, native Indians or even Hutterites as "ethnic groups" are misleading. French Canadians usually are not considered and do not consider themselves to be "ethnics" even in minority situations; Canada's aboriginal peoples are qualitatively different from "immigrant" ethnic groups; and the Hutterites are perhaps better understood as an extremist religious sect rather than as an exemplar of Canadian ethnic groups. It may be argued however, as Roberts and Clifton apparently do, that Hutterites represent the best empirical approximation of an "ideal case" among Canadian ethnic groups resisting assimilation. The "extremist" nature of this group, then, is seen to vividly provide social observers with valuable organizational lessons as to how all groups genuinely wishing to resist assimilation *must* be. Yet this assertion misconstrues the very nature of ethnic communities in Canada.

The Hutterites, contrary to most other ethnic groups, are an isolationist, secessionist colony whose very social structure is predicated upon doxies antithetical to modern social order. Such is not the case for other ethnic communities in Canada which in fact struggle to find their niche in both the Canadian polity and economy. The true "ideal case" for Canadian ethnic groups would be one which enjoys a high degree of integration into mainstream Canadian economic life while concurrently maintaining its own ethno-cultural identity. In this instance, one might more appropriately conceive of ethnic communities as *sub*-cultural groups whose distinctive cultural symbols and social structures exist within the parameters enunciated by the host culture.

There are, it seems, three fundamental factors which contribute to the preservation of living, distinctive ethnic communities in Canada:

1. Many ethnic groups in Canada *do* have the organizational capacity to ensure a viable degree of cultural continuity — e.g., schools, churches, social service organizations, clubs, media, etc.
2. Most ethnic groups in Canada are *not* attempting to maintain or revitalize an anachronistic socio-cultural system as are the Hutterites. Rather, their desire is to participate fully in modern industrial society, and they envisage their culture as dynamic and evolving within the suprastructure of an advancing Canadian social system.
3. A characteristic of Canadian society is its "structural pluralism" which allows and encourages diversity not merely in individual or symbolic realms, but also in everyday collective behavior, lifestyle and cultural matters. This applies, of course, to ethnic groups.

Notwithstanding the points above, it may be that ultimately, in the ceaseless advance of progress, we shall all become as one, the world truly a global village. In that future "brave new world," ethnic groups will surely not exist, but its arrival is many generations away. In the meantime, it would appear that ethnic groups in Canada have the will and resources to persist as structural realities for a protracted period.

Though one would not want to minimize the homogenizing effects of modern industrial society, it remains that as late as 1976, one national study (O'Bryon, Reitz and Kuplowska 1976) reported that only about a quarter of the members of Canada's major ethnic groups had "insufficient conversational" knowledge of their mother tongue, while approximately half used their ethnic language "every day" or "often." On a much smaller scale, research (Dawson 1981) into the English-Ukrainian Bilingual School Program in Edmonton public schools provides an example of how, despite itself, the muddled policy of multiculturalism is having some effect in abating language and cultural loss at least in that particular ethnic community. Children of Ukrainian origin enter the publicly sponsored and funded program at the kindergarten level with a flagging knowledge of the Ukrainian language and emerge, after grade six, with a significant degree of linguistic fluency and a greater knowledge and appreciation of Ukrainian culture.

The use of the Ukrainian language and the emphasis upon the child's Ukrainian heritage in the English-Ukrainian Bilingual Program serves to incorporate the Ukrainian culture into the everyday classroom experience of the students. This day-to-day exposure is something more than the "nostalgic allegiance" to a traditional culture described by Gans (1979) as "symbolic ethnicity" which is "felt" but not "lived." The bilingual program does not "teach about being ethnic" but is systematically structured to ethnicly contextualize quotidian student life. As the program was developed through the co-operative efforts of the Ukrainian churches, Ukrainian business interests and an array of cultural associations, it was envisioned and designed from the outset to be a vital link in the network of interdependent Ukrainian social institutions of Edmonton. Consequently, the program functions as a genuine structural support for the cultural integrity of the Ukrainian community.

The publicly run English-Ukrainian Bilingual Program and others like it (e.g., German, Hebrew, etc.) should not be equated with French bilingual or immersion programs which are developing across the country. These latter programs have as their goal simple linguistic fluency in the French language. The students who enroll in these programs are not subjected to a strong cultural component as are those in the Ukrainian program. Most important, however, is the fact that French immersion programs cater to anglophone students who wish to learn a second language, not to francophone communities in minority situations who are fearful of losing their ethnic identity. Hence, the emergence of bilingual or immersion French schools across Canada is in no way indicative of a resurgence of the structural components necessary to support French culture. On the other hand, continuing with our example, the Ukrainian bilingual program is intentionally structured to act as a mechanism to preserve and perpetuate the Ukrainian language and culture in succeeding generations of Canadians of Ukrainian origin.

It would also appear from data collected by the Edmonton Catholic School Board that Roberts and Clifton's (1981) arguments that link exogamy to "structural assimilation" are somewhat overstated. For example, in 1977–78, less than 60 per cent of the families which enrolled their children in the English-Ukrainian Bilingual Program claimed that both parents were Ukrainian origin. If having a child in a fully (50 per cent Ukrainian, 50 per cent English) bilingual school program is taken as one indicator of participation in Ukrainian community structure, then it could be said that the non-Ukrainian parents may well have married into the Ukrainian community. In this interpretation, the non-Ukrainian spouse is structurally assimilated into the Ukrainian ethnic group, not vice versa. Of course this example "proves" nothing, but it is clear that a facile equation of exogamy and assimilation is to be viewed with skepticism.

Also, this same research (Dawson 1981) indicates that it is precisely those ethnic groups most integrated economically and culturally into Canadian society (i.e., those who are most likely to hold what Roberts and Clifton (1981), after Brotz (1980), refer to as "bourgeois-democratic" habits and ideas) which work to maintain and expand their unique social structures. Perhaps these groups, now that they've "made it," feel "safe" enough to openly reassert their ethnicity.

While the data presented above do not demonstrate conclusively that many Canadian ethnic groups have the organizational capacity to ensure their cultural continuity, it is also true that Roberts and Clifton (1981) and others have not demonstrated that all Canadian ethnic groups do *not* have the necessary structural supports to maintain a unique cultural identity. Moreover, Roberts and Clifton (1981) set up exacting and extreme criteria for the demonstration of adequate structural boundaries (i.e., the Hutterites' colonies are the "ideal case") and then dismiss the existing structures of Canadian ethnic groups as insufficient. At the same time, they simply define away whatever cultural integrity ethnic groups may have been able to sustain as being merely "symbolic ethnicity" of little consequence.

In conclusion, though Canadian policy on multiculturalism is muddled, it is not without some basis in social reality. Though ethnic communities do face difficulties in their efforts to stem the tide of structural assimilation, many are proving to be quite successful in sustaining their traditional group affiliations and supporting structures, at least for the present and near future.

DISCUSSION QUESTIONS

1. Imagine that you have been commissioned by the government of Canada or Heritage Canada to frame legislation to help the ethnic groups who wish to maintain their culture. What will be your sug-

public-policy implications depend on the extent to which each model applies. The "discrimination" model focuses on social and institutional practices that discriminate against members of one group (or that favor members of another), undermining the "level playing field" called for by recent American political and legal rhetoric. This model clearly applied in many instances in the past, such as the exclusion of black baseball players from the major leagues prior to 1947 and the barrier against professional military careers for blacks before and during World War II. The educations provided blacks and whites by the South's racially segregated public school systems, which differed vastly in the levels of public support, are a paradigmatic example of racial differences that the discrimination model explains well.

In the discrimination model, equality can come about only when the barriers imposed by society are removed; but when they are removed, equality eventually ensues. The crucial assumption of this model is that in the absence of barriers, the groups would be proportionally equal at every level of society, Differing averages are thus *prima facie* evidence of discrimination, whatever the expressed intentions of the society or its record of law and administration; any lingering difference in the proportional representation of the races proves that the society is racist and justifies "affirmative action" and other restraints on its citizens.

To the limited extent that the book strives to explain the differences that it observes, *A Common Destiny* (Williams and Jaynes 1989) is rooted in the discrimination model. In its own words: "Black status results from American social institutions and the race relations that have developed within that institutional structure." The book ignores the alternative model, the "distributional" model, which explains the overlapping of the populations and their differing averages by referring to characteristics of the populations themselves. The distributional model understands differences between the races not simply in terms of the different opportunities available to people of different races; it is willing to consider the possibility that the different outcomes are also the product of differing average endowments of people in the two races.

The two models may both be partially correct. Facts exist, or could be found, that may help to account for disparities between the races whether or not we know or wish to know what they are. Thus, the distributional model's adherents would consider possible differences in athletic endowments in explaining the disproportionate presence of black basketball players in the National Basketball Association. Similarly, in accounting for differences in income, education, health, and so on, the model's proponents would examine individual traits that may be distributed differently among blacks and whites; these traits may help to explain both the observed differences in the average and the overlapping distributions at each level of income, education, and the rest.

A difference in the average levels of these things would not, according to the distributional model, by itself indict a society of racism. Similarly, the absence of a difference would not disprove charges of discrimination. *Any* average level of attainments could indicate a nondiscriminatory society provided that it correlated with the underlying distributions of traits. To the extent that the distributional model is correct, affirmative action and other equalizing constraints on people are less moral imperatives than the products of a political judgment.

Differences between blacks and whites are highly controversial, of course; the result is that any consideration of the distributional model (which everyone realizes is the alternative to the discrimination model) is taboo in polite company. *A Common Destiny* (Williams and Jaynes 1989) frankly states that something like the distributional model is offered by a majority of white (but not black) Americans when asked on surveys to explain black–white inequality. Even so, open discussion of the model is our obscenity, much as public discussion of sexuality was the Victorian obscenity.

OMISSIONS OF EVIDENCE

A Common D stiny (Williams and Jaynes 1989) says almost nothing about differe.ices between blacks and whites on standardized tests of intelligence or cognitive aptitude; what little it says is mostly wrong. No dimensio' of individual human variation has been measured as often as what' er it is that those tests test. The topic cannot have been omitted b' .use of a scarcity of data.

        :ks and whites cover more or less the same range on aptitude tests, br .sproportionately. Relatively more whites score high, and relatively more .s score low. On average, there is a difference of about one standard devi- .n between the two populations. In other words, to a first approximation, .ie average black is at the 16th percentile of the distribution of whites on tests of intellectual aptitude; the average white is at the 84th percentile of the distribution of blacks. In absolute numbers, of course, each race has many people throughout the scale, from top to bottom.

The difference in averages has been observed in hundreds of studies, involving thousands upon thousands of people, since objective testing began early in the century (Loehlin et al. 1975; Osborne and McGurk 1982). Notwithstanding some vague hints in the book, there is no clear evidence that the gap between the races has been closing recently or that it shrank when the economic gap between the races was shrinking. The legacy of slavery and of past and present discrimination cannot be discounted as a contributor to the racial gap in scores because its effects might be as profound as they are hard to measure or uproot.

But we do not know with any certainty where the difference comes from or what it would take for it to go away.

INTELLIGENCE AND ECONOMIC STATUS

The book occasionally attributes the black population's low average academic skills to its low average economic standing. Thus, it falls victim to the all-too-familiar logical error of thinking that the correlation between economic status and intelligence proves that status causes intelligence; it would be just as plausible to say that intelligence determines status and most plausible to claim that from generation to generation, the lines of causality run in both directions simultaneously (with intelligence contributing to eventual status and vice versa).

Evidence not presented in the book indicates that within each race, variations in status explain little of the variance in tested intelligence.[1] In other words, at each socioeconomic level, there are wide and overlapping distributions of test scores. This pattern suggests — though it does not prove — that the difference in the races' average socioeconomic status may not in and of itself account for much of the gap in the average scores.

Indeed, the reverse may, to some extent, be true. The productivity of workers in America today is correlated with their tested intelligence, as measured on conventional IQ tests or other comparable gauges of aptitude such as the federal government's General Aptitude Test Battery. The more demanding an occupation is cognitively, the higher the correlation between productivity and tested intelligence; even in the most routine and undemanding jobs, however, intelligence matters.

The two recent studies commissioned by the National Academy of Sciences cited above accept this correlation but disagree on how significant it is for the economy as a whole. The two studies agree, however, that the difference in tested aptitude is an important factor in the different economic conditions and prospects that confront blacks as compared with whites. The present book does not mention either of those earlier studies; it also ignores the scientific literature with which they grapple (Gottfredson 1986).[2] Nonetheless, no individual trait predicts as much about one's personal destiny in America as test scores. Given the hypothetical choice of being black with an IQ of 120 or white with an IQ of 80, one should choose the former to get ahead in America now or in the readily visible future.

A Common Destiny (Williams and Jaynes 1989) mentions a few studies that may eventually lead to educational improvement. As the book recognizes, some teachers teach more effectively than others, but they are not necessarily those who have taken the most education courses or who have other objective credentials. Good teaching remains somewhat mysterious. Some classrooms or schools appear to create a better climate for learning than others. The most effective education occurs with a stable faculty, a safe school, strong leadership from the administration, support from families, a serious emphasis on course content, and a willingness to condemn the bad academic work as well as to praise the good.

Having made these points, the book then neglects to point out that improving schools would not necessarily lessen the gap between blacks and whites. Nothing in the data indicates that the observed differences between the races are to any large extent explained by these variables; as far as we know, black and white children would profit equally from improvements in teacher effectiveness, school ambiance, and the like. Still, improving our schools is presumably desirable even if doing so would merely raise the average level of intellectual performance and leave the black–white gap largely intact.

CRIME

The book's discussions of other topics also ignore the possibility that distributional differences and not just discrimination might account for the observed differences between the races. After raising the question whether biases in the criminal-justice system might account for the differences between black and white rates of arrests, convictions, and imprisonments, the book concludes that there is a genuine, large, and growing disproportion in *crime* rates: blacks are increasingly more likely to break the law than whites. This is what most other studies of the subject now assert.

But then — virtually without supporting evidence — the book makes a claim that is far more common in the popular media than in the scholarly literature: "As long as great disparities in the socioeconomic status of blacks and whites remain, blacks' relative deprivation will continue to involve them disproportionately in the criminal justice system, as victims and offenders." If this is so, the relative deprivation of blacks must have grown in the United States front 1939 to 1985 since the proportion of black prisoners in those years rose from 26 percent to 46 percent of the total prison population. But *A Common Destiny* (Williams and Jaynes 1989) itself notes that relative deprivation decreased during that period.

The chapter on crime simply does not consider evidence that may support the distributional model's analysis of the racial difference in crime rates. There is, for instance, evidence showing that tested intelligence and other individual psychological traits are among the primary predictors of criminal behavior. Other evidence indicates that socioeconomic status and unemployment are by comparison weak predictors (Wilson and Herrnstein 1985; Wilson 1983).[3]

Scholars cannot yet explain why the rise in crime rates seems to be concentrated among those with particular individual traits. Some scholars have tried to account for those individual traits in terms of sociological forces — as the results of poverty or discrimination, for example — but they have not succeeded. In any event, unlike the authors of *A Common Destiny* (Williams and Jaynes 1989), most scholars at least acknowledge the ostensible power of individual traits in predicting criminality.

THE DANGERS OF DOGMA

This reluctance to pose obvious and important questions is the chief failure of *A Common Destiny*'s (Williams and Jaynes 1989) unwavering adherence to the discrimination model as the sole explanation of race differences. Life in a multiethnic society undoubtedly presents problems, and history provides many examples of attempted solutions that failed disastrously (Sowell 1989). We cannot expect to find workable answers easily or painlessly. It is easy for us today to point to racism or discrimination as the obvious source of our difficulties — but it may not be the sole source. To the extent that racism is not the whole story, we can hardly hope to discover constructive public policies when we deny or ignore the possibility that distributional factors may account for some of the differences between the races.

Suppressing the distributional model is not only unwanted but also harmful. Dogmatic adherence to the discrimination model inhibits thinking about the problems of multiethnic society while creating new problems. If cognitive ability predicts performance without regard to race, then affirmative-action programs that set different test-score criteria for blacks and whites in hiring or in admission to schools will result in different levels of performance. We can ignore this iron law of selection, but we cannot elude it; whether we realize it or not, we are often choosing between some level of disproportionate representation and some reciprocal level of differential performance. We eliminate the former at the cost of the latter. Depending on how different the hiring or admissions criteria are and how well the criteria correlate with performance, the result will be performance gaps of varying sizes between the races.

Such gaps are undesirable. They may give many blacks the impression that their earnest efforts to do well are unappreciated, and they may give whites the impression that blacks are usually found near the lower end of the performance distribution. On one side are the corrosive effects of repeated frustration; on the other side, the almost reflexive and often unwarranted expectations of poor performance. On one side is the belief that the government does too little to produce equality; on the other, the belief that it intrudes too much into private matters. Both sides sense that an injustice is perpetrated, but they understand the injustice differently. As a result of this difference, we may be exacerbating our problems instead of solving them.

NOTES

[1] The evidence for this statement is scattered in many empirical studies, but a secondary source for it is Arthur R. Jensen (1981).

[2] Gottfredson draws on an influencial program of research by industrial psychologists and others (prominently including John Hunter of Michigan State University and Frank Schmidt of the University of Iowa) dealing with the relation between intelligence test scores and economic productivity. Gottfredson has specifically addressed this relation's implications for racial differences in occupational status.

[3] These things are also summarized and discussed in a good many other primary and secondary sources — none of which is cited or mentioned in *A Common Destiny* (Williams and Jaynes 1989).

Understanding Black-White Differences
Robert M. Hauser, Gerald D. Jaynes,
and Robin M. Williams, Jr.

Indeed, in one sense, Herrnstein says little that requires a response; he himself explicitly acknowledges that even geneticists and sociobiologists do not know the source of black–white differences. But he seems to forget this refreshing admission in the balance of his essay, which presents an artful case for the theory that underlying differences in black and white intellectual endowments are the chief source of black–white differences in socioeconomic attainments.

Professor Herrnstein correctly observes that *A Common Destiny* (Williams and Jaynes 1989) (hereafter, the report) "suggests that the central determinant of black–white relations in America is discrimination — past or present, deliberate or inadvertent — by whites against blacks." We reviewed a massive accumulation of data that left no doubt that racial discrimination has been and continues to be (though to a much lesser extent) a pervasive fact of American life. Surely there can be no scientific objection to describing the extent and character of racial discrimination and to analyzing its deep consequences. To do so is not to advance a "discrimination model" if one means, as Herrnstein appears to, that discrimination is the source of all contemporary black–white differences that we regard as undesirable. Nothing could be further from our intentions.

Instead, the report goes to considerable lengths to emphasize that the current status of black Americans has many causes and is the outcome of complex historical processes. The report points to economic and demographic changes; to shifts in employment opportunities (e.g., the loss of jobs in the "rust belt"); to changes in public policies, especially with regard to political participation, education, and health; and to the behaviors of black Americans. It emphasizes the massive influence of the broader changes in American society since World War II. In short, the report does far more than present a simplistic portrait that attributes the condition of American blacks entirely to "discrimination."

Professor Herrnstein complains that the report ignores relevant science. Of course it does: a great many subjects might have been analyzed in the report, so we had to choose among them, making difficult judgments about the importance of different lines of inquiry.

We estimate that the editors had to omit close to two-thirds of the original manuscript prepared for the report. Many of the study participants have already fielded criticisms about several topics that were treated briefly or not at all, such as slavery as a source of family instability; contemporary instances of discrimination, violence, and harassment against blacks; gender, regional, and interurban differences among blacks; differences between blacks of West Indian heritage and those born in the United States; differences among minority groups; and important aspects of the transition from youth to adulthood.

The important question, then, is not whether the report was selective, but why. Early on, we decided that the theoretical propositions we included should satisfy three criteria. First, they had to cover areas in which there was scientific evidence that lead to sound conclusions. Second, they had to be relevant to public policy. Third, they had to help account for the observed changes in the status of blacks, or for the changes in the status differences between blacks and whites, that had occurred during the period that we were investigating. We are willing to defend the report on the basis of these criteria. Theories such as the one that Professor Herrnstein proposes, which attempt to explain black–white differences in socioeconomic attainments on the basis of the measured differences between blacks and whites in "indices of ability" (e.g., IQ tests), failed on all three of our criteria.

A major reason for our lack of interest in biological explanations of racial differences in ability or achievement is that changes in the gene pool could have had little, if any, effect on the changes in black–white differences that occurred over the forty-year span covered by the study. One simply cannot explain change by a constant. Thus, Herrnstein is wrong to suggest that the major theme of the report is the persistent and intractable difference between black and white life chances. Its major themes instead revolve around the massive and diverse *changes* in the status of black Americans — both favorable and unfavorable — that have occurred since World War II.

Contrary to Herrnstein's assumption, the report does not emphasize only deficiencies in the status of blacks. We found, for instance, that blacks are less likely than whites with similar social characteristics to drop out of high school; that blacks in the mid-1970s were more likely than whites with similar social characteristics to go to college; that black women's earnings are equal to those of white women; and that blacks are more likely to vote than whites with similar social and economic characteristics. The general lesson here is not the intractability of black–white differences, but the volatility of the condition of blacks, which is shaped by general social conditions, by changes in the economy and public policy, and by blacks' individual and collective strivings.

So long as genetic engineering and psychobiology have not advanced far enough to enable policymakers to alter people's genetic makeups, Herrnstein's differential-abilities model will lack clear policy implications. In a society that values the rights of individuals, knowledge about group differences — provided that the groups' distributions overlap — offers nothing useful to policymakers. Sadly, this fact was not so widely appreciated in an earlier period of our history when a Secretary of Education for the state of Alabama argued that the lesser abilities of black children, combined with considerations of fiscal efficiency, justified lower expenditures for educating black children than for educating white children.

Herrnstein seems to believe that the differential-abilities hypothesis negates various arguments for affirmative action and other remedial social programs. But this claim would be valid only in the extreme case in which black–white socioeconomic differences were due entirely to black–white ability differences — that is, if 250 years of slavery, followed by segregation and past and present discrimination, had had *no* impact upon black Americans today. Since this is clearly not the case, arguments for affirmative action that would apply in the absence of differences in the average abilities of blacks and whites remain valid. (Implementing affirmative-action programs might, however, be more difficult if black–white ability differences had to be factored in.)

If no one knows the true underlying distribution of abilities, or even understands how they interact with environmental factors, how should public policy be formulated? Professor Herrnstein seems to say that policymakers should assume that current conditions reflect an inalterable underlying reality. We say that policymakers should instead assume that equality would be the norm in the absence of discrimination; they should require society itself to prove that inequality is not the result of bias. Our society has been shaped by a past filled with pervasive oppression of blacks, and it cannot assume a neutral starting point.

Let us say a bit more about why we decided to include and emphasize certain materials, especially the NAEP tests — which have recently become the centrepiece of federal efforts to monitor progress toward national educational goals. Our objective was to find measurements of the levels and trends of black and white intellectual performance that would parallel the measures of educational enrollment and attainment that were obtained from census data. In our judgment, there are no such measurements of IQ; that is, none of the measurements have sufficient scientific quality to justify their inclusion in the report.

To be sure, it is possible to measure the difference between mean-performance levels of blacks and whites in one sample or another and for various years. But even under the best of circumstances, these data show virtually nothing about overall trends in mental ability — we do not know the trend of IQ in the U.S. population — and the various samples (and nonsamples) are so diverse and often so selective that they provide no evidence of trends in black–white differences (see, for example, Loehlin et al. 1975: Ch. 6; Humphries 1988).

Herrnstein, however, emphasizes test scores to claim that the measured differences "lend support to the impression that there are intractable race differences in the performance of cognitively demanding tasks." This statement asks readers to accept both an "impression" and the enormous assumption that the differences are racial and "intractable." In a matter of such grave importance, Herrnstein's argument requires more substantial support than impressions and assumptions can provide.

As an expert in the field, Herrnstein surely knows that research and experience over the years have gradually tempered the early enthusiasm for so-called IQ tests as measures of intelligence. Such tests have now come to be seen for what they are: indicators of a set of skills, including acquired language skills selected as components of academic aptitudes (see Sowell 1977). Thus, those who thought that intractable differences between blacks and whites were revealed by the Army Alpha testing in World War I had to confront the fact that many southern whites scored below northern blacks. The apparent racial inferiority of those southern whites, of course, reflected their lack of educational opportunities. Similarly, the "evidence" in the 1920s from tests at Ellis Island showing the inferior performance of European immigrants proved transitory.

The importance of schooling is what led us to emphasize the NAEP tests. Although these tests do not go back very far in time, they do provide absolute measures of performance for well-defined samples of age groups that can be compared across time and racial lines. Among the report's relevant findings is that blacks aged nine to seventeen improved between 1969 and 1984 in reading, mathematics, and science. Similarly, intercohort changes in literacy differences between blacks and whites, as measured in a census survey, point to decreasing differences in cognitive performance between blacks and whites.

Herrnstein, however, is too preoccupied with unobservable racial differences to be attentive to such positive developments. His preoccupation harms his analysis at all points. Thus, he notes that surveys of black and white preferences for racial housing patterns reveal that blacks and whites typically claim to prefer some level of racial mixing — although blacks usually prefer much higher percentages of blacks than do whites. Herrnstein then criticizes the report for failing to "infer ... that at some point blacks as well as whites would prefer to prevent additional blacks from moving into their neighborhoods. The dislike of predominantly black neighborhoods — common to whites *and* blacks — frustrates blacks' quest for equal access to housing" (Herrnstein's italics). Should we also conclude that whites who say that they prefer integrated neighborhoods seek to prevent additional whites from moving in? Of course not. Such whites instead express egalitarian and pluralistic values that are characteristically American. Unlike Herrnstein, who is preoccupied with black–white differences, we attribute similar values to the typical black.

Herrnstein's position, however, is more generally flawed than these specific criticisms suggest. Its crucial weakness is revealed in his contention that the report "wrongly ignores the evidence at the individual level that I discuss here." Here, Herrnstein makes unexamined assumptions concerning the meaning of "individual level" — assumptions that are built into subsequent statements such as his assertion that the report ignores a model that refers to "characteristics of the populations themselves." But Herrnstein fails to define "characteristics ... themselves." Similarly, he does not tell us what he means by "individual." Are Herrnstein's "individual traits," which "may be distributed differently among blacks and whites," to be understood as genetically determined, socially determined, or outcomes of complex life-course interactions? We are not told. Soon afterwards, however, Herrnstein informs us that "[*a*] *ny* average level of attainments could indicate a nondiscriminatory society provided that it correlated with the underlying distributions of traits" (Herrnstein's italics).

Thus, Herrnstein seems to assume that individuals' characteristics are somehow intrinsic, innate, and unaffected by the individuals' lives. But the conditions affecting many blacks, we know from undisputed evidence, range from lead poisoning and malnutrition to the hope-lessness induced by extreme poverty and lack of access to opportunities. Surely we also know that people are what they are in substantial measure because of the beliefs and values that they acquire in the course of their lives. We ignore this fundamental truth if we assume that "individuals" are monads, constituted by "characteristics" unrelated to the cultural environment that shapes them.

The natural sciences, to which Herrnstein's hypotheses would direct our attention, cannot as yet tell us what portion of the difference between black and white scores on IQ tests — which are, after all, social constructs — is explicable only by genetic factors. The social sciences can tell us, however, that black Americans have been under-nourished, physically and psychologically terrorized, and grossly undereducated for three centuries — and that this has begun to change only during the last two decades. For these reasons, it would be absurd to believe that Herrnstein's alternative explanations are sufficiently well-grounded to have required anything like equal treatment in *A Common Destiny* (Williams and Jaynes 1989).

DISCUSSION QUESTIONS

1. Outside class, discuss informally with your friends factors that account for racial differences in socio-economic achievements. Which of the two models (discrimination versus individual traits) seems to have popular support? For those who use a genetic explanation, introduce the idea that one cannot explain a changing phenomenon by a constant. What is their response? Does this argument make them change their view? Discuss some of their arguments with your classmates.

2. To what extent is the nature of black–white relations different in Canada from in the United States? What was the extent of slavery in Canada? What are various discriminatory experiences of the Canadian racial/ethnic minorities? Are they systemic?

3. Can affirmative action policies help ameliorate racial disparities in Canada?

4. What are possible backlashes against affirmative action policies?

5. Read the article "Our Secret Past" (Exhibit 3.4). Describe how various groups in Canada have been historically racialized. Can you give other examples?

Exhibit 3.4

Our Secret Past

Canada's history of discrimination has been kept so well hidden that a 1994 Canadian Civil Liberties Association survey found that: 91% of high school graduates didn't know that blacks had been refused entry to Canada on the basis of race and ethnicity; and 68% didn't know that voting rights had been denied to aboriginal Canadians.

There's a stain beneath the gloss that Canada has painted over its race relations. Gary Yee knows about it. In 1917, his grandfather came to Canada as an immigrant. But Mr. Yee's grandfather was Chinese, so the government forced him to pay a head tax of $500. This amounted to about two years' wages at the time. Only Chinese immigrants were forced to pay this tax.

Six years later, and before Gary's grandfather could bring his wife here, the Canadian government passed a law which banned any further Chinese immigration. In 1947, the exclusion law was repealed, but it was another five years before Mr. Yee's grandfather could get his wife into Canada and another 17 years before the last of his children was allowed in. He was an immigrant in good standing, but he was denied the rights all other immigrants enjoyed simply because he was Chinese.

But Mr. Yee's grandfather was not alone in suffering from the official racism of Canadian governments. East Indians would understand.

In 1914, a businessman, Gurdit Singh, chartered a Japanese ship, the *Komagata Maru*. He loaded up with 376 Indian passengers and headed for Canada. The vessel arrived at Victoria on 21 May, where everyone on board was vaccinated. They then sailed for Vancouver, where the harbour was lined with angry citizens. They were concerned that the *Komagata Maru* was carrying the advance guard of what would become a flood of East Indian immigrants.

The Canadian government refused to let the people on the ship come ashore. For two months, the ship sat in Vancouver Harbour, its passengers hungry and irritable. A large police force tried to board the ship, but it was turned back when the passengers pelted them with missiles. Eventually, the warship *Rainbow* was sent for. Looking down the barrels of naval guns was enough, and the *Komagata Maru* quickly weighed anchor and headed back to Calcutta.

These and other immigrant groups have suffered because of laws enacted against them. But perhaps no group in Canada has been discriminated against as much as our own Native people.

(continued)

Exhibit 3.4 *(continued)*

For almost a century, various Canadian governments were engaged in a systematic assault on Native people. The agent of the attack was the Indian Act, first passed in 1876. The goal: the destruction of Native culture and the assimilation of Native people into white society. The solution to what was called "the Indian problem" was simply to make a whole race of people disappear.

Under the Indian Act, travel and property rights were restricted. Many traditional ceremonies and rituals were outlawed. Indians even needed the government's permission to wear traditional costume off the reservation. Native languages were illegal under certain circumstances. And, of course, Indians could not vote in elections. But perhaps the cruelest aspect was the setting up of residential schools.

By 1920, it was compulsory for Indian parents to give up their children for education in these residential schools. Children as young as three were forced to live apart from the security of their families.

The children were constantly told about the worthlessness of the society from which they had been "rescued." Former students recall how countless times they were told they were dirty and lazy and no good.

The worst sin a child could commit was to speak his or her own language. The punishment for this was severe. At Thunderchild School, it could mean 100 lashes of a whip. Think about that for a moment — 100 lashes.

Escaping the lash of slave owners drove thousands of black people to Canada. For most, life here was better, but it wasn't free of racism.

- By the 1830s, many churches forced black worshippers to sit in a back gallery known as "Nigger Heaven."
- The Separate School Act of 1850 made it possible to force blacks into all-black schools; the last all-black school was still functioning in Alberta in 1960.
- In the 1850s, blacks were barred from many hotels in southern Ontario.
- In 1860, a theatre in Victoria banned blacks from the good seats.
- In 1924, blacks were ordered to stay out of public parks and swimming pools in Edmonton.

If Canadian governments in the past enacted racist laws, they were probably only reflecting the wishes of the people. Today, while there are still plenty of Canadians who would support such official racism, our governments are working hard to make their laws fair towards every racial group.

Source: "Our Secret Past," *Canada and the World Backgrounder,* Waterloo, ON: Taylor Publishing Consultants Ltd., Vol. 62, No. 5 (April 1996), pp. 16–17.

Glossary

Achieved status A social position that one assumes as a result of personal choice by learning skills or gaining credentials. It reflects personal ability and effort.

Affirmative action Policies designed to increase representation of members of disadvantaged groups in various occupations in relation to their proportion of the population.

Alienation The term, as originally used by Marx, refers to loss of control over one's work and product. It is a feeling of powerlessness from other people and from oneself.

Ascribed status A social position that one assumes at birth or receives involuntarily later in life.

Assimilation The process by which minority groups lose their distinctive culture and adopt that of the dominant group.

Authority Power that people perceive as legitimate rather than coercive.

Bourgeoisie In Marxism, they are the owners of the means of production (capital, raw materials, factories) who hire workers in order to produce products to sell for profit.

Capitalism A system of production in which a small group of people own the means of production, while a large group of people who do not have access to those means of production have to sell their labour power in order to earn enough to subsist.

Capitalists *See* bourgeoisie.

Charter groups The two original European groups (British and French) whose rights and privileges (such as language rights) are enshrined in the Canadian Constitution.

Class Although this concept is one of the most used concepts in sociology, there is little agreement among sociologists on its definition. Marxists define class in terms of an individual's location within the production process. Weberians, in contrast, define class in terms of an individual's access to life chances. Generally, it means the individual's relative location in a society based on wealth, power, prestige, or other valued resources.

Class conflict Antagonism between social classes in a society. Marx used this term to refer to the struggle between capitalists and workers because of their clash of interests.

Class consciousness In Marxism, this term refers to large groups of people who have similar class positions, who are aware of those positions, and are organized in order to achieve their class interests.

Class exploitation The process by which members of one class (e.g., capitalists) extract surplus value or surplus labour from members of another class (e.g., working class).

Commodity production Goods and services created for exchange in the market.

Communism A social system where there is no private ownership of the means of production and no state; all members of the society are economically, politically, and socially equal.

Consensus Agreement between individuals and groups on basic values. Social stability results from agreement by large groups of people on certain beliefs and values for a substantial period of time.

Correlation A regular relationship between two variables. The change in one variable is statistically associated with the change in the other.

Cultural capital A term used by Pierre Bourdieu to refer to people's assets, including their values, beliefs, attitudes, and competence in language and culture.

Culture of poverty The idea that poor people are responsible for their poverty because of their cultural values and attitudes, which prevent them from taking action to ameliorate their situation.

Dependency theory An explanation that wealth and riches in one region or country is generated by the exploitation and control of wealth and riches in another region or country.

Discrimination Unequal treatment of various groups. Actions of the dominant group that deny members of minority groups resources available to other groups.

Division of labour Task specialization of economic activities.

Domestic labour debate The body of research concerned with the status of homemakers within the capitalist economic system.

Domination Institutionalization of control of one group by another.

Dual labour market *See* split labour market.

Dual system theory The view that sees both capitalist and patriarchal systems as responsible for women's oppression.

Elite A small number of powerful people who occupy key positions in various institutions of society.

Employment equity Policies designed to ensure that men and women who perform tasks of similar nature in terms of skill, responsibility, difficulty, etc., receive equal pay. Such policies are intended to eliminate the effect of past discrimination by making available employment opportunities to the excluded groups.

Entrance groups Late immigrants whose group rights are not enshrined in the Canadian Constitution.

Equality of condition A belief in the equality of overall distribution of resources.

Equality of opportunity A view that all individuals should be given an equal chance to compete for higher education, status, and jobs.

Ethnocentrism The practice of judging members of another ethnic group by one's own ethnic standards. A belief in the superiority of one's own culture.

Family wage Male workers asked for sufficient wages to support themselves, their wives, and their children. The institutionalization of family wages is said to exclude women from employment and high-paying jobs.

Feminization of poverty The trend that women represent an increasing proportion of the poor.

Forces of production Natural and human resources necessary for the production process.

Functionalism A theory that views society as made of interdependent parts, with each part functioning to help produce social stability and consensus.

Gender inequality The relative position of men and women with respect to education, occupation, income, prestige, or other socio-economic resources.

Genocide The systematic annihilation of one group of people by another.

Hegemony A type of domination. The subordinate classes' consensus to capitalism is achieved through control over their thinking process. Ideological control.

Hierarchy Ranked positions with a society or social system.

Horticulture Technology-based hand tools for plant cultivation and harvest.

Human capital theory The idea that one's skill and productivity are the prime determinant of one's position in the hierarchy. The social skill level is also the key for economic growth.

Hunting and gathering Economic activities based on simple technology of gathering fruits and vegetables and hunting animals.

Ideology A set of charged normative and descriptive beliefs that justify and/or question that existing order of society.

Imperialism The practice of one state or group of people from one society extending its control over another state or country by economic penetration, exploitation, and/or force.

Individual discrimination One-to-one act by members of a dominant group that harms members of the minority group.

Institutional completeness The availability of various institutions necessary for a group's maintenance.

Institutional racism The established rules, procedures, and practices that directly and deliberately prevent full and equal involvement of the minority group members in society.

Intergenerational mobility Upward and downward social movement of individuals from one generation to another.

Interlocking directorships A situation where one person serves on the board of directors of two or more companies.

Labour theory of value Marx's view that the value of a product is a function of the labour time needed to produce that product.

Matriarchy A hierarchical social organization where women are in control of social, political, and economic institutions of society.

Mean Statistical term used to describe the sum of all the scores divided by the number of scores.

Means of production Land, tools, factories, and raw material needed for the production process.

Median The score that divides a distribution into two equal parts.

Melting pot The situation where various groups amalgamate and blend together so that there are no distinctive groups.

Meritocracy A social system in which one's position in society depends on one's effort and talent.

Minority A category of people distinguished by physical and/or cultural traits and who are often disadvantaged.

Mobility Movement of individuals from one status or class into another.

Monopoly Exclusive control of trade in some commodity by one individual, corporation, or other body.

Multiculturalism Policies designed to ensure cultural and ethnic maintenance of ethnic groups and to promote equality of opportunity for all ethnic groups in Canada.

Multinational corporations Large companies with headquarters in one country and economic activities and subsidiaries in other countries.

Occupational status attainment The process of attaining status within the social system.

Patriarchy Social organization where males dominate females.

Pay equity Policies designed to ensure equal pay for work of equal value.

Point system The system by which immigrants are evaluated based on characteristics such as age, education, skill, occupation, knowledge of official languages, etc., as a mechanism of being selected to immigrate to Canada.

Postindustrial society Society in which at least half of the labour force is involved in the tertiary sector of the economy.

Poverty line A level of income calculated on the basis of total income required to meet basic needs (food, shelter, and clothing), below which people are considered poor.

Power The ability to control other people despite their opposition.

Prejudice Negative judgement of individuals on the basis of assumed characteristics of the group to which the individual belongs. This judgement is usually not based on actual experience.

Prestige An individual's social status based on the general population's evaluation of occupations and positions.

Racism The belief that one group sharing certain physical characteristics is innately superior to another group with different characteristics.

Relations of production The relationship between social classes in the production process (e.g., how properties are owned, who controls them, who decides what to produce, etc.).

Reserve army of labour A part of the labour force that is drawn into the labour market when needed by capitalists and is pushed out of that market when no longer needed. Women and minority ethnic groups are said to constitute such a flexible labour supply.

Resource mobilization The process of supplying, attracting, and organizing resources to achieve collective goals.

Ruling class An economically dominant group that also controls the political institutions.

Sexism The belief that one sex is innately superior to the other. Stereotyped and derogatory attitudes or discriminatory practices, often toward one sexual group by another.

Sex-segregated occupations The extent to which any occupation is concentrated by males or females. The higher the concentration of one of the sexes in an occupation, the more that occupation is sex segregated.

Sexual harassment Unwelcome comments, gestures, or physical abuse that are sexual in nature.

Slavery Economic organization in which some individuals are the property of other individuals. Slaves can be bought and sold at the owners' wish.

Social inequality A pattern of social relationships when individuals have unequal access to resources and unequal opportunity to acquire them.

Socialism A society in which people are roughly equal, without private property or the means of production. Also, a social theory that advocates collective responsibility for the well-being of members of the society.

Social stratification Existence of structured inequality between groups of people in a society based on their access to material and non-material resources.

Social structure Large-scale and long-term patterns of organization in a society. These organizations are external to individuals and influence their behaviour and thought.

Sociobiology The study of the biological basis of human behaviour.

Socio-economic status One's social status in the stratification hierarchy based on education, occupation, and income.

Split labour market Division of the economy into two sectors — primary and secondary. The primary sector is more unionized and capital intensive with high-paying jobs than the secondary sector. Often, subordinate group members work in the secondary economic sector.

Standard deviation Measure of dispersion based on deviation from the mean.

Statistical discrimination The discrimination one receives based on the average characteristics of the group to which one belongs. Women, for example, may receive lower wages because an employer may believe that they will leave their jobs if their husbands are transferred to another city. The employer, in a sense, deducts insurance premiums from their wages under the assumption that the time used to train women employees will be wasted.

Stereotype A simplified belief about characteristics of a social group. Such a belief minimizes a group's differences and maximizes its similarity. It exaggerates based on too little information.

Structural assimilation The process by which ethnic groups are able to participate in the economic and social organization of the dominant ethnic group.

Subsistence wage The minimum wage needed to ensure the cost of living for the worker and his or her family based on the prevailing standards.

Surplus value According to Marx, it is the difference between wages paid to the workers and the value created by the workers in the act of producing commodities.

Treaty status Certain privileges and obligations passed on to the aboriginal people of Canada by their ancestors who signed treaties with the Canadian government.

Vertical mosaic A hierarchical ordering of members of various racial and ethnic groups based on their access to economic, political, ideological, and social resources. A vertical ordering of ethnic groups.

Visible minority Official government classification of non-white and non-Caucasian groups.

References

Abbott, S., M.B. Nikitovitch-Winer, and J. Worell. 1986. Three voices in opposition. *Society* 23(6):15–21.

Abraham, J.H. 1989. The divorce revolution revisited: A counter-revolutionary critique. *Northern Illinois Law Review* 9:251–98.

Alba, R., and G. Moore. 1982. Ethnicity in the American elite. *American Sociological Review* 47(3):373–82.

Alford, R. 1963. *Party and Society.* Chicago: Rand McNally.

Allen, M. 1992. Child-state jurisdiction. *Family Law Quarterly* 26:293–318.

Allen, S. 1982. Perhaps a seventh person? In *Race in Britain: continuity and change,* ed. C. Husbands. London: Hutchinson.

Amos, V., and P. Parmar. 1984. Challenging imperial feminism. *Feminist Review* 17 *Many Voices, One Chant: Black Feminist Perspectives.*

Anderson, C.C. 1982. Poverty and misery: An analysis and some implications for social intellectuals. *Canadian Journal of Education* 7(2):85–89.

Anderson, A.B., and J.S. Frideres. 1981. *Ethnicity in Canada: Theoretical Perspectives.* Toronto: Butterworths.

Anisef, P., F.D. Ashbury, and A.H. Turritten. 1992. Differential effects of university and community college education on occupational status attainment in Ontario. *Canadian Journal of Sociology* 17(1):69–84.

Anthias, F. 1980. Women and the reserve army of labour: A critique of Veronica Beechey. *Capital and Class* 10(Spring):50–63.

Anthias F., and N. Yuval-Davis. 1983. Contextualizing feminism — gender, ethnic and class divisions. *Feminist Review* 15.

Arias, I., and S.R.H. Beach. 1987. Validity of self-reports of marital violence. *Journal of Family Violence* 2:139–49.

Armstrong, P., and H. Armstrong. 1983a. Beyond sexless class and classless sex: Towards feminist marxism. *Studies in Political Economy*:7–43.

————. 1983b. More on marxism and feminism: A response to Patricia Connelly. *Studies in Political Economy* (Fall):179–84.

————. 1984. *The Double Ghetto.* 2d ed. Toronto: McClelland and Stewart.

Aronowitz, S. 1987. Too narrow a focus. *New Politics* 1(3):31–35.

Arthurs, H.W., D.D. Carter, J. Fudge, and H.J. Glasbeek. 1988. *Labour Law and Industrial Relations in Canada.* 3d ed. Toronto: Butterworths.

Babcock, B.A., A.E. Freedman, E.H. Norton, and S.C. Ross. 1975. *Sex Discrimination and the Law: Cases and Remedies.* Boston: Little, Brown & Co.

Baer, D.E., and R.D. Lambert. 1990. Socialization into dominant vs. counter ideology among university-educated Canadians. *Canadian Review of Sociology and Anthropology* 27(4):487–504.

Baker, E.F. 1964. *Technology and Women's Work.* New York: Columbia University Press.

Bakker, P. 1991. Some unions are more equal than others: A response to Rosemary Warskett's "Bank worker unionization and the law." *Studies in Political Economy* 34:219–33.

Baldwin, E. 1977a. The mass media and the corporate elite. *Canadian Journal of Sociology* 2(1):1–27.

————. 1977b. On methodological and theoretical "muddles" in Clement's media study. *Canadian Journal of Sociology* 2(2): 215–22.

Baltzell, E.D. 1958. *Philadelphia Gentlemen: The Making of a National Upper Class.* New York: Free Press.

Barber, B., and O.D. Duncan. 1959. Discussion of papers by Professor Nisbet and Professor Heberte. *The Pacific Sociological Review* 2(1):25–28.

Barnes, G.E., L. Greenwood, and R. Sommer. 1991. Courtship violence in a Canadian sample of male college students. *Family Relations* 40:37–44.

Barrett, M. 1980. *Women's Oppression Today.* London: Verso.

————. 1992. Psychoanalysis and feminism: A British sociologist's view. *Signs* 17:455–66.

Barrett, M., and M. McIntosh. 1985. Ethnocentrism and socialist feminism. *Feminist Review* 20.

Beauchesne, E. 1998. Child poverty worst on record. *The Windsor Star* (May 12):A6.

Beaujot, R., and P. Rappak. 1990. The evolution of immigrant cohorts. In *Ethnic Demography*, ed. S.S. Halli et al., 111–40. Ottawa: Carleton University Press.

Becker, G.S. 1964. *Human Capital.* Chicago: University of Chicago Press.

Beechey, V. 1977. Some notes of female wage labour in capitalist production. *Capital and Class* (3):45–66.

———. 1979. On patriarchy. *Feminist Review* 3.

Bell, D. 1973. *The Coming of Post Industrial Society.* New York: Basic.

Bell, E. 1989a. The petite bourgeoisie and social credit: A reconsideration. *Canadian Journal of Sociology* 14(1):45–65.

———. 1989b. A reply to Peter R. Sinclair. *Canadian Journal of Sociology* 14(3):393–94.

Bendix, R., and F.W. Howton. 1959. Social mobility in the American business elite. In *Social Mobility in Industrial Society*, eds. R. Bendix and S.M. Lipset. Los Angeles: University of California Press.

Berk, R.A., S.F. Berk, D. Loseke, and D. Rauma. 1983. Mutual combat and other family violence myths. In *The Dark Side of Families,* eds. D. Finkelhor, R.J. Gelles, G.T. Hotaling, and M.A. Straus. Beverly Hills: Sage.

Berkowitz, S.D. 1980. Structural and non-structural models of elites: A critique. *Canadian Journal of Sociology* 5(1):13–31.

———. 1984. Corporate structure, corporate control, and Canadian elites. In *Models and Myths in Canadian Sociology*, ed. S.D. Berkowitz, 233–62. Toronto: Butterworths.

Bianchi, S. 1981. *Household Composition and Racial Inequality.* New Brunswick, NJ: Rutgers University Press.

Black, E.R. 1974. The fractured mosaic: John Porter revisited. *Canadian Public Administration* 17(4):640–53.

Blackburn, R. 1971. Comments on: "Sex Politics: Class Politics." *New Left Review* 66:92–93.

Bland, L., and F. Mort. 1984. Look out for the "good time" girl: Dangerous sexualities as threat to national health. *Formations* 2. London: Routledge and Kegan Paul.

Blau, P., and O.D. Duncan. 1967. *The American Occupational Structure.* New York: Wiley.

Blishen, B. 1967. A socio-economic index for occupations in Canada. *Canadian Review of Sociology and Anthropology* 4(1):41–53.

———. 1978. Perception of national identity. *Canadian Review of Sociology and Anthropology* 15(2):128–32.

Blishen, B.R., and H.A. McRoberts. 1976. A revised socioeconomic index for occupations in Canada. *Canadian Review of Sociology and Anthropology* 13(1):71–79.

Blishen, B.R., W.K. Carroll, and C. Moore. 1987. The 1981 socioeconomic index for occupations in Canada. *Canadian Review of Sociology and Anthropology* 24(4):465–88.

Block, F. 1987. *Revising State Theory.* Philadelphia: Temple University Press.

———. 1992. Capitalism without class power. *Politics and Society*, 20:277–302.

Block, W.E., and M.A. Walker. 1982. *Discrimination, Affirmative Action, and Equal Opportunity*. The Fraser Institute.

Boserup, E. 1970. *Women's Role in Economic Development*. New York: St. Martin's Press.

Bottomore, T., and R. Brym, eds. 1989. *The Capitalist Class*. New York: Harvester Wheatsheaf.

Boulding, E. 1976. *The Underside of History*. Boulder, Co: Westview Press.

Boulet, J.A., and L. Lavallée. 1984. *The Changing Economic Status of Women*. Study prepared for the Economic Council of Canada. Ottawa: Minister of Supply and Services Canada.

Bourgeault, R. 1983. The development of capitalism and the subjugation of native women in northern Canada. *Alternate Routes* 6:109–40.

Boyd, M. 1985. Immigration and occupational attainments of native-born Canadian men and women. In *Ascription and Achievement: Studies in Mobility and Status Attainment in Canada*, ed. M. Boyd et al., 393–446. Ottawa: Carleton University Press.

———. 1990. Immigrant women: Language and socioeconomic inequalities and policy issues. In *Ethnic Demography*, ed. S.S. Halli et al., 275–96. Ottawa: Carleton University Press.

Brand, H. 1994. Inequality and immigration. *Dissent* (Summer): 404–12.

Brandwein, R.A., C.A. Brown, and E.M. Fox. 1974. Women and children lost: The social situation of divorced mothers and their families. *Journal of Marriage and the Family* 36:498–514.

Brantlinger, E. 1985. What low-income parents want from schools: A different view of aspirations. *Interchange* 16(4):14–28.

———. 1986. Aspirations, expectations, and reality-response to Olson and Weir. *Interchange* 17(1):85–87.

Braverman, H. 1974. *Labour and Monopoly Capital: The Degradation of Work in the Twentieth Century*. New York: Monthly Review Press.

Breines, W., and L. Gordon. 1983. The new scholarship on family violence. *Signs: Journal of Women in Culture and Society* 8:491–53.

Brenhardt, A., M. Morris, and M.S. Handcock. 1995. Women's gains or men's losses? A closer look at the shrinking gender gap in earnings. *American Journal of Sociology* 101(2):302–28.

———. 1997. Percentages, odds, and the meaning of inequality: A reply to Cotter et al. *American Journal of Sociology* 102(4):1154–62.

Breton, R. 1964. Institutional completeness of ethnic communities and the personal relations of immigrants. *American Journal of Sociology* 70:103–205.

————. 1978. Stratification and conflict between ethnolinguistic communities with different social structures. *Canadian Review of Sociology and Anthropology* 15(2):148–57.

Breton, R., W.W. Isajiw, W.E. Kalbach, and J.G. Reitz. 1990. *Ethnic Identity and Equality: Varieties of Experience in a Canadian City.* Toronto: University of Toronto Press.

Briskin, L. 1990. Identity politics and the hierarchy of oppression: A comment. *Feminist Review* 35(Summer):102–08.

Brody, D. 1987. Hill discounts larger context. *New Politics* 1(3):38–41.

Brooks, G.W. 1987. Racism and the drift toward oligarchy. *New Politics* 1(3):27–29.

Brotz, H. 1980. Multiculturalism in Canada: A muddle. *Canadian Public Policy* 6(1):41–46.

Brown, C. 1984. *Black and White in Britain: The Third PSI Survey.* London: Heinemann.

Browne, A. 1987. *When Battered Women Kill.* New York: Free Press.

Brownmiller, S. 1975. *Against Our Will: Men, Women and Rape.* New York: Simon & Shuster.

————. 1976. *Against Our Will: Women and Rape.* Harmondsworth: Penguin.

Brym, R. J. 1985. The Canadian capitalist class, 1965–1985. In *The Structure of the Canadian Capitalist Class.* Toronto: Garamond Press.

Brym, R.J., and B. Fox. 1989. *From Culture to Power: The Sociology of English Canada.* Toronto: Oxford University Press.

Brym, R.J., and R.L. Lenton. 1991. Distribution of anti-Semitism in Canada in 1984. *Canadian Journal of Sociology* 16(4):411–18.

————. 1992. Anti-Semitism in Quebec: Reply to Langlois. *Canadian Journal of Sociology* 17(2):179–83.

Bukharin, N. 1973. *Imperialism and World Economy.* New York.

Bureau of the Census. 1980. Families maintained by female householders 1970–1979. *Current Population Reports* Series P-23, no. 207. U.S. Dept. of Commerce.

————. 1981. Money income of families and persons in the United States: 1979. *Current Population Reports* Series P-60, no. 129. U.S. Dept. of Commerce.

Bureau of Labor Statistics. 1967. *Three Standards of Living for an Urban Family of Four Persons.* U.S. Dept. of Labor.

————. 1968. *Revised Equivalence Scale for Estimating Equivalent Incomes or Budget Costs by Family Types.* Bulletin no. 1570-2. U.S. Dept. of Labor.

Burlington, M. The legacy of slavery. *Academic Questions* (Fall):86–89.

Burnet, J. 1975. The policy of multiculturalism within a bilingual framework: An interpretation. In *Education of Immigrant Students,* ed. A. Wolfgang, 205–14. Toronto: Ontario Institute for Studies in Education.

———. 1978. The policy of multiculturalism within a bilingual framework: A stock taking. *Canadian Ethnic Studies* 10:107–13.

Burt, S. 1990. Canadian women's groups in the 1980s: Organizational development and policy influence. *Canadian Public Policy* 16(1)17–28.

Butler, S.S., and R.A. Weatherly. 1992. Poor women at midlife and categories of neglect. *Social Work* 37:510–15.

Cain, G. 1976. The challenge of segmented labour market theories to orthodox theory: A survey. *Journal of Economic Literature* 14:1215–57.

Campbell, B. 1987. *The Iron Ladies — Why Do Women Vote Tory?* London: Virago.

Campbell, C., and G. Szablowski. 1979. *The Superbureaucrats: Structure and Behaviour in Central Agencies.* Toronto: Macmillan.

Canada. 1971. *House of Commons Debates.* 28th Parliament, 3d session, vol. 8.

Canadian Human Rights Advocate. 1988. 4(7), August.

Canadian Human Rights Advocate. 1989a. 5(1), January.

Canadian Human Rights Advocate. 1989b. 5(2), February.

Canadian Human Rights Advocate. 1989c. 5(4), May.

Canadian Human Rights Advocate. 1989d. 5(8), September.

Canadian Labour Law Reporter. 1989. Don Mills: CCH Canadian Limited.

Carby, H. 1982. White women listen! Black feminism and the boundaries of sisterhood. In *The Empire Strikes Back: Race and Racism in 70s Britain.* London: Hutchinson, Birmingham University Centre for Contemporary Cultural Studies.

Carroll, W.K. 1984. The individual, class, and corporate power in Canada. *Canadian Journal of Sociology* 9(3).

———. 1986. *Corporate Power and Canadian Capitalism.* Vancouver: University of British Columbia Press.

Carroll, W.K., J. Fox, and M.D. Ornstein. Forthcoming. The network of directorate interlocks among the largest Canadian firms. *Canadian Review of Sociology and Anthropology.*

Case, K. 1976. The Chesire cat: Reconstructing the experience of medieval women. In *Liberating Women's History,* ed. B.A. Carroll. Chicago: University of Illinois Press.

Cass, B. 1988. Redistribution to children and to mothers: A history of child endowment and family allowances. In *Women, Social Welfare and the State,* ed. C. Baldock and B. Cass. Sydney: Allen and Unwin.

Central Statistical Office. 1983. *Social Trends* 13. London: HMSO.

Chaney, E.M., and M. Schmink. 1976. Women and modernization: Access to tools. In *Sex and Class in Latin America,* ed. Nash and Safa. New York: Praeger.

Cherlin, A.J. 1981. *Marriage, Divorce, Remarriage.* Cambridge: Harvard University Press.

———. 1990. The strange career of the "Harvard-Yale Study." *Public Opinion Quarterly* 54:117–24.

Chodos, R. 1973. *The CPR: A Century of Corporate Welfare.* Toronto.

Chorney, H., W. Clement, L. Panitch, and P. Phillips. 1977. The state and political economy. *Canadian Journal of Political and Social Theory* 1(3):71–85.

Clark, A. 1920. *Working Life of Women in the 17th Century.* New York: Harcourt, Brace, and How.

———. 1969. *The Working Life of Women in the Seventeenth Century.* New York: Kelly.

Clark, T.N., and R. Inglehart. 1991. The new political culture: An introduction. In *The new political culture,* ed. T.N. Clark and V. Hoffmann-Martinot. Forthcoming.

Clark, T.N., and S.M. Lipset. 1991. Are social classes dying? *International Sociology* 6(4):397–410.

Clawson, D., A. Neustadt, and D. Scott. 1992. *Money Talks: Corporate PACs and Political Influence.* New York: Basic.

Clement, W. 1974. The Changing Structure of the Canadian Economy. *The Canadian Review of Sociology and Anthropology. Aspects of Canadian Society.* 3–27.

———. 1975a. *The Canadian Corporate Elite: An Analysis of Economic Power.* Toronto: McClelland and Stewart.

———. 1975b. Inequality of access: Characteristics of the Canadian corporate elite. *The Canadian Review of Sociology and Anthropology* 12(1):33–52.

———. 1977a. *Continental Corporate Power: Economic Linkages Between Canada and the United States.* Toronto: McClelland and Stewart.

———. 1977b. The corporate elite, the capitalist class, and the Canadian state. In *The Canadian State,* ed. L. Panich. Toronto.

———. 1977c. Overlap of the media and economic elites. *Canadian Journal of Sociology* 2(2):205–14.

———. 1990. A critical response to "Perspectives on the class and ethnic origins of Canadian elites." *Canadian Journal of Sociology* 15(2):179–85.

Cockburn, A. 1996. Beat the devil. *The Nation* (April 6):9.

Connell, R. 1987. *Gender and Power.* Stanford: Stanford University Press.

Connelly, P.M. 1978. *Last Hired, First Fired: Women and the Canadian Work Force.* Toronto: Women's Press.

————. 1983. On marxism and feminism. *Studies in Political Economy* 12:153–61.

Corey, L. 1934. *The Decline of American Capitalism.* New York: Covici-Friede.

Cotter, D.A., J. DeFiore, J. Hermsen, M. Kowalewski, B. Marstellar, R. Vanneman. 1997. Same data, different conclusions: Comment on Bernhardt et al. *American Journal of Sociology* 102(4):1143–62.

Creighton, D. 1972. The decline and fall of the empire of the St. Lawrence. In *Towards the Discovery of Canada*, ed. D. Creighton. Toronto.

Crompton, R.E. 1991. Three varieties of class analysis: Comment on R.E. Pahl. *International Journal of Urban and Regional Research* 15:107–13.

Crystal, G. 1991. *In Search of Excess: Executive Compensation in the 1980s.* New York: Norton.

Cummins, J. 1994. Lien we live by: National identity and social justice. *International Journal of Sociology and Language* 110:145–54.

Cuneo, C. 1978. Class exploitation in Canada. *Canadian Review of Sociology and Anthropology* 15:284–300.

————. 1982. Class struggle and measurement of the rate of surplus value. *Canadian Review of Sociology and Anthropology* 19(3): 377–425.

————. 1984. Reconfirming Karl Marx's rate of surplus value. *Canadian Review of Sociology and Anthropology* 21(1):98–104.

Cuneo, C., and J. Curtis. 1975. Social ascription in the educational and occupational status attainment of urban Canadians. *Canadian Review of Sociology an Anthropology* 12(1):6–24.

Dahrendorf, R. 1959. *Class and Class Conflict in Industrial Society.* Stanford: Stanford University Press.

Darroch, A.G. 1979. Another look at ethnicity, stratification, and social mobility in Canada. *Canadian Journal of Sociology* 4(1):1–25.

————. 1981. Urban ethnicity in Canada: Personal assimilation and political communities. *Canadian Review of Sociology and Anthropology* 18(1):93–100.

Darroch, A.G., and M.D. Ornstein. 1980. Ethnicity and occupational structure in Canada in 1871: The vertical mosaic in historical perspective. *Canadian Historical Review* 61(3):305–32.

David, M., and T. Flory. 1989. Changes in marital status and short-term income dynamics. In *Individuals and Families in Transition*, eds. H.V. Beaton, D.A. Ganni, and D.T. Frankel, 15–22. Washington, DC: U.S. Bureau of the Census.

Davis, A. 1981. *Women, Race and Class.* London: The Women's Press.

Davis, K. 1953. Reply. *American Sociological Review* 18:394–97.

Davis, K. 1991. *City of Quartz.* London: Verso.

Davis, Kingsley, and Wilbert Moore. 1945. Some principles of stratification. *American Sociological Review* 10(April):242–49.

Dawson, D. 1981. The development of the English-Ukrainain Bilingual School Program in the Edmonton school system. *MS.* Faculty of Education, University of Alberta.

———. 1982. The structural realities of Canadian multiculturalism. A response to Roberts and Clifton. *Canadian Public Policy* 8(4):608–11.

Degrass, R.P. 1977. Development of Monopolies in Canada from 1907–1913. Master's thesis, University of Waterloo.

DeKeseredy, W.S. 1988. *Woman Abuse in Dating Relationships: The Role of Male Peer Support.* Toronto: Canadian Scholars' Press.

———. 1992. In defence of self-defence: Demystifying female violence against male intimates. In *Crosscurrents: Debates in Canadian Society,* ed. R. Hinch. Toronto: Nelson.

———. 1994. Addressing the complexity of woman abuse in dating: A response to Gardiner and Fox. *Canadian Journal of Sociology* 19(1):75–80.

DeKeseredy, W.S., and B.D. MacLean. 1990 Researching woman abuse in Canada: A left realist critique of the Conflict Tactics Scale. *Canadian Review of Social Policy* 25:19–27.

DeKeseredy, W.S., and R. Hinch. 1991. *Woman Abuse: Sociological Perspectives.* Toronto: Thompson Educational Publishing.

DeKeseredy, W.S., and K. Kelly. 1993. The incidence and prevalence of woman abuse in Canadian university and college dating relationships. *Canadian Journal of Sociology* 18(2):137–59.

DeKeseredy, W.S., K. Kelly, and B. Baklid. 1992. The physical, sexual, and psychological abuse of women in dating relationships: Results from a pretest for a national study. Paper presented at the annual meeting of the American Society of Criminology, New Orleans.

DeKeseredy, W.S., and M.D. Schwartz. 1993. Male peer support and woman abuse: An expansion of DeKeseredy's model. *Sociological Spectrum.* In press.

DeKeseredy, W.S., M.D. Schwartz, and K. Tait. 1993. Sexual assault and stranger aggression on a Canadian university campus. *Sex Roles.* In press.

Democratic Policy Committee, Staff Report. 1996. *Who is Downsizing the American Dream?* March 1. Washington.

Denich, B.S. 1974. Sex and power in the Balkans. In *Women, Culture and Society,* ed. M. Rosaldo and L. Lamphere. Stanford University Press.

Denton, M.A., and A.A. Hunter. 1984. Economic sectors and gender discrimination in Canada: A critique and test of Block and

Walker and some new evidence. *Labour Canada Women Bureau Series A: Equality in the Workplace* 6. Ottawa: Labour Canada Publications Distribution Centre.

Derrida, J. 1992. Force of law: "The mystical foundation of authority." In *Deconstruction and the Possibility of Justice*, eds. D. Cornell, M. Rosenfield, and D.G. Carlson. New York: Routledge.

———. 1967. *Writing and Difference.* Chicago: Alan Bass.

DiIorio, J.A. 1989. Being and becoming coupled: The emergence of female subordination in heterosexual relationships. In *Gender in Intimate Relationships: A Microstructural Approach*, eds. B.J. Risman and P. Schwartz. Belmont, CA: Wadsworth.

Dobash, R.E., and R. Dobash. 1979. *Violence Against Wives.* New York: Free Press.

———. 1988. Research as social action: The struggle for battered women. In *Feminist Perspectives on Wife Abuse*, eds. K. Yllo and M. Bograd. Beverly Hills: Sage.

Dobash, R., R.E. Dobash, M. Wilson, and M. Daly. 1992. The myth of sexual symmetry in marital violence. *Social Problems* 39:71–91.

Doeringer, P., and M. Piore. 1971. *Internal Labour Markets and Manpower Analysis.* Lexington: D.C. Heath.

Domhoff, G.W. 1970. *The Higher Circles: The Governing Class in America.* New York: Vintage.

———. 1990. *The Power Elite and the State.* New York: Aldine de Gruyter.

Dominion Bureau of Statistics. 1961–72. *Prices and Price Indexes.* Ottawa: Queen's Printer.

Douglas, T. 1976. The case for public ownership. In *The Big Tough Expensive Job*, ed. J. Laxter and A. Martin. Toronto.

Downes, A. 1995. *Corporate Executions.* New York: American Management Association.

Drache, D. 1977. Staple-ization: A theory of Canadian capitalist development. In *Imperialism, Nationalism and Canada*, ed. J. Saul and C. Heron, 15–33. Toronto.

D'Souza, D. 1996. In reply and summation. *Academic Questions* (Fall):89–91.

———. 1996. Relativism, racism, and a dysfunctional culture. *Academic Questions* (Fall):69–76.

Dubois, W.E.B. 1980. A reply to Stone. *Abridged from American Journal of Sociology* 13:834–38.

Duncan, G., and S. Hoffman. 1985. A reconsideration of the economic consequences of divorce. *Demography* 22:485–97.

Dutton, D.G., and K. Hemphill. 1992. Patterns of socially desirable responding among perpetrators and victims of wife assault. *Violence and Victims* 7:29–40.

Edwards, J. 1985. Language, diversity and identity. In *Linguistic Minorities, Policies and Pluralism*, ed. J. Edwards, 277–310. London: Academic Press.

Edwards, J. 1994. Rebuttal essay: Canadian update, and rejoinder to the comments. *International Journal of Language* 110:203–19.

Edwards, R., M. Reich, and T. Weisskopf. 1978. Imperialism. In *The Capitalist System*, eds. R. Edwards, M. Reich, and T. Weisskopf, 2d ed., Englewood Cliffs, NJ.

Ehrenreich, B., and D. English. 1978. *For Her Own Good.* Garden City, NY: Doubleday Anchor Press.

Ehrlich, C. 1981. The unhappy marriage of marxism and feminism: Can it be saved? In *Women and Revolution*, ed. L. Sargent, 109–33. Boston, MA: South End Press.

Eller, J.D. and R.M. Coughlan. 1993. The poverty of primordialism: The demystification of ethnic attachments. *Ethnic and Racial Studies* 16(2):183–202.

Elliot, S., D. Odynak, and H. Krahn. 1992. *A Survey of Unwanted Sexual Experiences Among University of Alberta Students.* Research report prepared for the Council on Student Life, University of Alberta. University of Alberta: Population Research Laboratory.

Emmerson, R.J., and P.N. Rowe. 1982. Professor Cuneo's analysis of class exploitation in Canada. *Canadian Review of Sociology and Anthropology* 19(2):279–89.

Engbersen, G. 1989. Cultures of long-term unemployment in the west. *The Netherlands Journal of Social Sciences* 25:75–96.

Engels, F. 1970. The origins of the family, private property and the state. In *Selected Works* 3, 204–316, eds. K. Marx and F. Engels. Moscow: Progress Publishers.

———. 1972. *The Origin of the Family, Private Property and the State.* New York: International Publishers.

———. 1975. The condition of the working class in England. In *Collected Works* 4, 295–664, eds. K. Marx and F. Engels. Moscow: Progress Publishers.

Epstein, C.F. 1986. Inevitabilities of prejudice. *Society* 23(6):7–15.

Erikson, R., and J.H. Goldthorpe. 1992. *The Constant Flux: Class Mobility in Industrial Societies.* Oxford: Oxford University Press.

Espenshade, T.J. 1979. The economic consequences of divorce. *Journal of Marriage and the Family* 41(August):615–25.

Esping-Anderson, G. 1990. *The Three Worlds of Welfare Capitalism.* Princeton, NJ: Princeton University Press.

Etzioni, A. 1969. *The Semi-Professions and Their Organization.* New York: The Free Press.

Evans, M. 1989. A comment on Nicky Hart. *New Left Review* 179:125–29.

Ezorsky, G. 1987. In affirmative action numbers count. *New Politics* 1(3):35–37.

Faludi, S. 1991. *Backlash.* New York: Crown Publishers.

Featherman, D.L., and R.M. Hauser. 1978. *Opportunity and Change.* New York: Academic.

Fee, E. 1973. The sexual politics of Victorian social anthropology. *Feminist Studies* 1(Winter–Spring).

Fennama, M., and H. Schijf. 1979. Analysing interlocking direc-torates: Theory and methods, *Social Networks* I:297–332.

Ferber, M., and J.A. Nelson, eds. 1993. *Beyond Economic Man: Feminist Theory and Economics.* Chicago: University of Chicago Press.

Ferguson, A., and N. Folbre. 1981. The unhappy marriage of patriarchy and capitalism. In *Women and Revolution,* ed. L. Sargent, 313–38. Boston, MA: South End Press.

Filer, R.K. 1990. Compensating differentials and the male-female wage gap: A comment. *Social Forces* 69(2):469–73.

Fillmore, C.J. 1990. Gender differences in earnings: A re-analysis and prognosis for Canadian women. *Canadian Journal of Sociology* 15(3):275–300.

———. 1985. A comparison of historical estimates of gender occupational segregation between Canada and the United States, 1931–1981. Paper presented at the Annual Meetings of the Ontario Sociology and Anthropology Association, Waterloo, Ontario.

———. 1991. Gender differences in earnings: A response to Nakamura. *Canadian Journal of Sociology* 16(2):202–03.

Findlay, P.C. 1975. Multiculturalism in Canada: Ethnic pluralism and social policy. In *Education of Immigrant Students,* ed. A. Wolfgang, 215–24. Toronto: Ontario Institute for Studies in Education.

Fineman, M.L. 1986. Illusive equality: On Weitzman's *Divorce Revolution. American Bar Foundation Research Journal:* 781–90.

Finkelman, L. 1992. *Report of the Survey of Unwanted Sexual Experiences Among Students of U.N.B.-F. and S.T.U.* University of New Brunswick: Counselling Services.

Firestone, S. 1970. *The Dialectic of Sex.* New York: William Morrow and Company.

Flanagan, T. 1989. The agricultural argument and original appropriation: Indian lands and political philosophy. *Canadian Journal of Political Science* 22(3):589–606.

Flax, J. 1995. Race/gender and the ethics of difference—A reply to Okin's "Gender Inequality and Cultural Differences." *Political Theory* 23(3):500–16.

Folbre, N., and H. Hartmann. 1989. The persistence of patriarchal capitalism. *Rethinking Marxism* 2(4):90–96.

Foot, D.K., 1994. Canada's unemployment-immigration linkage: Demographic, economic, and political influences. *Canadian Journal of Sociology* 19(4):513–23.

Forcese, D. 1975. *The Canadian Class Structure.* Toronto: McGraw-Hill Ryerson.

Foreman, A. 1977. *Femininity as Alienation.* London: Pluto Press.

Forse, M. 1986. La diversification de la societé française vue a traverse le mariage et l'idéologie. *The Tocqueville Review* 7:223–33.

Foss, J.E., 1996. Is there a natural sexual inequality of intellect? A reply to Kimura. *Hypatia* 11(3):24–46.

Fox, B.J. 1993. On violent men and female victims: A comment on DeKeseredy and Kelly. *Canadian Journal of Sociology* 18(3):321–24.

Fox, B.J., and J. Fox. 1986. Women in the labour market, 1931–1981: Exclusion and competition. *Canadian Review of Sociology and Anthropology* 23:1–21.

Fox, B., and M. Ornstein. 1986. The Canadian state and corporate elites in the post-war period. *Canadian Review of Sociology and Anthropology* 23:481–506.

Fraiman, S. 1997a. Diversity in adversity: The retreat from affirmative action. *National Women's Studies Association* 9(1):39–43.

———. 1997b. Power not plurality: A response to Estella Lauter and Ranu Samantrai. *National Women's Studies Association* 9(1):54–56.

Francis, D. 1986. *Controlling Interest: Who Owns Canada?* Toronto: Macmillan.

Frank, A.G. 1967. *Capitalism and Underdevelopment in Latin America.* New York.

———. 1969. *Capitalism and Underdevelopment in Latin America.* Revised and enlarged. New York.

———. 1972. *Lumpen-Bourgeoisie and Lumpen-Development: Dependence, Class and Politics in Latin America.* New York.

Frank, A. et al, eds. 1986. *The Encyclopedic Dictionary of Sociology,* 3d ed. Guildford, Connecticut: Dushkin.

Friedan, B. 1963. *The Feminine Mystique.* New York: Dell Publishing.

Furstenberg, F.F. 1987. The divorce dilemma: After the revolution. *Contemporary Sociology* 16:556–58.

Gans, H. 1979. Symbolic ethnicity: The future of ethnic groups and cultures in America. *Ethnic and Racial Studies* 2:1–20.

Gardiner, J. 1975. Women's domestic labour. *New Left Review* 89:47–72.

Gardner, R. 1975. Historical trends in Canadian class relationships: A note on some contemporary interpretations. Paper presented at the annual meetings of the Canadian Sociology and Anthropology Association, Edmonton, Alberta.

Gartner, R. 1993. Studying women abuse: a comment on DeKeseredy and Kelly. *Canadian Journal of Sociology* 18(3):313–19.

Gates, H.L. Jr. A response: Multiculturalism and its discontents. *The Black Scholar* 24(1):16–17.

Gerth, H.H., and C. Wright Mills. 1958. *From Max Weber, Essays in Sociology.* New York: Oxford University Press.

Giddens, A. 1980. *The Class Structure of the Advanced Societies.* New York: Harper and Row.

Gitlin, T. 1993. From universality to difference: Notes on the fragmentation of the idea of the left. *Contention* 2(2):15–40.

———. 1994. Wither the left: A reply to David C. Roper. *Contention* 3(2):205–06.

Glaberman, M. 1996. Marxism and class consciousness. *Labour/Le Travail* 37:233–41.

———. 1987. Class is a missing element. *New Politics* 1(3):58–61.

Goldberg, S., 1986a. Reaffirming the obvious. *Society* 23(6):4–7.

———. 1986b. Utopian yearning versus scientific curiosity. *Society* 23(6):29–39.

Goldthorpe, J. 1966. Social stratification in industrial society. In *Class, Status and Power*, 2d ed, eds. Bendix and Lipset, 648–59. New York: Free Press.

Goldthorpe, J.H. 1980. *Social Mobility and Class Structure in Modern Britain.* Oxford: Clarendon Press.

Goldthorpe, J.H., and G. Marshall. 1992. The promising future of class analysis. *Sociology* 26:381–400.

Gordon, A.D., and M.J. Buhle. 1976. Sex and class in colonial and nineteenth century America. In *Liberating Women's History*, ed. B.A. Carroll. Chicago: University of Illinois Press.

Gordon, M. 1964. *Assimilation in American Life.* New York: Oxford University Press.

Gordon, S. 1987. *Women in the Labour Force: A Case Study of the Manitoba Jobs Fund.* Winnipeg: Manitoba Advisory Council on the Status of Women.

Gottfredson, L.S. 1986. Societal consequences of the *g* factor in employment. *Journal of Vocational Behavior* 29:379–410.

Gough, I. 1972. Marx's theory of productive and unproductive labour. *New Left Review* 76:47–72.

Gould, K. 1990/91. Dialogue on Quebec 1970. *Quebec Studies* 11:63–73.

Gray, J.P. 1987. Do women have higher social status in hunting societies without high gods? *Social Forces* 65(4):1121–31.

Grayson, J.P. et al. 1979. The Canadian literary elite: A socio-historical perspective. *Canadian Journal of Sociology* 3(3):291–308.

Griffin, A. 1984, *Quebec: The Challenge of Independence.* Cranbury, NJ: Associated University Press.

Griffin, N. 1989. Reply to Professor Flanagan. *Canadian Journal of Political Science* 22(3):603–06.

Grosby, S. 1994. The verdict of history: The inexpungeable tie of primordiality — A response to Eller and Coughlan. *Ethnic and Racial Studies* 17(1):164–71.

Grusky, D.B. 1986. American social mobility in the nineteenth and twentieth century. Ph.D. thesis, Department of Sociology, University of Wisconsin—Madison.

Guimond, S., D.L. Palmer, and G. Begin. 1989. Education, academic program and intergroup attitudes. *Canadian Review of Sociology and Anthropology* 26(2):193–216.

Guimond, S., and D.L. Palmer. 1994. The politics of Canadian social scientists: A comment on Baer and Lambert. *Canadian Review of Sociology and Anthropology* 31(2):184–95.

Gulick, J. 1986. Nurturing the nature controversy. *Society* 23(6): 22–23.

Gunderson, M. 1976. Work patterns. In *Opportunity for Choice*, ed. G. Cook. Ottawa: Information Canada.

Guppy, N. 1992. Does school matter? An invited comment on Anisef, Ashbury, and Turritten's differential effects of university and community college education on occupational status attainment in Ontario. *Canadian Journal of Sociology* 17(1):85–88.

Haffey, M., and P.M. Cohen. 1992. Treatment issues for divorcing women. *Families in Society* 73:142–48.

Haggag Youssef, N. 1974. *Women and Work in Developing Societies.* Berkeley, CA: Institute of International Studies.

Hamilton, R. 1978. *The Liberation of Women: A Study of Patriarchy and Capitalism.* London: George Allen and Unwin.

Hamilton, R. 1997. Theorizing gender, sexuality and family: Feminism and psychoanalysis revisited. In *Feminism and Families: Critical Policies and Changing Practices*, ed. M. Luxton, 192–230. Halifax: Fernwood Publishing.

Hamilton, R., and M. Pinard. 1977. Poverty in Canada: Illusion and reality. *Canadian Review of Sociology and Anthropology* 14(2):247–52.

Harris, K. 1989. New alliances: Socialist-feminism in the eighties. *Feminist Review* 31(Spring):34–54.

Hart, N. 1985. Gender and the rise and fall of class politics. *New Left Review*:19–47.

Hartmann, H. 1976. Capitalism, patriarchy, and job segrega-tion by sex. *Sign: Journal of Women in Culture and Society* 1(Spring).

———. 1979. Capitalism, patriarchy and job segregation by sex. In *Capitalist Patriarchy and the Case for Socialist Feminism*, ed. Z. Eisenstein. New York: Monthly Review Press.

―――. 1981a. The unhappy marriage of Marxism and Feminism: Towards a more progressive union. In *Women and Revolution: A Discussion of the Unhappy Marriage of Marxism and Feminism*, ed. L. Sargent. Boston: South End Press.

―――. 1981b. Summary and response: Continuing the discussion. In *Women and Revolution*, ed. L. Sargent, 363–73. Boston: South End Press.

Harvey, D. 1982. *The Limits to Capital.* Oxford: Basil Blackwell.

Harvey, E., and I. Chartner. 1975. Social mobility and occupational attainment of university graduates. *Canadian Review of Sociology and Anthropology* 12(2):134–49.

Hauser, R.M., and D.B. Grusky. 1984. Comparative social mobility revisited. *American Sociological Review* 49:19–38.

―――. 1987. Cross-national variation in occupational distributions, relative mobility chances and intergenerational shifts in occupational distributions. Draft paper.

Hauser, R.M., G.D. Jaynes, and R.M. Williams Jr. 1990. Understanding black–white differences. *Public Interest* 99:110–19.

Heap, J.L. 1972. Conceptual and theoretical problems in *The Vertical Mosaic. Canadian Review of Sociology and Anthropology* 9(2):176–87.

Heap, J.L., ed. 1974. *Everybody's Canada: The Vertical Mosaic Reviewed and Re-Examined.* Toronto: Burns and MacEachern.

Herrnstein, R.J. 1990a. Still an American dilemma. *The Public Interest* 99:3–17.

―――. 1990b. On responsible scholarship: A rejoinder. *The Public Interest:*120–27.

Hewlett, S. 1986. *A Lesser Life.* New York: William Morrow.

Hill, A.C. 1970. Protective labor legislation for women: Its origin and effect. New Haven, CN: Yale Law School. Mimeographed.

Hill, H. 1987a. Herbert Hill replies. *New Politics* 1(3):61–71.

―――. 1987b. Race, ethnicity and organized labor: The opposition to affirmative action. *New Politics* 1(2):31–82.

Himmelweit, S., and S. Mohun. 1977. Domestic labour and capital. *Cambridge Journal of Economics* 1(March).

HMSO. 1995. *Share Ownership.* London.

Hochschild. A. 1989. *The Second Shift: Working Parents and the Revolution at Home.* New York: Viking.

Hodgkinson, C. 1982a. Wealth and happiness: An analysis and some implications for education. *Canadian Journal of Education* 7(1):1–13.

―――. 1982b. Greed, dyspepsia, and dispair: A confutation of professor Anderson. *Canadian Journal of Education* 7(2):90–93.

Hoff, J. 1991. *Law, Gender, and Injustice.* New York: New York University Press.

Hoffman, S., and G. Duncan. 1988. What are the economic consequences of divorce? *Demography* 25:641–45.

Hoffman, S., and J. Holmes. 1976. Husbands, wives, and divorce. In *Five Thousand American Families — Patterns of Economic Progress*, eds. G. Duncan and J. Morgan, 23–75. Ann Arbor, MI: Institute for Social Research.

Holden, K.C., and P.J. Smock. 1991. The economic costs of marital dissolution. *Annual Review of Sociology* 17:51–78.

Hole, J., and E. Levin, eds. 1971. Politics of ego: A manifesto for New York Radical Feminists. *Rebirth of Feminism*. New York: Quadrangle Books.

Hollway, W. 1983. Heterosexual sex: power and desire for the other. In *Sex and Love*, eds. S. Cartledge and J. Ryan. London: The Women's Press.

Hooks, B. 1982. *Ain't I A Woman: Black Women and Feminism*. London: Pluto.

Hotaling, G.T., and D.B. Sugarman. 1986. An analysis of risk markers and husband to wife violence: The current state of knowledge. *Violence and Victims* 1:101–24.

Hout, M. 1982. The association between husbands' and wives' occupations in two-earner families. *American Journal of Sociology* 88:397–409.

———. 1988. More universalism, less structural mobility. *American Journal of Sociology* 93(March):1358–400.

———. 1989. *Following in Father's Footsteps: Social Mobility in Ireland*. Cambridge, MA: Harvard University Press.

Hout, M., and R.M. Hauser. 1992. Hierarchy and symmetry in social mobility. *European Sociological Review* 8:239–66.

Hull, G., P.B. Scott, and B. Smith, eds. 1982. *But Some of Us Are Brave: Black Women's Studies*. New York: The Feminist Press.

Humphries, J. 1975. Women: Scapegoats and safety valves in the Great Depression. *Review of Radical Economics* 1(Spring):98–121.

———. 1977. Class struggle and the persistence of the working-class family. *Cambridge Journal of Economics* 1:241–58.

Humphries, L.G. 1988. Trends in levels of academic achievement of blacks and other minorities. *Intelligence* 12:231–60.

Hunter, A. 1976. "Class and status in Canada." In *Introduction to Canadian Society*, eds. G.N. Ramu and S.D. Johnson. Toronto: Macmillan.

———. 1986. *Class Tells: On Social Inequality*. 2d ed. Toronto: Butterworths.

Hutcheson, J. 1978. *Dominance and Dependency*. Toronto.

Inglehart, R. 1990. *Cultural Shift in Advanced Industrial Society*. Princeton: Princeton University Press.

Innis, H. 1956. *Essays in Canadian Economic History.* Ed. M.Q. Innis. Toronto.

International Confederation of Free Trade Unions. 1996. *The Globe Market — Trade Unionism's Greatest Challenge.* Brussels.

Isajiw, W.W. 1983. Multiculturalism and the integration of the Canadian community. *Canadian Ethnic Studies* 15(2):107–17.

———. 1990. Ethnic-identity retention. In *Ethnic Identity and Equality: Varieties of Experience in a Canadian City,* ed. R. Breton et al., 34–91. Toronto: University of Toronto Press.

Jackson, S. 1992. Towards a historical sociology of housework: A materialist feminist analysis. *Women's Studies International Forum* 15:153–72.

Jacob, H. 1988. *Silent Revolution.* Chicago, IL: University of Chicago Press.

Jacobs, J.A., and R.J. Steinberg. 1990a. Compensating differentials and the male–female wage gap: Evidence from the New York state comparable worth study. *Social Forces* 69(2):439–68.

———. 1990b. Compensating differentials and the male–female wage gap: A Reply to Filer. *Social Forces* 69(2):475–78.

Jaffa, H.V. 1996. On the racism industry. *Academic Questions* (Fall):83–85.

Janes, R.R. 1994. Personal, academic and institutional perspectives on museums and first nations. *Canadian Journal of Native Studies* 14(1): 147–56.

Jencks, C. 1982. Divorced mothers, unite. *Psychology Today* (November).

Jencks, C., and P. Petersen, eds. 1991. *The Urban Underclass.* Washington, DC: Brookings Institute.

Jensen, A.R. 1981. *Straight Talk About Mental Tests.* New York: The Free Press.

Johnson, B.D. 1992. Campus confidential. *MacLean's* (November 9):43–46.

Johnson, C. 1996. Does capitalism really need patriarchy? Some old issues reconsidered. *Women's Studies International Forum* 19(3): 193–202.

Johnson, L. 1974. *Poverty in Wealth: The Capitalist Labour Market and Income Distribution in Canada.* Toronto: New Hogtown Press.

Johnston, J. 1973, *Lesbian Nation; The Feminist Solution.* New York: Simon and Schuster.

Kalbach, W.E. 1970. *The Impact of Immigration on Canada's Population.* Ottawa: Queen's Printer.

Kalbach, W.E., and W.W. McVey. 1971. *The Demographic Basis of Canadian Society.* Toronto: McGraw-Hill.

Kalleberg, A.L., and I. Berg. 1987. *Work and Industry: Structures, Markets, and Processes.* New York: Plenum Press.

Kanter, R.M. 1977. *Men and Women of the Corporation.* New York: Basic Books.

Kaufman, M. 1987. The construction of masculinity and the triad of men's violence. In *Beyond Patriarchy,* ed. M. Kaufman. Toronto: Oxford University Press.

Kazi, H. 1986. The beginning of a debate long due: Some observations on "Ethnocentrism and Socialist-Feminist Theory." *Feminist Review* 22:87–91.

Kelly, K. 1994. The politics of data. *Canadian Journal of Sociology* 19(1):81–86.

Kelly, K., and W.S. DeKeseredy. 1993. Developing a Canadian national survey on woman abuse in university and college dating relationships: Methodological, theoretical and political issues. *Journal of Human Justice.* In press.

Kelly, L. 1988. *Surviving Sexual Violence.* Minneapolis: University of Minnesota Press.

Kennedy, L.W., and D.G. Dutton. 1989. The incidence of wife assault in Alberta. *Canadian Journal of Behavioural Science* 21:40–54.

Kessler-Harris, A. 1975. Stratifying by sex: Understanding the history of working women. In *Labor Market Segmentation.* Lexington, MA: D.C. Heath and Company.

———. 1976. Women, work and the social order. In *Liberating Women's History.* Chicago: University of Illinois Press.

Kimura, D. 1992. Sex differences in the brain. *Scientific American* (September):81–87.

Kinder, D.R. 1986. The continuing American dilemma: White resistance to racial change 40 years after Myrdal. *Journal of Social Issues* 42(2):151–71.

Klatch, R.E. 1987. *Women of the New Right.* Philadelphia: Temple University Press.

Klein, I. 1985. Three models of explaining ethnic strife: Sociobiology, new-marxism and rational choice. *Canadian Ethnic Studies* 17(3):91–99.

Knight, G. 1979. Work orientation and mobility ideology in the working class. *Canadian Journal of Sociology* 4(1):27–41.

Koedt, A., ed. 1972. *Radical Feminism.* New York: Quadrangle Press.

Kornhauser, R.R. 1978. *Social Sources of Delinquency: An Analytic Appraisal of Models.* Chicago: University of Chicago Press.

Korpi, W. 1972. Some problems in the measurement of class voting. *American Journal of Sociology* 78:627–42.

———. 1983. *The Democratic Class Struggle.* London: Routledge and Kegan Paul.

Koss, M.P., and C.A. Gidycz. 1985. Sexual experiences survey: Reliability and validity. *Journal of Consulting and Clinical Psychology* 50:455–57.

Koss, M.P., C.A. Gidycz, and N. Wisniewski. 1987. The scope of rape: Incidence and prevalence of sexual aggression and victimization in a national sample of higher education students. *Journal of Consulting and Clinical Psychology* 55:162–70.

Koss, M.P., and C.J. Oros. 1982. Sexual experiences survey: A research instrument investigating sexual aggression and victimization. *Journal of Consulting and Clinical Psychology* 50:455–57.

Krahn, H.J., and G.S. Lowe. 1988. *Work, Industry and Canadian Society*. Scarborough: Nelson Canada.

Krashinsky, M. 1987. The returns to university schooling in Canada: A comment. *Canadian Public Policy* 13(2):218–21.

Kulchyski, P. 1995. Aboriginal peoples and hegemony in Canada. *Journal of Canadian Studies* 30(1):60–68.

Labour Canada. 1987. *Equal Pay for Work of Equal Value*. Cat. No. L44-1778/86. 2d ed. Ottawa: Minister of Supply and Services Canada.

Lacan J. 1968. *The Language of the Self*. New York. Delta Books.

Lacapra, D. 1987. *History and Criticism*. Ithaca, NY: Cornell University Press.

Lacoste, D. 1989. *Brief Presented to the Task Force on Barriers to Women in the Public Service of Canada*. Ottawa: The Professional Institute of the Public Service of Canada.

Lamanna, M.A., and A.C. Riedmann. 1985. *Marriages and Families*. Belmont, CA: Wadsworth.

Lampard, R. 1996. Might Britain be a meritocracy? A comment on Saunders. *Sociology* 30(2):387–93.

Laner, M.R., and J. Thompson. 1982. Abuse and aggression in courting couples. *Deviant Behavior* 3:229–44.

Langford, T. 1994. Strikes and class consciousness. *Labour/Le Travail* 33:107–37.

Langlois, S. 1992. The distribution of anti-Semitism in Canada in 1984. *Canadian Journal of Sociology* 17(2):175–78.

Laurin, C. 1978. French language charter. *Canadian Review of Sociology and Anthropology* 15(2):115–27.

Lautard, E.H., and D.J. Loree. 1984. Ethnic stratification in Canada. *Canadian Journal of Sociology* 9(3):333–44.

Lautard, E.H., and N. Guppy. 1990. The vertical mosaic revisited: Occupational differentials among Canadian ethnic groups. In *Race and Ethnic Relations in Canada*, ed. P.S. Li, 189–208. Toronto: Oxford University Press.

Lauter, E. 1997. Toward diversity. *National Women's Studies Association* 9(1):44–48.

Laxer, G. 1985. Foreign ownership and myths about Canadian development. *Canadian Review of Sociology and Anthropology* 22:311–45.

Lebowitz, M.A. 1988. Trade and class: Labour strategies in a world of strong capital. *Studies in Political Economy* 27(Autumn):137–48.

———. 1990. Trade and class revisited. *Studies in Political Economy* 33(Autumn):193–96.

Lees, S. 1986. Sex, race and culture: Feminism and the limits of cultural pluralism. *Feminist Review* 22:92–102.

Leibowitz, L. 1978. *Females, Males, Families: A Biosocial Approach.* North Scituate, MA: Duxbury Press.

Lenin, V.I. 1970. Imperialism, the highest stage of capitalism. In *Selected Works,* V.I. Lenin, 667–768. Moscow.

Levitt, K. 1971. *Silent Surrender.* Toronto.

Levy, F. 1987. *Dollars and Dreams: The Changing American Income Distribution.* New York: Russell Sage Foundation.

Lewenhak, S. 1977. *Women and Trade Unions: An Outline History of Women in the British Trade Union Movement.* London: Ernest Benn.

Li, P.S. 1978. The stratification of ethnic immigrants: The case of Toronto. *Canadian Review of Sociology and Anthropology* 15:31–40.

———. 1988. *Ethnic Inequality in Class Society.* Toronto: Thomson Educational Publishing.

Lichtenstein, N. 1987. An Unbalanced Rendering. *New Politics* 1(3):53–55.

Lieberson, S. 1970. *Language and Ethnic Relations in Canada.* New York: John Wiley.

Lindblom, C. 1977. *Politics and Markets.* New York: Basic.

Lipset, S.M. 1981 [1960]. *Political Man: The Social Bases of Politics.* Baltimore: Johns Hopkins University Press.

———. 1985. *Consensus and Conflict.* New Brunswick, NJ: Transaction Books.

———. 1990. The death of the third way: Everywhere but here, that is. *The National Interest* 20:25–37.

Lipset, S.M., and R. Bendix. 1991 [1959]. *Social Mobility in Industrial Society.* New Brunswick, NJ: Transaction Books.

Little, M. 1983. Divorce and the feminization of poverty. Paper presented at the meetings of Sociologists for Women in Society, American Sociological Association, August 30.

Liu, T.P. 1991. Race and gender in the politics of group formation: A comment on notions of multiculturalism. *Frontiers* 12(2):155–65.

Loehlin, J.C., L. Gardner, and J.N. Spuhler. 1975. *Race Differences in Intelligence.* San Francisco: W.H. Freeman.

Lonsdorf, B.J. 1991. The role of coercion in affecting women's inferior outcomes in divorce. *Journal of Divorce and Remarriage* 16:69–106.

Lopreato, J. 1965. *Vilfredo Pareto: Selections from His Treatise.* New York: Harcourt Brace Jovanovich.

Lowe, M. 1978. Sociobiology and sex differences. *Journal of Women in Culture and Society* 4(1):118–25.

———. 1980. Reply to Ralls. *Journal of Women in Culture and Society* 5(3):546–47.

Lubin, M. 1985. Review of Quebec: The challenge of independence. *Quebec Studies* 3:240–43.

Lupul, M.R. 1982. The political implementation of multiculturalism. *Journal of Canadian Studies* 17(1):93–102.

———. 1983. Multiculturalism and Canada's white ethnics. *Canadian Ethnic Studies* 15(1):99–107.

MacMillan, C.M. 1990. Explaining support for language rights: A comment on "Political Culture and the Problem of Double Standards." *Canadian Journal of Political Science* 23(3):531–36.

Magas, B. 1971. Sex politics: Class politics. *New Left Review* 66:69–91.

Makepeace, J.M. 1983. Life events stress and courtship violence. *Family Relations* 32:101–09.

———. 1986. Gender differences in courtship victimization. *Family Relations* 35:383–88.

Mandel, E. 1968. *Marxist Economic Theory.* London.

———. 1975a. The industrial cycle in late capitalism. *New Left Review* 90: 3–26.

———. 1975b. *Late Capitalism.* London: New Left Books.

Manitoba Labour. 1989. *Pay Equity in Manitoba — A Discussion Paper.* 2d ed. Winnipeg: Pay Equity Bureau.

Mansnerus, L. 1995. The divorce backlash. *Working Woman* 20 (February):41–45.

Manza, J. 1992. Classes, status groups, and social closure: A critique of neo-Weberian social theory. *Current Perspectives on Social Theory* 12:275–302.

Manza, J., and C. Brooks. 1996. Does class analysis still have anything to contribute to the study of politics? — Comments. *Theory and Society* 25:717–24.

Marceau, J. 1977. *Class and Status in France: Economic Change and Social Immobility.* New York: Oxford University Press.

———. 1989. *A Family Business? The Making of an International Business Elite.* New York: Cambridge University Press.

Marchak, P. 1979. *In Whose Interests.* Toronto.

Marchak, M.P. 1989. The ideology of free trade: A response to Smith. *Canadian Public Policy* 15(2):220–25.

Mare, R.D. 1980. Social background and educational continuation decisions. *Journal of the American Statistical Association* 75:295–305.

———. 1981. Change and stability in educational stratification. *American Sociological Review* 46:72–87.

Markland, S. 1990. Structures of modern poverty. *Acta Sociologica* 33:125–40.

Marshal, G. 1991. In defence of class analysis: A comment on R.E. Pahl. *International Journal of Urban and Regional Research* 15:114–18.

Marshall, G., and A. Swift. 1995. Social mobility — Plus ça change. *Prospect* (November).

Marx, K. 1906. *Capital* I. Chicago: Charles H. Kerr & Co.

———. 1954. *Capital* I. Moscow: Progress Publishers.

———. 1967. *Capital* I–III. New York: International Publishers.

Massey, D.S. 1990. American apartheid: Segregation and the making of the underclass. *American Journal of Sociology* 96:329–57.

Massey, D.S., and M.L. Eggers. 1990. The ecology of inequality: Minorities and the concentration of poverty, 1970–1980. *American Journal of Sociology* 95:1153–88.

May, Kathryn. 1998. PSAC wins pay equity battle. *The Windsor Star* (July 30):A1–A2.

McBride, T.M. 1977. The long road home: Women's work and industrialization. In *Becoming Visible*. New York: Houghton Mifflin.

McCraw, M.L. 1978. Medical care costs lead rise in 1976–77 family budgets. *Monthly Labor Review* 101(11):33–36.

McLaughlin, S.D. 1978. Occupational sex identification and the assessment of male and female earnings inequality. *American Sociological Review* 43:909–21.

McNally, D. 1990. Socialism or protectionism? *Studies in Political Economy* 31(Spring):159–68.

McNeely, R.L., and G. Robinson-Simpson. 1987. The truth about domestic violence: A falsely framed issue. *Social Work* 32:485–90.

McRoberts, K. 1991/92. Separate agendas: English Canada and Quebec. *Quebec Studies* 13:1–11.

Meiksins, P., and E. Meiksins-Wood. 1985. Beyond class? A reply to Chantal Mouffe. *Studies in Political Economy* 17(Summer):141–65.

Melli, M. 1986. Constructing a social problem: The post-divorce plight of women and children. *American Bar Foundation Research Journal* 1986:759–72.

Menskikov, S. 1969. *Millionnaires and Managers.* Moscow.

Meyers, M. 1996. A call for compensatory consideration. *Academic Questions* (Fall):79–83.

Michels, R. 1962. *Political Parties.* New York: The Free Press.

Migrant Women Speak. 1978. London: Search Press/World Council of Churches.

Miles, A. 1983. Economism and feminism: Hidden in the household — A comment on the domestic labour debate. *Studies in Political Economy* 11:197–209.

Miles, R. 1982. *Racism and Migrant Labour.* London: Routledge and Kegan Paul.

Miles, R., and A. Phizacklea. 1980. *Labour and Racism.* London: Routledge and Kegan Paul.

Miller, S. 1981. Harvard hyphenates America. *The American Spectator* 14(5):28–31.

Millett, K. 1971. *Sexual Politics.* New York: Avon Books.

Mills, C.W. 1946. The middle class of middle-sized cities. *American Sociological Review* 11:520–29.

Mincer, J., and S.W. Polacheck. 1974. Family investments in human capital: Earnings of women. *Journal of Political Economy* 82:76–111.

Mingione, E. 1991. The new urban poor and the crisis of citizenship/welfare systems in Italy. Paper presented at the Working Conference on Pauverté, immigrations et marginalités urbaines dans les sociétés avancées. Paris, Maison Suger, May.

Mirza, H.S. 1986. The dilemma of socialist feminism: A case for black feminism. *Feminist Review* 22:103–05.

Mitchell, C. 1993. Multiculturalism: The coded reinscription of race in contemporary education discourse. *The Black Scholar* 23(3,4): 71–74.

Mitchell, J. 1971. *Women Estate.* Harmondsworth: Penguin Books.

———. 1974. *Psychoanalysis and Feminism.* New York: Pantheon Books.

Molyneux, M. 1981. Socialist societies old and new: Progress towards women's emancipation. *Feminist Review* 8.

Moore, W.E. 1953. Reply. *American Sociological Review* 18:397.

———. The Tumin-Moore polemics — Remaining points of disagreement. *American Sociological Review* 28.

Moore, S., and D. Wells. 1975. *Imperialism and the National Question in Canada.* Toronto.

Morgan, L.A. 1991. *After Marriage Ends.* Newbury Park, CA: Sage.

Morton, W.L. 1961. *The Canadian Identity.* Toronto: University of Toronto Press.

Mouffe, C. 1989. Working-class hegemony and the struggle for socialism. *Studies in Political Economy* 12:7–26.

Mullins, P. 1991. The identification of social forces in development as a general problem in sociology: A comment on Pahl's remarks on class consumption relations as forces in urban and regional development. *International Journal of Urban and Regional Research* 15:119–26.

Nakamura, A. 1990. Gender differences in earnings: A comment. *Canadian Journal of Sociology* 15:463–69.

Nakamura, A., M. Nakamura, and D. Cullen. 1979a. *Employment and Earnings of Married Females.* Ottawa: Minister of Supply and Services Canada.

———. 1979b. Job opportunities, the offered wage, and the labour supply of married women. *American Economic Review* 69:787–805.

Nakamura, A., and M. Nakamura. 1981. A comparison of the labour force behaviour of married women in the United States and Canada, with special attention to the impact of income taxes. *Econometrica* 49:451–89.

———. 1985. A survey of research on the work behaviour of Canadian women. In *Work and Play: The Canadian Labour Market* 17, ed. W.C. Riddell. Ottawa: Ministry of Supply and Services Canada.

Nakhaie, M.R. 1995. Ownership and management position of Canadian ethnic groups in 1973 and 1989. *Canadian Journal of Sociology* 20(2):167–92.

———. 1998. Asymmetry and symmetry of conjugal violence. *Journal of Comparative Family Studies.* Forthcoming.

Nakhaie, M.R., and J.E. Curtis. 1998. Effects of class positions of parents on educational attainment of daughters and sons. *Canadian Review of Sociology and Anthropology* 35(4):545–77.

Naylor, R.T. 1972. The rise and fall of the third commercial empire of the St. Lawrence. In *Capitalism and the National Question in Canada,* ed. G. Teeple. Toronto.

Naylor, T. 1975. *A History of Canadian Business 1867–1914 II.* Toronto: J. Lorimer.

National Center on Women and Family Law. 1983. Sex and economic discrimination in child custody awards. *Clearinghouse Review* 16 (April).

Neiman, L. 1984. Wage discrimination and women workers: The move towards equal pay for work of equal value in Canada. *Labour Canada Women's Bureau Series A: Equality in the Workplace,* No. 5. Ottawa: Labour Canada Publications Distribution Centre.

Nestel, G., J. Mercier, and L.B. Shaw. 1983. Economic consequences of midlife change in marital status. In *Unplanned Careers,* ed. L.B. Shaw, 109–25. Lexington, MA: Lexington Books.

Newman, P.C. 1975. *The Canadian Establishment* 1. Toronto: McClelland and Stewart.

———. 1989. *The Canadian Establishment* 1. Reissued with a new introduction. Toronto: McClelland and Stewart.

Niosi, J. 1981. *Canadian Capitalism: A Study of Power in the Canadian Business Establishment.* Trans. by R. Chodos. Toronto: James Lorimer.

Nisbet, R.A. 1959. The decline and fall of social class. *Pacific Sociological Review:* 11–17.

———. 1966. *The Sociological Tradition.* New York: Basic Books.

Nisbet, R. 1975. Public opinion versus popular opinion. *The Public Interest* 41(Fall):166–92.

Nock, D. 1982. Patriotism and patriarchs: Anglican Archbishops and Canadianization. *Canadian Ethnic Studies* 14(3):79–94.

Oakley, A. 1974. *Women's Work: The Housewife Past and Present.* New York: Vintage Books.

O'Bryon, K.G., J.G. Reitz, and O.M. Kuplowska. 1976. *Non-Official Languages: A Study in Canadian Multiculturalism.* Ottawa: Queen's Printer.

O'Conner, J. 1975. Productive and unproductive labor. *Politics and Society* 5(3):297–336.

Ogmundson, R. 1980a. Liberal ideology and the study of voting behaviour. *Canadian Review of Sociology and Anthropology* 17(1):45–54.

———. 1980b. Review of "Ethnicity and ethnic relations in Canada." *Canadian Ethnic Studies* 12(3): 148–49.

———. 1990. Perspectives on the class and ethnic origins of Canadian elites: A methodological critique of the Porter/Clement/Olsen tradition. *Canadian Journal of Sociology* 15(2):165–78.

———. 1992. Commentary and debate. *Canadian Journal of Sociology* 17(3):313–25.

———. 1993. At the top of the mosaic: Doubts about the data. *American Review of Canadian Studies* (Autumn):373–86.

Ogmundson, R., and J. McLaughlin. 1992. Trends in the ethnic origins of Canadian elites: The decline of the BRITS? *Canadian Review of Sociology and Anthropology* 29(2):227–42.

———. 1994. Changes in an intellectual elite 1960–1990: The Royal Society revisited. *Canadian Review of Sociology and Anthropology* 31(1):1–13.

Okin, S.M. 1991. Economic equality after divorce. *Dissent* 38:383–87.

———. 1994. Gender inequality and cultural differences. *Political Theory* 22(1):5–24.

———. 1995. Response to Jane Flax. *Political Theory* 23(3):511–16.

Okun, L. 1986. *Woman Abuse: Facts Replacing Myths.* Albany: SUNY Press.

Olsen, D. 1980. *The State Elite.* Toronto: McClelland and Stewart.

Oppenheimer, V.K. 1973. Demographic influence on female employment and the status of women. *American Journal of Sociology* 78:946–61.

Osborne, R.T., and F.C.J. McGurk. 1982. *The Testing of Negro Intelligence,* vol. 2. Athens, GA: Foundation for Human Understanding.

Ostry, S., and M.A. Zaidi. 1979. *Labour Economics in Canada.* 2d ed. Toronto: Macmillan.

Overbeek, H. 1980. Financial capital and crisis in Britain. *Capital and Class II:*99–120.

Pahl, R.E. 1989. Is the emperor naked? Some questions on the adequacy of sociological theory in urban and regional research. *International Journal of Urban and Regional Research* 13(4):709–20.

————. 1991. R.E. Pahl replies. *International Journal of Urban and Regional Research* 15:118,127–29.

————. 1993. Does class analysis without class theory have a promising future: A reply to Goldthorpe and Marshal. *Sociology* 27(2):253–58.

Pakulski, J. 1982. *Elite Recruitment in Australia: A Comparative Study*. Miami: Books Australia.

————. 1993. The dying of class or Marxist class theory. *International Sociology* 8(3):279–92.

Pakulski, J., and M. Waters. 1996a. The reshaping and dissolution of social class in advanced society. *Theory and Society* 25:667–91.

————. 1996b. Misreading status as class: A reply to our critics. *Theory and Society* 25:731–36.

Park, L., and F. Park. 1973. *Anatomy of Big Business*. Toronto.

Parkin, F. 1971. *Class Inequality and Political Order*. New York: Praeger.

————. 1972. *Class Inequality and Political Order*. London: Paladin.

————. 1974. Strategies of social closure in the maintenance of inequality. Presented at the Eighth World Congress of Sociology. Toronto (August 24).

————. 1979a. *Marxism and Class Theory: A Bourgeois Critique*. New York: Columbia University Press.

————. 1979b. *Class Inequality and Political Order*. London: MacGibbon and Kee.

Parkman, A.M. 1992. *No-Fault Divorce*. San Francisco, CA: Westview.

Parmar, P. 1982. Gender, race and class: Asian women in resistance. Centre for Contemporary Cultural Studies.

Parr, J. 1990. *The Gender of Breadwinners*. Toronto: University of Toronto Press.

Parsons, T., ed. 1964. *Max Weber: The Theories of Social and Economic Organization*. New York: The Free Press.

————. 1970. Equality and inequality in modern society or social stratification revisited. In *Social Stratification*, ed. E.O. Laumann, 13–72. New York: Bobbs-Merrill.

Pateman, C. 1988. *The Sexual Contract*. Oxford: Basil Blackwell.

————. 1996. A comment on Johnson's "Does capitalism really need patriarchy?" *Women's Studies International Forum* 19(3): 203–05.

Pattison, S., ed. 1985. *Financial Post Survey of Industrials*. Toronto: Financial Post.

Perlo. V. 1957. *The Empire of High Finance*. New York.

Petchesky, R. 1979. Dissolving the hyphen: A report on marxist feminist groups 1–5. In *Capitalist Patriarchy and the Case for Socialist Feminism*, ed. Z. Eisenstein. New York: Monthly Review Press.

Peters, T.J., and R.H. Waterman. 1982. *In Search of Excellence.* New York: Warner Books.

Peterson, R.R. 1989. *Women, Work and Divorce.* Albany, NY: State University of New York Press.

———. 1996a. Re-evaluation of the economic consequences of divorce. *American Sociological Review* 61(3):528–36.

———. 1996b. Statistical errors, faulty conclusions, misguided policy: Reply to Weitzman. *American Sociological Review* 61(3): 538–41.

Pettigrew, T. 1990. Is race friction between blacks and whites in the United States growing and inevitable? In *The Sociology of Race Relations: Reflection and Reform,* 15–27. New York: The Free Press.

Phillips, A. 1987. *Divided Loyalties: Dilemmas of Sex and Class.* London: Virago.

Phillips, A., and B. Taylor. 1986. Sex and skill. In *Waged Work: A Reader,* ed. Feminist Review, 54–61. London: Virago.

Phillips, K. 1991. *The Politics of Rich and Poor: Wealth and the American Electorate in the Reagan Aftermath.* New York: Harper.

Phizacklea, A., ed. 1983. *One Way Ticket: Migration and Female Labour.* London: Routledge and Kegan Paul.

Piedalue, G. 1976. Les groupes financiers au Canada 1900–1930. *Revue d'Histoire de l'Amerique Française* 30:1.

Pike, R.M. 1981. Sociological research on higher education in English Canada 1970–1980: A thematic review. *Canadian Journal of Higher Education* 11(2):1–25.

Pineo, P., and J. Porter. 1967. Occupational prestige in Canada. *Canadian Review of Sociology and Anthropolgy* 4(1):24–40.

———. 1985. Ethnic origin and occupational attainment in Canada. In *Ascription and Achievement: Studies in Mobility and Status Attainment in Canada,* ed. M. Boyd et al., 357–92. Ottawa: Carleton University Press.

Piore, M. 1975. Notes for a theory of labour market stratification. In *Labour Market Segmentation,* eds. R. Edwards, M. Reich, and D.M. Gordon. Toronto: D.C. Heath.

Polacheck, S.W. 1979. Occupational segregation among women: Theory, evidence and a prognosis. In *Women in the Labour Market,* ed. C. Lloyd. New York: Columbia University Press.

Polanyi, K. 1944. *The Great Transformation.* Boston: Beacon Press.

Polikoff, N.D. 1986. Review of *The Divorce Revolution* by Lenore J. Weitzman. *American Bar Association Journal* 72:112–16.

Porter, J. 1957. The economic elite and the social structure in Canada. *Canadian Journal of Economics and Political Science* 23:376–94.

———. 1965. *The Vertical Mosaic.* Toronto: University of Toronto Press.

———. 1970. Research biography of a macrosociological study: The vertical mosaic. In *Macrosociology: Research and Theory*, ed. J. Coleman et al., 149–82. Boston: Allyn and Bacon.

———. 1972. Conceptual and theoretical problems in the vertical mosaic: A rejoinder. *Canadian Review of Sociology and Anthropology* 9(2):188–89.

———. 1975. Foreword. In *The Canadian Corporate Elite*, W. Clement. Toronto: McClelland and Stewart.

———. 1979. Power and freedom in Canadian democracy. In *Measure of Canadian Society: Education, Equality and Opportunity*, ed. J. Porter, Ch. 9, 207–40. Toronto: Gage.

Power, M. 1983. From home production to wage labour: Women as a reserve army of labour. *Review of Radical Political Economics* 15:71–91.

Pratt, L. 1982. Energy: Roots of national policy. *Studies in Political Economy* 7(Winter).

Prechel, H., 1990. Steel and the state: Industry politics and business policy formation, 1940–1989. *American Sociological Review* 55:648–68.

Presthus, R. 1974. *Elites in the Policy Process*. Cambridge: Cambridge University Press.

Probert, B. 1989. *Working Life*. Melbourne: McPhee Gribble.

Pross, A.P. 1990. Typologies, claims, institutions and the capacity for discourse: A reply. *Canadian Public Policy* 16(2):209–13.

Przeworski, A., and J. Sprague. 1986. *Paper Stones: A History of Electoral Socialism*. Chicago: University of Chicago Press.

Putnam, R. 1976. *The Comparative Study of Political Elites*. Englewood Cliffs: Prentice-Hall.

Raftery, A.E., and M. Hout. 1993. Maximally maintained inequality: Expansion, reform, and opportunity in Irish education, 1921–1975. *Sociology of Education* 66:41–62.

Ralls, K. 1980. Comment on Lowe's "Sociobiology and Sex Differences." *Journal of Women in Culture and Society* 5(3):544–46.

Ramazanoglu, C. 1986. Ethnocentrism and socialist–feminist theory: A response to Barrett and McIntosh. *Feminist Review* 22:83–102.

Rees, A. 1954. Industrial conflict and business fluctuations. In *Industrial Conflict*, eds. A. Kornhauser, R. Dubin, and A. Rose. Toronto: McGraw-Hill.

Reich, R. 1991. *The Work of Nations*. New York: Knopf.

Reinharz, S. 1986. Patriarchal pontifications. *Society* 23(6):23–29.

Reiter, R.R., ed. 1975. *Toward an Anthropology of Women*. New York: Monthly Review Press.

Reitz, J. 1985. Language and ethnic community survival. In *Ethnicity and Ethnic Relations in Canada*, eds. R.M. Bienvenue and J.E. Goldstein, 105–23. Toronto: Butterworths.

Rent, C.S., and G.S. Rent. 1977. More on offspring-sex preference: A comment on Nancy E. Williamson's "Sex Preferences, Sex Control, and the Status of Women." *Journal of Women in Culture and Society* 3(2):505–13.

Rey, L. 1971. Comments on: "Sex Politics: Class Politics." *New Left Review* 66:93–96.

Reynolds, V. 1978. Race and ethnicity: A sociobiological perspective. *Ethnic and Racial Studies* 1(4):401–11.

———. 1980a. Sociobiology and discrimination: A rejoinder. *Ethnic and Racial Studies* 3(4):482.

———. 1980b. Sociobiology and the idea of primordial discrimination. *Ethnic and Racial Studies* 3(3):303–15.

Rich, A. 1980. Compulsory heterosexuality and lesbian existence. *Sings* 5:631–60.

Rich, H. 1976a. The vertical mosaic revisited: Toward a macro-sociology of Canada. *Journal of Canadian Studies* 11:14–31.

———. 1976b. Inequality of access. *Canadian Review of Sociology and Anthropology* 13(3):352–53.

———. 1991. Observations on "Class and ethnic origins of Canadian elites" by Richard Ogmundson. *Canadian Journal of Sociology* 16(4):419–23.

———. Forthcoming. John Porter's sociology and liberal democracy. *Canadian Journal of Sociology*.

Richardson, R.J. 1982. Merchants against industry: An empirical study. *Canadian Journal of Sociology* 7:279–96.

Roberts, L., and E. Boldt. 1979. Institutional completeness and ethnic assimilation. *Journal of Ethnic Studies* 7(2): 103–08.

Roberts, L.W., and R.A. Clifton. 1981. Exploring the ideology of Canadian multiculturalism. *Canadian Public Policy* 8(1):88–94.

Robertson, D. 1984. *Class and the British Electorate*. Oxford: Basil Blackwell.

Robinson, R., and D.S.G. Goodman, eds. 1996. *The New Rich in Asia*. London: Routledge.

Roediger, D. 1987. Three problems in Hills' major contribution. *New Politics* 1(3):46–48.

Roper, D.C. 1994. Wither the left: A reply to Todd Gitlin. *Contention* 3(2):201–04.

Rosaldo, M., and L. Lamphere, eds. 1974. *Woman, Culture and Society*. Stanford, CA: Stanford University Press.

Rose, S. et al. 1984. *Not in Our Genes: Biology, Ideology and Human Nature*. Harmondsworth: Penguin.

Rosen, L., and R. Bell. 1966. Mate selection in the upper class. *Sociological Quarterly* 7:157–66.

Rosen, S. 1987. Human capital. In *The New Palgrave: A Dictionary of Economics*, vol. 2, eds. J. Eatwell, M. Milgate, and P. Newman. London: The Macmillan Press.

Rosenfeld, R.A. 1983. Sex segregation and sectors: An analysis of gender differences in returns from employer changes. *American Sociological Review* 48:637–55.

Ross, D.P., E.R. Shillington, and C. Lochhead. 1994. *The Canadian Fact Book on Poverty—1994.* Ottawa: The Canadian Council on Social Development.

Rothstein, R. 1993. Immigration dilemmas. *Dissent* (Fall):455–62.

Rowbotham, S. 1973. *Hidden from the History: 300 Years of Women's Oppression and the Fight Against It.* London: Pluto Press.

Rubin, G. 1975. The traffic in women: Notes on the "Political economy of sex." In *Toward an Anthropology of Women*, ed. R. Reiter. New York: Monthly Review Press.

Russell, D. 1986. *The Secret Trauma: Incest in the Lives of Girls and Women.* New York: Basic.

Russell, J. 1984. Commentary. *Alternate Routes* 7:169–72.

Rushton, J.P. 1988a. Race differences in behaviour: A review and evolutionary analysis. *Personality and Individual Differences* 9(6):1009–24.

———. 1988b. The reality of racial differences: A rejoinder with new evidence. *Personality and Individual Differences* 9(6): 1035–40.

Ryan, M. 1975. *Womanhood in America from Colonial Times to the Present.* New York: New Viewpoints.

Saffioti, H. 1978. *Women in Class Society.* New York: Monthly Review Press.

Salvatore, N. 1987. Race, ethnicity and organized labor. *New Politics* 1(3):22–26.

Samantrai, R. 1997. On being the object of concern. *National Women's Studies Association* 9(1):49–53.

Sargent, L., ed. 1981. *Women and Revolution: A Discussion of the Unhappy Marriage of Marxism and Feminism.* Boston: South End Press.

Saunders, D.G. 1986. When battered women use violence: Husband abuse or self-defence? *Violence and Victims* 1:47–60.

———. 1988. Wife abuse, husband abuse, or mutual combat? A feminist perspective on the empirical findings. In *Feminist Perspectives on Wife Abuse*, eds. K. Yllo and M. Bograd. Beverly Hills: Sage.

———. 1989. Who hits first and who hits most? Evidence for the greater victimization of women in intimate relationships. Paper presented at the annual meeting of the American Society of Criminology, Reno, Nevada.

Saunders, P. 1995. Might Britain be a meritocracy? *Sociology* 29(1):23–41.

Sayers, J. 1982. Psychoanalysis and personal politics. *Feminist Review* 10:91–95.

Schlegel, A. 1986. Logic, gender and power. *Society* 23(6):21–22.

Schreiber, E.M., 1980. Class awareness and class voting in Canada: A reconsideration of the Ogmundson thesis. *Canadian Review of Sociology and Anthropology* 17(1):37–44.

Schwartz, M.D., and W.S. DeKeseredy. 1993. The return of the "battered husband syndrome" through the typification of women as violent. *Crime, Law and Social Change.* In press.

Schwarzschild, S.S. 1987. American history marked by racism. *New Politics* 1(3):56–58.

Scott, J.F. 1971. *Internalization of Norms: A Sociological Theory of Moral Commitment.* Englewood Cliffs, NJ: Prentice-Hall.

Scott, J. 1994. Class analysis: Back to the future. *Sociology* 28(4):933–42.

Secombe, W. 1973. The housewife and her labour under capitalism. *New Left Review* 83:3–24.

Segal, L. 1990. *Slow Motion.* London: Virago.

Seiling, S.B., and H. Harris. 1991. Child support awards: Links with alimony and in-kind support. *Journal of Divorce and Remarriage* 16:121–35.

Shaiken, H. 1984. *Work Transformed: Automation and Labor in the Computer Age.* New York: Holt, Rinehart and Winston.

Sharp, R., and R. Broomhill. 1988. *Short-Changed: Women and Economic Policies.* Sydney: Allen and Unwin.

Shavit, Y., and H.P. Blossfeld. 1992. *Persistent Inequality: Changing Educational Stratification in Thirteen Countries.* Boulder, CO: Westview.

Shorrocks, A.F. 1987. U.K. wealth distribution: Current evidence and future prospects. In *International Comparisons of the Distribution of Household Wealth,* ed. E. Wolff, 29–50. New York: Oxford University Press.

Simeral, M.H. 1978. Women and the reserve army of labour. *The Insurgent Sociologist* 8:164–79.

Simmons, A.B. 1994. Canadian immigration policy in the early 1990s: A commentary on Veugelers and Klassen's analysis of the breakdown of the unemployment–immigration linkage. *Canadian Journal of Sociology* 19(4):525–34.

Sinclair, P.R. 1989. Social credit and social class: A comment on "The petite bourgeoisie and social credit: A reconsideration." *Canadian Journal of Sociology* 14(3):390–92.

Skocpol, T. 1990. Sustainable social policy: Fighting poverty without poverty programs. *The American Prospect* (Summer).

Smeeding, T.M. 1991. Cross-national comparisons of inequality and poverty position. In *Economic Inequality and Poverty: International Perspectives*, ed. L. Osberg, 39–59. Armonk, NY: Sharpe.

Smith, D.A. 1972. The determinants of strike activity in Canada. *Relations Industrielles/Industrial Relations* 27(4):663–78.

Smith, M.D. 1977–78. The battered husband syndrome. *Victimology* 3–4:499–509.

———. 1987. The incidence and prevalence of woman abuse in Toronto. *Violence and Victim* 2:173–87.

———. 1990a. Patriarchal ideology and wife beating: A test of a feminist hypothesis. *Violence and Victims* 5:257–73.

———. 1990b. Socio-demographic risk factors in wife abuse: Results from a survey of Toronto women. *Canadian Journal of Sociology* 15:39–58.

———. 1993. Familial ideology and wife abuse. Unpublished manuscript. North York, ON: LaMarsh Research Programme on Violence and Conflict Resolution.

Smith, M.R. 1979. A comment on Knight's "Work orientation and mobility ideology in the working class." *Canadian Journal of Sociology* 4(2):155–61.

Smith, M. 1989. A sociological appraisal of the Free Trade Agreement. *Canadian Public Policy* 15(1):57–71.

Sniderman, P.M., and P.E. Tetlock. 1986a. Symbolic racism: Problems of motive attribution in political analysis. *Journal of Social Issues* 42(2):129–50.

———. 1986b. Reflections on American racism. *Journal of Social Issues* 42(2):173–87.

Sniderman, P.M., J.F. Fletcher, P.H. Russell, and P.E. Tetlock. 1989. Political culture and the problem of double standards: Mass and elite attitudes toward language rights in the *Canadian Charter of Rights and Freedoms. Canadian Journal of Political Science* 22(2):259–84.

———. 1990. Reply: Strategic calculation and political values — The dynamics of language rights. *Canadian Journal of Political Science* 23(3):537–44.

Snyder, D. 1975. Institutional setting and industrial conflict: Comparative analyses of France, Italy, and the United States. *American Sociological Review* 40(3):259–78.

Sørenson, A. 1992. Estimating the economic consequences of separation and divorce: A cautionary tale from the United States. In *Economic Consequences of Divorce: The International Perspective*, eds. L.J. Weitzman and M. MacLean, 263–82. New York: Oxford University Press.

Sova, G., ed. 1988. *The 1988 Corpus Almanac and Canadian Sourcebook.* Toronto: Southam Communications.

Sowell, T. 1977. New light on the black IQ controversy. *New York Times Magazine* (March 27):56–65.

———. 1984. *Civil Rights: Rhetoric or Reality?* New York: Morrow.

———. 1989. Affirmative action: A worldwide disaster. *Commentary* (December).

Spånt, R. 1987. Wealth distribution in Sweden: 1920–1983. In *International Comparisons of the Distribution of Household Wealth,* ed. E. Wolff, 51–71. New York: Oxford University Press.

Spencer, M.R. 1994. Multiculturalism, political correctness and the political diversity. *Sociological Forum* 9(4):547–67.

Statistics Canada. 1974, 1975. *Manufacturing Industries of Canada.* Ottawa: Information Canada.

———. 1981. *Canada's International Investment Position 1977.* Ottawa.

———. 1986. *The Labour Force,* December 1985, Cat. No. 71-001. Ottawa: Minister of Supply and Services Canada.

———. 1987. *Earnings of Men and Women,* Cat. No. 13-217. Ottawa: Minister of Supply and Services Canada.

Steinmetz, S.K. 1977–78. The battered husband syndrome. *Victimology* 3–4:499–509.

Stevenson, P. 1980. Accumulation in the world economy and the international division of labour. *Canadian Review of Sociology and Anthropology* 17:3.

Stirling, K.J. 1989. Women who remain divorced: The long-term economic consequences. *Social Science Quarterly* 70:549–61.

Stone, A.H. 1980. Is race friction between blacks and whites in the United States growing and inevitable? *Abridged from American Journal of Sociology* 13:676–97.

Straus, M.A., and R.J. Gelles. 1986. Societal changes and change in family violence from 1975 to 1985 as revealed by two national surveys. *Journal of Marriage and the Family* 48:465–79.

———. 1990. *Physical Violence in American Families.* New Brunswick, NJ: Transaction Publications.

Straus, M.A., R.J. Gelles, and S.K. Steinmetz. 1981. *Behind Closed Doors: Violence in the American Family.* New York: Anchor Books.

Sugarman, D.B. and G.T. Hotaling. 1989. Dating violence: Prevalence, context, and risk markers. In *Violence in Dating Relationships: Emerging Social Issues,* ed. M.A. Pirog-Good and J.E. Stets. New York: Praeger.

Sugarman, S.D. 1990. Dividing financial interests on divorce. In *Divorce Reform at the Crossroads,* eds. S.D. Sugarman and H.H. Kay, 130–65. New Haven, CT: Yale University Press.

Sweeny, R. 1980. The evolution of financial groups in Canada and the capital market since the second world war. Master's thesis, Université du Québec à Montréal.

Symons, T.H.B. 1975. *To Know Ourselves*. Ottawa: Association of Universities and Colleges of Canada.

Szalai, J. 1996. Why the poor are poor in post-1989 Hungary. *New Internationalist* May.

Szelenyi S., and J. Olvera. 1996. The declining significance of class: Does gender complicate the story? *Theory and Society* 25(5):725–30.

Szymanski, A. 1977. Is U.S. imperialism resurgent? *New Left Review* 101:144–52.

Taeuber, A.F., K.E. Taeuber, and G.G. Cain. 1966. Occupational assimilation and the competitive process: A reanalysis. *American Journal of Sociology* 72:273–85.

Taylor, B. 1983. *Eve and the New Jerusalem: Socialism and Feminism in the Nineteenth Century*. London: Virago.

Taylor, K.W. 1991. Racism and Canadian immigration law. Paper presented at the meetings of the Canadian Sociology and Anthropology Association. Kingston, ON. Also forthcoming in *Canadian Ethnic Studies*.

Tepperman, L. 1975. *Social Mobility in Canada*. Toronto: McGraw-Hill Ryerson.

Thistle, S. 1992. Between two worlds. Ph.D. diss., Department of Sociology, University of California, Berkeley.

Thornton, A. 1986. The fragile family. *Family Planning Perspectives* 18:243–44.

Thurow, L. 1995. Companies merge; Families break up. *New York Times*, September 3:11.

Tollett, K.S. 1991. Racism and race-conscious remedies. *The American Prospect* (Spring):91–101.

Tong, R. 1989. *Feminist Thought: A Comprehensive Introduction*. London: Unwin Hyman.

Townsend, P., P. Corrigan, and U. Kowarzick. 1987. *Poverty and Labour in London*. London: Low Pay Unit.

Treiman, D.J., and K. Terrell. 1975. Women, work, and wages — trends in the female occupational structure since 1940. In *Social Indicator Models*, eds. K.C. Land and S. Spilerman. New York: Russell Sage Foundation.

Treiman, D.J., and H.I. Hartmann. 1981. *Women, Work, and Wages: Equal Pay for Work of Equal Value*. Washington: National Academy Press.

Trivedi, P. 1984. To deny our fullness: Asian women in the making of history. *Feminist Review* 17 *Many Voices, One Chant: Black Feminist Perspectives*.

Tumin, M. 1953. Rejoinder. *American Sociological Review.* 18:398.

Tyree, A. 1985. Tracking a ghost to test a theory. *Social Science Quarterly* 66:668–74.

Urquhart, M.C., and K.A. Buckley, eds. 1965. *Historical Statistics of Canada.* Toronto: Macmillan.

Useem, M. 1984. *The Inner Circle.* New York: Oxford University Press.

Useem, M., and J. Karabel. 1986. Paths to corporate management. *American Sociological Review* 51:184–200.

Usher, D. 1980a. How should the redistributive power of the state be divided between federal and provincial governments? *Canadian Public Policy* 6(1):16–29.

———. 1980b. A reply. *Canadian Public Policy* 6(4):667–69.

———. 1995a. The interests of English Canada. *Canadian Public Policy* 21(1):72–84.

———. 1995b. A reply. *Canadian Public Policy* 12(1):94–106.

Vaillancourt, F., and I. Henriques. 1986. The return of university schooling in Canada. *Canadian Public Policy* 12(3):449–58.

Van den Berg, A., and M.R. Smith. 1984. Correcting Cuneo's corrections. *Canadian Review of Sociology and Anthropology* 21(1):92–97.

Van den Berghe, P. 1978. Race and ethnicity: A sociological perspective. *Ethnic and Racial Studies* 1(4):401–11.

———. 1980. Sociobiology and discrimination: A comment on Vernon Reynolds. *Ethnic and Racial Studies* 3(4):475–83.

Van Loon, R., and M. Whittington. 1976. *The Canadian Political System.* 2d ed. Toronto: McGraw-Hill.

Varga, E. n.d. *The Great Crisis and Its Political Consequence.* New York: International Publishers.

Varley, D. 1938. On the computation of the rate of surplus value. *Science and Society* 2(3):393–96.

Veltmeyer, H. 1977. Political economy: A question of theory. *Canadian Journal of Political and Social Theory* 2(1):171–73.

Veugelers, J.W.P., and T.R. Klassen. 1994a. Continuity and change in Canada's unemployment–immigration linkage. *Canadian Journal of Sociology* 19(3):351–69.

———. 1994b. Canadian immigration policy: A Reply to Foot and Simmons. *Canadian Journal of Sociology* 19(4):535–40.

Vogel, L. 1973. The earthly family. *Radical America* 7(July–October):9–50.

———. 1981. Marxism and feminism: Unhappy marriage, trial separation or something else? In *Women and Revolution,* ed. L. Sargent, 195–217. Boston, MA: South End Press.

Wacquant, L. 1993. Red belt, black belt: Articulating color, class, and place in Chicago's ghetto and the Parisian periphery. Unpublished manuscript. Forthcoming in *International Journal of Urban and Regional Research*.

Walby, S. 1990. *Theorizing Patriarchy*. Oxford: Basil Blackwell.

Waltzer, K. 1987. The need to explore distinctions. *New Politics*. 1(3):41–46.

Ward, K.B., and F.C. Pampel. 1985a. Structural determinants of female labor force participation in developed nations, 1955–75. *Social Science Quarterly* 66:654–67.

———. 1985b. More on the meaning of the effect of the sex ratio on female labor force participation. *Social Science Quarterly* 66:675–79.

Warskett, R. 1988. Bank worker unionization and the law. *Studies in Political Economy* 25:41–73.

Watkins M.H. et al. 1968. *Foreign Ownership and the Structure of Canadian Industry*. Ottawa.

Watson, W. 1995. Home fame: Comments on "The Interests of English Canada." *Canadian Public Policy* 21(1):85–93.

Weaver, H.R., and R.B. Parton. 1979. Replication and contamination of relational variables. *Canadian Review of Sociology and Anthropology* 16(2):134–49.

Weinbaum, B. 1976. Women in transition to socialism: Perspectives on the Chinese case. *Review of Radical Political Economics* 8 (Spring).

Weir, R. 1986. Low-income parents — What they want from schools. *Interchange* 17(1):82–84.

Weir, S. 1987. Looking beyond union bureaucracy. *New Politics* 1(3):48–52.

Weiss, R.S. 1984. The impact of marital dissolution on income and consumption in single-parent households. *Journal of Marriage and the Family* 46:115–27.

Weitzman. L.J. 1985. *The Divorce Revolution: The Unexpected Social and Economic Consequences for Women and Children in America*. New York: The Free Press.

———. 1986. Bringing the law back in. *American Bar Foundation Research Journal*: 791–97.

———. 1992. Alimony: Its premature demise and recent resurgence in the U.S. In *Economic Consequences of Divorce: The International Perspective*, eds. L.J. Weitzman and M. MacLean, 247–62. New York: Oxford University Press.

———. 1996. The economic consequences of divorce are still unequal: Comment on Peterson. *American Sociological Review* 61(3):537–38.

West, A.W. 1994a. Personal, academic and institutional perspectives on museums and first nations. *Canadian Journal of Native Studies* 14(1):147–56.

———. 1994b. Why I don't like museums: A reply to the commentary "Personal, academic and institutional perspectives on museums and first nations by Robert R. Janes." *Canadian Journal of Native Studies* 14(2):363–68.

West, D.A. 1996. Hegemony and the representation of aboriginal politics. *Journal of Canadian Studies* 31(1):137–40.

West, E.G., and S.L. Winer. 1980. Will federal centralization help the poor? *Canadian Public Policy* 6(4):662–67.

Williams, A.P. 1989. Social origins and elite politics in Canada. *Canadian Journal of Sociology* 14(1):67–88.

Williams, W.E. 1996. Justice in the process, not in the results. *Academic Questions* (Fall):76–79.

Williams, R., and G.D. Jaynes, eds. 1989. *A Common Destiny: Blacks and American Society.* Washington, DC: National Academy Press.

Williamson, N.E. 1976. Sex preference, sex control, and the status of women. *Journal of Women in Culture and Society* 1(4):847–62.

———. 1977. A reply to Rent and Rent's "More on Offspring-Sex Preference." *Journal of Women in Culture and Society* 3(2):513–15.

Wilson, E. 1981. Psychoanalysis: Psychic law and order. *Feminist Review* (8):63–78.

Wilson, J.Q., ed. 1983. *Crime and Public Policy.* San Francisco: ICS Press.

Wilson, J.Q., and R.J. Herrnstein. 1985. *Crime and Human Nature.* Simon and Schuster.

Wilson, W.J. 1978. *The Declining Significance of Race.* Chicago: University of Chicago Press.

———. 1987. *The Truly Disadvantaged: The Inner City, the Underclass, and Public Policy.* Chicago: University of Chicago Press.

———. 1990. Race-neutral programs and the democratic coalition. *The American Prospect* 1(Spring):74–81.

Winn, C. 1985. Affirmative action and visible minorities: Eight premises in quest of evidence. *Canadian Public Administration* 11(4):684–700.

Winnipeg Free Press. 1982. Foreign investment doubles in Canada, November 9.

Wolff, E. 1991. The distribution of household wealth: Methodological issues, time trends, and cross-sectional comparisons. In *Economic Inequality and Poverty: International Perspectives,* ed. L. Osberg, 92–133. Arrnonk, NY: Sharpe.

Wollstonecraft, M. 1971. *A Vindication of the Rights of Women.* New York: Source Book Press.

Womack, R.G. 1987. Civil rights and the A.F.L.-C.I.O. *New Politics* 1(3):29–30.

Wong, R.S-K., and R.M. Hauser. 1992. Trends in occupational mobility in Hungary under socialism. *Social Sciences Research* 21:419–44.

Woodhouse, B.B. 1990. Towards a revitalization of family law. *Texas Law Review* 69:245–90.

The World Bank. 1995. *World Development Report 1995.* Washington.

Wright, E.O. 1990. Explanation and utopia in Marxism and feminism. Paper presented at the annual meeting of the American Sociological Association, Washington, DC, August 11–15.

———. 1985. *Classes.* London: Verso.

———. 1996. The continuing relevance of class analysis — Comments. *Theory and Society* 25:693–716.

Yanz, L., and D. Smith. 1983. Women as a reserve army of labour: A critique. *Review of Radical Political Economics* 15:92–106.

Young, I. 1981. Beyond the unhappy marriage: A critique of dual systems theory. In *Women and Revolution,* ed. L. Sargent. Boston: South End Press.

Zaretsky, E. 1976. *Capitalism, the Family and Personal Life.* New York: Harper and Row.

Zeitlin, M. 1989. *The Large Corporation and Contemporary Classes.* Cambridge: Polity.

Zellner, H. 1975. The determinants of occupational segregation. In *Sex, Discrimination, and the Division of Labour,* ed. C.B. Lloyd. New York: Columbia University Press.

Zuboff, S. 1988. *In the Age of the Smart Machine: The Future of Work and Power.* New York: Basic.

Zuckerman, M., and N. Brody. 1988. Oysters, rabbits and people: A critique of "Race Differences in Behaviour" by J.P. Rushton. *Personality and Individual Differences* 9(6):1025–33.

Credits

We wish to thank the authors, publishers, and copyright holders for permission to reprint the selections in this book, which are listed below in order of appearance.

Part One

Kingsley Davis and Wilbert E. Moore. Abridged from "Some Principles of Stratification," *American Sociological Review*, Vol. 10 (1945), pp. 242–49.

Melvin M. Tumin. Abridged from "Some Principles of Stratification: A Critical Analysis," *American Sociological Review*, Vol. 18 (1953), pp. 387–93.

Terry Nichols Clark and Seymour Martin Lipset. Abridged from "Are Social Classes Dying?" *International Sociology*, Vol. 6, No. 4 (1991), pp. 397–410. Reprinted by permission.

Mike Hout, Clem Brooks, and Jeff Manza. Abridged from "The Persistence of Classes in Post-Industrial Societies," *International Sociology*, Vol. 8, No. 3 (1993), pp. 259–77. Reprinted by permission.

Carl J. Cuneo. Abridged from "Class Exploitation in Canada," *Canadian Review of Sociology and Anthropology*, Vol. 15, No. 3 (1978), pp. 284–300. Reprinted by permission.

Axel van den Berg and Michael R. Smith. Abridged from "On 'Class Exploitation' in Canada," *Canadian Review of Sociology and Anthropology*, Vol. 19, No. 2 (1982), pp. 263–78. Reprinted by permission.

Wallace Clement. Abridged from "Inequality of Access: Characteristics of the Canadian Corporate Elite," *Canadian Review of Sociology and Anthropology*, Vol. 12, No. 1 (1975), pp. 33–52. Reprinted by permission.

R. Ogmundson. Abridged from "Perspectives on the Class and Ethnic Origins of Canadian Elites: A Methodological Critique of the Porter/Clement/Olsen Tradition," *Canadian Journal of Sociology*, Vol. 15, No. 2 (1990), pp. 165–77. Reprinted by permission.

William K. Carroll. Abridged from "The Canadian Corporate Elite: Financiers or Finance Capitalists?" *Studies in Political Economy*, Vol. 8 (1982), pp. 89–114. Reprinted by permission.

Paul Stevenson. "Capital and the State in Canada: Some Critical Questions on Carroll's Finance Capitalists," *Studies in Political Economy*, Vol. 12 (1983), pp. 163–167. Reprinted by permission.

Part Two

Heidi Hartmann. Abridged from "The Unhappy Marriage of Marxism and Feminsm: Towards a More Progressive Union," in Lydia Sargent, ed., *Women and Revolution*, Boston, MA: South End Press, 1981, pp. 1–41. Reprinted by permission.

Iris Young. Abridged from "Beyond the Unhappy Marriage: A Critique of the Dual Systems Theory," in Lydia Sargent, ed., *Women and Revolution*, Boston, MA: South End Press, 1981, pp. 43–69. Reprinted by permission.

Carol Johnson. Abridged from "Does Capitalism Really Need Patriarchy? Some Old Issues Reconsidered," *Women's Studies International Forum*, Vol. 19, No. 3, pp. 193–202. Reprinted by permission of Elsevier Science.

Carole Pateman. "A Comment on Johnson's 'Does Capitalism Really Need Patriarchy?'" *Women's Studies International Forum*, Vol. 19, No. 3, pp. 203–205. Reprinted by permission of Elsevier Science.

Catherine J. Fillmore. Abridged from "Gender Differences in Earnings: A Re-Analysis and Prognosis for Canadian Women," *Canadian Journal of Sociology*, Vol. 15, No. 3 (1990), pp. 275–300. Reprinted by permission.

Alice Nakamura. Abridged from "Gender Differences in Earnings: A Comment," *Canadian Journal of Sociology*, Vol. 15, No. 4 (1990), pp. 463–69. Reprinted by permission.

Walter DeKeseredy and Katharine Kelly. Abridged from "The Incidence and Prevalence of Woman Abuse in Canadian University and College Dating Relationships," *Canadian Journal of Sociology*, Vol. 18, No. 2 (1993), pp. 137–59. Reprinted by permission.

Bonnie J. Fox. "On Violent Men and Female Victims: A Comment on DeKeseredy and Kelly," *Canadian Journal of Sociology*, Vol. 18, No. 3 (1993), pp. 320–25. Reprinted by permission.

Lenore J. Weitzman. Abridged from *The Divorce Revolution: The Unexpected Social and Economic Consequences for Women and*

Children in America, New York: The Free Press, a division of Simon & Schuster, Inc., 1985, pp. 337–43. Copyright © 1985 by Dr. Lenore J. Weitzman. Reprinted by permission.

Richard R. Peterson. Abridged from "A Re-Evaluation of the Economic Consequences of Divorce," *American Sociological Review*, Vol. 61 (1996), pp. 528–36. Reprinted by permission.

Part Three

Michèle Barrett and Mary McIntosh. Abridged from "Ethnocentrism and Socialist-Feminist Theory," *Feminist Review*, Vol. 20 (1985), pp. 23–47. Reprinted by permission.

Caroline Ramazanoglu. "Ethnocentrism and Socialist-Feminist Theory: A Response to Barrett and McIntosh," *Feminist Review*, Vol. 22 (1986), pp. 83–86. Reprinted by permission.

R. Ogmundson and J. McLaughlin. Abridged from "Trends in the Ethnic Origins of Canadian Elites: The Decline of the BRITS?" *Canadian Review of Sociology and Anthropology*, Vol. 29, No. 2 (1992), pp. 227–42. Reprinted by permission.

M. Reza Nakhaie. Abridged from "Vertical Mosaic among the Elites: The New Imagery Revisited," *Canadian Review of Sociology and Anthropology*, Vol. 34, No. 1 (1997), pp. 1–24. Reprinted by permission.

Camille Laurin. Abridged from "French Language Charter," *Canadian Review of Sociology and Anthropology*, Vol. 15, No. 2 (1978), pp. 115–27. Reprinted by permission.

Bernard Blishen. "Perceptions of National Identity," *Canadian Review of Sociology and Anthropology*, Vol. 15, No. 2 (1978), pp. 128–32. Reprinted by permission.

Peter Kulchyski. "Aboriginal Peoples and Hegemony in Canada," *Journal of Canadian Studies*, Vol. 30, No. 1 (1995), pp. 60–68. Reprinted by permission.

D.A. West. "Hegemony and the Representation of Aboriginal Politics in Canada," *Journal of Canadian Studies*, Vol. 31, No. 1 (1996), pp. 137–40. Reprinted by permission.

Lance W. Roberts and Rodney A. Clifton. "Exploring the Ideology of Canadian Multiculturalism," *Canadian Public Policy*, Vol. 8, No. 1 (1982), pp. 88–94. Reprinted by permission.

Don Dawson. "The Structural Realities of Canadian Multiculturalsim: A Response to Roberts and Clifton," *Canadian Public Policy*, Vol. 8, No. 4 (1982), pp. 608–11. Reprinted by permission.

R.J. Herrnstein. Abridged from "Still an American Dilemma," *The Public Interest*, No. 98 (Winter 1990), pp. 3–17. © 1990 by National Affairs, Inc. Reprinted by permission of the author.

Reader Reply Card

We are interested in your reaction to *Debates on Social Inequality: Class, Gender, and Ethnicity*, by M. Reza Nakhaie. You can help us to improve this book in future editions by completing this questionnaire.

1. What was your reason for using this book?

   ❑ university course ❑ college course ❑ continuing education course
   ❑ professional   ❑ personal   ❑ other (please specify) _____
     development   interest   _____

2. If you are a student, please identify your school and the course in which you used this book.

3. Which chapters or parts of this book did you use? Which did you omit?

4. What did you like best about this book?

5. What did you like least?

6. Please identify any topics you think should be added to future editions.

7. Please add any comments or suggestions.

8. May we contact you for further information?

   Name: _____

   Address: _____

   _____

   Phone: _____

   E-mail: _____

(fold here and tape shut)

MAIL ➤ POSTE

Canada Post Corporation / Société canadienne des postes

Postage paid
If mailed in Canada

Port payé
si posté au Canada

**Business
Reply**

**Réponse
d'affaires**

0116870399   01

0116870399-M8Z4X6-BR01

Larry Gillevet
Director of Product Development
HARCOURT BRACE & COMPANY, CANADA
55 HORNER AVENUE
TORONTO, ONTARIO
M8Z 9Z9